BLAKE IN CONTEXT

STEWART CREHAN

BLAKE
IN
CONTEXT

GILL AND MACMILLAN

HUMANITIES PRESS

First published in 1984 by
Gill and Macmillan Ltd
Goldenbridge, Dublin 8
with associated companies in
Auckland, Dallas, Delhi, Hong Kong,
Johannesburg, Lagos, London, Manzini,
Melbourne, Nairobi, New York, Singapore,
Toyko, Washington

©Stewart Crehan 1984

Published in 1984 in USA and Canada by
Humanities Press Inc.
Atlantic Highlands, New Jersey 07716

Gill and Macmillan SBN 0 7171 1313 2
Humanities Press ISBN 0-391-02855-3

Origination by Galaxy Reproductions Limited, Dublin.

Printed and bound in Great Britain by
Biddles Ltd., Guildford and King's Lynn

Contents

List of Illustrations
(between p. 182 and p. 183)

T. Gainsborough, *The Morning Walk*
(Reproduced by courtesy of the Trustees of The National Gallery)

H. Fuseli, *The Nightmare*
(The Goethe Museum, Frankfurt am Main: Freie Deutsche Hochstift — Frankfurt am Main)

J.-L. David, *Oath of the Horatii*
(Musée du Louvre/Cliché des Musées Nationaux — Paris)

William Blake, *Satan, Sin and Death*
(courtesy of The Henry E. Huntington Library and Art Gallery, California)

J. Barry, *King Lear Weeping over the Dead Body of Cordelia*
(Reproduced by courtesy of the Trustees of The National Gallery, London)

William Blake, *God creating Adam*
(The Tate Gallery, London)

William Blake, *America*, Plate 8
(courtesy of The Auckland Public Library, New Zealand)

William Blake, *America*, Plate 10
(courtesy of The Auckland Public Library, New Zealand)

William Blake, *The Angel Michael binding Satan*
(courtesy of The Fogg Art Museum, Harvard University)

William Blake, *The Blossom, Songs of Innocence*
(by permission of the Houghton Library, Harvard University)

William Blake, *The Ancient of Days*
(Whitworth Art Gallery, University of Manchester)

H. Fuseli, *The Debutante*
(The Tate Gallery, London)

Illustrations

William Blake, *Jerusalem*, Plate 25
  (by permission of the Houghton Library, Harvard University)

William Blake, *The Wise and Foolish Virgins*
  (courtesy of The Metropolitan Museum of Art, New York)

William Blake, *The Body of Abel found by Adam and Eve*
  (The Tate Gallery, London)

Acknowledgments

I would like to thank the following for their help, guidance and encouragement during the writing of this book: Paul Arnold, Alan Bold, Doris Hare, Geoffrey Keynes, Michael Kidron, Ilse Mwanza, Lewis Nkosi, C. P. Richardson, Anne and Harry Rothman, Paul Stigant, Prayag Tripathi, Peter Wyeth, and Kate and Edith.

Introduction

Underpinning this study of Blake is the premise that poetry and visual art always have a social context and a social function, which in class society assumes a specific class character. Artistic work is a complex process involving many choices and decisions, constraints, 'leaps', intuitions, and re-workings, but this process has to take place within the larger social process. Moreover, it is this larger context that gives the creative act shape and meaning. The need to master reality through art presumes certain social conditions of creative work which are, in fact, its *raison d'être*, albeit masked by Romantic and modernist theories of art and the views of the artist. Without a coherent social context, significant form and intelligible content disappear altogether.

By 'context' I do not mean the positivist's 'milieu', the literary historian's social, political or historical 'background', or the idealist's 'background of ideas', but *class* content, a particular moment in the class struggle. Since art and literature always present us with some kind of picture of the world, and since the ruling class's picture of the world is always the ruling picture, any art or literature that presents us with a new picture of the world must be a product of new class forces. History is a unified process. Within any historical period, contradictory class forces, whether in an open or covert manner, face each other and fight it out ideologically and artistically as well as politically. Thus by seeing the visual art or literature of a period in its class context we can grasp its deeper content, so often obscured by later commentary and analysis. Certain questions then take on a new dimension. For example, how is it that, during the 1780s and 1790s, some of the best poetry in English could be written in such popular 'oral' forms as the song and the ballad (Burns's songs, Blake's *Songs*, Wordsworth's and Coleridge's *Lyrical Ballads*)? Why does David's art gain in such intensity, austere concentration and emotive force between the early 1780s and 1793, the year of *The Death of Marat*? And so on. In these questions, social and political context, artistic form and content, are inextricably bound together.

In his *Literature and Revolution*, Trotsky cut through the dichotomy of 'pure' versus 'tendentious' art as follows:

> Keeping on the plane of scientific investigation, Marxism seeks with the same assurance the social roots of the 'pure' as well as of the tendentious art. It does not at all 'incriminate' a poet with the thoughts and feelings which he expresses, but raises questions of a much more profound significance, namely, to which order of feelings does a given artistic work correspond in all its peculiarities? What are the social conditions of these thoughts and feelings? What place do they occupy in the historic development of a society and of a class? And, further, what literary heritage has entered into the elaboration of the new form? Under the influence of what historic impulse have the new complexes of feelings and thoughts broken through the shell which divides them from the sphere of poetic consciousness? The investigation may become complicated, detailed or individualised, but its fundamental idea will be that of the subsidiary role which art plays in the social process.[1]

These are the questions a Marxist approach keeps to the fore. The search for *overt* social and political meanings is unnecessary, given that a work of art does not have to be socially explicit or politically tendentious in order to provoke a highly-charged, partisan response. Genteel, eighteenth-century taste, for example — that is, the taste of the landed gentry — generally regarded mountains as horrid, disorderly protuberances; when poets and painters began to find them inspiring, the shift in attitude this betokened was quickly understood. Both history and artistic taste were moving away from those positions held by the landed gentry and royalist aristocracy. Absolutism in France had seen its rule mirrored in the tamed, geometric shapes of palace and and chateau gardens. The 'liberal' English landowners preferred theirs to be played out in natural-seeming, 'improved' landscape gardens. But the titanic forces that had pushed up the earth's great mountain ranges, that were felt in 'the raging of the stormy sea', and that were eventually to push aside centuries of monarchical, aristocratic rule, were beyond the mental horizons of either. The artistic expression of violent, creative energy, which is associated with Romanticism (and with the work of Blake in particular) emerges out of the great movement that began with the rebellion of the American colonies in 1775, erupted with more far-reaching consequences when the Parisian masses rose in 1789, and raged throughout Europe for the next sixty years.

Revolutionary epochs teach us that no artistic form or style is ever politically or ideologically neutral. Nor are they ideologically fixed: forms and styles 'belonging' to one class can be appropriated by another and so transformed. In times of open class warfare, not only the choice and handling of particular subjects, but all aesthetic signs and techniques acquire a significance peculiarly heightened by their underlying class content. Compare, for example, the restless, onward surge of Milton's blank verse paragraphs in *Paradise Lost* with the bounded formality of Dryden's rhyming couplets in *Absalom and Achitophel*: the former act out the movement of a revolutionary bourgeois consciousness; the latter uphold the urbane 'moderation' of pro-royalist conservatism. With the passage of time, however, the deep social content of aesthetic signs tends to get obscured, as the bourgeoisie becomes incapable of seeing the logic of its own revolutionary past. The art and literature of the bourgeois-democratic epoch are neatly folded back into the drawer marked 'Age of Romanticism'. Works of art once considered challenging, shocking or unacceptable because of their social implications are made 'safe', either by ignoring the ways in which they might challenge modern class society, or by gathering them into a museum-ised, timeless 'World of Art', where they remain, carefully valued, priced and labelled, in the hands of the art and literary establishment. Art is de-politicised, 'aestheticised'.

De-historicising, de-politicising and aestheticising art is the principal aim of formalism. Formalist criticism, which remains the dominant tendency in bourgeois criticism, implies a kind of severed consciousness, a historical amnesia which relates to the present through an ostrich-like distaste for all social determinants in artistic matters. The larger these social and political determinants loom, the less secure and more nervous that distaste becomes. (Some formalists have thus adopted a 'Marxist' — or rather neo-Althusserian — terminology in order to reconcile the two approaches. Concepts such as the 'semi-autonomy' of art merely justify and uphold the *autonomy* of art and ideas, and hence the social autonomy of artists and intellectuals, while appearing to give ground to economic, social and political determinants.) When the social meaning and class content of a particular work of art are so deeply embedded, forgotten or unresearched as to be entirely absent to the average modern viewer, the formalist critic or 'aesthetician' is only too happy to take advantage of such ignorance (being, as a rule, incurious himself in these matters). Since all that apparently remains is the aesthetic object in front of him or her, the critic can safely ignore its complex social and historical roots (aside from mentioning dates, authentication, circumstances of composition, when first published or exhibited, etc.), and concentrate on the aesthetic form.

In epitomising the *meaning* of a work, however, bourgeois criticism frequently resorts to subjective impressions and perennial, supra-historical thoughts and feelings. Thus one critic, discussing J. M. W. Turner's most famous painting, *The Fighting Temeraire*, asks: 'Why grieve over the end of a ship?'[2] (The picture shows a little steamer tugging an elegant old sailing ship to her last berth at sunset.) He then guesses at the meaning of the painting by saying that 'life' is an unending, cold and meaningless journey. But English patriots at the time had no difficulty in seeing what the painting was about. The grand old ship in Turner's painting was the main victor at the Battle of Trafalgar. (The *ship*, that is, not the sailors who manned her. Ships are powerful metaphors.) What is going on in the picture? 'The old *Temeraire* is dragged to her last home by a little, spiteful, diabolical steamer.' Thus wrote Thackeray, on seeing the painting at the Academy exhibition in 1839 (the year of the People's Charter). His references to the 'slow, sad, and *majestic*' ship and the 'foul, lurid, red-hot, *malignant* smoke' of the 'diabolical *steamer*' (my italics), have enough implicit historical awareness, class bias and political content in them to make further comment unnecessary. Thackeray knew *his* 'Turner' better than some modern critics.

Turner's paintings are nearly all 'history paintings', in that the particular vision, impression and mood they capture have the feel and importance (especially in the larger canvasses) of a unique historical moment, in which past, present and future are momentarily fused. But each hard-won vision, perceived in a shifting reality, and felt as an emotional as well as aesthetic unity, makes the viewer poignantly or vividly aware that in this endless process of change, with its moments of tension, danger, upheaval and calm, everything is relative and nothing is permanent. Such is the vision engendered by an unprecedented process of social, industrial and technological change, and it makes Turner, in the opinion of this writer, the most important artist Britain has so far produced. Turner's pictures of the world invoke a sense of the *transience* of observable reality, a dialectical awareness of which visual art had, prior to that time, been incapable.

The art of Turner and Constable (Constable's giving us a new sense of outdoor freshness and light) continues a tradition established in England by George Stubbs and Joseph Wright of Derby, in that it grows out of a scientific and empirical perception of nature. Here, landscapes predominate. The art of David, Barry, Fuseli, Flaxman and Blake is of another order: ideologically man-centred, less empirically-governed, it relies heavily on artistic precedent and ideal forms. Here, what is capable of being empirically or naturalistically represented is severely limited, depending for the most part on a conceptual, iconographic and symbolic view of reality, where the conceptual 'reality' is determined compositionally by the picture frame. The difference between these two orders of visual representation is not only generic (one topographical, the other anthropo-centric). It is also a historical and class difference: whereas the growth of the new industrial bourgeoisie in England gave fresh impetus to the development of the empirical and scientific outlook, encouraging in art a more sensuous, detailed appreciation of nature and a closer study of certain natural phenomena (such as animals, plants, light, clouds, trees and water), the commercial and urban petty bourgeoisie were more conscious of their place within the social and political framework and of the need to reform or revolutionise the social order. Hence Flaxman's purified, austere classicism and Blake's intense, 'visionary' schematism.

Criticism of the old order could be said to begin, in terms of 'visual ideology', with the neoclassical rejection of rococo decorativeness and softness in the 1760s, and reach its climax with the hard linearity and uncompromising spirituality of Blake's 'visions of Eternity' in the 1790s. But it is Turner and Constable (Turner beginning in the 1790s) who represented, through their fusion of empirical perception and imaginative art, the most fruitful advances in their own time. (In poetry, too, it is the fresh, detailed perception of nature and richly sensuous experience, such as we find in Wordsworth and Keats, that was *historically* most significant and had the greatest influence in the Victorian period.)

Much of Blake's poetry and art embodies the 'spirit of revolt' characteristic of Romanticism. Blake is often called a 'rebel', but this can become another a-historical label. After all, who among avant-garde Western artists in the twentieth century is not a 'rebel'? It is easy, for example, to trace a line from Blake to Carlyle, to D. H. Lawrence, to the manifestoes of the 'counter-culture' during the late 1960s and early 1970s. The revolt is by times transcenden-talist, libertarian, anarchist and utopian, though writers such as Herbert Marcuse have employed Marxist concepts in their attack on the Urizenic, 'one-dimensional' society. The critique that accompanies this revolt is roughly as follows: capitalist social relations have created a techno-cratic society, perverting and killing the basic, spontaneous human emotions, subordinating all human activity to the profit motive and the drive for so-called economic efficiency. The appearance of labour power as a commodity, an abstract quantity whose exchange value can be measured, brings with it a profound dehumanisation and crushing of the human spirit. Since art is essentially an affirmation of 'life', of the spontaneous and the creative as against the regimented and the mechanised, true art is essentially anti-capitalist (and, incidentally, anti-'totalitarian'). The artist by his very nature cannot help but be a rebel.[3]

Blake is rightly seen as one of the first embodiments of this kind of artistic revolt. But there is a danger, both of confusing it with the *modern* revolt — and hence, as we shall see, with modernism — and of obscuring the historical *context* within which it arose. What were the social conditions that led to this original Blakean revolt, with its rejection of 'Bacon, Newton, Locke'?

Blake, a hosier's son and a London engraver, was born into and remained part of a social class that had a long tradition of radical dissent behind it. It was vigorously active in the late eighteenth-century revolt against the landed and mercantile aristocracy, and was equally vigorous in opposing the new social order of industrial capitalism. Yet whereas in the former it was largely successful (since the industrial bourgeoisie was also anti-aristocratic and anti-mercantile), in the latter it was doomed to fail. Across the Channel, it was the most revolutionary force for change in the French Revolution, and the one most bitterly disappointed in its aim for a libertarian, democratic republic. Blake, as I shall argue, was an artistic representative of this class of small masters, craftsmen and artisans who, in England, had been the backbone of anti-Royalist agitation in London during the 1640s, were the most articulate element in the movement of popular radicalism between 1792 and 1820, and would be finally destroyed as a social force during the 1860s. While their militant actions helped to usher in bourgeois democracy, the new capitalist relations of production worsened their position as independent producers, and their economic role progressively declined. This, then, is the context of Blake's art and the Blakean 'revolt'.

Yet it is only part of the answer. Blake's ideological revolt was not merely a response to contemporary realities; it can also be seen as the continuation of hitherto submerged traditions. As Jack Lindsay has pointed out:

> Blake cannot be understood unless there is seen in him the re-emergence of the submerged revolutionary traditions that had carried on mainly among the craftsmen and small tradesmen of the towns. Enriched, the Ranter tradition burst out to meet the new situation in which total revolutionary change at last again seemed possible.[4]

This view of Blake was first put forward by A. L. Morton in his study of Blake and the Everlasting Gospel in 1958. Morton discovered a close affinity between Blake's ideas and those of the antinomians, Ranters and other radicals of the seventeenth century, who comprised both a lower-class breakaway from Puritan Independency, and a millenarian upsurge following the execution of the king and the defeat of the Levellers. The climacteric came in 1649-50. In the 1790s the old ideas suddenly flared up again, finding a new revolutionary context in which — at least for those who held them — 'their time had come'. Such a phenomenon of re-birth, strongly reflected in Blake's work, indicates an aspect of the late eighteenth-century 'religious revival', with its importance for the Romantic movement, that had not been noted in sufficient detail until E. P. Thompson's *The Making of the English Working Class* (1963). (I deal with this phenomenon, and its special relevance to Blake, more fully in the last chapter.)

Popular protest and resistance prior to the emergence of the organised working class — one thinks of bread riots, millenarian meetings, machine-breakings, insurrectionary conspiracies, etc. — was frequently violent and spontaneous, often with defensive, 'craftist' and backward-looking aims, and a conspiratorial, secret-society type of organisation as its source and nucleus. (The crucial exception is, of course, the London Corresponding Society. Yet despite its democratic organisation and discipline, it lacked the collective consciousness and deep class solidarity that was to weld together the working-class reform societies, trade union and cooperative movements of the industrial north.) Some of the ideological features of this pre-working-class, popular resistance — in particular, millenarianism and radical mysticism — are echoed in Blake's work. Partly reflecting his later social isolation, a subversive content is found clothed in the language of ancient symbolic tradition; poetry with a forceful directness and immediacy can be found among dense thickets of mystico-philosophical explication; rousing calls to 'Young Men of the New Age' are accompanied by labyrinthine researches into private psychology in the form of mythological psycho-dramas, which are presented as part-cosmic, part-historical conflicts, but which may be interspersed with such straight-from-the-shoulder declarations as: 'Their God/I will not worship in their Churches, nor King in their Theatres', utterances that leap out at the reader quite unexpectedly:

> Satan! Ah me! is gone to his own place, said Los.
>   Their God
> I will not worship in their Churches, nor King in
>   their Theatres.
> Elynittria! whence is this Jealousy running along
>   the mountains . . .

The effect is like a lightning flash in the murky darkness or a voice suddenly distinct after mumbling in a distant corner. (This passage was, however, written in 1803-4, at a time when the mass revolutionary tide had long since subsided.) 'Syntagmatic' conventions are thus denied.

The class that spoke through Blake and other radicals like him presented a major threat to the ruling hegemony, yet it was incapable, seeing that the bourgeoisie was unwilling, of leading a successful struggle for democratic reform. Though radicalism spread among manufacturers, shopkeepers and wealthier tradesmen, they were often susceptible to aristocratic pressures and ideas of bourgeois gentility, aspiring to a world of fashion, taste and respectability. The smaller masters, craftsmen and artisans, on the other hand, were less tied, yet they had little economic future in the long run as a social class; for the majority, proletarianisation or pauperisation was their fate, a fate that was more drawn-out in the capital than in the industrial north and midlands. Combinations of artisans and craftsmen —

Sucked into industrialism

both political and economic — were one reason for the Combination Acts, it is true; however, there was a strong element of individualism, competitiveness and élitism among the skilled craftsmen, especially in the London luxury trades. Even the poorest of independent producers, while prepared to combine with their fellows in a common cause, prized, above all, their 'master-less' freedom: many a hand-loom weaver preferred to starve at his own loom rather than be able to eat as a mill-owner's wage slave. After 1795, when the reaction set in, the war had begun to bite, and the prospect of parliamentary reform had receded, artisans, labourers and the poor turned increasingly towards religious solutions, while a tiny radicalised minority took up insurrectionary methods. This too finds its reflection in Blake's work. What, above all, has to be seen in this period is that the English bourgeoisie was not prepared for a political revolution. The manufacturers sheltered under the monarchy, with its government of landowners, rich merchants and royal hangers-on, rather than daring to awaken Albion to revolution. The governing class also acknowledged, in the words of Lord Liverpool, that 'England could not have survived the Napoleonic Wars without the steam-engine.' The English bourgeoisie, while it welcomed the events of 1789, had already had its revolution in the seventeenth century and saw no need for another. It behaved according to its own class interests. The war with France, launched by the conservative aristocracy and mercantile monopolists, especially those with West Indian interests (who did not bargain for yellow fever and Toussaint l'Ouverture), was at first opposed by the Whig gentry and liberal middle class, yet if the Tories saw France as a political threat, the bourgeoisie soon came to see it as an economic threat. The real reason for the political impotence of the Foxites was not the Terror or the so-called war fever, but international competition, loss of trade and the threat to exports, and, at home, the threat of combinations and higher wages. Hence the war was an opportunity to crush a major rival and discipline restive wage-earners. For the Tories, France meant an 'armed doctrine' that threatened their very existence with invasion and popular subversion. Though 'Church and King'

mobs were organised, it was the plebeian masses — of whom
Blake was a representative — who stood firm in their
opposition to the war, and retained a large measure of
sympathy for revolutionary France.

The contours of a revolutionary art are not determined
solely by the emotional and spiritual shape of the artist's
own life, but are inseparable from the wider struggle. The
image of the artist one draws from Blake has a deep social
significance: it is that of a heroic worker-intellectual, a
muscular artisan whose raw material consists of the human
suffering, anger and yearning he sees around him, and whose
artistic function is the production of truth and beauty out
of the midst of war, ugliness and falsehood. The following
passage, from *Jerusalem* (1804-20), gives some idea of the
heroic burden Blake felt he was taking upon his shoulders.
The speaker is Los, the blacksmith-poet who struggles with
Urizen, master-architect of capitalism and enemy of the
poetic imagination. The subject is the war, and those who
continue hypocritically to promote it:

Awkwardness arm'd in steel, folly in a helmet of gold,
Weakness with horns & talons, ignorance with a
                                        rav'ning beak,
Every Emanative joy forbidden as a Crime
And the Emanations buried alive in the earth with
                                        pomp of religion,
Inspiration deny'd, Genius forbidden by laws of
                                        punishment,
I saw terrified. I took the sighs & tears & bitter groans,
I lifted them into my Furnaces to forge the spiritual
                                        sword
That lays open the hidden heart. I drew forth the pang
Of sorrow red hot: I work'd it on my resolute anvil:
I heated it in the flames of Hand & Hyle & Coban
Nine times. Gwendolen & Cambel & Gwineverra
Are melted into the gold, the silver, the liquid ruby,
The crysolite, the topaz, the jacinth & every previous
                                        stone.
Loud roar my Furnaces and loud my hammer is
                                        heard.

I labour day and night. I behold the soft affections
Condense beneath my hammer into forms of cruelty,
But still I labour in hope, tho' still my tears flow
                                                  down:
That he who will not defend Truth may be compell'd
                                              to defend
A Lie: that he may be snared and caught and snared
                                            and taken:
That Enthusiasm and Life may not cease; arise,
                                        Spectre, arise!

In spite of the difficulties presented here for a reader
unfamiliar with Blake's longer works, it is not difficult,
surely, to sense the heroic struggle that is going on, or to
catch the rising tone of anger, militancy and aggressive
confidence as the speaker, even while his 'tears flow down'
(not in pity only, but in pity and wrath), becomes conscious
of his strength, and challenges the hypocritical falsehood of
his 'Spectre' with a defiant command. In some ways, Blake's
struggle is Miltonic — especially if we see it in terms of the
solitary artist's spiritual battle against powerful worldly
forces. The content of that lonely struggle must, however,
be placed in its historical context before it can be fully
understood, together with its modes of discourse.

This study is therefore offered as one contribution to the
Marxist approach to literature and art, concentrating on the
work of a single artist-poet. If anything, I have concentrated
on Blake in order to explore certain problems and to develop
a method of analysis. The approach is selective and thematic
rather than all-embracing and chronological, while each
chapter (apart from the three on visual art) may be read
almost as a self-contained essay. If this gives a 'synchronic'
rather than 'diachronic' feel to the book as a whole, the
basic approach nevertheless remains historical. I am not a
'Blakean' and do not subscribe to any cultist appreciation
of his work. I have tried to explain Blake's famed 'uniqueness' in historical terms — taking the poetry and the visual
art together — rather than leaving it as an inexplicable
mystery. If I am consequently accused of reductivism, of
overstressing art's 'subsidiary role in the social process' and

hence of neglecting art's inherent laws, then this is because there are too many books on Blake that analyse the art, poetry and ideas (especially the ideas) and forget the social process. This is not intended as another work of literary-cum-art criticism, though detailed interpretations of specific poems and paintings are undertaken. My main concern is the social and historical context within which an artist such as Blake emerges, and how this context makes necessary a revolution in artistic form and practice. As long as the formalists continue to hold sway in all discussions of art and literature, the historical-materialist approach will repeatedly stress art's historical and class content, guided by an understanding of the primacy of social laws over artistic ones.

1

The Romantic Artist

One of the best-known records of William Blake is Samuel Palmer's letter, written in 1855, to Blake's future biographer Alexander Gilchrist:

> In him you saw at once the Maker, the Inventor; one of the few in any age: a fitting companion for Dante. He was energy itself, and shed around him a kindling influence; an atmosphere of life, full of the ideal . . .
>
> He was a man without a mask; his aim single, his path straightforwards, and his wants few; so he was free, noble, and happy . . .
>
> His eye was the finest I ever saw: brilliant, but not roving, clear and intent, yet susceptible; it flashed with genius, or melted in tenderness. It could also be terrible. Cunning and falsehood quailed under it, but it was never busy with them. It pierced them, and turned away. Nor was the mouth less expressive: the lips flexible and quivering with feeling. I can yet recall it when, on one occasion, dwelling upon the exquisite beauty of the parable of the Prodigal, he began to repeat a part of it; but at the words, 'When he was yet a great way off, his father saw him', could go no further; his voice faltered, and was in tears.

Here is another record of the artist as restless life source:

> Picture to yourself a man of approximately fifty years of age, small rather than of medium size, but with a very powerful, stumpy figure, compact and with a notably strong bone structure . . . with restless, glowing and when his gaze is fixed, even piercing eyes . . . intelligent and full of life, offering a mingling or an occasional momentary alteration of the heartiest amiability and

shyness ... now a merrily and freely spoken word; again, immediately after, a relapse into gloomy silence ...

His remarks were all made with the greatest unconcern and without the least reserve, and whatever he said was spiced with highly original, naive judgements or humorous fancies. He impressed me as being a man with a rich, aggressive intellect, an unlimited, never resting imagination.

This is Beethoven, recorded by Friedrick Rochlitz in 1822.

In both passages we see a portrait of the Romantic Genius, in harmony with something other than his immediate environment; whose every word, glance, even movement of the lips, is expressive of the intense, contradictory life within; a personality deeply marked by suffering (Blake's tears, Beethoven's 'gloomy silence'), yet honest, open, and even childlike ('a man without a mask', 'the greatest unconcern ... without the least reserve ... naive judgements ... humorous fancies'); a Rousseauesque individual whose noble simplicity ('free, noble, and happy') and spontaneous warmth ('the heartiest amiability') seem to go with dramatic changes of mood ('it flashed with genius, or melted in tenderness. It could also be terrible. .... It pierced them and turned away', 'now a merrily and freely spoken word; again, immediately after, a relapse into gloomy silence'); an individual whose awesome insights and piercing vision ('it could be terrible. Cunning and falsehood quailed under it'; 'piercing eyes ... a rich, aggressive intellect, an unlimited, never resting imagination') spring from a passion for social justice, liberty and brotherhood, and the power to imagine, through artistic creation, a transcendent ideal. Such individuals have a godlike power; larger than life, they seem to burst the integuments of a conservative social order by their very existence.

The Romantic artist — as 'genius' and individual creator — is the cumulative outcome of three historical periods: the Italian Renaissance, the Elizabethan Age, and the period of the French and industrial revolutions. Michelangelo, Leonardo, Shakespeare, Beethoven and Blake are examples of artists whose creative energies have almost mythic status.

The liberating creative power of such artists could never have been released in times of stable conformity. The merchant princes of the Italian city-states, the Elizabethan sea-dogs, the leaders of the French Revolution and the industrial pioneers in England were also 'exceptional individuals'.

In broad terms, the free, individual creative artist, culminating in the figure of the Romantic artist, begins to appear at the moment when feudal social relations are decisively challenged. Bourgeois social relations, once they are juridically fixed as a system of contractual obligations between free individuals, ideologically reinforce the 'free individual' as the dominant and typical human subject. In the period of the bourgeois-democratic revolution (1776-1848) the dissolution of feudal-aristocratic bonds breaks the material and spiritual ties that bind the artist to his ecclesiastical, courtly, landed or corporate patrons, and makes possible his emergence as a freely creating individual whose source of creative potentiality lies in his 'own' personality and way of perceiving. Once the closed yet personal bonds of the client-patron relationship have given way to the impersonal exchanges of an expanding market in books and visual art, the artist becomes a 'liberated' individual creating for an unknown buying public:

> The nineteenth century exhibition presents the new social role of the work of art as a merchandise, in conformity with the creation of a competitive market economy. The artist has to enter the same social relations; his product now is competitive and he exhibits in the market. What he has to sell is his own creation, his own personality, his uniqueness.[1]

This goes some way towards explaining why the Romantics, despite the common threads of Romantic ideology, are so *different* — a fact that has led some critics and art historians to despair of ever defining the nature of Romanticism. Blake might nevertheless seem to confute this 'market' thesis, in that he tried to absorb the role of that spectre, the commercial middleman (whether publisher, printer, print-seller, or gallery owner), by printing, selling and exhibiting his works himself, so opting out of an impersonal market relationship. Yet he still depended on the middleman for commissions, and his 'recusancy' tended to push him back into the arms of patrons, a situation he likewise rebelled against when it curbed his individual creativity. With his etching process, his 'illuminated books', and his rejection of the middleman, Blake simply pushed the principle of artistic freedom and individuality further than anyone else.

There is, then, a deep connection between Romanticism and the emergence of 'free' individuals who are encouraged to produce commodities in competition with other 'free' individuals. The conflict between the expanding productive forces and the 'unfree' nature of the existing relations of production, relations sanctioned by the 'undemocratic', 'illiberal' nature of dominant political institutions, could only be resolved, at least in France, through a political revolution. The hard-fought bourgeois-democratic freedoms (such as free trade and a liberal constitution) found their artistic expression in the movement known as Romanticism. Romantic yearning and expansiveness, the desire to unite with a constantly changing, expansive reality, also parallels the 'constant revolutionising of production, uninterrupted disturbance of all social conditions, everlasting uncertainty and agitation' that Marx saw as the distinguishing feature of the bourgeois epoch. The Romantic artist is hence the embodiment of individualistic 'freedom', a freedom that, as Caudwell has shown, is the quintessential bourgeois illusion.

When the Third Estate declared itself the National Assembly in June 1789, most English observers — liberal aristocrats and moderate supporters of parliamentary reform — hailed the event as a victory for constitutional monarchy on the English model. Few had any notion that a profound change in human affairs had only just begun. It was not until February 1790, when Edmund Burke made a historic speech in the House of Commons, that upper-class opinion in England began to shift decisively against the French Third Estate, whose reliance on popular pressure and agitation caused alarm in England, where it was feared that the property of the rich might face similar dangers. Burke 'wished

the House to consider, how the members would like to have
their mansions pulled down and pillaged, their persons
abused, insulted and destroyed; their title-deeds brought
out and burned before their faces, and their families driven
to seek refuge in every nation throughout Europe'.[2] The
liberal bourgeoisie and landed gentry, represented in the
Commons by Whigs such as Fox and Sheridan, maintained
an open Francophile attitude until the declaration of war by
England in 1793.

Blake, as an English Jacobin, strongly identified with the
aspirations of the *menu peuple* and *sans-culottes*, the small
masters, craftsmen and artisans who made up the bulk of
the most advanced sections of the Parisian masses. English
Jacobinism was not a middle-class movement, but a movement of politically conscious artisans and small tradesmen
who were opposed to the monarchy, aristocracy, the tax
system and all distinctions of status. They were not only
for parliamentary reform but, in the words of English
Jacobinism's main ideologue, John Thelwall, were for 'a
large and comprehensive system of reform'. Blake's poem
The French Revolution, written in 1790-91 for Joseph
Johnson, the radical publisher (it was printed, though never
published), is not only anti-clerical but deeply republican
in sentiment. The Revolution is the beginning of a new
world, a cataclysmic upheaval in which all forms of tyranny,
oppression and superstition are being challenged and overthrown by the masses, whose power and actions are suggested
by the poem's elemental imagery. This passage, in which
La Fayette faces the troops, is typical:

> Like a flame of fire he stood before dark ranks,
>   and before expecting captains:
> On pestilent vapours around him flow frequent
>   spectres of religious men, weeping
> In the winds; driven out of the abbeys, their naked
>   souls shiver in keen open air;
> Driven out by the fiery cloud of Voltaire, and
>   thund'rous rocks of Rousseau,
> They dash like foam against the ridges of the army,
>   uttering a faint feeble cry.

The imagery, though at times strident and inflated, conveys the feeling of an enormous release of hitherto imprisoned energies, the unleashing of vast human potentialities whose vastness acquires for Blake the scale of a cosmic event, as if the earth itself were given birth. Politics and history are never, however, lost sight of:

> . . . in folds of the robe the crown'd adder builds
> and hisses
> From stony brows; shaken the forests of France,
> sick the kings of the nations,
> And the bottoms of the world were open'd, and the
> graves of arch-angels unseal'd:
> The enormous dead lift up their pale faces and look
> over the rocky cliffs.

Steeped in the language of biblical prophecy, this London engraver and religious 'enthusiast' (in 1789 he was, it seems, a Swedenborgian and member of the New Jerusalem Church) found in the French Revolution a source of poetic inspiration that corresponded with his class's vision of a world violently, yet gloriously, erupting.

With that glorious eruption came a stupendous laval flow of imaginative writing, very close in spirit to the visions of the seventeenth-century Ranters and Diggers, though with a corrosive, satirical bite and poetic intensity unprecedented in English:

> Prisons are built with stones of Law, Brothels with
> bricks of Religion.
> The pride of the peacock is the glory of God.
> The lust of the goat is the bounty of God.
> The wrath of the lion is the wisdom of God.
> The nakedness of woman is the work of God.
> Excess of sorrow laughs. Excess of joy weeps.
> The roaring of lions, the howling of wolves, the raging
> of the stormy sea, and the destructive sword, are
> portions of eternity, too great for the eye of man.

Such poetic energy is never one man's personal possession. Engendered by the actions of the revolutionary masses, who tore down the old moral codes, breaking the power of the monarchy and its church, it belongs, one might say, not simply to 'humanity' but to a humanity that has not yet been born.

The influence of the rebellious masses thus forged 'new complexes of feelings and thoughts' — feelings and thoughts that, since they were hitherto 'unpoeticised' and perhaps only half-realised, '[broke] through the shell which divides them from the sphere of poetic consciousness'.[3] The vision of an 'unborn humanity', the cleansed perception of a society of the future, is anticipated by means of a revolutionary leap in artistic consciousness. This leap did not happen through some inexplicable imaginative act — through the sudden 'visions' and 'prophecies' of innate, individual genius — but occurred as a *dialectical break* with the dominant ideology: responsive to and changed by the eruption of new mass forces, of new cries and new sensibilities, the plebeian artist himself becomes an arena of conflict, of revolutionary development and struggle. New class content shatters the old artistic forms, and a dialectical art, encompasing within itself 'contrary' states and 'contrary' visions, is born.

The 'act of creation', in the era of Romanticism, is individualistic and innovative. The work of art *appears* as the organic issue of an individual sensibility, spurning imitative, rule-governed production within a previously laid-down, shared tradition. Neoclassical imitation and the reliance on classical models is decisively rejected. Instead, the originality of individual genius is affirmed. As Edward Young puts it in *Conjectures on Original Composition* (1759), an original 'rises spontaneously from the vital root of genius; it grows, it is not made'. Imitations, on the other hand, 'are often a sort of *manufacture*, wrought up by those *mechanics, art* and *labour*, out of pre-existent materials not their own'. Raymond Williams, in *Culture and Society 1780-1950* (1958), ties this in with Burke's organicism and the emergent reaction against industrialism. Yet it was Burke who, in his *Reflections*, argued for the inheritance by posterity of previously laid-down constitutional laws, and the never-ending reliance on 'analogical precedent, authority and example', referring to the Revolution Settlement of 1688. Paine's riposte in *The Rights of Man* (1791) was that no parliament or generation of men in any country has the power of 'binding and controlling posterity', and that every age and generation 'must be free to act for itself, *in all cases*, as the ages and generations which preceded it. The vanity and presumption of governing beyond the grave, is the most ridiculous and insolent of all tyrannies'. In art as in politics, latent and hitherto unrealised energies are liberated. Each work of art positions its readers 'inside' the personality of its individual creator, who is, at the same time, swept along by forces beyond his individual control. Yet this desire to *innovate*, which derives from a sense of revolutionary necessity, a subjective impulse to explore the hidden depths of personality (i.e. the unconscious), and a compulsive need for renewed growth and continuous 'self-creation', is accompanied at the same time by a *social* drive towards technical innovation, the continuous revolutionising of technique inherent in the capitalist mode of production itself, which, in the period of Romanticism, is historically progressive. (The modernist obsession with technical innovation for innovation's sake is, on the other hand, paralleled by a *decline* in the wider benefits of technical innovation, as large areas of the underdeveloped or 'Third World' starve, and tens of millions in the advanced, industrial countries become permanently unemployed.)

At this point, revolutionary Romanticism expresses the progressive energies of the Enlightenment. When Joseph de Maistre attacked those who 'have a certain fierce and rebellious pride which does not compromise with anything', who 'find fault in every authority' and 'hate anything above them', and who, if allowed, 'will attack everything, even God, because he is master',[4] he was indicting the Romantic rebel as much as the atheist and materialist *philosophes* he had in mind. But when the Jacobin republic degenerated into the Directory, and the Directory turned into Empire, and the steam engines of Boulton and Watt were heard in a hundred textile mills, the social relations of modern bourgeois society emerged in all their prosaic, and for many, miserable greyness. The dreams of the Enlightenment faded. Perfectibility, utility and the clear light of reason were gods with feet of clay. Wordsworth and Coleridge, disillusioned with the

failure of their earlier hopes of a new society, adopted more
conservative attitudes. Southey's Toryism was the most
complete defection. 'You have your salary; was't for that
you wrought?' was Byron's gibe.[5] Blake's was a subtler
and more complex change, yet one that reflects, in its own
way, the broader pattern. The return of many Romantics,
at first seduced by the Enlightenment's critique of religion,
to 'spiritual' values based on faith and the 'holiness of the
Heart's affections',[6] a process repeated in Carlyle, whose
idealism resembles that of Blake, reflects, in part, the
restoration throughout Europe of a church order temporarily
de-stabilised by the French Revolution and Napoleon's
armies. Hence, the profound effects of the Concordat
between Napoleon and Pope Pius VII in 1801. T. E. Hulme
called Romanticism 'spilt religion',[7] but there were really
two Romanticisms: one that spilt it, and one that poured
it back. On a less intellectual level, the slogan of the
Birmingham mob who destroyed Joseph Priestley's library
and laboratory in 1791 was clear enough. It was: 'No
Philosophers — Church and King forever'.

When we look at the radical change in poetry that came
about with Romanticism, it is soon evident that its principal
achievements are a new lyrical intensity and a greater organic
complexity, allied to the adoption of both popular and more
'open-ended' modes and forms. Between personal, subjective
content and popular form (in Wordsworth's and Coleridge's
Lyrical Ballads, for example) there is often a tension that
remains unresolved, echoing, perhaps, the somewhat uneasy
alliance that developed between the new middle-class
intelligentsia and the popular masses. Allan Rodway has
periodised English Romanticism as follows: first, a pre-
Romantic phase of Sensibility, interpreted as 'unpurposive
pity, which seems, psychologically speaking, to be a sign of
guilt and a substitute for reformism'.[8] Next, the French
Revolution, and the poetry of Blake. This is where
Romanticism in England is usually said to begin. The period
of Wordsworth's greatest creativity, and, within that, of a
more passive and negative opposition, spans the years 1795-
1800. The years 1804-15 are a time of relative stasis, of

religious revival and the 'period of the pseudo-romantics' such as Moore, Campbell and Scott.[9] 1815 to 1824 sees the resurgence of the radical reform movements, the transition from Waterloo (1815) to Peterloo (1819), the Cato Street conspiracy (1820) and subsequent reaction, and the mature works of Shelley and Byron.

In the period of English Romanticism all artistic forms and modes underwent radical changes, while new forms and modes came into being. Since it was a period of intense repression and violent, as well as non-violent mass protest, a period in which the whole future of humanity seemed to be at stake, it was thus, pre-eminently, a period of *crisis*, hence of emotional crises and what has been called 'crisis poetry'. (The apparently spontaneous, unplanned nature of capitalist production, with its boom-slump cycle; the accelerated dynamic of social life as a whole, and the birth of the modern class struggle, have left their indelible mark on the personality structure and psyche of every writer and artist.) In Romantic poetry, older, classical forms such as the ode were re-vitalised and transformed, while the rhythms and metres that had dominated in the period after 1660 were either supplanted or made new. Thus appropriate places to begin are the lyric and the English decasyllabic line, the verse form that dominated English poetry from Chaucer to Tennyson. By focusing on this latter form — as a kind of 'test case' — we shall perhaps be able to assess more concretely the nature of the radical change that came about.

The lyric, as has often been said, is the chief glory of the Romantic movement. The change from sentiment and sensibility to Romantic feeling is the change from an *attitude* or a *stance towards* something, to direct *involvement* and *empathy*, from self-conscious pity to a passionate intensity and single-minded absorption that come from the exercise of the creative imagination, or — in the case of Keats's famous sparrow — a new 'negative capability', an unmediated, innocent perception of the world. From concrete externals, seen by an observer as part of a physical universe existing in time and space, a world of material objects and processes, we move to the concrete symbols of an inner, spiritual reality, a reality that exists beyond or outside time and space and obeys no material laws, only the laws of a subjective consciousness. Romantic feeling enacts a movement away from mechanistic materialism towards subjective idealism. The laws of matter and the laws of thought appear to belong to different epistemological universes. The Romantic poet, through the lyric, explores states of the soul, subjective psychic processes. Natural landscapes are neither simply 'out there', as objectively real landscapes passively observed, nor are they wholly under man's control: they are landscapes of the mind or soul of the poet, or exist in and for themselves, uncontrolled by man. (By a circuitous route, natural objects, such as Wordsworth's daffodils, that have a unique existence independent of man, nevertheless have to be *perceived* as 'themselves', and are thus vivid proof of a 'uniquely individual' perception.) Romantic feeling, finally, generates a faith in the possibility of social change through an improvement or revolution in interpersonal relations, a belief that social change can come about by a return to 'nature' or to natural feeling. The fact that interpersonal relations rest on socio-economic foundations is not usually perceived by the Romantic poet, since objective economic analysis and in particular political economy are felt to be somehow destructive of the human soul.

It has often been said that the origin and foundation of poetry is rhythm, or rhythmically heightened speech. According to George Thomson, 'the language of poetry is essentially more primitive than common speech, because it preserves in a higher degree the qualities of rhythm, melody and fantasy inherent in speech as such'.[10] Rhythm itself, he argues, is related both to work and to the mimetic dance.

Romantic poets, like many twentieth-century modernists, felt the need to go back to primal *origins*, back to the 'real foundations' of poetry, in an attempt to re-vitalise it at the deepest level and overcome the moribund formalism and decorativeness of eighteenth-century poetry. The decasyllabic line, simply because of its dominance, was bound to be affected in this period of radical change and transformation.

The basic rhythm of the English decasyllabic line is iambic — that is, an unstressed followed by a stressed syllable (^{x} ´). This line is sometimes called an iambic pentameter — a line of verse composed of five feet, each one an iamb, with a caesura after the second foot. The entry into English of the iambic decasyllabic line, it could be argued, partly reflects the assimilation into the language of large numbers of disyllabic compound verbs carrying iambic stress (such as 'refléct', 'sustáin', etc.) during the Middle English period, due to French and Latin borrowings. The rise of the new, 'refined' syllabic metres, which were opposed to the more rugged, alliterative, *stressed* (rather than syllabic) verse of the Anglo-Saxon oral and popular tradition, accompanied the growth of post-Norman courtly culture.

(It might be worth finding out, in this regard, whether or not all revolutions in poetic metre have been accompanied by, and even largely caused by, major shifts in the basic rhythms of the spoken language, or shifts in the way rhythms previously neglected, suppressed, or unheard are then heard, adopted and used — all of which is closely bound up with political, social and economic changes. Thus from the old, pre-feudal clan system, with its alliterative verse and predominantly trochaic rhythms based on intrinsic Germanic stress patterns, we move to the feudal period, with its French-influenced syllabic metres, then to the bourgeois-aristocratic hegemony of the eighteenth century, with its closed, decasyllabic rhyming couplets, then to the era of bourgeois democracy, with its mixture of transformed 'hegemonic' and popular forms, and finally to the cross-cultural anarchy and experimentation of the modern era, with its ubiquitous, metreless *vers libre*.)

For centuries the dominant rhythm in English verse, reflecting a dominant courtly-aristocratic culture, was iambic. Other, non-iambic rhythms, or verse based on the number of beats or stresses, was associated with the older, indigenous alliterative tradition, and with popular forms such as the song, nursery rhyme and ballad, and was therefore either subordinated, suppressed or contained by the iambic decasyllabic line. Only Milton, it seems, was daring enough in his use of the decasyllabic line to combine enjambment with an opening down-beat in the next line, thereby producing a spondee (´´) at the most palpable point, as in:

> In the Beginning how the Heav'ns and Eárth
> Róse out of Chaos: Or if Sion hill
> Delight thee more, and Siloa's Brook that flówd
> Fást by the Oracle of God; I thence . . .

Here, the repeated spondee sets up a true counter-rhythm, full of productive conflicts and tensions; the verse is 'unfettered', energetically alive, and continually changing, shifting and pressing forward in the great strides of Milton's verse paragraphs. It releases and celebrates the deep rhythmic potentialities of the language, instead of suppressing or containing them; unlike the verse couplets of Denham, Dryden, Pope and Cowper, it unflinchingly harnesses the rhythmic energies they can only absorb, and so becomes a kind of model for eighteenth-century liberal poets such as Thomson, and Romantic poets such as Wordsworth and Keats. (Blake eventually eschewed the iambic, decasyllabic line altogether, just as he eschewed the use of oils in painting, and there were important reasons for this.)

The typically 'Augustan' rhyming couplet, with its regular iambic rhythm and Latinate diction, is a symbolic enactment of a certain kind of 'order'; of political balance and compromise; of antitheses that are aesthetically contained; of 'correctness', 'refinement', and a supple, 'natural' decorum. In the following example, from Pope's *Windsor-Forest*, the intrinsic iambic rhythm and the metre, which are so well suited to detached or thoughtful reflection (as in: 'When I consider how my light is spent', or: 'The curfew tolls the knell of parting day'), and the feel of easy, unhurried discourse, have become inseparable from the dominance of a particular *class* and class viewpoint, mirrored in the subject matter of the passage:

> When milder autumn summer's heat succeeds,
> And in the new-shorn field the Partridge feeds,
> Before his Lord the ready Spaniel bounds,
> Panting with hope, he tries the furrow'd grounds,
> But when the tainted gales the game betray,
> Couch'd close he lies, and meditates the prey;

Secure they trust th' unfaithful field, beset,
Till hov'ring o'er 'em sweeps the swelling net . . .
See! from the brake the whirring Pheasant springs,
And mounts exulting on triumphant wings.
Short is his joy; he feels the fiery wound,
Flutters in blood, and panting beats the ground.
Ah! what avail his glossy, varying dyes,
His purple crest, and scarlet-circled eyes,
The vivid green his shining plumes unfold,
His painted wings, and breast that flames with gold?

Although this passage describes a lively action, the lines are
fairly regular. The most irregular are, appropriately, the four
that describe the shooting of the pheasant:

Sée!/from the brake the whirring Pheasant springs,
And mounts exulting/on triumphant wings.
Shórt is his joy;/he feels the fiery wound,
Flúttẽrs in blood,/and panting beats the ground.

Although in the last two lines a caesura falls after the fourth
syllable, and although in the first there is a hint of a second
caesura after 'brake', the lines are not strictly regular because
an iambic rhythm is not established at the beginning of each
line, the fourth beginning with an emphatically trochaic
word, 'flutters'. Such irregularities are, of course, the strength
of the decasyllabic line, with its contrapuntal rhythms.
Perfect regularity would, as the Augustans well knew, be of
all things the most boring and monotonous. Yet it could be
argued that non-iambic rhythms are only present as a
temporary disturbance, however pleasurable or necessary to
the whole, and that when the disturbance has been quelled,
a normal kind of regularity is resumed. To put it less crudely,
the rhyming couplet succeeds in absorbing non-iambic
rhythms by the very manner in which it introduces them.

In the blank verse of Wordsworth's *Prelude*, we can see
how the poet exploits a far more liberal and expressive
variety of rhythms and rhythmic patterns, still *within* the
'absolutist' hegemony of a fundamentally iambic rhythm
and decasyllabic metre, yet seeming to break all the metrical
rules:

> And in the frosty season, when the sun
> Was set, and visible for many a mile
> The cottage windows through the twilight blaz'd,
> I heeded not the summons: — happy time
> It was, indeed, for all of us; to me
> It was a time of rapture: clear and loud
> The village clock toll'd six; I wheel'd about,
> Proud and exulting, like an untired horse,
> That cares not for its home. — All shod with steel,
> We hiss'd along the polish'd ice, in games
> Confederate, imitative of the chace
> And woodland pleasures, the resounding horn,
> The Pack loud bellowing, and the hunted hare.
> So through the darkness and the cold we flew,
> And not a voice was idle; with the din,
> Meanwhile, the precipices rang aloud,
> The leafless trees, and every icy crag
> Tinkled like iron, while the distant hills
> Into the tumult sent an alien sound
> Of melancholy, not unnoticed, while the stars,
> Eastward, were sparkling clear, and in the west
> The orange sky of evening died away.

The whole movement of the passage, while not so poundingly spondaic and forceful as Milton's (which would not perhaps be suitable here anyway), has a nervy resilience, an alert responsiveness to the movement of thoughts and feelings as they are recollected — above all, a sense of pace as it springs, runs along, holds back then springs again (demonstrating well the principle of 'reculer pour mieux sauter'), that one finds in energetic yet disciplined prose. In particular, the frequent enjambments go with an apparent disregard, syntactically, for metric verse as a container of phrase units (as in

> while the distant hills
> Into the tumult sent an alien sound
> Of melancholy,)

and a freedom in which the words seem to express their own rhythms, instead of being confined in a regular metre. There is rhythmical counterpoint too: 'clear and loud/The village clóck tóll'd síx' has six beats (thus, as it were, 'telling' the chimes) of which the last three form three consecutive beats, or what the Greeks called a molossus; this is carried on in 'úntíred hórse' and, further down, in 'Páck lóud béllowing', like a rhythmical motif of the kind used by Beethoven, acting as a memory of something that has gone before, or an anticipation — here, a slightly sinister one — of something to come. Again, there is an apparently free and expansive discursiveness, with the appearance of thoughts spontaneously occurring, as in

> I heeded not the summons: — happy time
> It was, indeed, for all of us; to me
> It was a time of rapture . . .

There is the cluster of unstressed syllables, typical of speech, as in

Confederate, imitative of the chace

— where, imitatively, the syllables chase the word 'chace', so that the irregularity (as with the Augustans) has a precise function. (The last line in the passage, as a cadence point, is a perfectly regular iambic pentameter.) The passage seems to want to be prose, and therefore 'natural' (betraying a continuity with certain Augustan aesthetic norms), yet the more we look at it, the more we feel a masterful verse technique binding it together, and this tension between an almost rebellious freedom ('I heeded not the summons') and a kind of magisterial authority — a tension that is present both in the verse itself and in the juxtaposition (as we read the passage) of heedless youth and a wiser, adult consciousness that has suffered and felt — is what gives the whole passage its power and strength.

One tendency of English Romantic verse is therefore towards greater *freedom* and *variety*, corresponding with a desire for greater individual freedom of expression within society as a whole. (Hence the bourgeois paradigm of 'the individual versus society', where society becomes the polar opposite of the individual.) The element of binding restraint — the 'absolutism', for example, of the ten-syllable line, beginning and ending in an iamb — thus corresponds with the need for some socially-determined obligation or duty, whether this is to the state, the law, tradition, or simply one's fellow human beings. The logic of individual freedom, on the other hand, is a total absence of such restraint or coercion, in other words, *absolute freedom*, the anarchist principle that the individual be permitted to develop freely, unhampered by laws, duties or obligations. The false consciousness that this kind of extreme individualism represents has been frequently exposed. The anarchist demand for absolute freedom of the individual (in essence a utopian hypostatisation of 'free' capitalist competition) implies a revolt against *all* forms of external authority, cooperation and social organisation. In the artistic field, and in poetry in particular, anarchist principles can result in a dissipation and empty formlessness as wearisome as any of the binding rules against which they rebel. In this regard, *vers libre* (as a revolt against the dominance of the Alexandrine, corresponding at a certain point to a denial of the legitimacy of the French state and its institutions) and 'free verse', are far more difficult to handle than regular verse forms, simply because in this case the poetic form, not having been laid down *for* the poet, has to be freshly created *by* him each time he makes an attempt at poetic creation. Unless some kind of formal principle or formal basis external to the poet is made use of — even at the level of gesture or ironic allusion — the result is often likely to be a collapse into formlessness and aimless experimentation, a modernist or Dadaist travesty of Romantic spontaneity. Free form thus imposes a far heavier responsibility on the individual creative artist (a surviving, neo-Romantic genotype) than the handling of an established poetic or verse form. Untrapped steam may be 'free', but only steam that has been trapped in cylinders and seeks an outlet can drive engines. Free verse, if it is to drive *poetic* engines, must at least be contained by certain rhythmic, formal principles.

These remarks are relevant to Blake, since Blake — at least in his poetry — pushed the freedom principle further than any other English Romantic poet, even to the extent of writing a free verse poem — the first of its kind in English.

As far as the iambic pentameter or decasyllabic line is concerned, Blake's earliest poetry already shows a straining against its rhythmic restrictions. The four poems to the

seasons in *Poetical Sketches* (1783) are in blank verse, and
the freedoms taken are Miltonic:

> The hills tell each other, and the list'ning
> Vallies hear; all our longing eyes are turned
> Up to thy bright pavilions: issue forth,
> And let thy holy feet visit our clime. ('To Spring')

The supposedly underlying iambic rhythm is here replaced
by the trochaic, as at: 'téll eăch', 'óthĕr', 'líst'nĭng', 'Vállĭes',
'áll oŭr', 'lóngĭng', 'Úp tŏ', 'íssŭe' and 'vísĭt'. This disruptive
trochaic rhythm heightens the feeling of a rapidly approaching change, conveying a mood of excited expectancy; the
poet does not merely *respond* to change but *urges* it ('íssŭe
forth'; 'vísĭt our clime'), thus preventing any 'Augustan'
relapse into some easy, confident expectation or passive
observation. The Romantic response to nature is subjective
in the sense that the poet is no longer merely an observer,
but an active participant, often trying to fuse his mind
or will with external reality — a reality that is itself in
constant flux and change.

By 1789 Blake has more or less abandoned the decasyllabic
line (frequently used in *Poetical Sketches*, and used only
once in *Songs of Innocence*, in *The Little Black Boy*) for
the fourteener, or fourteen-syllable line, while his development of the short lyric shows a preference for trochaic
metres and triple (e.g. dactylic) rhythms over iambic ones.
The effect is twofold: with the fourteener, a greater —
perhaps dangerously greater — freedom and variety as to
rhythmic patterns; with the song, a greater liveliness, freshness and purity than had existed in English since the time
of Shakespeare.

It is easy to see how Blake came to adopt the fourteener.
Divided into one iambic four-stressed, and one iambic three-
stressed line, it is the basic metre and stanza form of the
ballad, as in the ballad *Gwin, King of Norway (Poetical
Sketches);*

> Thĕ gód ŏf wár iŝ drúnk wĭth blóod;
> Thĕ eárth dŏth faínt aňd faíl;
> Thĕ sténch ŏf blóod măkes síck thĕ héav'ns;
> Ghŏsts glút thĕ thróat ŏf héll!

> O what have Kings to answer for,
> Before that awful throne!
> When thousand deaths for vengeance cry,
> And ghosts accusing groan!

The same metre re-appears in *Night (Songs of of Innocence)*, where it is joined to the triple (3/4) rhythm used in *The Ecchoing Green* ('Thĕ Sún dŏes ăríse,/Ănd măke háppў thĕ skíes'), to produce an original stanza form:

> Thĕ sún dĕscéndĭng ĭn thĕ wést,
> Thĕ évenĭng stár dŏes shíne;
> The birds are silent in their nest,
> And I must seek for mine.
> Thĕ móon lĭke ă flówer
> Ĭn héavń's hĭgh bówer,
> Wĭth sílĕnt dĕlíght
> Sĭts ănd smíles ŏn thĕ níght.

In *Holy Thursday* (which first appears in *An Island in the Moon*, c. 1784-5) the metre is explicitly written as a fourteener: 'Thĕ chíldrĕn wálkĭng twó & twó ĭn gréy & blúe & gréen'. The next stage is to treat this syllabic metre with the freedom that Blake had hitherto treated the pentameter, by abandoning rhyme, upsetting the iambic rhythm (which, in the line just quoted, is as regular as the march of the Charity-School children) and varying the caesura, and then by breaking the syllabic count. Add to this process the influence of Macpherson's Ossianic prose-poems, and the result is *Tiriel* (1789) where, but for the frequency of end-stopped lines (the only metrical restriction, it seems, that Blake consistently imposes upon himself in this poem), the effect could have been to destroy the sense of metre altogether, hence to revert to non-metrical prose or to produce something akin to free verse (and if the latter, then the *appearance* of the fourteener line on the page would have been wholly misleading). As it is, it is doubtful whether the free fourteener presents anything like the underlying, *felt* regularity even of Miltonic blank verse: the movement towards 'free verse', or towards what Gerard Manley Hopkins called 'sprung rhythm', seems to be irresistible.

The lines in *The French Revolution* (1791) are written as

lines of verse, but there is constant enjambment, no regular syllabic count, no obviously regular underlying rhythm, no regular number of stresses in each line and a bewildering variety of cadences — in fact little to show us that this is verse, apart from the fact that it appears on the page as lines of verse. If regularity has been abandoned, what is it that we must look for? What are the underlying principles? What, in other words, makes this verse, rather than forceful, impassioned prose? Closer examination reveals a loose anapestic, seven-stressed (septenary) line with frequent dactylic counterpoint, though the frequency of spondees and clusters of stressed syllables (e.g. 'féet,/Hánds, héad, bósom') makes it exceptionally difficult to scan.

The next stage, then, is free verse itself:

> Rintrah roars & shakes his fires in the burden'd air;
> Hungry clouds swag on the deep.
>
> Once meek, and in a perilous path,
> The just man kept his course along
> The vale of death.
> Roses are planted where thorns grow,
> And on the barren heath
> Sing the honey bees.
>
> Then the perilous path was planted,
> And a river and a spring
> On every cliff and tomb,
> And on the bleached bones
> Red clay brought forth . . .

The unit here is not the metrical line and the formal stanza, but the *phrase* and the *unit of sense*. A hundred years before the 'modernist revolution', Blake had shattered the carapace of poetic metre, allowing the expressive phrase and the poetic *argument* (the quotation is from 'The Argument' at the beginning of *The Marriage of Heaven and Hell*), rather than some predetermined metrical pattern, to dictate the poetic form. Its rhythmic 'feet' tread a new 'perilous path'.

The *Book of Urizen* (1794) uses a stressed, non-syllabic pattern of three to four (usually four) stresses or beats per line, but in *Vala, or the Four Zoas* (1797) there is a return

to the basic fourteener line, where an exact syllabic count of
fourteen syllables can often be made, though any regular
iambic rhythm has long since been overthrown:

> But when fourteen summers & winters had revolved
> > over
> Their solemn habitation, Los beheld the ruddy boy
> Embracing his bright mother, & beheld malignant fires
> In his young eyes, discerning plain that Orc plotted
> > his death.

Though each of these lines contains exactly fourteen syllables,
only the second (whose caesura comes one syllable too
early) approximates a regular fourteener.

The one statement made by Blake concerning his verse
technique is in 'To the Public', prefacing his epic poem,
Jerusalem:

> When this Verse was first dictated to me, I consider'd a
> Monotonous Cadence, like that used by Milton &
> Shakespeare & all writers of English Blank Verse, derived
> from the modern bondage of Rhyming, to be a necessary
> and indispensable part of Verse. But I soon found that in
> the mouth of a true Orator such monotony was not only
> awkward, but as much a bondage as rhyme itself. I there-
> fore have produced a variety in every line, both of
> cadences & number of syllables. Every word and every letter
> is studied and put into its fit place; all are necessary to
> each other. Poetry Fetter'd Fetters the Human Race.

Here, in a nutshell, is the Romantic revolt against metrical
restrictions, taking the form of a revolt against 'English
Blank Verse', which remained the dominant verse form in
English poetry up to Tennyson. Blake gives us no clue as
to what his own metrical principles are, except to say that
there is 'a variety in every line' and that 'Every word and
every letter is studied and put into its fit place'. The democratic expansiveness of Whitman's verse; the revolt against
'unsprung' metre and the iambic pentameter which we
associate with Hopkins and Pound (the former re-affirming
the *Germanic* roots of English); the free, prosaic philosophis-
ing in McDiarmid's poetry; the verse of a neo-Blakean

'visionary' such as Ginsberg, and the later poetry of Ted Hughes, another mythopoeic iconoclast — in brief, the revolt against 'fettered' verse and the ordered, rational world-view, begins, if it begins anywhere, with Blake. The revolt has created more problems than it has solved: the search for appropriate forms continues, a search impelled, not by a homogeneous reading public or a shared body of social and aesthetic values (since these have become shattered and fragmented beyond any hope of their synthesis — short of a socialist revolution — in some 'common culture'), but by the creative will or mind of the individual poet himself, as he journeys towards self-realisation and personal 'truth'.

Alongside this Romantic need for greater freedom and variety of expression, and one of the central features of Romanticism, is the so-called 'revolt against the tyranny of Reason'. For Blake, classical reason demanded a confinement and contraction of the feelings and senses, a wilful exclusion of that faculty through which the 'spiritual man' perceives infinity. Urizenic man shuts himself up in a cavern whose chinks are the five senses (parodying Locke's model of passive receptivity). He sees the sun only as a round disc of fire 'somewhat like a Guinea' (an appropriate simile), whereas the spiritual man sees 'an Innumerable company of the Heavenly host crying "Holy, Holy, Holy is the Lord God Almighty"'. This is Blake's answer to the alienated vision of capitalism and Newtonian science, symptoms of man's Fall from Eternity:

> And many said, 'We see no Visions in the darksom air.
> Measure the course of that sulphur orb that lights the
> darksom day:
> Set stations on this breeding Earth & let us buy & sell.'
> (*The Four Zoas*, Night II)

> And as their eye & ear shrunk, the heavens shrunk
> away:
> The Divine Vision became First a burning flame, then
> a column
> Of fire, then an awful fiery wheel surrounding earth
> and heaven,

> And then a globe of blood wandering distant in an
> unknown night . . .
> They look forth: the Sun is shrunk: the Heavens
> are shrunk
> Away into the far remote . . .
>
> (*Jerusalem*, Plate 66)

The first passage is also applicable to the measuring Babylonians, whose 'economic calculations were made on the basis of astronomical calculations . . . The upper and nobler half of mathematics was concerned with the heavens and the other half was concerned with buying and selling and satisfying tax demands on earth' (Bernal, 1972, 28). The second reflects advances in astronomical science. For John Donne, the new Copernican philosophy had called 'all in doubt'; the Neoplatonic correspondences had been lost and the element of fire 'quite put out'. After Galileo, 'heaven' was 'abolished' (as Brecht's Galileo puts it, but historically it was Giordano Bruno who came to that revolutionary conclusion). Man was no longer the centre of the universe. The mechanists turned the cosmos into a clock-like machine and God into a Divine Watchmaker (though this was not Newton's conception); then, with Herschel's discovery (in 1781) of the planet Uranus, and, even more spectacularly, of other remote galaxies — vast aggregations of individual stars with dark voids in between — the human world shrank to the size of an atom, while the heavenly bodies flew off into space, 'wandering distant in an unknown night'. Blake's Isaiah, when asked: 'does a firm perswasion that a thing is so, make it so?' replies: 'All poets believe that it does, & in ages of imagination this firm persuasion removed mountains'. D. H. Lawrence, who was of the 'firm perswasion' that the moon was made of phosphorus, echoes Blake when he laments the contraction of human vision and the loss of 'the great living cosmos of the "unenlightened" pagans':

> Petty little personal salvation, petty morality instead of cosmic splendour, we have lost the sun and the planets, and the Lord with the seven stars of the Bear in his right hand. Poor, paltry, creeping little world we live in, even the keys of death and Hades are lost.
>
> (*Apocalypse*, 26-7)

Such is the repeated refrain of anti-rationalism since the seventeenth century. Yet Blake's reaction has its own context.

According to one writer, the anti-rationalist revolt erupted when

> ... strong irrational forces, hitherto kept in check by a traditionalist and hierarchic society, had been unleashed by the Revolution, a turn of events which the Romantics regarded as highly auspicious. In a sense it might be said that the explosion of irrational, or subconscious impulses that characterised so many aspects of the Revolution was the signal for the Romantic battle against Reason.[11]

Such a notion of 'irrational forces' betrays, of course, its own class viewpoint. The September massacres and the 'Terror' were seen by conservatives as the violent upsurge of wild, irrational forces, whereas the slaying of tens of thousands in a single battle during the Seven Years' War was greeted by no such reaction, at least among ruling-class circles, since wars and violence initiated by monarchical states were regarded as a necessary part of 'policy' in an imperfect world. Others view Romantic ideology as the result of a cumulative intellectual change. Thus T. J. Diffey:

> ... it is evident that the enormous changes in thought and sensibility between Locke and, say, Blake, were not achieved in sudden and inexplicable leaps for which philosophy and the aesthetics of the eighteenth century leave us totally unprepared.[12]

Explanations for this change, however, cannot be found in the 'history of ideas'.

> Morality, religion, metaphysics, and other ideologies, and their corresponding forms of consciousness ... have no history, no development; it is men, who, in developing their material production and their material intercourse, change, along with this their real existence, their thinking and the products of their thinking. Life is not determined by consciousness, but consciousness by life.[13]

Any explanation must, in other words, avoid sharing 'in each historical epoch the illusions of that epoch'.[14]

Locke's famous *tabula rasa* image and his image of the mind as a kind of house, *furnished* with ideas conveyed in from outside, give the impression of the mind as a passive receiver or container. Thinking, doubting, believing, reasoning and willing he calls 'the different actings of our own minds; which we being conscious of, and observing in ourselves, do from these receive into our understandings as distinct ideas as we do from bodies affecting our senses'.[15] Mental activity, as such, is not the highest awareness in Locke's scheme of things, but *observation: 'observing in ourselves'* the 'different actings of our minds'. These 'actings', which are conveyed into our 'understandings', we receive 'as distinct ideas'. The highest level is that of the *privileged observer*, receiving ideas from an objective source that is always external. The manifold 'actings' of our own minds are not fully conscious of themselves as actings, but rather become the *objects* of a higher consciousness. Sensation is not, in Locke, practical-sensuous activity, but always a 'conveyance' from outer to inner.[16]

This alienated objectivity nevertheless reflects a social advance. The growth of technique, of commodity production and of trade in the later seventeenth century meant an increase in the exchange and circulation of manufactured goods, coins and paper money. (The Bank of England was founded in 1694, four years after the publication of Locke's *Essay Concerning Human Understanding*.) Objects of labour — that is, goods and money — suddenly appear to have an independent existence and hence laws of their own, seen from the viewpoint of the individual subject as privileged observer. The circulation of paper banknotes, for example, enables the Bank to lend more money than it actually possesses. The new financial machinery, once regulated, can operate more or less autonomously, without the need for constant government intervention, just as in the natural universe moving particles and bodies, once set in motion by the Supreme Being, behave according to fixed mechanical laws; divine intervention is no longer required. Social relations themselves tend to become reified as relations between inanimate, quantifiable, weighable objects in motion. Without this kind of reifying objectivity, itself the product of a new kind of social alienation, Newtonian physics would have been impossible.

In aesthetics, value is attributed to objective form rather than to the creative process by which it comes into being. This object of appreciation always has a social utility: it must communicate, combing the *utile* with the *dulce*. The imagination, as a shaping power, is barely distinguished from the fancy, that faculty of inventing fictitious entities (such as the centaur and the unicorn) by re-arranging the already seen and known. New knowledge can only come from empirical experience and reasoning; imagination or fancy may discover new beauties, but not new knowledge.

With Romanticism, the human subject, no longer determined by the environment, becomes the active creator of the world in which he lives. Whereas classical reason had 'misread' the domain of exchange and circulation as a set of fixed, unhistorical laws, Romanticism 'misreads' the production sphere as a process of individual creation and innovation freed of social restraints. The rapid expansion of the productive forces is misinterpreted as the result of individual rather than social forces. Imagination is re-defined as a higher, more active, more all-embracing human faculty than the understanding. Perception is not passive but creative; the work of art is valued, not as a finished object to which nothing can be added or taken away, but as a unique, living organism, whose inner life and meaning are beyond the grasp of reason. Poetry of the imagination strives towards infinity. As Derrida would put it, 'it always signifies again and differs'.[17]

Blake's reaction against Lockean empiricism is an assertion of the unlimited powers of the subject over those of the object. Laws of thought established by the recognition of objective laws are, as it were, overturned. Freed from external restraint, the individual consciousness can perceive the infinite: 'Man's perceptions are not bounded by organs of perception; he perceives more than sense (tho' ever so acute) can discover'; 'The desire of Man being Infinite, the possession is Infinite & himself Infinite . . . He who sees the Infinite in all things, sees God. He who sees the Ratio only, sees himself only'; 'As none by travelling over known lands can find out the unknown, So from already acquired knowledge Man could not acquire more: therefore an universal Poetic Genius exists'; 'If the doors of perception were cleansed every thing would appear to man as it is, infinite'. Locke had already dismissed this desire for union with the infinite as beginning 'at the wrong end':

> I thought that the first step towards satisfying several inquiries the mind of man was very apt to run into, was, to take a survey of our own understandings, examine our own powers, and see to what things they were adapted. Till that was done I suspected we began at the wrong end, and in vain sought for satisfaction in a quiet and sure possession of truths that most concerned us, *whilst we let loose our thoughts into the vast ocean of Being; as if all that boundless extent were the natural and undoubted possession of our understandings*, wherein there was nothing exempt from its decisions, or that escaped its comprehension.[18] (my italics)

Locke found it necessary to define the limits of knowledge, to find the horizon 'which sets the bounds between the enlightened and dark parts of things — between what is and what is not comprehensible by us'.[19] Only in this way could knowledge advance. Blake, not surprisingly, woefully parodies what the sensationalists and materialists had actually argued. Reason for them was not the mere 'Ratio' of the already known, a journey across 'known lands' where nothing previously unknown could be discovered, or an arbitrary, Urizenic setting of limits and horizons. It was the systematic inquiry into the knowable and as yet unknown by application of the known — in other words, the testing of plausible hypotheses and the refining of theories by precise observation and experiment. In Blake's own time, when the Romantic imagination still operated on the premise that air and water were indivisible elements, chemists such as Cavendish and Priestley were isolating new elements such as hydrogen and oxygen, from which Lavoisier synthesised a chemical compound: water.

Blake did, however, discover important facts about perception that Locke hardly recognised. In 1799 he told

Dr Trusler:

> I see Every thing I paint In This World, but Every body
> does not see alike. To the Eyes of a Miser a Guinea is more
> beautiful than the Sun, & a bag worn with the use of
> Money has more beautiful proportions than a Vine filled
> with Grapes. The tree which moves some to tears of joy
> is in the Eyes of others only a Green thing that stands in
> the way . . . As a man is, So he Sees. As the Eye is formed,
> such are its powers.

The statement that 'Man's perceptions are not bounded by
organs of perception' is the familiar notion that there is a
supersensual realm which the spiritual man, but not the
natural man in us, perceives. Priestley's answer was that 'the
powers of sensation or perception or thought, as belonging
to man, have never been found but in conjunction with a
certain organised system of matter; and therefore, these
powers necessarily exist in, and depend upon, such a
system'.[20] However, when Blake writes: 'As a man is, So he
Sees', he goes beyond Priestley's naturalistic determinism.
Perception is not determined by the objective imprint of
external phenomena in this case, but by *ideological viewpoint*.
The viewpoints of the humble cottager and the improving
capitalist farmer may be so different as to bring up a
fundamental disagreement in their perception of the same
object in front of them. For the cottager, this object is a
living organism full of memories, associations and possibly
even spirits (like the tree filled with angels Blake saw as a
child); for the capitalist farmer, whose only concern is
profit, it is merely 'a Green thing that stands in the way'.[21]
 Blake's revolutionary insight arose out of the class struggles
and ideological conflicts of the 1780s and 1790s. He was
impelled towards a dialectical mode of thinking — recognising
what *The Anti-Jacobin* (November 27, 1797) called 'the
natural and eternal warfare of the POOR and the RICH'. This
was the progressive element that had been notably absent
from empiricism and mechanical materialism: 'Without
Contraries is no progression. Attraction and Repulsion,
Reason and Energy, Love and Hate, are necessary to Human
existence.'

Blake's dialectic owes much to Paracelsus, and to Jacob Boehme (1575-1624), a 'boisterous young shoemaker, prosperous, energetic, and immersed in the active mercantile life of his town',[22] whose works were re-issued in William Law's edition between 1764 and 1781, and who, in his own time, had condemned the 'greedy stiffnecks . . . who sweat and bleed the poor, oppressed and distressed'.[23] Radical Behmenist sects had existed in England in the seventeenth century. In *Aurora* (1612), good and evil, wrath and love, sympathy and antipathy, are contrary principles from which all substantial being or 'body', that is, existence, is generated. Opposing the dogmatism of ruling theology, Boehme saw everything in the universe, including God (since God was everywhere in the universe), as a dynamic interplay of opposing forces. 'A quality', said Boehme, 'is the mobility, surging, or drive of a thing'.[24] In alchemy, the agent of change is fire, which for Boehme seemed to epitomise the all-consuming, self-consuming passion for freedom, the 'wrathful, harsh, strong, bitter desiring source . . . which has all essences of life in it and is the vitality'.[25] Fire contains conflicting opposites, it is the 'desiring source', the freedom principle, and the supreme agent of change. This brings us close to Blake's fire symbolism: one thinks of Orc, the fiery god of revolution in *America* ('Fires inwrap the earthly globe, yet man is not consum'd'), of Fuzon, and of Los's fires.

Since Blake's dialectic is applicable to psychic as well as social forces, idealist readings are all too easy. Thus Stephen Prickett:

> Attraction and repulsion, reason and energy, love and hate are not abstractions, or qualities of the 'spiritual worlds' described in such unconvincing detail by Swedenborg, but qualities of the human mind, which is alive, unified and dynamic, and therefore in a process of constant change.[26]

Later, the division between Heaven and Hell is interpreted as 'a division between the conscious and unconscious'.[27] (This is surely truer of Reason and Energy than it is of Heaven and Hell: Blake's Hell is much more conscious than the Angelic Heaven.) What this 'human mind' with its dynamic qualities actually is is hard to discover. Yet it seems to contain everything and to be responsible for everything, as another critic, glossing Blake, declares: 'Dark satanic mills arise in towns because men have dark satanic mills in their minds.'[28] We need other ways of approaching Blake's revolt against these dark satanic mills if we are to avoid explaining it in terms of the human mind rebelling against itself. What were the roots of Blake's revolt against the rational tyranny he so powerfully mythologised? As I shall try to show, it was bound up with the historic predicament of those classes who resisted — violently in the case of the Luddites — the social and economic effects that science, the scientific method and the applications of science were having on them.

The spectacular achievements of mathematics in the seventeenth century inspired, as Bredvold has critically shown, a *furor mathematicus*, the utopian dream of a universal mathematical science, a science of man as well as of nature. The premises behind Descartes's mathematical ethics, Spinoza's 'geometrical demonstration of ethics', Weigel's 'Euclidian Ethics', and Leibniz's 'logic of life', found their most bizarre application in John Craig's *Theologiae Christianae Principia Mathematica*, or 'Mathematical Principles of Christian Theology' (1699). Yet the idea of a universal human science persisted. In 1844 Marx was still anticipating its triumph. Acknowledging that 'the natural sciences have penetrated all the more *practically* into human life, through their transformation of industry', and that they 'have prepared the emancipation of humanity, even though their immediate effect may have been to accentuate the dehumanising of man', he showed how,

> if industry is conceived as an *exoteric* form of the realization of the *essential human faculties*, one is able to grasp also the *human* essence of nature or the *natural* essence of man. The natural sciences will then abandon their abstract materialist, or rather, idealist, orientation, and will become the basis of a *human* science, just as they have already become — though in an alienated form — the basis of a really human life.[29]

In Blake, the social and psychic impact of science in its 'alienated form' is resisted with a fury far more desperate in its defence of what he felt to be 'a really human life', than the hopes of those victims of the *furor mathematicus* were ardent in their attempts to embrace human life. A parallel, if less anguished resistance is felt in other Romantic poets.

By analysing certain phenomena, the scientist abstracts and quantifies, and by doing so hives off those aspects of the object that are irrelevant for the purpose of the analysis. (Colour, texture and smell are an example in the case of classical mechanics, whose aim is to establish the quantifiable laws of motion of physical bodies, not to describe physical or sensuous qualities.) For the Romantic, analysis or dissection of anything *living* is a kind of blasphemy, provoking a chill of horror. How can living beings be treated as objects? For Blake, 'every thing that lives is Holy' — and thus should not be analysed. As he told the followers of 'Bacon, Newton & Locke', 'You . . . murder by analysing'; while Wordsworth said: 'We murder to dissect.' If philosophy is analytical reason, then Keats (who once drew flowers in the margins of his notebook as a medical student) abhorred its cold touch. Coleridge compared his own incurable habit of *self*-analysis or self-'watching' to a self-coiling serpent, or a water-boatman whose shadow is cast on the bottom of a stream; mental self-analysis, where the mind actually watches itself watching itself, became a kind of spiritual hell, a punishment for the abuse of those creative powers that God had given him.

Blake had seen the surgeon Sir William Hunter demonstrating human anatomy to drawing students at the Royal Academy, using partly-dissected Tyburn corpses which the Academy had purchased for its anatomy classes. (Corpses taken from Tyburn for purposes of dissection were the cause of several popular riots and attacks on the surgeons.) Thereafter, drawing from nature only 'deadened' his imagination. In *An Island in the Moon* (1784-5), surgery is the personified child of 'old corruption'. He forms 'a crooked knife', and runs about 'with bloody hands/To seek his mother's life'.[30] In Chapter 3 of *Jerusalem* a ritual sacrifice takes place at

Stonehenge, whose chains of stone are themselves 'Reasonings'. The victim's blood stains the defenders of Moral Law:

> They take off his *vesture whole* with their Knives
> of flint,
> But they *cut asunder* his inner garments, searching
> with
> Their cruel fingers for his heart, & there they enter
> in pomp,
> In many tears, & there they erect a temple & an altar.
> (my italics)

In 'Night the First' of *Vala, or The Four Zoas*, Tharmas asks Enion (who has looked into the secret soul of him she loved):

> Why wilt thou Examine every little fibre of my soul,
> Spreading them out before the sun like stalks of flax
> to dry?
> The infant joy is beautiful, but its anatomy
> Horrible, Ghast & Deadly; nought shalt thou find in it
> But Death, Despair & Everlasting brooding Melancholy.

Probing like this is a kind of jealous, unhealthy spying, but anatomy, surgery, scientific analysis and spying were probably associated in Blake's mind as techniques of the enemy. All work against artistic creation, which seeks to express organic wholeness and the expansive dynamism of life, whose constant self-renewal and unrepeatable moments of joy, creative vision, and sudden fusions of the inner and outer worlds are what fire the creative imagination. The truly creative artist exerts, not one side of himself, but his *whole being* in the act of imaginative creation. What he imaginatively perceives and creates are living, organic wholes. When the power of analytical reason takes over, it spiritually destroys and kills, crippling the act of creation.

The aim of all scientific analysis and experiment is the establishment of general or universal laws through the testing of hypotheses. The particular act of analysis, or the particular experiment that demonstrates such causal laws, is not a unique event, but can be repeated *ad infinitum*. These general laws are then reimposed on reality through a higher form of conceptualisation and practical control over reality. They later become the pivots of an education system whose curricular content is more and more abstract and generalised. For Blake, however, the artist's knowledge is always concrete and particular: 'To Generalize', he wrote, 'is to be an Idiot. To Particularize is the Alone Distinction of Merit. General Knowledges are those Knowledges that Idiots possess.' The rejection of 'destructive' analysis is thus consistent with Blake's rejection of abstract laws, which he sees as cloudy generalisations issuing from the dark, oppressive shadow of the Tree of Mystery. Moral Law and the scientific method are repudiated as the 'generalising Demonstrations of the Rational Power'; art and true science, on the other hand, 'cannot exist but in minutely organised Particulars'.

The 'generalising Demonstrations' of 'Bacon, Newton & Locke' were also a threat to a way of life that saw no need for, and indeed strongly resisted, scientific analysis and systematic rationalisation. What faith, magic, kinship values and an informal education had instilled, no university-trained priest or academy-trained natural philosopher was going to eradicate. The truth was that the old way of life and the popular culture rooted in it *had* to be finally destroyed if, as the apostles of progress declared, society was to advance.

Blake's revolt is not therefore simply against rational analysis and the general laws of science *per se*, but against their *social consequences*. The key passage is this, from *Jerusalem* (Chapter 4, Plate 91), which takes us to the heart of the matter:

> He who would see Divinity must see him in his
> Children,
> *One first*, in friendship & love, *then a Divine Family*,
> & in the midst
> Jesus will appear; so he who wishes to see a Vision,
> a perfect Whole,
> Must see it in its Minute Particulars, Organised, & not
> as thou,
> O Fiend of Righteousness, pretendest; thine is a
> Disorganised
> And snowy cloud, brooder of tempests & destructive
> War.

You smile with pomp & rigor, you talk of benevolence
& virtue;
I act with benevolence & Virtue & get murder'd time
after time.
You accumulate Particulars & murder by analysing,
that you
May take the aggregate, & you call the aggregate
Moral Law.
And you call that swell'd & bloated Form a Minute
Particular;
But General Forms have their vitality in Particulars,
& every
Particular is a Man, a Divine Member of the Divine
Jesus. (my italics)

Analysis and aggregation have produced 'a Disorganised/And
snowy cloud . . . tempests & destructive War'. The 'Particulars'
(and 'every/Particular is a Man') have been 'murdered' by
analysis, then re-combined as an aggregate, a false, indefinite
totality, a 'bloated' General Form embodying the 'Moral
Law' of society. In other words, the 'Rational Power' has
blighted the whole social organism. Blake's revolt against
the tyrannical primacy of reason stems from the fact that the
scientific method is now being applied to *society as a whole*.
What emerges is a social catastrophe: 'a Disorganised/And
snowy cloud . . . tempests & destructive War.'

In order to understand the context of Blake's revolt,
therefore, we should consider not merely his rejection of
'Bacon, Newton & Locke', but the spread of the scientific
method itself — how, in particular, the empirical method
employed in the natural sciences came to be applied, by
the end of the eighteenth century, in the new, so-called
'social sciences', creating new fields (or, as a consistent
Romantic would see it, new monsters) such as moral
philosophy (rationalist and utilitarian), sociology, and political
economy. Within the latter, and one of the most crucial areas
from our point of view, there emerged the analysis and
systematisation of the production process itself, which was
both a result of, and a spur to the development of industrial
capitalism. As workers, human beings became 'factors of

production' for the maximisation of profit, not ends in themselves. Analysis and aggregation, as we shall see, were not merely 'spiritual' threats, but threatened the economic and social position of that class which Blake, as a creative artist, represented.

David Hartley, following Locke's conjecture that 'morality is capable of demonstration as well as mathematics',[31] sought to put psychology and moral philosophy on a scientific basis. All sensation begins with simple ideas or elementary sense impressions. Through their association concepts are formed. Thus our 'Passions and Affections can be no more than Aggregates of simple ideas united by Association'.[32] These aggregates can in turn be re-analysed into their constituent parts or simple ideas. Bentham later tried to mathematise human passions and affections with his famous moral calculus outlined in his *Principles of Morals* (1789), where pleasure and pain are measured on a statistical scale. Utilitarianism calculated maximum social utility on the basis of sum totals or aggregates of individual happiness, the kind of rational calculation that justified the capitalist accumulation of maximum profits as a means of bringing about general happiness. Yet the system emerged as one of ruthless exploitation, where the wealth of the few continued to be amassed at the expense of the many; it became 'a Disorganized/ And snowy cloud, brooder of tempests & destructive War' — not, as the Benthamite reformers had hoped, a society in which the greatest happiness of the greater number would be achieved. Malthus was more phlegmatic in his *Essay on the Principle of Population* (1798), dismissing William Godwin's system of social equality outlined in *An Enquiry Concerning Political Justice* as 'little better than a dream, a beautiful phantom of the imagination', having proved as a quasi-scientific law the principle that wealth and productivity cannot increase faster than population. Hence, 'Man cannot live in the midst of plenty. All cannot share alike the bounties of nature.'

Analysis, or reducing something to its simplest parts, then aggregation of these parts into a new whole, was the method Adam Smith and others applied to the work process. That 'something' was *living labour*. Since the 'greatest improvement in the productive powers of labour' was brought about by the division of labour, this was to be applied within the workshop itself: 'by reducing every man's business to some one simple operation, and by making this operation the sole employment of his life, necessarily increases very much the dexterity of the workman'.[33] The human consequences of 'making this operation the sole employment of his life' did not go unrecognised, yet specialisation was an inevitable process. After close observation and analysis of the various work processes, each job was split up into its detailed operations. Work was then re-organised on the basis of these simple operations, the aim being higher productivity and an enhanced rate of profit. Alexander Chisholm, Wedgwood's secretary at the Etruria pottery works during the 1790s, carried out such an analysis, and discovered that 273 out of 278 workers were already specialists. Increased mechanisation, the scientific analysis of skilled handicrafts into their constituent detailed operations, and hence the more 'efficient' (and more dehumanising) re-organisation of the work process resulted in the de-skilling of the worker, the cheapening of labour power, and a greater degree of control exerted by the calculating brain of the capitalist — a rational tyranny that Andrew Ure, in his *Philosophy of Manufactures* (1835) cynically endorsed.

This, then, became the new moral law of capitalist rationality. As Marx stated, 'the analysis of a process of production into its particular phases . . . coincides completely with the decomposition of a handicraft into its different partial operations'.[34] The modern factory is an aggregate, not of independent, skilled craftsmen but of 'partial operations' performed by de-skilled, detail labourers — 'hands' not 'men'. Once they have been isolated and conceptualised, the operations. Work was then re-organised on the basis of these away from him, split up and shared out among one-job specialists until a new 'Reasoning Power', embodying the power of capital over labour, confronts the degraded worker (whose mind has effectively been taken away from him) as an alien force: 'the worker is brought face to face with the intellectual potentialities of the material process of production as the property of another and as a power which

rules over him'.[35] What is this power but Urizen? It is
not merely 'manual' work that is atomised in this new
division of labour, but the creative 'soul' of the worker
himself:

> You accumulate Particulars & murder by analysing,
> > that you
> May take the aggregate, & you call the aggregate
> > Moral Law . . .

Only through accumulating particular individuals within
factories, where 'every man's business' has been reduced to
'one simple operation', can modern capitalist accumulation
take place. The 'whole man', both as craftsman and as
potentially creative artist (which Blake, as craftsman and
artist, sets out to defend) is 'murdered', with no room left
for craft or creativity. The intellectual and creative potentiality inherent in the work carried out by the skilled craftsman
has been abstracted and hence appropriated as capitalist
Reason, which now rules over the propertyless, de-skilled
wage worker 'as the property of another'.

Art thus becomes a desperately defended area, the one
sphere of human activity — if we exclude the sexual act —
that remains outside and resists this kind of dehumanising
rational control. Hence the need of the Romantic artist at
times to mystify artistic creativity, and to give a special,
unique status to the artist himself. It is not merely *skill* (which
is vulnerable) that makes an artist, but *sensibility*. Alienated
from the increasingly harsh social realities of degrading wage
labour and the mechanised factory, art is driven into utopia,
fantasy and escapism, or underground into the unconscious.
Yet an art that is produced by alienated individuals is inevitably an alienated art, whatever its therapeutic aim.

Romanticism, though tied to the liberal capitalist spirit
through its expression of the 'bourgeois illusion' of individual
freedom, is not, then, a simple expression of the bourgeois
epoch. Rather, it issues forth as the product of a historic split
within the intelligentsia. In the period of early industrial
capitalism, empirical knowledge and scientific progress, and
the attempts of reformers to cushion the harsh effects of
capitalist exploitation and the boom-slump cycle, do not

succeed in dispelling the social misery, fear and anxiety caused by an oppressive and fundamentally irrational social system. The increasing mastery over natural laws leads, paradoxically, to greater social disorder: the modern class struggle cannot be comprehended within a rationalist, empirical view of man and society; huge new gaps in man's knowledge thus appear on the heels of scientific-industrial advance. Fear, uncertainty and anxiety, the psychological unease and traumatic alienation caused by massive demographic uprooting and the forcible dispossession of land, property and means of production; the widespread social and economic dislocation brought about by the enclosure movement, the growth of the modern factory system, the Napoleonic war and its aftermath, all create conditions for spiritual crisis, a cognitive and normative void in man's explanation of the world which is partly answered, psychologically, by religion, but which is also met in the quasi-ritualistic, therapeutic forms of much Romantic poetry and art, the psychological necessity for tales of terror and horror, and the Romantic involvement with superstition, ghosts, dreams, magic, myth and symbol.

These latter expressions should not be seen merely as exercises in Gothicism, medievalism and the sublime — that is, simply as part of a literary and artistic cult. They also reflect, or at the very least indicate, the existence of a *popular culture*, a network of beliefs, superstitions and magical practices that, contrary to the myths of progressive and enlightened orthodoxy, had by no means died out by the end of the eighteenth century.[36] This was the fertile soil in which religious enthusiasm, the attack on deism and natural religion (articulated most forcefully by Blake), popular millenarianism and — through its emotional sympathy, if not always direct contact, with the common people — Romantic poetry, were able to grow and flourish. The *Athenaeum* in 1828 denounced the continuing flood of popular almanacs as 'utterly uninfluenced by any modes of thinking which have marked the emancipation of the present generation from ignorance and credulity'. Though rationalist and scientific attitudes were vigorously propagated throughout the eighteenth century, the vast mass of the population were untouched by scientific knowledge. Most trades and crafts were able to advance without any need for scientific training. In 1800 formal science was still not an established part of the education system.[37] Most histories of magic, alchemy and astrology end around 1700, but the symbolism and the sense of power these practices gave were deeply rooted in popular consciousness. In the age of the water frame and the power loom, of steam and gas-lighting, supernatural forces were still at work. Angels and fairies, heavenly influences and unseen emanations, ghosts and spirits, were very much alive, especially in Scotland, Wales and rural England. The eighteenth-century magus, as wise man or cunning woman, still had access to occult mysteries, even if not to the 'great'. They spoke to the uneducated and semi-educated majority, those who looked to miracles, divine intervention and magical aids for answers and solutions, rather than to physicians (whom they feared and mistrusted), priests (whose God was not their God), lawyers and politicians (who exploited them), or men of formal learning (whose vocabulary and cold detachment were alienating). Prophets and millenarians, however, had a broader appeal: Sir Richard Bulkeley, an Irish baronet, was a follower of Abraham Whitlow, a 'levelling' prophet during the reign of Queen Anne, while the scholarly interests of the Whig M.P. Nathaniel Brassey Halhed actually confirmed his belief, at a time of acute political crisis (1794-5), that Richard Brothers, an ex-naval lieutenant on half pay, was a descendant of David and Nephew of the Almighty. Blake's art and ideas cannot be properly understood outside the context of this popular non-rationalist culture.[38]

The French Revolution had been prepared, philosophically, by the ideas, as well as the technical and scientific advances, of the Enlightenment. But in England the bourgeoisie, though nursed on the ideas of Bacon, Locke and rational Dissent, and increasingly aware of the possibilities of science, feared the growing power of the masses and compromised with conservative reaction during the wars with France. (This is probably why, in *The Four Zoas*, Urizen degenerates from Prince of the Enlightenment to reactionary tyrant: he can build his palace of reason in the sky but he cannot cope with the perplexing monsters of the abyss, nor with the arguments of Orc, and so hardens into a scaly Satanic dragon.) If science had been appropriated by the bourgeoisie and served its interests, Neoplatonism and occult ideas were associated with the radical sects thrown up by the Civil War. 'Magic's very success during the Interregnum', says Keith Thomas, 'may have helped to accelerate its rejection by scientists, anxious to shake off overtones of sectarian radicalism.'[39]

Since, however, the key to revolutionary Romanticism, as I have argued, is the bourgeois-democratic revolution itself, with its belief that once oppressive man-made institutions are removed, the infinite potential of every individual will be realised and progress will be achieved, it became possible for certain radical, middle-class strains to applaud science, technology and the factory system as liberating forces, at the same time displaying a deep attachment to nature. (Shelley's passion for science is of relevance here.) The 'mixed', early Romanticism of Wright of Derby is of this type. So too is the later Romanticism of the minor poet Ebenezer Elliott, best-known for his *Corn-Law Rhymes* (1831), but also the author of a remarkable poem entitled 'Steam at Sheffield' (1840). Carlyle praised the poetry of this 'red son of the furnace' in an essay in the *Edinburgh Review* of 1832, while Symons's *The Romantic Movement in English Poetry* (1909) devotes four pages to him. A connection with Blake lies in Elliott's unshakeable belief in the liberating energies of his time: only by harnessing the powers of nature can mankind free itself from superstition, tyranny and poverty.

> Oh, there is glorious harmony in this
> Tempestuous music of the giant, Steam,
> Commingling growl, and roar, and stamp, and hiss,
> With flame and darkness! Like a Cyclops' dream,
> It stuns our wondering souls, that start and scream
> With joy and terror . . .
>
> > . . . he stands
> Before this metal god, that yet shall chase
> The tyrant idols of remotest lands,
> Preach science to the desert, and efface
> The barren curse from every pathless place
> Where virtues have not yet atoned for crimes.[40]

Through the impersonal, superhuman qualities of these new, *man-made* rhythms and harmonies, the poet discovers a capacity for emotional transcendence. In *formal* terms, of course, the poem remains 'fettered' by its iambic rhythm, which not even steam power can break.

> Poor blind old man! what would he give to see
> This bloodless Waterloo! this hell of wheels;
> This dreadful speed, that seems to sleep and snore,
> And dream of earthquake![41]

The mixture of joy and terror is provoked by that beauty the Romantics called 'sublime'; here, however, it is not nature herself but man's conquest of nature — 'This bloodless Waterloo' — that is sublime.

There is, of course, no hint in Elliott's poem of capitalist exploitation or the degradation brought about by the factory system. Its ideological stance is one-sided, whereas Blake's is complex and many-sided. (Even in Wright's painting *Experiment on a Bird with a Windpump* the message of confidence in a new scientific age is given a very ambivalent rendering.) There are nevertheless certain tensions. The two sides of Elliott's personality — nature-lover and radical iron-founder — sit somewhat uneasily together. Though science and industry's conquest of nature have disturbed nature's balance ('The falcon, wheeling near,/Turns, and the angry crow seeks purer skies' to avoid the towering, dense smoke), this victory is still seen as part of 'Nature's plan'. Blake, however, saw the conquest as a coercive *confinement*, rather than liberation of energy; energy is never mechanical, since machines are not alive: according to this vitalist conception, only life has energy. In *The Four Zoas* Urizen's sons use 'immense machines' to compel the sun, 'like a fierce lion in his chains', to descend; the 'hoarse wheels' and 'terrific howlings' of the wild beasts that drag the sun's chariot are drowned by the sound of instruments as the sun is put into the 'temple of Urizen'. Elliott ignores the fact that steam power, celebrated in Romantic fashion as a liberating release and harnessing of energy, robbed working men of their creative energies. Hence, in this context, the importance of Blake's critique of the moral law of the new economic system. Yet even with Blake, the dominant contradiction remained unresolved: how, for example, could the Poetic Genius, already fragmented by the workshop division of labour, be restored through the mere championing of that same Poetic Genius? The new contradictions could not be honestly confronted by writers such as Elliott, who remained ideologically tied to the capitalist development of industry; rather, they were glossed over. One might add, as a coda, that Marx's own development from romantic humanist to prophet of the proletarian revolution was the most instructive in showing where their future resolution lay. The advent of revolutionary socialism marked a sharp break with romantic humanism, and at the same time carried forward its revolutionary content, raising it to a higher level.

2

The Artist in the City

'I behold London, a human awful wonder of God'

South of Tiborn Road, the northern limit of the parish of
St James, Westminster, lay some pasture ground. Once every
six weeks its grazing cattle would look up and stare, with
animal dumbness, at a noise behind the houses lining the
road. A procession of rumbling carts, soldiers, officers,
clergymen and onlookers was making its way from Newgate
gaol to the place of execution. Each cart contained a prisoner,
with hands bound, and a coffin. It was hanging day, which
meant it was a fair day — a day of shows and crowds. At the
north-east corner of Hyde Park, seated in a grandstand,
people of fashion were staring in anticipation at a deliciously
terrifying spectacle: the large gallows known as 'Tyburn
tree'. For them it was to be a ritual sacrifice, a display of the
law's power, and an emotional catharsis: in their linen, lace
and velvet, they were going to feel a savage excitement, a
thrill of horror, and then pity for each wretch as he or she
dropped and swung. Down below, mingling among the
crowd that had gathered, future attractions were picking
pockets.

In 1665 a new horror overshadowed the 'fatal tree' near
'ever-weeping Paddington'. Watching turned into flight.
Those with estates in the country or enough money to leave
the city did so, leaving the poor to die in their tens of
thousands, and the depleted authorities to cope with something they could neither understand nor properly control.
The number of dead and dying became unmanageable, so
'plague pits' were hurriedly dug. One of these, together
with a pesthouse, was on Lord Craven's pasture land between

Tyburn Road and the future Silver Street. The overworked
and frightened sextons had failed to make this pit deep
enough, and the naked corpses, tipped wholesale from death
carts (still a spectacle to morbid watchers), lay half-covered
in shallow troughs. Bodies rapidly decomposed in the
summer's heat, till the stench became intolerable. Lord
Craven proposed covering the area with a layer of unslaked
lime, but this proved impossible. Even the Great Fire was
unable to remove the stigma of the area, whose unhygienic
(and unfashionable) associations made planners and
speculative builders proceed with caution. Yet in the long
run nothing could stop them. By 1673 Christopher Wren
had signed a plan for a square to be erected just south of
Pesthouse Fields, on the estate of Lord Craven. The square,
called Golden Square, was built during the 1680s, and into
its neat, spacious, red-bricked mansions moved bishops,
lords, duchesses, ambassadors and gentlemen, with their
entourage of wives and children, butlers, servants and maids.

This movement was part of a general migration from East
to West. The bourgeoisie and *nouveaux riches* of the City,
who seemed to increase with every trading ship that came up
the Thames, were building themselves new houses, so setting
off a westward expansion. The 'enemy', as Fielding put it
in 1752, 'broke in', and 'the circle of the People of Fascination . . . retreated before the foe to Hanover Square: whence
they were once more driven to Grosvenor Square and even
beyond it, and that with so much precipitation, that had they
not been stopped by the walls of Hyde Park, it is more than
probable they would by this time have arrived at Kensington.'[1]
The landed and genteel classes were thus driven to the
'polite' end of town, with its parks, palaces, fine views and
healthy air, socially and geographically removed from the old
wooden houses, narrow courts and crooked streets of the
City end. In the fields of Westminster were laid squares,
terraces, and straight, wide streets. Gradually an expanding
grid of streets and habitations appeared, whose regular
patterns, sharp outlines and repetitive uniformity, seen in
every two-dimensional façade and in every formally elegant
square, were the product of geometric, financial and social
calculation. To the East, crowded weavers' cottages, dingy

workshops and the din of looms and hammers were a growing accompaniment to the private bargains being made in City coffee-houses. M. D'Archenholz wrote in 1791 that the difference between East and West, 'which extends to drinking and eating, amusements, dress, and manner of expression, occasions a kind of hatred between the inhabitants of each.'[2] But as the class division between the City bourgeois and the West-end 'nob' grew, the various classes who fed, clothed, served and worked for both also grew.

Once Golden Square was built, the way was clear for further development. Over the bones of the dead, new streets and buildings began to appear. Plans of master architects were gradually materialised in brick and stone. Across Pesthouse Fields was laid Marlborough Street, named after Queen Anne's famous duke. Down the east side was laid Poland Street, and along the south side, Silver Street. In 1725 a parish workhouse was placed in a corner of the large burial ground where the pesthouse and plague pit had been. Paupers were set to work on a wide variety of tasks, such as silk weaving and the making of quilted petticoats, for which new workshops were built after 1742. By 1734 a new development had pushed out a limb westwards into Pesthouse Close. Its breadth earned it the name of Broad Street. Lord Craven's new leases, numbers 14-28 on the north side, comprised a solid four-storey Georgian terrace which, like the other houses in Broad Street, attracted the 'better sort' of tradesmen, craftsmen and professional people: an architect, a composer, a family of harpsichord-makers, a surgeon, several carpenters and a landscape gardener all lived in the street at various times. (Later, Golden Square and Broad Street were to become associated with artists and musicians.) In 1753 a new well-to-do tradesman moved into the house on the corner, No. 28. His name was James Blake, a master hosier from Rotherhithe, who had married one Catherine Armitage the previous year. It was above this hosier's shop, on 28 November 1757, that William Blake, the second son of James and Catherine, was born.

When Blake was born, London was a vast city of about 600,000 people, twenty times bigger than Bristol, England's second largest city. By 1801 its size was 900,000 — an average increase of seven thousand people a year. Migrants from the countryside, victims of the agricultural revolution, flocked into the city, so that as London got richer, it also got poorer. To M. D'Archenholz, a visitor to London in 1788, it appeared 'wonderful, that the crowds of poor wretches who continually fill the streets of the metropolis, excited by the luxurious and effeminate life of the great, have not some time or another entered into a general conspiracy to plunder them.'[3] They almost did in June, 1780, when for a whole week the Gordon rioters plundered and set fire to the houses of the rich, and freed prisoners from Newgate. The metropolitan ruling class was never to forget this traumatic event.

The rationalist ideal of 'order' and 'regularity' (in which *some* licence and *some* variety were to be tolerated) found an aesthetic parallel in Georgian terraces and Augustan couplets, in 'composed' pictorial (as well as gardened) landscapes, and in the authoritative poses and settled demeanours that looked down at one from solid, stuccoed walls. Yet the repeated patterns of brick terraces and poetic couplets, with their gracefully varied rhythms, hardly matched the physical and verbal rhythms of London's workshops, printing houses, taverns and teeming streets. 'In the London streets the populace is supreme', wrote D'Archenholz.[4] Yet who was to speak for them?

The harvest of eighteenth-century rational improvement in mass urban terms was increasing poverty and social misery. New inmates filled the gaols, workhouses and madhouses, placing a growing burden on the parish authorities, and bringing urgent calls for institutional reform. The condition of those without rights or property is expressed in the following statistic. In 1793, when England launched its war on the young French Republic, one in every six females in London (not counting kept mistresses) was a prostitute — from the girls of eight or nine who solicited at night from the shadows, to the more favoured courtesans in Ring's Place, near St James, where Fox, the leader of the Whig opposition, was a frequent visitor. But, as one observer noted, if this abuse, 'the natural consequence of luxury and superabundance', were to be reformed, 'such a reformation, in a country like England, would be attended with the most pernicious consequences to trade and commerce.'[5] He was right. Prostitution was socially and economically ingrained in the urban system.

The ruling order was 'improving' the look of the city, lighting and paving the streets, bringing (after 1784) a more centralised rationality into almost every sphere of administration, yet it could not prevent the rise of pauperism and crime, what it called 'disorder' (and still does), or the growth of popular radicalism. In spite of its partial embrace (at least verbally) of the view that certain reforms were necessary, when English Jacobinism reared its head the combined ruling-class response was not reform, but repression. Property, it said, had to be safeguarded. Parliament remained unreformed. Laws against thieves and poachers became increasingly savage, and capital statutes ran into the hundreds. After 1794, when the Jacobin 'threat' in England was evidenced in the growth of mass organisations, ruling-class political terror was the order of the day. An atmosphere of revolution and counter-revolution, of riots, armed conspiracies, plots, informers and spies, generated by the eruption of a new, world-historical conflict as the French revolutionary armies overturned monarchical systems of government throughout Europe, made the 1790s quite different from any previous period. A new historical dynamic was opening up, a new era of social crisis and class struggle out of which the modern working class was born.

Blake's life and art were forged and moulded by this new dynamic. Though as a Londoner he was not immediately hit by the rise of the factory system, as a *working* Londoner it was impossible for him to remain free of its effects or to be merely an observer. Like other plebeian, self-taught intellectuals, he aimed further than those whose outlook was bound by formal eighteenth-century categories such as 'order', 'nature', 'reason' and 'moral law'. Blake's iconoclasm and modernity are the product of a radical, lower-class response to the 'pressure of the times'. They are also the product of an experience which, unlike that of poets such as Wordsworth and Shelley, is rootedly urban. Blake is arguably the first modern poet of the city.

Before analysing Blake's varied responses to the city in which he lived we need, therefore, to consider the hard facts of his life as a Londoner.

Blake tried on more than one occasion to free himself physically from the city, but the serpentine coils of 'the darkening Thames' held him till the end (although as an old man he was still able to see the river's 'cheating waves' as bars of gold when the sunlight was reflected in them). Blake's entrapment in London is poignant and instructive. Unlike Wordsworth, for whom seclusion in the Cumbrian landscape, far from the city, became a spiritual necessity; or Byron, who could lambast English society from his secure Italian exile; or Shelley, who, on hearing of the Peterloo Massacre, wrote *The Mask of Anarchy* in distant Florence — unlike them, Blake never enjoyed anything more than a precarious refuge deep in 'Albion's bosom', encompassed by many enemies: servants of the Beast and the Whore, 'ignorant Hirelings', and those who either misunderstood him, mocked and betrayed him or sensed that his art was a threat to their existence. It is important to remember all this. Blake never, as a 'humble' engraver, tasted Shelley's freedom. Dreams of personal liberty were a luxury for someone who, unlike Wordsworth, never enjoyed an annuity or a pension. Apart from his three years on the Sussex coast, Blake's working life was spent either in, near or a few minutes' walk from the house in Soho where he was born.

When Blake married in 1782, he moved to 23 Green Street, Leicester Fields, about five minutes away. Two years later, on the death of his father, he moved to No. 27 Broad Street, and set up a print shop with an ex-fellow apprentice, James Parker. (The number twenty-seven became symbolic of imperfection; twenty-eight Blake saw as a perfect number.) When the partnership fell through, the Blakes moved round the corner to No. 28, Poland Street, where Blake's beloved younger brother Robert died in 1787. From 1790 to 1800 Blake was in Lambeth (the 'house of the Lamb') across the river, about half an hour from Golden Square by Westminster Bridge. (In *Jerusalem* the 'Daughters of Albion' cry: 'from Lambeth/We began our foundations, lovely Lambeth!') Returning to London in 1803 after his three years' 'slumber' on the Sussex coast, Blake took rooms in tiny South Molton Street, Soho, just off Oxford Street, and ten minutes' walk from Broad Street, where his elder brother James ran the hosiery and haberdashery business. In the last six years of his life Blake occupied a couple of poky rooms on the first floor of No. 3 Fountain Court, off the Strand.

An engraver like Blake required a certain kind of patronage, most of it London-based, in order to survive. His best years, from 1789 to 1795, were years of relative independence. Yet both the hard, linear style he learned from Basire and his own artistic originality made him unfashionable at a time when he came to depend on patronage — that is, after 1795-96. In 1803 he asked William Hayley, the Sussex poet whose patronage had proved an intolerable burden:

> How is it possible that a Man almost 50 Years of Age, who has not lost any of his life since he was five years old without incessant labour & study, how is it possible that such a one with ordinary common sense can be inferior to a boy of twenty, who scarcely has taken or designs to take a pencil in hand, but who rides about the Parks or Saunters about the Playhouses, who Eats & drinks for business not for need, how is it possible that such a fop can be superior to the studious lover of Art can scarcely be imagin'd. Yet such is somewhat like my fate & such it is likely to remain. Yet I laugh & sing . . .

Fashionable London spurned its most original artist, an artist whose illustrations to the Book of Job are the most outstanding examples of line engraving Britain has ever produced. Yet for much of his life, being unable to live solely on the sales of his original work, Blake had to mask his inward bitterness and resentment from 'the customer' — from the connoisseurs, enthusiasts and art collectors, the world of dealers, publishers and print-shop owners — in other words, the art market and the patrons on whom he depended for a living.

> And because I am happy & dance & sing,
> They think they have done me no injury . . .

The chimney sweeper's words are strangely echoed in their author's fate. He could laugh and sing, knowing that to resist the prostitution of his skills and talents in fashionable London was to court ridicule, obloquy and the threat of starvation. Yet (putting a brave face on it), 'as Man liveth not by bread alone, I shall live altho' I should want bread'.

Blake's working life came to be circumscribed physically, socially and materially. He never left the south of England, and hence never saw the Italian masterpieces he so admired, Republican France, the iron industry of Shropshire, or the textile mills of the industrial north (though he must have known and read about them). He understood his own circumscribed personal position with a kind of wry sadness, tinged with intellectual irony:

> To God
> If you have formed a circle to go into,
> Go into it yourself and see how you would do.

Blake was a rebel, seeking through creative labour his release from a Urizenic system. He knew what it was like to be enclosed within the Circle of Destiny, racked on the revolving wheels of Newton and chained to the mill of life's daily grind. Yet he saw, with a liberating insight, that the gaoler also confines himself — perhaps more so than those he incarcerates in his 'system'. In the famous *Ancient of Days* design, in which God (that is, Urizen) circumscribes the world with his compasses or 'dividers', we see that the 'creator', in order to confine others, has also drawn a perfect circle around himself.

As a boy (thick-set, snub-nosed and red-haired), Blake would make off with friends down Oxford Street, then along Tottenham Court Road, till suddenly they would reach fields, farms and villages — a short journey of some ten or fifteen minutes. The dust of the city behind them, their first stop would be the Jew's-harp-House, a tea-garden near Tottenham Court. Then, if the weather was hot, they would take one of the paths through the fields, find the nearest pond or stream, and take off their clothes. That one child-hood pleasure, of rushing naked into the cool water on a hot summer's day, remained with Blake all his life. Childhood memories became nostalgically interwoven with the vision of Jerusalem:

> The Jews-harp-house & the Green Man,
> The Ponds where Boys to bathe delight,
> The fields of Cows by Willans Farm
> Shine in Jerusalem's pleasant sight.
>
> She walks upon our meadows green,
> The Lamb of God walks by her side:
> And every English Child is seen,
> Children of Jesus & his Bride,
>
> Forgiving trespasses . . .

In the poem *Summer*, in *Poetical Sketches* (1783), the figure of Summer is an Apollonian sun-god, then a youth with 'ruddy limbs and flourishing hair' who, though divine, is suddenly very human in his desire — proudly and swiftly acted upon — for cool, sensual gratification:

> Beneath our thickest shades we oft have heard
> Thy voice, when noon upon his fervid car
> Rode o'er the deep of heaven; beside our springs
> Sit down, and in our mossy vallies, on
> Some bank beside a river clear, throw thy
> Silk draperies off, and rush into the stream;
> Our vallies love the Summer in his pride.

It is as natural to 'rush into the stream' when in the mossy vallies as it is for the river itself to run in the vallies. Sexual associations are subtly suggested in sound and image; one feels as if one is returning to a purifying stream of life, whose movement is expressed in the poem's free-flowing, run-on lines. This, then, is no Anglican baptism, but a total immersion. Here is the *essential* current of life, in which innocent desire continually seeks to immerse itself. Yet the poet is aware of its fragility. In the 'contrary' poem, *To Winter*, winter is 'the direful monster' who 'strides o'er the groaning rocks' and 'freezes up frail life'. The oppositions of the later poetry — fire and stone, water and ice. Energy and Reason — are already here in embryonic form.

In *Holy Thursday (Songs of Innocence)* the adult observer

sees thousands of charity-school children processing throug the streets of London, 'Till into the high dome of Paul's they like Thames waters flow'. By seeing them in this way he has, one could say, imaginatively entered the purifying stream. However, this time we are in the heart of the city, not in the 'mossy vallies'. The regimental pauper children walk two abreast behind grey-headed beadles, who have 'wands as white as snow' (i.e. rods that symbolise cold authority, and that may have beaten the children). This is hardly a free-flowing stream. The children are being channelled through the streets by a regulating authority, 'like Thames waters' with its built-up banks. If we fail to see the irony behind Blake's use of the simile, we misread the poem.

The Thames thus becomes a symbol of bitter disillusion-ment:

> Why should I care for the men of Thames,
> Or the cheating waves of charter'd streams,
> Or shrink at the little blasts of fear
> That the hireling blows into my ear?
>
> Tho' born on the cheating banks of Thames,
> Tho' his waters bathed my infant limbs,
> The Ohio shall wash his stains from me:
> I was born a slave, but I go to be free.

How far Blake got in his plans to emigrate to America (the Ohio was praised in a book by Imlay, Mary Wollstonecraft's lover) we do not know. Probably not very far. What is significant is the phrase 'cheating waves of charter'd streams', where 'cheating' and 'charter'd' combine in sound and meaning. The Thames was not a river one could simply dive into on a hot summer's day. Since its banks were lined with the quays and wharves where the goods of chartered com-panies were unloaded, it was difficult even to get near the water.

The offer of freedom and escape promised by the commerce-stained river is therefore a cheat, since what seems to be offered is actually denied. The poet has been 'cheated' of his freedom. In his hope that the Ohio will wash away the 'stains' of the Thames, the poet is also implying that the stained, or 'dirty Thames' (as he wrote in the first

n) has cheated him of the kind of baptismal ... that rushing into 'a river clear' could give, and ... e in the Thames's polluted waters means, both ... d metaphorically, to be stained with the filth of ... ial profiteering. Again, the river is 'cheating' because ... arter'd', in the sense that it is laden with goods carried by ... e ships of chartered companies, such as the East India Company. The idea of trading as 'cheating' had a long history. In *The Law of Freedom* (1649) Gerrard Winstanley wrote: '[buying and selling] is the law of the conqueror, but not the righteous law of creation: how can that be righteous which is a cheat?' Finally, the word 'cheat' had another, more grisly, connotation in Blake's day: 'the cheat' was the gallows, and to be 'cheated' meant to be hanged. Interconnected strands of the urban experience now begin to emerge. To live in the capital city is to be contaminated by 'cheating' commerce, it is to be cheated of one's freedom, it is to be dominated by powerful monied interests, and it is to live under permanent threat of the gallows.

In *The Chimney Sweeper (Songs of Innocence)* the act of rushing into a 'river clear' has been transformed into a more poignant symbol of liberation. The new sweep, Tom Dacre, cries when his head is shaved, but is consoled by his friend (who is the speaker in the poem). That night Tom has a dream in which thousands of sweepers are 'Lock'd up in coffins of black',

> And by came an Angel who had a bright key,
> And he open'd the coffins & set them all free;
> Then down a green plain leaping, laughing they run,
> And wash in the river, and shine in the Sun.

Though prophetic, this transformation is an indictment of a terrible urban reality from which the sole escape is to dream of the after-life. Only when the sweepers are dead will the soot of their oppression be washed away. Meanwhile, the Angel who 'frees' Tom's companions offers more platitudes that will reconcile him to his work when he awakes:

> And the Angel told Tom, if he'd be a good boy,
> He'd have God for his Father, & never want joy.

Even in his dream, Tom is unable to escape from moralising humanitarians. The final stanza, with its ironic last line, exposes a contradiction:

> And so Tom awoke and we rose in the dark,
> And got with our bags & our brushes to work.
> Tho' the morning was cold, Tom was happy & warm;
> So if all do their duty they need not fear harm.

Though Tom is 'happy & warm' in his trusting innocence, we, the readers, recognise that nothing external has really changed. The sweeps still have to rise in the dark with their bags and brushes. Thus the poem shows us how comforting dreams of escape can actually reconcile us to our oppression.

There is, however, an even deeper irony. The Angel who 'frees' the sweeps from their coffins is the same Angel who reconciles Tom to his work; Tom's fear of early death and incarceration in a black coffin has been removed, since Tom will be 'freed' from this coffin by the Angel. But the 'coffins of black' are also the narrow, twisting chimneys of eighteenth-century London houses and mansions, in which many child sweepers met their end. How, from *these* 'coffins of black', can the Angel free Tom's companions? The answer, of course, is that he cannot. The only 'freedom' lies in death. (Porter's Act of 1788, which sought to limit the sweepers' hours of work and raised the minimum age to eight, was mild in its reforms, yet even this mild legislation could not be implemented.) The Angel in Tom's dream is Tom's own imprisoning trust. Tom and the speaker need not *fear* harm, but as long as they clean chimneys and believe what they are told, harm will come to them.

True freedom for Blake thus came to mean freeing oneself from the dominant ideology. In the poem *Milton* (1804), the baptismal metaphor returns, not as an escapist dream, but as a self-purification from mechanistic, sceptical philosophy. Man is redeemed through the free exercise of his creative imagination, through 'Inspiration':

> To cleanse the Face of my Spirit by Self-examination,
> To bathe in the Waters of Life, to wash off the Not
> > Human,

I come in Self-annihilation & the grandeur of
                              Inspiration,
To cast off Rational Demonstration by Faith in
                              the Saviour,
To cast off the rotten rags of Memory by Inspiration,
To cast off Bacon, Locke & Newton from Albion's
                              covering,
To take off his filthy garments & clothe him with
                              Imagination . . .

To 'cast off the rotten rags of Memory' and 'to wash off the
Not Human' means that one has been *wearing* those rotten
rags and is oneself tainted with the 'Not Human'. This is
so for a very important reason: as social beings, none of us
is untainted.

On the other hand, if ideological contamination (which
goes with what the Radicals called 'Old Corruption') is social,
there can be no purely individual road to a higher innocence.
That too is social. Blake understood the threefold nature of
ruling-class ideology as a means of social control: it represents
and upholds, first of all, the political domination of the few
over the many, it is woven into the pattern of everyday life,
and — most important — the many come to *internalise* it,
thus internalising both their own subordination to the
ruling few and their acceptance of the prevailing moral and
social structure.

In an early fragment known as *Then she bore pale Desire*,
the moral contamination is analysed in the paradoxical terms
of engendering, making pregnant and breeding on the one
hand, and spreading contagion and pestilence on the other.
The moral system of society is allegorically dissected, producing a genealogical tree of ugly, human passions and
vices. At the top is Pride, whose fear of losing dominion
breeds Envy and Hate, Envy in turn engendering — in a
profound Blakean insight — 'Satire, Foul Contagion'. The
insight is profound because the poet (who wrote his satire
An Island in the Moon, in which he appears as Quid the
Cynic, at a time when he was entertaining commercial
ambitions) sees that a certain kind of satire, 'from which
none are free', is still bound by the status quo, since its
contagious cynicism is bred by a hidden envy of Old

Corruption, personified as 'Pride'. This satire is like a corroding poison; from its nether parts flows the black river (antithesis of the purifying stream) of Desire denied. That Blake is analysing the urban and political system together is evident from his question: 'alas, in Cities where's the man whose face is not a mask unto his heart?' The act of generation (understood in its widest sense) in a system where the dominion of Pride turns artistic creativity into satire, rebellion into hate and slander, and intellect into policy and guile, reproduces, not the Tree of Life, but what Blake called the Tree of Mystery, the corrupt political and priestcraft-ridden system psychologically exposed in *The Human Abstract*. The first step in preventing the breeding of those 'reptiles in the mind' such as envy, mistrust and self-love, or in halting the spread of that pestilence bred by him 'who desires but acts not', is to unmask the human heart, to strip away the masks that those 'in Cities' wear.

For the city is uniquely a place of 'pestilence', given that any viral or bacterial infection is communicated most rapidly where large concentrations of people and unhygienic conditions are found together. Though bubonic plague had been eradicated from Blake's London, its memory and associations (*vide* 'Pesthouse Close') remained. Images of plague, pestilence and contagion in Blake's work derive both from this memory of the Great Plague of London and from biblical tradition, but the images themselves take on new, 'Blakean' meanings.

The plagues which the Lord sends down on the land of Egypt in *Exodus*, and His threat to disobedient Israelites in *Leviticus* that 'when ye are gathered together within your cities, I will send the pestilence among you', established a tradition of belief in which 'plagues' were seen as God's punishment on a wicked or disobedient, city-dwelling humanity. This belief was not held by Blake. The avenging, jealous God of the Old Testament is transposed into royal tyranny. Plagues have an earthly cause. Thus plagues are associated with reactionary and oppressive forces, or (in moral, psychological terms) with the fogs and standing lakes of inactivity, restraint and sexual repression.

In the poem *Tiriel*, King Tiriel (who combines the qualities of Oedipus, King Lear and possibly George III) calls on pestilence in order to punish his 'cursed sons':

> Where art thou, Pestilence, that bathest in fogs &
> standing lakes?
> Rise up thy sluggish limbs & let the loathsomest of
> poisons
> Drop from thy garments as thou walkest . . .

But the pestilence redounds on *all*, turning the royal palace into a 'noisom place' from which the aged Tiriel has to be guided by his daughter. The ironic reversal (the would-be punisher punishing himself) is a travesty of Old Testament examples, heralding the death of all tyrannical power. Pestilence is associated with the priests of the *ancien régime* in *The French Revolution*; with Marie Antoinette, 'the beautiful Queen of France', in a notebook poem; and, in *America*, with 'Albion's Angels' (the armies of George III), whose plagues, sent as a punishment to the rebel colonies, recoil across 'the limbs of Albion's Guardian', repulsed by the revolutionary flames of Orc.

In one series of pictures, however, Blake explored the theme of the plague (in this case, the Great Plague of 1665) with a far greater intensity than he ever did in his poetry. The 1978 Tate exhibition of Blake's work brought together for the first time Blake's five workings of this one subject, done over a period of about twenty years.[6] The first sketch, with its small Stothard-like figures and disparate centres of interest, evokes little more than poignant sentiment, the sweetheart dying in her lover's arms verging on the sentimental. Gradually, however, the original composition is made firmer and stronger; the principal figures and groups are more clearly and forcefully foregrounded, and a Fuseli-like, mannerist (or rather, expressionist) emphasis is given to postures and faces. In the final version there is great emotional power, starkness and concentration. Blake pondered the subject of the plague until he felt he had plumbed its deepest meanings and paradoxes, expressing them in purely visual terms.

The final picture, a London street scene, is a simple contrast of verticals and horizontals, against which are set six figures in various drooping or bending attitudes. On the extreme left, a male holds in his arms the body of a female, who has probably just at that moment died. The proximity of the two heads, hers hanging in death, his rigid with shock, his heavy-browed eyes staring out in horror, only serves to stress their unbridgeable separateness. This is no 'lovers' tragedy', but something more frightening. From left to right across the centre of the picture, two males, heads repetitively drooping, slowly bear a long, heavy, dark coffin while from a door behind them another anonymous, head-drooping coffinbearer emerges. The coffin itself, like an oblong rain cloud, dominates the picture. To the right a grave-digger, newly struck with the plague, is falling over his spade as he digs, his posture echoing that of the group on the extreme left. In the middle distance, as we look down the de Chirico-like empty street, the smoke and flames of a fire can be seen.

One meaning of this picture lies in the idea — visually presented — that during a plague 'each dies alone' when, paradoxically, that death is the result of infection or contagion from another human being. There is no communication or mutual response between the figures. Since a 'plague' by definition is the communication of a disease between many people living close together, the isolated separateness of these drooping, dying, stricken figures is far more horrific than the idea of a common fate. The *real* horror, which is suggested visually, is that of urban alienation. The feeling of individual isolation, of 'strangeness' and emptiness, is powerfully conveyed.

Estrangement and isolation are the spiritual void induced by an oppressive system. Nothing is more acceptable to authoritarian rule than a cowed people who bottle up their feelings, evade the truth of their situation, and look for private solutions. Blake's antinomianism rested on the principle that submission and obedience to existing law is incompatible with human dignity and freedom. In *The Law of Freedom*, Winstanley had written: 'I am assured that, if it be rightly searched into, the inward bondages of the mind, as covetousness, pride, hypocrisy, envy, sorrow, fear, desperation and madness, are all occasioned by the outward bondage that one sort of people lay upon another.' For Blake, the inward bondage of 'mind-forg'd manacles' was to be 'heard' in the streets of London themselves, in those streets where, as D'Archenholz observed with unconscious irony, the populace was 'supreme'.

London is a poem in which the urban experience has been gathered, concentrated and distilled to the point where every word has a terrible, corrosive force. The poem's damning vision of a whole society burns like acid into our brains:

> I wander thro' each charter'd street,
> Near where the charter'd Thames does flow,
> And mark in every face I meet
> Marks of weakness, marks of woe.
>
> In every cry of every Man,
> In every Infant's cry of fear,
> In every voice, in every ban,
> The mind-forg'd manacles I hear.
>
> How the Chimney-sweeper's cry
> Every black'ning Church appalls;
> And the hapless Soldier's sigh
> Runs in blood down Palace walls.
>
> But most thro- midnight streets I hear
> How the youthful Harlot's curse
> Blasts the new born Infant's tear,
> And blights with plagues the Marriage hearse.

Though clearly a poem of protest, *London* transcends the rhetoric of contemporary radical protest in several important ways. First of all, the 'I' of the poem does not overtly accuse, but simply wanders through 'each charter'd street', passively recording what he sees and hears. The lack of any overt crusading outburst makes the signs of social misery ('Marks of weakness, marks of woe') seem all the more inescapable. Their presence overwhelms us. The monotonous repetitions of the first two stanzas ('charter'd', 'marks' and 'every'), together with the Johnsonian generality of 'the 'hapless Soldier's' and 'the youthful Harlot's', register an ineluctable — that is, *social* condition. The perception of a doomed and rotten society is *heard* rather than seen: what we see we can choose not to see, but what we hear is less easily shut out. Individual moral outrage or denunciation is redundant in a poem whose shock effect lies in the objective force of the human images themselves.

This is, of course, a mark of Blake's success as a poet. In Book VII of *The Prelude*, Wordsworth describes how as an idle resident he walked London's streets, observing, with wonder and awe, the 'endless stream of men and moving things'. Recording a never-ending spectacle, the poet suggests a multitudinous yet confusingly trivial variety of human specimens, but it is interesting to note that the three central figures in Blake's poem — the chimney sweeper, the soldier and the harlot — do not occur anywhere in Wordsworth's compendious observations. Although they loom large in Blake's urban landscape, they were not *empirically* the obvious figures to choose.

Contemporary social protest often added the threat of divine vengeance, but in Blake's poem no heavenly judgment is needed, since both the judgment and the threat come from within the urban system itself. Biblical, apocalyptic allusions are present, but the workings of society revealed in the poem have an apocalyptic logic of their own. The voice of protest has been objectified. The millenarian Richard Brothers wrote of London:

> her streets are full of Prostitutes, and many of her houses are full of *crimes*; it is for such exceeding great wickedness that St. John *spiritually* calls *London* in his chapter (Revelation 11:8) by the name of *Sodom....For my designation is, and the commands of God to me are, that I shall walk through the great thoroughfare-street of the city, to pronounce his judgements, and declare them irrevocable ...*[7]

And a follower of Brothers, Thomas Taylor, addressed the 'opulent possessors of property' as follows:

> Know you, that the cries of the Widow, Fatherless Children, and the defenceless oppressed Poor, are come up unto the ears of the Lord of *Hosts*. He is ready to

undertake their cause: and if you repent not of your evil deeds, *He will consume you*, with the breath of his mouth.[8]

In Blake's *London* the possibility of that kind of judgment and repentance is excluded, since what is exposed is not 'crimes', 'wickedness' and 'evil deeds', but *a whole social system*.

The images in the last two stanzas show how established religion is bound up with exploitation, politics is bound up with war, and marriage is bound up with prostitution. The chimney sweeper's cry, instead of coming 'up unto the ears of the Lords of *Hosts*', casts a pall over every 'black'ning Church', whose blackness, caused by the smoke from the chimneys that the sweeps clean, and darkening, instead of brightening, the lives of those who live under it, makes the target — here, the guilty clergy's hypocritical concern — concretely visible. The 'hapless Soldier's sigh' is not heard by God, but becomes visible as blood running down 'Palace walls'. The image both exposes and indicts the 'hapless' soldier's *true* enemy, which is not Republican France, but king, parliament and archbishop who, from the safety of their respective palaces, urge poor labouring men to die for their country, fighting the foreigner. The image, however, is ambiguous, and as such contains a prophetic warning: the blood could one day be the oppressor's. Finally, it is not the breath of the Lord that consumes, but the 'Harlot's curse'. The curse is syphilis, whose contagion indiscriminately blinds the new-born infant and turns the marriage bed into a 'hearse'. But the plagues with which the harlot blights the 'Marriage hearse' are also symbolic. They are a *verbal* curse on the confining hypocrisy of legalised, monogamous marriage itself.

The vision is in some ways not unlike that of Dickens in *Bleak House*: the infection and contagion of Tom-all-Alone's, a pestilential, criminal-infested London slum where poor Joe lives, shall, we are told, 'work its retribution, through every order of society, up to the proudest of the proud, and to the highest of the high. Verily, what with tainting, plundering, and spoiling, Tom has his revenge.'[9] Dickens, however, is here using apocalyptic rhetoric in order to terrify the bourgeoisie into doing something about places like Tom-all-

Alone's. Blake, through the youthful harlot, is voicing a far more sweeping social 'curse'; a curse that, since it exposes an institution even Dickens held sacred (publicly, if not in private) is far more destructive.

London is a poem of political and social protest; it is also a poem about London, and the experience of living in London. The freedom to wander the streets is shown to be illusory when a mercantile system that annuls the rights of the majority is so complete that even the Thames is 'charter'd'. By his 'marking' the speaker relates to others at a less than human level, in a vast city where all are strangers. As E. P. Thompson has shown, the word 'mark' would have had a number of associations for Blake's readers. Revelation 13:17 speaks of 'the mark of the beast' on those who buy and sell. London's streets were full of the cries of street-sellers, in which Blake's speaker hears only 'mind-forg'd manacles'. The freedom to buy and sell shackles 'every Man' — *including* the speaker — in a de-personalising system based, not on genuine human contact, but on the exchange of goods and money. There is no possibility within the speaker's mode of perception, trapped as he is in this impersonal system, of hearing a street-cry, say, as a poetic utterance, an assertion of something human behind the figure of the seller. (To illustrate this point, a 'flower man' during the French wars was heard to cry: 'All alive! all alive! Growing, blowing; all alive!' and a blind man, accompanied by his wife and children, cried his mats and brooms in rhyming couplets, ending: 'So I in darkness am oblig'd to go;/To sell my goods I wander to and fro.')[10] Blake's speaker, as a 'free' individual wandering the streets, marks every other 'free' individual not as a person, but as a face with 'marks' in it. Into every face he meets he also draws the marks of his *own* weakness and woe; he tellingly picks out, with a deceptive lack of conscious choice, those most degraded by the system, a system in which the labour-power of infants and the charms of female children could be bought in the streets.

The urban experience in *London* is not only alienating, but is one in which growing violence and incipient revolt are strongly felt. Though the speaker makes no direct accusation, rising protest is heard in the tone of voice, from 'I wander' to

'But most . . .'. The poem moves from a kind of weary aim-
lessness (suggested by the long vowel sounds in 'charter'd'
and 'mark(s)') to the shocked exclamations ('How . . .' etc.)
of stanza three, with its emphatic trochaic rhythm, to the
verbal violence of the climactic final stanza, with its rasping
'curse', 'Blasts', 'blights' and 'plagues'. The poem is a violent
crescendo of verbal sounds and meanings, held within a
tightly disciplined form. Its hyperbolic extremism is an
imaginative revelation of a whole urban process, as the poem
moves from alienation and distress to inarticulate violence.

Blake saw the city imaginatively. He perceived in its
familiar landmarks, its streets, buildings, people and places
not empirical facts, but *symbols*, a symbolic reality behind
the surface appearance. What he saw in London, he interpreted imaginatively. Tyburn, for example (where the last
public execution took place in 1783), became symbolic of
the cruelty of Moral Law masking as religion, a Satanic
horror that revealed its true nature in the ritual sacrifice of
human beings. 'London Stone' (an ancient relic, now built
into the Bank of China) was, Blake believed, the stone on
which the Druids slaughtered their victims, and became
another symbol of the petrified dogmatism of state religion
and conservative ideology. (Other symbolic London places
in Blake's poetry might include the Tower of London –
which was a prime target for the Spencean insurrectionists
in 1816-1820 – St Paul's Cathedral, Westminster Abbey,
Lambeth, Golden Square, Hampstead, and 'the fields from
Islington to Marybone'.)

The work of the builders, so much in evidence in Blake's
London, exerted a strong influence on his poetry. In *Vala,
or The Four Zoas*, Urizen, 'the great workmaster' and master
architect of a mechanistic universe, builds the 'Mundane
Shell' enclosing the material world:

> In human forms distinct they stood round Urizen,
> prince of light,
> Petrifying all the human imagination into rock & sand.
> Groans ran along Tyburn's brook, and along the river
> of Oxford
> Among the Druid temples. Albion groaned on
> Tyburn's brook . . .

> Then rose the builders; first the architect divine his plan
> Unfolds — the wondrous scaffold reared all round the
> > infinite.
> Quadrangular the building rose, the heavens squared
> > by a line.
> Trigon & cubes divide the elements in fine bonds;
> Multitudes without number work incessant; the hewn
> > stone
> Is placed in beds of mortar mingled with the ashes
> > of Vala.
> Severe the labour, female slaves the mortar trod,
> > oppressed.

The free-ranging allusions, transitions and sudden connections are an example of a radical urban consciousness. Blake here links together the vengeance of the law, the dreaming spires of Oxford, which he calls 'Druid temples' (dark satanic mills of learning cruelly divorced from life), the Rational Being of the Deists, abstract geometry, analytical thought (dividing 'the elements in finite bonds'), and the exploitation of human labour. The consequence of this labour is the enslavement of the labourers themselves. The scale of Urizen's planning is horribly impressive, but Blake does not forget 'minute particulars': he has seen and records the fact that women tread mortar on London's building sites.

Pitt's counter-revolutionary war turned London into Babylon. In *Jerusalem*, Albion laments:

> The walls of Babylon are souls of men, her gates
> > the groans
> Of nations, her towers are the miseries of once happy
> > families.
> Her streets are paved with destruction, her houses
> > built with death,
> Her palaces with hell & the grave, her synagogues
> > with torments
> Of every-hardening despair, squared & polished with
> > cruel skill.
> Yet thou wast lovely as the summer cloud upon my
> > hills
> When Jerusalem was thy heart's desire in times of
> > youth & love.

Neo-classical architecture is here the mark not of civilised values, but of barbaric oppression. Walls, streets, palaces and churches have been built on the East India trade and the slave trade — on exploitation and death. In a time of war, when cities fed upon empire and trade, and trade fed upon death, the capitals of Europe became places of 'ever-hardening despair':

> The voice of wandering Reuban echoes from street
>   to street
> In all the cities of the nations; Paris, Madrid,
>   Amsterdam.
> The corner of Broad Street weeps, Poland Street
>   languishes;
> To Great Queen Street & Lincoln's Inn, all is distress
>   & woe.

The passages that perhaps strike the deepest chord, however, are those that evoke the essential contradiction of modern urban life, namely its atomised collectivity. A man who, as Samuel Palmer said, was 'without a mask', and whose 'times of youth & love' were bound up with feelings of spontaneous affection, openness and shared enjoyment, could only rebel against a social condition in which, though packed together like grains of sand, individuals had become atomised and privatised — aggregates of atoms, each isolated in hardened separation:

> Every house & den, every man bound; the shadows
>   are filled
> With spectres, & the windows wove over with curses
>   of iron.
> Over the doors *Thou shalt not*, and over the chimneys
>   *Fear* is written.

The urban abyss could nevertheless become a place of energetic delight when its human potentialities began to be realised, as happened during the rise of popular radicalism, the time when, as Blake puts it in *The Marriage of Heaven and Hell*, 'the Eternal Hell revives'. This was in the years 1790-1793. After 1795, under the effects of Pitt's repressive legislation, the organising spirit of popular radicalism evaporated. According to E. P. Thompson, the movement 'was not extinguished when the corresponding societies were broken up, Habeas Corpus suspended, and all 'Jacobin' manifestations outlawed. It simply lost coherence. For years it was made inarticulate by censorship and intimidation. It lost its press, it lost its organised expression, it lost its sense of direction.'[11] It was in these hard times that the full horror of the urban abyss was felt, when atomisation, a sense of impotence and a sickening isolation were symptomatic of a whole movement turning in upon itself. (A parallel phenomenon is the revolutionary movement in Russia after the defeat of 1905.) This historic experience is what Blake seems, in part, to be describing in Night VI of *The Four Zoas*, written around 1797:

> In cruel delight
> Los brooded on the darkness, nor saw Urizen with
> a Globe of fire
> Lighting his dismal journey thro the pathless world
> of death,
> Writing in bitter tears & groans in books of iron
> & brass
> The enormous wonders of the Abysses, once his
> brightest joy.
>
> For Urizen beheld the terrors of the Abyss wandring
> among
> The ruind spirits, once his children & the children
> of Luvah.
> Scard at the sound of their own sigh that seems to
> shake the immense
> They wander Moping, in their heart a Sun, a Dreary
> moon,
> A universe of fiery constellations in their brain,
> An Earth of wintry woe beneath their feet, & round
> their loins
> Waters or winds or clouds or brooding lightnings
> & pestilential plagues.
> Beyond the bounds of their own self their senses
> cannot penetrate:

As the tree knows not what is outside of its leaves
                                        & bark
And yet it drinks the summer joy & fears the winter
                                        sorrow,
So in the regions of the grave none knows his dark
                                        compeer
Tho he partakes of his dire woes & mutual returns
                                        the pang,
The throb, the dolor, the convulsion in soul
            sickening woes . . .

In the second chapter of *Jerusalem* Los walks through the streets of London, searching the cause of urban oppression with anguished perplexity. (This parallels Urizen's exploration of his dens.) The lost people are Pharoah's slaves:

Fearing that Albion should turn his back against the
                                        Divine Vision,
Los took his globe of fire to search the interiors of
                                        Albion's
Bosom, in all the terrors of friendship entering
                                        the caves
Of despair & death to search the tempters out,
                                        walking among
Albion's rocks & precipices, caves of solitude
                                        & dark despair,
And saw every Minute Particular of Albion degraded
                                        & murder'd,
But saw not by whom; they were hidden within in
                                        the minute particulars
Of which they had possess'd themselves, and there
                                        they take up
The articulations of a man's soul and laughing throw
                                        it down
Into the frame, then knock it out upon the plank,
                                        & souls are bak'd
In bricks to build the pyramids of Heber & Terah.
                                        But Los
Search'd in vain; clos'd from the minutia, he walk'd
                                        difficult.

Later, Los sees 'every Minute Particular harden'd into grains of sand,/And all the tenderness of the soul cast forth as filth & mire'. Every human being is a minute particular, yet every-where minute particulars are degraded, murdered, turned into clay for bricks or hardened into insensitive atoms. (Blake's horror of reification occasionally took on a paranoid-schizoid quality, yet here the imagery of petrification and atomisation is a profound critique, indicting as one system atomistic philosophy, capitalist individualism, and the reduction of human beings to objects in a society where labour power is as marketable as the bricks it is hired to produce.) Los's perplexity and confusion are, however, also Blake's:

> What shall I do? what could I do if I could find these
> Criminals?
> I could not dare to take vengeance, for all things
> are so constructed
> And builded by the Divine hand that the sinner
> shall always escape,
> And he who takes vengeance alone is the criminal
> of Providence.
> If I should dare to lay my finger on a grain of sand
> In way of vengeance, I punish the already punish'd.

The words 'constructed/And builded' have a special irony. The conclusion is that vengeance is futile and only com-pounds the crime, since individuals are not responsible for this state of affairs. Then who is? Blake seems at this point to be hamstrung by his new liberal doctrine of compassion and the forgiveness of sins. If the sinner always escapes, heads can never roll and social justice can never be imple-mented. (This is the very opposite of the violent retribution which the Messiah brings in the Book of Revelation.) It is not unfair to conclude that the Divine hand has constructed things this way in order to frustrate, change and maintain the system — a kind of predestinarian pessimism Blake would have no doubt disclaimed, yet that is where his argument seems to lead.

Brutalising hardness, insensitivity and indifference are characteristic of the mass urban experience in modern capitalist society. But the phenomenon began to be observed long ago. A German visitor to London in 1782, witnessing a funeral procession, wrote:

> A few bearers make their way as well as they can through the crowd, and several mourners follow. As for the rest of the populace, they take no more notice than if a haycart were driving past . . . it seems to me that in a populous city such a funeral as this is all the more unseemly because of the indifference of the spectators . . . The man being borne to his grave might never have belonged to the rest of humanity.[12]

In Blake's cowed city, where 'spectres' — human ghosts or shadows of men — wander through the streets over the doors of whose houses *'Thou shalt not'*, and over whose chimneys *'Fear'* is written, in such a city, social existence is like a graveyard:

> So in the regions of the grave none knows his dark
>   compeer
> Tho he partakes of his dire woes & mutual returns
>   the pang . . .

Engels later described London's 'dark regions of the grave' and its 'harden'd . . . grains of sand' with an analytical force:

> The brutal indifference, the unfeeling isolation of each in his private interest becomes the more repellent and offensive, the more these individuals are crowded together, within a limited space. And, however much one may be aware that this isolation of the individual, this narrow self-seeking is the fundamental principle of our society everywhere, it is nowhere so shamelessly barefaced, so self-conscious as just here in the crowding of the great city. The dissolution of mankind into monads of which each one has a separate principle and a separate purpose, the world of atoms, is here carried out to its utmost extreme.[13]

To 'wash off the Not Human', the inhuman individualism and individual isolation of this urban system, meant for Blake a heroic task of re-uniting a divided, atomised humanity. Part of Los's 'terrible' labour is to beat with his hammer the

hypocritic Selfhoods on the Anvils of bitter Death.
I am inspired. I act not for myself; for Albion's sake
I now am what I am.

Unlike Wordsworth, Blake did not — *could* not — reject
the city. He was too attuned to its rhythms, too much fired
by its contradictions, its possibilities of change. Atomisation
and despair were the 'bad side' of a vast human potentiality,
a paradoxical impotence whose enforcement was *proof* of
an infinite power that had, somehow, to be contained. Blake
thus reacted to what he heard and saw, not with gaping
surprise and wearied confusion, but with intimate knowledge
and critical insight, perceiving veiled connections, and searching with deep and often turbulent emotions the human
implications. He responded with love, anger, bitterness and
compassion to the sufferings, hopes and anxieties of the
oppressed, to the vagabonds who lit fires for warmth, the
children who, like 'jewels', ran down the gutters of the
streets 'as if they were abhorr'd', the young girls who weaved
and span in Lambeth's Royal Asylum for Female Orphans
and the Lambeth Charity School, the men who died on the
gallows or in the wars, leaving behind widows and children,
and all those who were tied to 'The Looms & Mills & Prisons
& Work-houses of Og & Anak'.

Blake's art had, in its own terms, a redemptive and
salutary mission. In *The Four Zoas*, Los and Enitharmon
prepare Golgonooza (the new Golgotha, replacing the old
Golgotha of Tyburn) as a protective sanctuary for poor
wandering spectres. In *Jerusalem* Los continues to build:

Here, on the banks of the Thames, Los builded
Golgonooza,
Outside of the Gates of the Human Heart beneath
Beulah
In the midst of the rocks of the Altars of Albion.
In fears
He builded it, in rage & in fury. It is the Spiritual
Fourfold
London, continually building & continually decaying
desolate.

There is no rural escapism, no sentimental utopianism in Blake.

Rural escapism was in any case difficult for some-one who knew about the decay of village life, saw the fields of his youth being absorbed into a periurban and suburban sprawl, and would have known (as a market-gardener's son-in-law) that all around London itself, the country was being transformed to supply the city. The difficulty of Los's labour is felt in the irony of his redemptive vision 'continually building & continually decaying desolate', just like that process of building and decay with which he is surrounded. Yet Blake could see, in the *human* part of this 'human awful wonder of God', its capacity for self-regeneration. London was a living creature, a living being that would one day 'awaken' (as we may suppose it began to do in the years 1790-1793). It would become a 'Spiritual Fourfold London'. It was Blake's commitment to this vision that gave him hope:

> I write in South Molton Street, what I see and hear
> In regions of humanity, in London's opening streets.

Unlike the speaker in *London*, the poet here perceives 'opening' rather than 'charter'd' streets. The change shows that at least there is the possibility of *imaginatively* breaking out of the system.

3

Radical Innocence

The late eighteenth century was a period in which the condition of children began to arouse the religious and moral concern of the enlightened middle class. Yet behind this concern, with its insistence on the need for 'reform', lay the objective needs of a new economic system, one that was based on wage labour, the regulated working day, and the institution of the nuclear family (as a unit of *consumption* rather than production). 'Irreligion', idleness and crime among working-class children were some of the obstacles to the new system; Evangelical groups in the 1780s saw a need to extend elementary education, which up to that time had been confined to the charity schools founded by the Society for Promoting Christian Knowledge. The Evangelicals were quick to recognise both the problem and the solution: a proletariat that had been trained to think of itself as, and to behave like, a disciplined and docile labour force, was far better than one compelled, unwillingly, to submit to a life of drudgery.

Children became an object of concern, not because they were poor but because they were undisciplined. Public concern was therefore on the whole a class reaction rather than a humane one. That is, while it is true that the plight of the chimney sweeps, the increase in child labour and the unscrupulous exploitation of charity-school children aroused the indignation of reformers and philanthropists, their concern for the most part was for something called 'society', rather than for the children themselves. Thus Robert Raikes, the leading publicist of the Sunday School movement, wrote in his Journal in 1783 that 'a reformation in society' was only practicable 'by establishing notices of duty, and practical habits of order and decorum, at an early age'. A change of manners through moral and religious education, i.e. the socialisation of children into the 'natural order' of class society, is what Raikes emphasises. The reactionaries opposed education of any kind for the poor. They were worried, particularly after 1792, by 'the pernicious doctrines of seditious writers', and hence were for keeping the lower orders ignorant; the 'progressives', on the other hand, saw the need for at least a semi-literate workforce who had, at the same time, been carefully immunised against these 'pernicious doctrines'. Hannah More, for example, praised 'the excellent institution of Sunday schools for training religious servants' — that is, servants (the word also applied to wage labourers) who were loyal, well-behaved and God-fearing.[1] Religion was seen as a means of teaching the potentially lawless the ways of obedience and service. Instilled into these servants was the belief that their humble station had been allotted to them by God, for, as one writer to the *Gentleman's Magazine* wrote in 1797, 'Society cannot possibly subsist without them.' Any thought of escape or evasion was branded as sinful. Licentious thoughts and rebellious desires were the moral weeds that a religious obedience alone could eradicate.

This, as Peter Coveney says in *The Image of Childhood*, was 'that other "eighteenth century"' of harsh moralising tracts, in which all the sensuousness and sensibility of Rousseau died. Rousseau's advocacy of natural, organic growth, of an education that simply allowed the child to pursue his or her natural desires, was unacceptable and indeed frightening to those obsessed with the idea of an ordered, rule-governed social framework. To be so obsessed was to be blind to human potentiality. It was to deny the possibilities of unlimited growth inherent in every human being. Life itself, particularly its infantile manifestation, must have seemed dangerous and frightening to many Evangelicals. Whereas Rousseau could say: 'Love childhood, indulge its sports, its pleasures, its delightful instincts . . . Why rob these innocents of the joys which pass so quickly, of that precious gift which they cannot abuse?'[2] that 'other' eighteenth century saw the untamed instinct of the child as the source of all evil. The loving father in that appalling early nineteenth-century manual, *The History of the Fairchild Family*, tells his offspring: 'Our hearts by nature, my dear children, are full of hatred.'³ By 1872 this book had passed through twenty-five editions. It was not Rousseau who won out in the end, but the Mrs Trimmers, the Hannah Mores and Mrs Sherwoods.

The liberal-democratic educational revolution has yet to be completed. The principles of liberal democracy in education have proved unable, on their own, to extend much beyond the privileged freedoms enjoyed by the sons and daughters of the middle class and upper working class. For those continually hemmed in by economic and cultural constraints — those, for example, for whom police and school are often synonymous — the nostalgic re-creation of childhood innocence, and the concept of moral evolution through the cultivation of the individual sensibility, must seem a peculiarly irrelevant kind of preoccupation. Which is one reason why Blake's *Songs of Innocence and of Experience* have the immediacy that Wordsworth's poetry relating to childhood often lacks.

The theme of lost childhood innocence is found in the seventeenth century in the poetry of Vaughan and Traherne. Henry Vaughan's *The Retreate* begins:

> Happy those early dayes! when I
> Shin'd in my Angell-infancy.

It continues:

> When on some gilded Cloud, or flowre
> My gazing soul would dwell an houre,
> And in those weaker glories spy
> Some shadows of eternity;
> Before I taught my tongue to wound
> My conscience with a sinful sound,
> Or had the black art to dispence
> A sev'rall sinne to ev'ry sence,
> But felt through all this fleshly dresse
> Bright shootes of everlastingnesse.

Vaughan's recollection of his 'Angell-infancy' and his lament for its loss in a corrupt world compares closely with Wordsworth's recollection of the 'visionary gleam' and his own sense of loss in the famous ode on *Intimations of Immortality from Recollections of Early Childhood*. There is in both a partial reconstruction, in adult terms, of something the poet can never regain, and hence a feeling of self-dissociation. There is no exuberant re-kindling of innocence, as in Blake, only its distant echo and saddened recollection. In lesser poets this often ends in what Coveney calls 'the cul-de-sac of debilitating regret'.[4] That is one approach.

The other is to create an innocent object. When observing children, Wordsworth tends to weave around them certain images, thoughts and feelings, as in the following, written of a child three years old:

> Light are her sallies as the tripping fawn's
> Forth-startled from the fern where she lay couched;
> Unthought-of, unexpected, as the stir
> Of the soft breeze ruffling the meadow-flowers . . .

The child has become a part of nature, like the solitary Lucy Gray upon 'the lonesome wild', or 'H.C.', six years old, who becomes

> . . . a dew-drop, which the morn brings forth,
> Ill fitted to sustain unkindly shocks,
> Or to be trailed along the solitary earth;
> A gem that glitters while it lives,
> And no forewarning gives;
> But, at the touch of wrong, without a strife
> Slips in a moment out of life.

In the poem *We Are Seven*, where the speaker encounters childhood innocence in a little cottage girl eight years old, there is, significantly, an ironic failure of communication. The poem is in a simple stanza form and uses the simplest vocabulary, but it remains nevertheless a poem written within an adult consciousness. This is not to say that many of Wordsworth's poems are not readily available to children (what child does not know 'I wandered lonely as a cloud . . .'?), but it illustrates that Wordsworth, unlike Blake, was more concerned with the adult's view of childhood than with children themselves. There is too often a hint of the sentimental, or an element of adult egoism and restraint, possibly resulting from the adoption of a particular kind of moralising didacticism, that is wholly absent from Blake's *Songs of Innocence*. This is only partly qualified by Wordsworth's preparedness, on occasions, to deflate his own ego and pomposity.

The *Songs of Innocence*, etched in 1789, were designed and written for children. Here is the opening song:

Introduction

Piping down the valleys wild,
Piping songs of pleasant glee,
On a cloud I saw a child,
And he laughing said to me:

'Pipe a song about a Lamb!'
So I piped with merry chear.
'Piper, pipe that song again.'
So I piped: he wept to hear.

'Drop thy pipe, thy happy pipe;
Sing thy songs of happy chear:'
So I sung the same again,
While he wept with joy to hear.

'Piper, sit thee down and write
In a book that all may read.'
So he vanish'd from my sight,
And I pluck'd a hollow reed,

And I made a rural pen,
And I stain'd the water clear,
And I wrote my happy songs
Every child may joy to hear.

The piper's 'pleasant glee' in 'the valleys wild' conjures up the genie-like vision of a child 'on a cloud', who tells him to play his pipe, play again (since children love to hear things repeated), then to sing, and finally to write his songs in 'a book that all may read'. As the child commands, so the piper obeys. 'Normal' adult-child relations have been reversed. The songs are not being handed *down* to children, but have been inspired *by* them. In reciprocating the spirit of the 'laughing'

child, the piper becomes a poet of Innocence, writing 'happy songs' that 'Every child may joy to hear'. The first poem in the collection thus acts out its own coming into being. With its lively staccato rhythm, its repeated words and simple narrative progression, it sings the song of its own creation.

Before we include Blake in the Romantic cult of childhood, we should be aware of two things: first, that his songs neither express lost innocence nor create an object around which the poet weaves his fancy, but are songs *of* Innocence; second, that this Innocence does not reside in the child as a separate being, but is acted out in the *relationship* established in the first song between piper and child. In the frontispiece illustration to the *Songs*, the piper looks up at a symbolic naked child who floats on a cloud between embracing trees. The entwined trunks of the right-hand tree, symbolising human love, the mingling branches, and the mutually answering elements in the composition, suggest a reciprocating, harmonious relationship. Such a relationship, freed of moral and social restraints, is essential if the poet is to be a poet of Innocence. The 'innocent' poet's function is to celebrate life rather than to inculcate ideas; to bind himself to children, not through the 'rules' of 'society' but through spontaneity, pleasure and a love of life; and to liberate, instead of repressing, those pleasures and desires we felt when we ourselves were children.

If 'Innocence' has nothing to do with simple naiveté or ignorance, what is its ideological content? Before we can properly answer this question, we need first to set the *Songs of Innocence* in their literary and religious context.

In form and style the *Songs* belong partly to a popular nursery-rhyme tradition and partly to the eighteenth-century tradition of hymns and songs written for children. Examples of this latter genre are Isaac Watts's *Divine and Moral Songs for the Use of Children* (1715), Charles Wesley's *Hymns for Children* (1763), Christopher Smart's *Hymns for the Amusement of Children* (1775), and Mrs Laetitia Barbauld's *Hymns in Prose for Children* (1787). Watts's *Divine and Moral Songs* were by far the most popular, even into the nineteenth century, and bear a close relation to some of Blake's songs, as Pinto (1957) has shown. Comparison between Watts and Blake is instructive.

The first lesson drummed into the child in Watts's songs is that God is everywhere and is invisible. He exists as a rather terrifying Omnipresence who sees the child's every little deed, even the most private, and, as he watches, writes them down in his great Account Book. Watts's God is an authoritarian father, the state within the family. As Watts said in *A Discourse on the Way of Instruction by Catechisms:* 'if Parents take no Care to inform their Children of the Duty they owe to God, they will quickly find that children will pay very little Duty to their Parents'.[5]

Next, the child is told that he or she, far from being innocent, is sinful, having inherited original sin at birth. Several songs expound this repellent doctrine.

> Our father ate forbidden fruit,
>   And from his glory fell,
> And we, his children, thus were brought
>   To death and near to hell.

In other words, the puritanical guilt of that *other* father, the one who 'ate forbidden fruit' in the act of procreation with the mother, is transferred onto the child. Within the bourgeois family, where sexual repression and separate roles are the norm, the child is seen as a potential rebel filled with sinful impulses that have to be curbed.

The third lesson is that we are continually being punished for our sins, whatever these sins may be. The children who called the prophet Elisha a 'bald-head' were, we learn, torn limb from limb by 'two raging bears' amid 'blood and groans and tears'. The parent raises his eyes to heaven, the child following and repeating:

> Great God, how terrible art thou
>   To sinners e'er so young!
> Grant me thy grace, and teach me how
>   To tame and rule my tongue.

The reality of God's power was, of course, made painfully tangible. The virtuous child is he who learns to obey his parents and behave according to the moral law.

The fourth lesson is that God appreciates industry and despises idleness. Emblems of individual accumulation and the profitable employment of time abound, such as the little busy bee who improves 'each shining hour', or the ant, traditionally an emblem of thrift and prudence:

> But I have less sense than a poor creeping ant,
> If I take not due care of the things I shall want.

(Blake undercut this 'business' morality in *The Marriage of Heaven and Hell* when he wrote: 'The busy bee has no time for sorrow'.)

In Watts the child, already carrying the seed of sin, enters a world that is itself full of corruption and sin. Tainted with both from birth, he must work and save to fend off temptation, and will probably spend his time saving money as he will spend his life trying to save his soul. (Sexually, too, he will no doubt 'save' himself.) Clearly, Watts's *Divine and Moral Songs* are intended to be used by parents of the same puritan, middle-class background as their author, parents whose children, albeit instilled with a sense of guilt, have been chosen by divine providence not to be poor:

> Not more than others I deserve,
>   Yet GOD hath given me more.
> For I have food while others starve,
>   Or beg from door to door.

The smug gratitude such an awareness inevitably breeds is in striking contrast to the identification with the suffering of others expressed in Blake's *On Another's Sorrow*. Whereas Watts's songs encourage an attitude of self-regard and bourgeois individualism, Blake's songs radiate the non-individualistic, sharing values of the popular, democratic community. (Blake's 'Innocence' is, in a deep sense, *communal* rather than individualistic.)

The *Songs of Innocence* are therefore in part an answer to the *Divine and Moral Songs* of Isaac Watts. Open, sharing relationships provide the free-flowing medium into which the child is introduced. Blake's 'Innocence' is a world without barriers. It is the living expression of joyous energy, a world from which Watts's God has entirely disappeared.

In *The Lamb*, the child spontaneously identifies with the lamb, whose 'softest clothing, wooly, bright' is a symbol of the love which the lamb's maker bears to his creation, and which, in the design, the child is about to touch by touching the lamb. The answer to the question, 'Little Lamb, who made thee?' is answered by the child himself:

> Little Lamb, I'll tell thee,
> Little Lamb, I'll tell thee:
> He is called by thy name,
> For he calls himself a Lamb.
> He is meek, & he is mild;
> He became a little child.
> I a child, & thou a lamb,
> We are called by his name.
> Little Lamb, God bless thee!
> Little Lamb, God bless thee!

Though this could sound like the obedient repetition of Christian doctrine, the child makes it his own, clothing it in language of the utmost simplicity. The child makes no differentiation between the maker of the lamb and the lamb itself, between the infant Jesus and himself as a child. All 'are called by his name'.

In *A Cradle Song* the mother, as she sings her lullaby, reaches the same kind of perception as the child in *The Lamb*. Maker and made, the divine and the human, herself and Jesus as protector and protected, are all fused in a single vision.

> Sweet babe, in thy face
> Holy image I can trace.
> Sweet babe, once like thee,
> Thy maker lay and wept for me.
>
> Wept for me, for thee, for all,
> When he was an infant small.
> Thou his image ever see,
> Heavenly face that smiles on thee,
>
> Smiles on thee, on me, on all;
> Who became an infant small.
> Infant smiles are his own smiles;
> Heaven & earth to peace beguiles.

Admittedly, the religious ideology is more overt here, and would be uncomfortable if we were told that an 'infant small' wept for the sins of humanity. One should rather read into it that Christ weeps because he feels the *sorrows* of humanity. There is also a hidden retort to Isaac Watts in the fusion of the human and the divine. In Watts' *A Cradle Hymn* the lot of Jesus and that of the child are heavily contrasted: 'Soft and easy is thy cradle;/Cold and hard thy Saviour lay'. Watts is continually suggesting that kind of distinction, which Blake's innocent vision overcomes.

The *Songs of Innocence* are all about relatedness, caring, interdependence and responsiveness, indicative of an organic kinship-bound community. The *Introduction* binds together the poet of Innocence and 'every child'; *The Little Boy Found* brings together a little boy and his father; *The Shepherd* and *A Cradle Song* sing of the indivisible oneness of protector and protected; the indulgent nurse in *Nurse's Song* bends to the desires of her charges who are playing on the green, thus instinctively following Rousseau's precepts. *Spring, Laughing Song* and *The Ecchoing Green* are spirited, joyous celebrations of play, fun, laughter and glad company.

The Ecchoing Green evokes an idyllic village community.

The Ecchoing Green

The Sun does arise,
And make happy the skies;
The merry bells ring
To welcome the Spring;
The skylark and thrush,
The birds of the bush,
Sing louder around
To the bells' cheerful sound,
While our sports shall be seen
On the Ecchoing Green.

Old John, with white hair,
Does laugh away care,
Sitting under the oak,
Among the old folk.

They laugh at our play,
And soon they all say:
'Such, such were the joys
When we all, girls & boys,
In our youth time were seen
On the Ecchoing Green'.

Till the little ones, weary,
No more can be merry;
The sun does descend,
And our sports have an end.
Round the laps of their mothers
Many sisters and brothers,
Like birds in their nest,
Are ready for rest,
And sport no more seen
On the darkening Green.

The structure of this poem testifies to Blake's poetic crafts-
manship. In the first stanza, everything seems to enliven
everything else; in the second stanza, this energised responsiveness is continued in the laughter of the old folk; in the
third, the poem wraps itself up in village slumber. The
threefold structure (morning, noon and evening) is simple
enough, befitting both the subject and the setting, but the
last two lines give a subtle feeling of evening stillness and
quiet, when sounds no longer heard echo in the memory.
The first four lines of the poem spring into life, while the
first four lines of the last stanza convey the children's
tiredness (in the long-vowelled 'weary', 'more' and 'sport',
and the heavy alliteration of 'does', 'descend' and 'end').

The 'our' in the first stanza indicates a youthful speaker,
or possibly a collective utterance by the children. In stanza
two 'we' is the old folk as former children, extending the
idea of collective enjoyment and 'Ecchoing' participation. In
the final stanza the 'we' has become 'them' (in 'Round the
laps of *their* mothers'), which suggests another viewpoint:
that of an observer. After the immediacy and expectancy
of the first stanza and the responsive reminiscence of the
second, comes the impersonality of the third: 'And sport
no more seen'. In this withdrawal, is there perhaps a passing

of something more profound? As the shadows lengthen and the sounds of children die away, longer perspectives begin to darken the village green.

In the original etching, the poem runs over two plates, whose designs give a feeling of security, communal fulfilment and ripening physical love. This love is quite open: on the second plate a boy, reclining on a vine branch, hands down a bunch of grapes to a girl who reaches up to receive it. (Her white hat looks like a halo.) With his left arm the boy grips the braided double stem of the vine, which has woven itself into a love-knot. The motif appears in the intertwined, limb-like trunks of the tree in the frontispiece illustration as a symbol of earthly love. Elsewhere, vines and other climbing plants twine themselves round stronger stems, symbolising both the dependence of the child on parental love, and the Rousseauesque principle of natural growth; the weaker plants do not cling parasitically (like ivy — which appears in *Songs of Experience*), but freely twine themselves round stronger supports as, reaching, they grow skywards.

Innocence being a state of the soul from which no spontaneous desires are excluded, it is not surprising that it should include physical love. Love in Innocence is a barrier-less continuum. Rigidly separate categories, such as 'sex', 'nature', 'childhood' and 'adulthood', do not exist. Where there is so much intertwining, mutual identification and responsive openness, one thing simply passes or grows into another.

In this regard *The Blossom* is one of the happiest of Blake's 'happy songs':

The Blossom

Merry, Merry Sparrow!
Under leaves so green
A happy Blossom
Sees you swift as arrow
Seek your cradle narrow
Near my Bosom.

Pretty, Pretty Robin!
Under leaves so green

> A happy Blossom
> Hears you sobbing, sobbing
> Pretty, Pretty Robin,
> Near my Bosom.

Simple, direct words and a pervasive trochaic rhythm go with the utterance of joyous sensations. The same rhythm and the use of two- and three-beat lines are also found in nursery rhymes. The following, for example, makes similar use of rhythmic syncopation and playful repetition:

> Gilly Silly Jarter,
> She lost a garter,
>   In a shower of rain.
> The miller found it,
> The miller ground it,
>   And the miller gave it to Silly again.

The changes of beat and time (which may have gone with a hopping or skipping game) are here quite puckish. In Blake, the use of one two-beat line to every two three-beat lines creates a more expressive effect, so that the beat we miss at the beginning of the line: 'A happy Blossom' makes the 'A ha-' sound, as we say it, like an ecstatic release or cry of pleasure.

There has been a good deal of critical discussion of this poem. Wicksteed bravely suggested that its subject was sexual intercourse, the erect phallus symbolised by the sparrow 'swift as arrow', and the post-orgasmic state by the sobbing robin. Hirsch took a contrary view. The speaker, he says, is Earth, the blossom is a symbol of birth, and the robin is the soul imprisoned in the body. Gillham, taking the same line as Wicksteed, added that the blossom 'tends to be aware of the male sexual organ almost as a sort of pet'.[6] Keynes, likewise agreeing with Wicksteed, says that the 'maiden', 'with her prospective motherhood, is an ideal figure to the male during the act of generation'.[7] Holloway says the poem has nothing to do with sex at all: it is simply about a young girl who, having plucked 'flowers in spring-time', puts them you-know-where. 'Green leaves, twittering or singing birds, blooming flower and girl with her young bosom . . . belong simply but jubilantly together.'[8] It is sometimes astonishing how poems can provoke this kind of critical nonsense.

The poem and design are about blossoming motherhood and birdlike infancy (which is sometimes merry, sometimes 'sobbing'), and, at a higher level, about life and love — including sexual love, which is pleasurable, and without which there would be no human life at all. But does 'sexual' have to mean exclusively the sexual act? According to our 'either/or' critics, yes. But an instinctive sexuality is surely *in*clusive, not *ex*clusive. It begins in the relationship between parent and child. As Freud was to show, a child has a fully developed capacity for love long before puberty. For this reason, Freud felt — as did Blake — that the clergy should have no hand in children's education: the stress on religious and moral ideals and the non-recognition or suppression of infantile sexuality only help to build a dam in the child's mind against its own natural impulses. What Freud empirically proved, Blake intuited. *The Blossom* is thus about sexuality in its widest sense.

The speaker of the poem is, of course, the Blossom herself. She is a mother, not a 'maiden', and is represented in the illustration as a 'mother-madonna' (the phrase is Erdman's) sitting on a flame-like leaf with an infant in her lap, i.e. her 'cradle narrow'. The flame-like vegetation is phallic, as Wicksteed suggests, but sexual intercourse is not the only act of love the poem and illustration express. Winged infant figures — 'naked joys' — are seen among the flaming spray near the mother. Two (not mentioned by Wicksteed) are actually embracing. They appear to mark a stage in earthly love's natural growth, completed in a seventh, wingless figure with arms raised on the right. Lapped near the maternal bosom, embracing each other, or celebrating sexual awareness, Blake's innocents are initiated stage by stage into ripe sexual love. The poem itself is a unique fusion of two ideas that a repressed sexuality, with its Oedipal guilt, will always dissociate: the early reliance on maternal love, and the performance in later life of the sexual act. In showing us that adult sexuality begins near the maternal bosom, Blake was more than a hundred years ahead of his time.

Innocence, once nurtured in the family, seeks to realise

itself in the wider world, conceived ideally as a
family. Divisions between parents and children,
classes, races and religious, are thus imaginatively ov

The Divine Image quietly subverts the dominant
of self-righteous patriotism, and perceives that h   -y,
albeit divided into separate nations and religions, is really one:

> Then every man, of every clime,
> That prays in his distress,
> Prays to the human form divine,
> Love, Mercy, Pity, Peace.
>
> And all must love the human form,
> In heathen, turk, or jew;
> Where Mercy, Love & Pity dwell
> There God is dwelling too.

Though such sentiments have now become the stock-in-trade
of liberal humanists, in Blake's time they were those of revolutionary democrats. The hidden suggestion that 'all religions
are one' may be set against the proselytising zeal of the late
eighteenth-century Evangelicals, whose hope of imposing
'civilisation' and Christianity on the benighted heathen was
more important than a recognition of common humanity
with the 'heathen' — a common humanity so often obscured
by the apparently alien nature of 'savage' customs.

In *The Little Black Boy* (which Coleridge thought the
best poem in the collection), an African child, probably
destined to become a West Indian slave, addresses the white
boy in far-off England, and looks forward to a time

> When I from black and he from white cloud free,
> And round the tent of God like lambs we joy.

The poem is Blake at his most Swedenborgian, particularly
in its symbolism. (Swedenborg believed that the New Church
would rise in Africa.) It prophesies a time of harmony,
when the spiritually superior black boy will have taught the
white boy the ways of spiritual love. In *Holy Thursday*, the
sight of thousands of charity-school children in St Paul's
is transformed into a vision of 'multitudes of lambs' who,
'like a mighty wind', raise to heaven the voice of song 'with

harmonious thunderings'. The language of biblical prophecy suggests that the adult speaker of the poem has intuitively perceived a mighty force for change in these 'multitudes of lambs'.

The designs for *Songs of Innocence* have their own visual eloquence. David Erdman has revealed a symbolic significance even in the lettering. The designs as a whole convey the freshness, energy, variety and plenitude of a world newly made. Flowers, birds, human figures, angels and other 'minute particulars' fill every corner, lie on vine branches, fly in the blue sky, recline in title letters or in scrolls; efflorescent, flame-like vegetation, as in *The Divine Image*, swirls with sexual energy and the freedom of unrestrained growth. One's first visual response to the book is often that of breath-catching exhilaration at the sheer beauty of the conception, which is a community of loving responses, where sports, games, play, mutual exchanges, climbing, flight, embracing, resting and sleeping — all the motions and gratified desires of 'the human form divine', delicately mirrored in the natural forms of trunks, branches, vines and flowers — require no other justification other than to say that they are alive. 'Every thing that lives is Holy.'

Such a vision was, however, as precarious as it was fulfilling. Blake's Innocence is neither nostalgic in its pastoralism nor escapist in its utopianism. There is always a critical force behind it: Innocence therefore implies Experience.

On Another's Sorrow connects the love nurtured in the family ('Can a father see his child/Weep, nor be with sorrow fill'd?') with a wider love, declaring, with some urgency, its faith in the spontaneous nature of human sympathy. It asks rhetorically how we can fail to share our children's sorrow or that of other children, and the urgency of the questions and the repeated answer ('O! no, never can it be!/Never, never can it be!') imply that this lack of sympathetic emotion is all too possible. The impassioned assertion thus carries an ironic force. Innocence is not naiveté; the social criticism which is here implied is made explicit in *Songs of Experience*.

The social criticism in *A Dream*, however, has proved too subtle for most readers. The poet uses the traditional emblem of the ant or 'emmet', but does something quite new with it.

A Dream

Once a dream did weave a shade
O'er my Angel-guarded bed,
That an Emmet lost its way
Where on grass methought I lay.

Troubled, 'wilder'd, and forlorn,
Dark, benighted, travel-worn,
Over many a tangled spray,
All heart-broke I heard her say:

'O, my children! do they cry?
Do they hear their father sigh?
Now they look abroad to see:
Now return and weep for me?'

Pitying, I drop'd a tear;
But I saw a glow-worm near,
Who replied: 'What ailing wight
Calls the watchman of the night?

I am set to light the ground,
While the beetle goes his round:
Follow now the beetle's hum;
Little wanderer, hie thee home.'

According to Holloway, 'the point of the poem is that all the ant's striving and effort *do it no good*'; the glow-worm, who 'does nothing but sit and shine', sets the 'way of life' before the lost ant, and 'the wisdom of the poem comes to [the poet] in pastoral innocence and idleness'.[9] This, he argues, answers conventional homilies regarding sluggards (deriving from Proverbs 6:6: 'Go to the ant, thou sluggard; consider her ways, and be wise') and the need to be a prudent, hard-working individual. But is the poem a song in praise of dreamy idleness? Hardly: the dreamer's imagination is active, not idle. The lost ant 'comes' to him in the dream as an 'it', but is changed by him into a forlorn and travel-worn mother. Then, with child-like make-believe, he places a glow-worm nearby to guide her. The 'watchman of the night' is not 'idle' either, but *caring,* and helps poor Mrs Emmet on her way home — where, in her imagination (and in the poet's) she

hears her children and husband cry, sigh and weep for her —
by telling her to follow 'the beetle's hum'. Interdependence
and caring are the whole point of the poem. In the imagination
of the 'Angel-guarded' dreamer, all the creatures in his dream
have a compassionate concern for others, as he has for them
(being his own creations). It is this that unites them.

Yet there is a poignant, bitter irony here we should not
miss. The parish watch, or constable — a nightly reminder
(with his *musket* as well as lantern) of urban crime — has
become in the dream a compassionate glow-worm; and the
parish beadle (so often, under the Poor Laws, responsible for
separating families) becomes, in this child-like vision, a
'beetle', guiding the lost mother back to her family. We are
reminded of the realities of life in Blake's London: of
poverty and homelessness, of social indifference, and the
fact that our compassionate dreams change nothing. On the
other hand, this make-believe is not to be confused with a
childish escape into 'pastoral innocence and idleness'. By
awakening us to our real responsibilities, Blake's poem is a
quietly biting comment on how things really stand.

The immediate vicinity of Broad Street and its associations
were forever imprinted on the poet's mind. Behind Dufours
Place, a narrow cul-de-sac that led off Broad Street on the
Blakes' side, was the parish workhouse known as 'the nurses'
houses'. In the 1760s the overseers adopted the practice of
boarding out the younger pauper children with nurses in
Wimbledon. *The Nurse's Song*, which consists of a dialogue
between a nurse and her charge, has an illustration showing
the 'green', with low hills in the background. It could very
easily be Wimbledon Common. As Geoffrey Keynes remarks,
'the weeping willow in the right-hand margin is perhaps a
reminder that not all life is fun and games'.[10]

The most socially direct of the *Songs of Innocence* is *The
Chimney Sweeper*, where the shocking casualness of the
opening ('When my mother died I was very young,/And my
Father sold me . . .'), the authentic details (sleeping in
soot, the boys' shaved heads, rising to work with brushes in
the dark) and the terrible irony of the final line, with its
monosyllabic baldness ('So if all do their duty they need not
fear harm') — all bitterly protest that such things should not

be, however much the victims may be mollified. The chimney sweeper's innocent trust is cruelly abused, but the speaker who consoles Tom is a victim too. Tom's innocence here is close to naiveté, as is the speaker's in *Holy Thursday* (who seems curiously innocent of the realities behind the stage-managed procession).

Writers of children's literature in Blake's day nearly always assumed that the children they wrote for would not be poor themselves. This, of course, is not surprising. Much the same is true today: how many present-day books for children depict high-rise blocks, police harrassment, black children in decaying inner city areas, poverty, overcrowding and broken homes? Yet Blake refused, when writing his songs, to push into the distance the equivalent social realities of his own time. Poor or 'lost' children are not some vague backdrop occasionally visited by providence and grace. For whom, then, did Blake write his illuminated songs? Whether they ever got into the hands of artisans' children, kindly nurses, liberal charity-school governors, progressive educational reformers and the like we shall probably never know. The price which the 'Author & Printer' of the *Songs of Innocence* was asking in 1793 was five shillings — the price of a week's bread for a journeyman or three days' wages for an agricultural labourer. The chances of such a book entering working homes would therefore appear to be fairly slim.

More relevant is Blake's break with the middle-class literary tradition, from Isaac Watts to Mrs Barbauld (though he owed something to both these writers). As one example of educational literature *to be used*, the *Songs of Innocence* are unique: neither seeking to socialise children into the norms and codes of class society, nor cultivating an individual sensibility, they psychologically prepare both parent and child for an open, free, democratic society. They were intended as songs from which the parents could learn as much as their children. They undercut the kind of religious teaching advocated for the poor by Evangelical reformers. They encourage freedom, love and play, not discipline, restraint and a repressed, guilt-ridden fear. Combining the values of the old community with a new, radical Christianity, they educate parents and children for a democratic future, not according to individualistic, middle-class values, but according to communal ones. Above all, they educate the educators into a healthy relationship with children: parents can no longer hide behind an unseen, divine authority once the divine and the human have become one. Many of the songs act out, in their form, language, rhythm and structure, a free and active growth, in which relatedness, responsiveness and sharing come before self. The 'morality' of Blake's Innocence is Exuberance: whereas the cisterns of other writers contained, this fountain overflows.

4

The Politics of Experience

When Blake issued *Songs of Innocence and of Experience* in a single bound volume in 1794, he etched and coloured a new title page. It shows the expulsion of Adam and Eve from the Garden of Eden, fleeing amid blood-red flames, with — in one version — a flash of sulphurous yellow between them, echoed in their leaf-girdled bodies. Over Adam's bent figure are the words: 'Shewing the Two Contrary States of the Human Soul'.

The biblical Fall thus provides the model for Experience. Yet *Songs of Innocence and of Experience*, like many of Blake's other works, shows a radical re-handling of traditional (in this case, biblical) ideas and symbols. The songs rely on a previous knowledge of these in order to present a view of the world that subverts orthodoxy. As a creative artist the poet is not bound by any pre-given set of meanings. Thus in the *Introduction* to *Songs of Experience*, the lines

> The Holy Word
> That walk'd among the ancient trees,
>
> Calling the lapsed Soul,
> And weeping in the evening dew

are a clear reference to Genesis 3:8: 'And they heard the voice of the Lord God walking in the garden in the cool of the day: and Adam and his wife hid themselves from the presence of the Lord God amongst the trees of the garden'. But in line 10, the repetition in 'And fallen, fallen light renew!' is deceptive, since the first 'fallen' can easily refer to the Holy Word itself, while *Earth's Answer* indicts a jealous, patriarchal authority that has imprisoned the female 'lapsed Soul' in a fallen and therefore oppressive world *created by the same patriarchal authority.* In this way Blake's antinomian 'heresy' re-interprets his original sources, just as antinomians such as John Saltmarsh (d. 1647), or the Ranters, Diggers, and other radicals of the seventeenth century had freely interpreted the Scriptures according to an 'inner light'. Like them, Blake obeyed 'the kingdom within', rather than establishment doctrine — the Moral Law of the ruling class. Such free interpretation also made the Scriptures live in a contemporaneous present. As Winstanley said: 'We may see Adam every day before our eyes walking up and down the street.' Blake's modern Adam and Eve, however, do not fall into sin by disobeying an interdiction (the command not to eat of the forbidden tree), but rather find themselves caught in a web of moral laws and interdictions whose rationale is as mysterious as their consequences — if the laws are obeyed — prove to be psychologically catastrophic. The speakers in *The Angel* and *My Pretty Rose Tree* have both 'heard' an interdiction (not to reveal the 'heart's delight', not to accept an offer of adulterous love), and the result is another kind of fall: repressing natural instincts merely blights and poisons the emotions.

It is the idea of a taboo, the 'Thou shalt not' — though such an idea recurs in myths, legends and folktales throughout the world — that Blake objects to. Why does God put a forbidden tree there in the first place? And what, really, is the modern meaning of this tree? In *The Human Abstract* the tree of knowledge becomes the tree of Mystery, a symbol of oppressive authority, where the ruling class, in a negative withdrawal, hides its fear and hatred of the poor behind a mask of pity, love and holiness. Some kind of ideological apparatus is needed to maintain the rule of 'Cruelty' (the abstract personification of political and religious tyranny). The tree of Mystery, whose 'dismal shade' spreads over Cruelty's head, is its symbol. The speaker of *A Poison Tree* is the cruel, vengeful God of Genesis writ small. (Blake knew of the poisonous upas tree of Java, whose milky sap was used for arrow poison, from Erasmus Darwin's *Loves of the Plants*.) Following an interdiction not to reveal his anger ('I told it not'), the speaker nurtures his repressed wrath into a tree of deceitful friendship which he intends for his 'foe', tempting him to steal into his garden and so eat of the enticing, forbidden fruit ('an apple bright') that proves to be the poison of the avenger's hate: 'In the morning glad I see/My foe outstretch'd beneath the tree.'

There are other ways in which Blake — again, following radical tradition — modifies his sources. The idea of the female soul imprisoned in a fallen material world, which derives from religious Platonism, and which Kathleen Raine has made so much of in *Blake and Tradition*, acquires political overtones: the 'break of day' in the *Introduction* is not just liberation from an earthly prison, but freedom from an oppressive system. Even Blake's Gnosticism — the idea that the material world is the creation of a cruel demiurge rather than that of a loving God — is re-worked into an indictment of the existing social and political order.

Experience is the 'contrary state' of Innocence. Since Blake was thirty-two when he issued *Songs of Innocence*, and since the composition of some 'contrary' poems may be only a few months apart, it has been accepted that the change from Innocence to Experience cannot be explained by any 'fall' from Innocence experienced in the poet's own life. Nor can the change be explained as a result of Blake's disillusionment and altered feelings towards the French Revolution. Biographical and historical explanations having been ruled out, it has therefore become the critical fashion to view the two spiritual 'states' as timeless opposites, to hold them in the mind as perpetually opposed, and compare 'contrary' poems with each other, such as *The Lamb* with *The Tyger*, *On Another's Sorrow* with *The Human Abstract*, the two *Nurse's Songs*, the two *Chimney Sweeper* poems, and so on. This is justified by the fact that poems in *Experience* parallel and satirise poems in *Innocence*. Thus in *On Another's Sorrow* the 'innocent' speaker asks:

> Can I see another's woe
> And not be in sorrow too?

and in *The Human Abstract* the 'experienced' speaker cynically retorts:

> Pity would be no more
> If we did not make somebody Poor . . .

Yet it is difficult not to connect the contrary 'states' with differing contexts, reflecting the transition from one kind of social (and hence spiritual) existence to another. Although they arguably do much more, *Songs of Innocence* instil into the reader the kind of relatedness, openness, responsiveness and caring values that are generated within a popular community. Such values have their roots, of course, in an older, rural way of life. The fragility of Innocence is also the fragility of that way of life (and the spiritual 'state' associated with it) in the face of momentous social changes. Blake's Innocence and Experience, therefore, are not only 'contrary states of the human soul' but, in social, historical terms, mark an irreversible transition, an unprecedented change from one kind of society to another.

There are many ways in which this change might be characterised. E. P. Thompson, for example, has called it an 'experience of immiseration' that came upon working people

> in a hundred different forms; for the field labourer, the loss of his common rights and the vestiges of village democracy; for the artisan, the loss of his craftsman's status; for the weaver, the loss of livelihood and of independence; for the child, the loss of work and play in the home; for many groups of workers whose real earnings improved, the loss of security, leisure and the deterioration of the urban environment.[1]

Blake's Experience is in one sense the experience of social misery, of poverty without the safety net of communal concern and mutual obligation. Individualism has bred social indifference:

Holy Thursday

Is this a holy thing to see
In a rich and fruitful land,
Babes reduc'd to misery,
Fed with cold and usurous hand?

Is that trembling cry a song?
Can it be a song of joy?
And so many children poor?
It is a land of poverty!

And their sun does never shine,
And their fields are bleak & bare,
And their ways are fill'd with thorns:
It is eternal winter there.

For where-e'er the sun does shine,
And where-e'er the rain does fall,
Babe can never hunger there,
Nor poverty the mind appall.

It is not merely the poverty that appals, but the lack of any love or genuine concern.

With the break-up of the old communities, a moral and spiritual vacuum was created for which Methodist chapels were hardly an answer. As R. M. Martin put it in 1834, '[the communities] seem to have lost their animation, their vivacity, their field games and their village sports; they have become a sordid, discontented, miserable, anxious, struggling people, without health, or gaiety, or happiness'.[2] From the communal joy of *The Ecchoing Green*, where children play on the green watched by village elders, we come to this:

The Garden of Love

I went to the Garden of Love,
And saw what I never had seen:
A Chapel was built in the midst,
Where I used to play on the green.

And the gates of this Chapel were shut,
And 'Thou shalt not' writ over the door;
So I turn'd to the Garden of Love
That so many sweet flowers bore;

And I saw it was filled with graves,
And tomb-stones where flowers should be;
And Priests in black gowns were walking their rounds,
And binding with briars my joys & desires.

Innocent village love has been curbed and blighted by an interfering priesthood, who bring only guilt, penance and joylessness. (The poem has a Buñuel-like dream quality.)

The transition to an industrial capitalist society eventually destroyed what remained of the old pre-industrial way of life. Working people were urged to adopt alien patterns of thinking and acting by the new, vigorous, 'industrious' middle class, with its armies of educational reformers, its philanthropists, its societies for the reformation of manners, its Evangelical societies, nonconformist chapels, and young, ardent ministers recruited from the artisan class. Older communal values, though in some ways renewed in the urban, working-class environment, were replaced at first by an atomised collectivity (thus aiding the process of religious conversion). Capitalism required a larger market of 'free labourers' in order to expand, and, like Blake's tree which some only see as 'a Green thing that stands in the way', the old communities were an obstacle to progress. It was also during this period that sanctified church marriage and the modern nuclear family began to be imposed more firmly on society as a whole.

Songs of Experience is in some ways a reaction to the 'compulsory sex morality' that is bound up with these two latter institutions. The conjugal pair depicted on the title page are bound together in mutual guilt and sexual tension; as the flames of sexual warfare and constantly erupting jealous battles swirl over them, Eve lies almost enticingly under the guilt-tormented Adam. Blake did not, of course, subscribe to the doctrine of original sin. He merely used the biblical Fall as a metaphor. Human beings are perhaps only 'in sin' when they are mentally imprisoned by social conventions and institutions, upon whose limiting constraints both Church and State depend.

During the 1790s Blake became intensely critical of monogamous marriage and the nuclear family. Yet unlike Shelley, the daring and freedom of whose personal life required much expensive wandering and exile, Blake held back from libertarian personal solutions. He certainly *contemplated* various kinds of 'escape', such as emigration and a communitarian life in America; and there is the story that he once suggested to his wife that they form a *menage à trois*, to which his wife responded with tears of hurt indignation. But his new-found libertarian ideas, fired by his reading of Rousseau and his association with radicals such as William

Godwin and Mary Wollstonecraft, were never put into practice: his childless marriage, bringing with it so much discontent, tension and heartache — and yet, in the end, so much solace — was to last forty-five years right up to his death.

In terms of the changes imposed on personal life in the seventeenth and eighteenth centuries, the Marriage Acts were some of the most important pieces of legislation. Marriage had always been founded on canon law, but in spite of the rules governing incest and divorce, there had been little actual control over the sexual and family life of ordinary working people. In fact before the Council of Trent in 1563 no religious ceremony needed to be performed when two people got married. Church marriages were not necessary, and clandestine marriages were common. An Act passed in 1694 stated that no person could marry without a licence, unless banns had first been published, while all births had to be registered by the parson. Lord Hardwicke's Marriage Act of 1753 finally outlawed 'clandestine' marriages, and stipulated that *all* marriages had to be solemnised according to the rites of the Church of England in the parish church of one of the two parties, in the presence of a clergyman and two witnesses. (Thus Blake, though a Dissenter, married Catherine Boucher in St Mary's Anglican church, Battersea, in his wife's parish.)

Behind this legislation lies a long-drawn-out, deep-going change in English social *mores*. With the expansion of commodity production, the extended family retreated; the nuclear family began to take over, and 'loose morals' (associated with the old rural way of life) were reformed. The old sociability thus also retreated. 'Everywhere', says Phillipe Ariès, the nuclear family 'reinforced private life at the expense of neighbourly relationships, friendships, and traditional contacts. The history of modern manners can be reduced in part to this long effort to break away from others, to escape from a society whose pressure had become unbearable.'[3]

Christian, monogamous marriage and the nuclear family rely heavily on the following related concepts: the mystic union, sealed by sacrament, of a single pair; the need for individual privacy — which, according to Ariès, was quite foreign to the medieval tradition of openness and neighbourliness, since it tended to stifle 'the activity of social relations';[4] the invention, then romanticising of childhood as a separate state, reflecting the new status of children in the non-productive nuclear family; and romantic love, which, though adulterous in the courtly love tradition, emotionally fulfils the ideal of Christian marriage, an ideal defined by Lord Penzance in 1866 as 'the voluntary union for life of one man and one woman, to the exclusion of all others'.

We all know what romantic love is. It's: 'O, my Luve's like a red red rose/That's newly sprung in June', and 'Roses are flowering in Picardy,/But there's never a rose like you'. Yet of all the blooming and blushing, or beautifully frail roses of literature, none compares with Blake's 'sick' rose. Something, surely, is terribly wrong. How can a rose be sick?

The Sick Rose

O Rose, thou are sick!
The invisible worm
That flies in the night
In the howling storm,

Has found out thy bed
Of crimson joy:
And his dark secret love
Does thy life destroy.

In the etched design, two female figures wearily droop on the rose's briar stems, while a caterpillar (symbol in Blake of priesthood) devours a leaf on the tree-like rose bush. The tail of the burrowing worm sticks out of the ball-like crimson rose, curling round the waist of a symbolic female who has lain in the centre of the blossom; her arms are outstretched in a possibly despairing gesture. The whole is a highly-charged symbol.

Whether Blake's English Rose is Woman, Beauty, or Romantic Love itself, there is from the outset something distinctly unhealthy about her. This is because she is a male invention, the idealised projection of a one-sided male consciousness. This false idealisation does two things: it serves, first, as a cover for male sexual politics — the desire of the male to *own* the female and so dominate her; and it creates a split between 'spiritual' and 'physical' love, repressing the latter for the sake of the former. The result is an 'invisible worm/That flies in the night'; the sexual act is considered sinful, and so becomes a deed of darkness to be done in secret, something unacceptable to the conscious mind.

If the whole idea of Romantic Love is unhealthy, then the invisible worm is a kind of avenger (unlike the merry sparrow that, 'swift as arrow', seeks its 'cradle narrow' in *The Blossom*). Night-borne and storm-laden, its rapid quest and destruction of the sick rose might be profoundly shocking, but at least it has acted. Perhaps the idealised romantic rose ought to be destroyed after all.

Sexual politics between man and woman are carried through into the relations between father, mother and child, and thus affect the child's whole life. This we can see from the extremely revealing notebook poem *Infant Sorrow*, the first two stanzas of which appear under the same title in *Songs of Experience*. (I have retained some of the deletions.)

Infant Sorrow

My mother groan'd, my father wept;
Into the dangerous world I leapt,
Helpless, naked, piping loud,
Like a fiend hid in a cloud.

Struggling in my father's hands
Striving against my swaddling bands,
Bound & weary, I thought best
To sulk upon my mother's breast.

When I saw that rage was vain,
And to sulk would nothing gain,
Turning many a trick & wile,
I began to soothe & smile.

And I sooth'd day after day
Till upon the ground I stray;
And I smil'd night after night,
Seeking only for delight.

And I saw before me shine
Clusters of the wand'ring vine
And many a lovely flower & tree
Stretch'd their blossoms out to me.

(But many a Priest — del.)
My father then with holy look,
In his hands a holy book,
Pronounc'd curses on my head
And bound me in a mirtle shade.

(I beheld the Priests by night;
They embrac'd (my mirtle — del.) the blossoms bright:
I beheld the Priests by day;
Underneath the vines they lay — del.)

Like to serpents in the night
They (altered to He) embrac'd my (mirtle — del.)
                                    blossoms bright
Like to holy men by day,
Underneath the vines they lay.

So I smote them & their gore
Stain'd the roots my mirtle bore;
But the time of youth is fled,
And grey hairs are on my head.

One is invited to read much into this: [the birth of the baby
is a sorrow for the mother and a threat to the father; the
authoritarian reflex is to repress infantile energies, yet the
infant's 'rebellion' is only a response to the conditions of
his birth and upbringing (swaddling clothes were, incidentally,
condemned by Rousseau); subdued, the infant falls back on
his mother, but impotence only spurs on revenge, desire for
which is hidden beneath what the child sees as a cunning
disguise ('many a trick & wile'), but probably isn't; an
Oedipal obsession with the father as somebody interfering
and omnipresent ('many a Priest') then takes over, thwarting
and blighting the youth's sexual impulses; father-son rivalry
dominates the young man's marriage; symbolic parricide
(or rather clergicide) then stains the marital relationship, so
that the husband feels himself robbed of youth and joy
before his time.]

Another notebook poem called *In a Mirtle Shade* is more specifically about the married state. The second stanza sounds like a *cri de coeur*:

> Why should I be bound to thee,
> O my lovely mirtle tree?
> Love, free love, cannot be bound
> To any tree that grows on ground.

Father and priest are again thought of together in: 'Oft (the priest beheld — del.) my father saw us sigh'.

A more subtle indictment of bourgeois marriage is *My Pretty Rose Tree*:

> My Pretty Rose Tree
>
> A flower was offered to me,
> Such a flower as May never bore;
> But I said 'I've a Pretty Rose-tree',
> And I passed the sweet flower o'er.
>
> Then I went to my Pretty Rose-tree,
> To tend her by day and by night;
> But my Rose turn'd away with jealousy,
> And her thorns were my only delight.

The loyal husband, having rejected 'a flower as May never bore', returns to his wife to 'tend her by day and by night', implying, perhaps, that this diligent care will expunge his infatuation, exonerate him in his wife's eyes, and compensate for his missed opportunity. Through the legal right of male possession, he expects to enjoy the flowers of his domesticated 'Rose-tree', symbolising his wife's function as passive sexual object, regular producer and pretty piece of decoration. Yet she turns away jealously, an affronted yet conspiring victim of a bonded relationship — refusing him in order to teach him a lesson. The speaker's hurt tone of voice, in: 'And her thorns were my only delight', is that of a surprised yet knowing cynic, whose ironic appeal for sympathy ('my only delight') reveals his self-centredness.

Introduction and *Earth's Answer* are also about 'the marriage problem', the latter ending with a call for free love as part of a revolutionary programme. The 'Bard' calls on Earth, the 'lapsed Soul', to return:

Turn away no more
Why wilt thou turn away?
The starry floor,
The wat'ry shore,
Is giv'n thee till break of day.

But 'Earth' hears in the voice of the Bard only a cruel, jealous, selfish possessor, who cultivates her for himself alone, in shameful secrecy:

Does spring hide its joy
When buds and blossoms grow?
Does the sower
Sow by night,
Or the plowman in darkness plow?

Break this heavy chain
That does freeze my bones around.
Selfish! vain!
Eternal bane!
That free Love with bondage bound.

But the strongest indictment of compulsory sex morality, and the most impassioned calls for free love, are to be found in *Visions of the Daughters of Albion* (1793), where the sexual politics of Experience seem to have been transcended by a new, 'higher' Innocence. Oothoon, the 'soft soul of America', is bound back to back (in the colour illustration) with the slave-owner Bromion, who has raped and possessed her, and cries out to her now jealous lover, Theotormon:

I cry: Love! Love! Love! happy happy Love!
         free as the mountain wind!
Can that be Love that drinks another as a sponge
         drinks water,
That clouds with jealousy his nights, with weepings
         all the day,
To spin a web of age around him, grey and hoary, dark,
Till his eyes sicken at the fruit that hangs before
         his sight?
Such is self-love that envies all, a creeping skeleton
With lamplike eyes watching around the frozen
         marriage bed.

But silken nets and traps of adamant will Oothoon
                                                    spread,
And catch for thee girls of mild silver, or of furious
                                                    gold.
I'll lie beside thee on a bank & view their wanton play
In lovely copulation, bliss on bliss, with Theotormon:
Red as the rosy morning, lustful as the first born beam,
Oothoon shall view his dear delight, nor e'er with
                                                    jealous cloud
Come in the heaven of generous love, nor selfish
                                                    blightings bring.

Blake is not indicting individuals but a system. It was Godwin
who stated, after much reflection and analysis, that '[the]
abolition of the present system of marriage appears to involve
no evils', and who wrote: 'So long as I seek to engross one
woman to myself, and to prohibit my neighbour from
proving his superior desert and reaping the fruits of it, I am
guilty of the most odious of all monopolies.'[4]

There is a strong sense, in *Songs of Experience*, of the
appalling mental and emotional harm people in a modern
repressive society inflict on themselves and on each other.
Those most imprisoned within it seem to be divorced from
nature and production, and hence from what is natural and
productive in themselves. (The other side of the coin is a
new bitterness and violence.) Blake shows us how obedience
to an external moral law and the dictates of state religion
leads to *self*-repression and a defensive withdrawal into
secretive self-interest that always diminishes us as human
beings. The naive, altruistic clod in *The Clod & the Pebble*
may be trodden with the cattle's feet, but the selfish pebble
is incapable of any responsive feelings. With her modesty and
coyness, the female speaker in *The Angel* has hidden from
the world (and from her 'Angel') a love which, because of
missed chances, will never be fulfilled. Thus Desire has
withered. A bleak unproductive landscape of sterile resentment, yearning and regret, of fear, guilt and joylessness; a
world dominated by priests and fathers, the church and the
chapel, has replaced the open, responsive, communal world
of *Innocence*.

And yet coercive conformity to a code that is built on social injustice and economic inequalities will always provoke protest and resistance. Repression often claims to have succeeded at the very moment when new fire breaks out. Children in *Songs of Experience* are no longer 'innocent', but are able to see through the system. Three poems bring this out: *The Chimney Sweeper, The Little Vagabond*, and *A Little Boy Lost*.

The child who is able to articulate an 'adult' political awareness is usually the product of extreme social circumstances: one thinks of 'street-wise' kids in the black ghettoes and slums of New York and Chicago; of war-damaged young survivors afer the bombardment of Tel-al-Zatar refugee camp in the Lebanon; or the black children involved in mass strikes against the Bantu Education system in South Africa. With its street vagabonds, infant chimney sweeps, child street-sellers of all kinds, charity schools and parish workhouses for destitute children, London in the 1790s must have been similarly traumatising and rapidly maturing for thousands of children — especially at a time when popular reform societies were radicalising the urban masses in their hundreds of thousands.[5]

In *The Chimney Sweeper*, the condition of the child sweeper is captured by the adult speaker of the poem in a single vivid image:

> A little black thing among the snow,
> Crying 'weep! weep!' in notes of woe!

The sweep is an atom, a 'little black thing' among millions of other atoms, an object people use to clean their chimneys. Yet this 'thing', when asked by the speaker where its mother and father are, shows a burning resentment at paternal hypocrisy:

> [They] are gone to praise God & his Priest & King,
> Who make up a heaven of our misery.

The sweep, who is at first a pitiable object to the speaker of the poem, is not only aware of his condition, but has seen through the religion of those who have caused his misery.

State religion, the religion of the Accuser, is for Blake the real evil, not the so-called 'sins' which the Accuser condemns. It is a gloomy Protestantism, sin-obsessed, that teaches the happy child to 'sing the notes of woe', simply *because* he is happy. In *The Little Vagabond*, Blake's child of Experience has imbibed ideas uncannily similar to those of the seventeenth-century Ranters:

> Dear Mother, dear Mother, the Church is cold,
> But the Ale-house is healthy & pleasant & warm;
> Besides I can tell where I am used well,
> Such usage in heaven will never do well.
>
> But if at the Church they would give us some Ale,
> And a pleasant fire our souls to regale,
> We'd sing and we'd pray all the live-long day,
> Nor ever once wish from the Church to stray.
>
> Then the Parson might preach, & drink, & sing,
> And we'd be as happy as birds in the spring;
> And modest dame Lurch, who is always at Church,
> Would not have bandy children, nor fasting, nor
>
> > birch.
>
> And God, like a father rejoicing to see
> His children as pleasant and happy as he,
> Would have no more quarrel with the Devil or the
>
> > Barrel,
>
> But kiss him, & give him both drink and apparel.

All this is deceptively innocent: the child simply asks for health and warmth. In fact, he is a *persona* through whom the poet endorses a revolt, begun in the previous century, against a moral law that excluded from grace all those whom it saw as sinners and reprobates — meaning, more often than not, the lower classes. Singing, dancing, and drinking in ale-houses gave the Puritan middle-class conscience sufficient cause for a quarrel with the Devil. If *that* was their Devil, argued the Ranters, then 'Devil is God, Hell is Heaven, Sin Holiness, Damnation Salvation'.[6] Antinomians and Ranters regularly met in ale-houses. Thomas Edwards, in his *Gangraena*, a compendious indictment of 'gangrenous' heresies written in 1646, spoke of 'an antinomian preacher in

London' who 'on a fast day said it was better for Christians to be drinking in an ale-house, or to be in a whore-house, than to be keeping fasts legally'.[7] Writing in the same year, the Suffolk parson John Eachard (who, according to Christopher Hill, 'spoke up for the common soldiers in 1645') declared: 'Eat of Christ, therefore, the tree of life, at supper, and drink of his blood, and make you merry'.[8] Blake's young speaker has exposed the life-denying, cruel nature of a religion and an education he has come to associate with cold cheerlessness and corporal punishment. (The 'Church' in the first line of the poem is not merely a building, but the institution.) To be given ale, warm clothes, and a good diet, thereby preventing rickets, is more 'heavenly' to the boy's mind than having to do penance for alleged sins. But for these things to happen, the God of 'them up there', instead of fearing and hating the Devil whom 'they' connect with 'us down here', will have to learn to 'kiss him'.

The boy in *A Little Boy Lost* has acquired a realistic, down-to-earth outlook on life, and has become aware that his 'Father' (the priest) is only a human being like himself. Such a clear-sighted wisdom it is the aim of a religious-based education to stamp out. Hence, one of the lessons learned from *Songs of Innocence* encounters authoritarian resistance. In other words, this kind of education seeks to *prevent* the development of any independent thought in the child, since it might turn out to be critical of authority. In one stanza — indeed, in one phrase — Blake strikes at the heart of the Evangelical movement; its fanaticism and sense of missionary dedication are seen as nothing but the pathological manifestation of a cruelly repressive urge:

> The Priest sat by and heard the child,
> In trembling zeal he siez'd his hair;
> He led him by his little coat,
> And all admir'd the Priestly care.
>
> And standing on the altar high,
> 'Lo! what a fiend is here!' said he.
> 'One who sets reason up for judge
> Of our most holy mystery.'

The weeping child could not be heard,
The weeping parents wept in vain;
They strip'd him to his little shirt,
And bound him in an iron chain;

And burn'd him in a holy place,
Where many had been burn'd before:
The weeping parents wept in vain.
Are such things done on Albion's shore?

While the phrases 'trembling zeal' and 'Priestly care' are ironically precise, the vision of the child's punishment turns into a hyperbolic, anticlerical satire. On the other hand, the line 'One who sets reason up for judge' could be a definite contemporary reference: perhaps the little boy has heard some of the arguments of Tom Paine. The poem thus works on several levels.

If Innocence and Experience represent 'contrary states', they also represent, or imply, *social* states so different as to be incompatible. Here, it is not simply material or physical *circumstances* that are important, but *social relationships*, relationships that either provide or fail to provide the needed psychological protection when circumstances change (the sort of psychological protection enjoyed by the chimney sweeper in *Innocence*). The children in *Experience*, who are without that protection, have become 'wise', and once this occurs, the old, instinctive trust can never be regained.

Songs of Innocence and of Experience are thus about the irrevocable change from one way of life and one sensibility to another, a change experienced with much greater sharpness in a period of rapid upheaval. The moral law of factory and chapel was replacing inherited custom and the communality of village life. It is not 'ideas', but social change and social conflict that stimulate dialectical thought. For Blake the movement of contemporary history became neither a succession of rational 'improvements' nor a repeated upsurge of blind, irrational forces. It was a struggle of 'contraries', a struggle that had to be fought out in the 'soul' of every man. If there is a sense in which the French Revolution and the intensifying political conflicts in England led to the writing of *Songs of Experience*, then it can be seen in the way the songs express not 'disillusionment' or a cynical awareness of social and psychological realities, but a new *dialectical* awareness. Blake's Innocence already *implies* Experience, but it is doubtful whether Blake had fully conceived his two 'contrary states' by 1789 — in spite of the fact that dialectical thinking had become natural to him by that time. (In his annotations to Swedenborg's *Divine Love*, written about 1789, Blake wrote: 'Good & Evil are here both Good & the two contraries Married', and: 'Heaven & Hell are born together'.)

In this context, Blake's Innocence is certainly the spiritual 'contrary' of Experience, but it is not, as it stands, a true *dialectical* 'contrary': it is too weak an alternative, too fragile a critique to withstand the withering cynicism of Experience: 'Pity would be no more/If we did not make somebody Poor'. Blake's Experience, in fact, contains its *own* dialectical 'contraries', since it is a *power struggle* and not merely a 'state'. Rulers and ruled, rich and poor, priests and laity, parents and children, teachers and taught, male and female, husband and wife; romantic idealism *versus* cynical realism, monogamous marriage *versus* free love and/or prostitution — *everywhere* there is the opposition of 'married contraries', as a result of which a new dynamic has opened up. These points should be borne in mind when considering the best-known of Blake's 'Songs of Experience', *The Tyger.*

Blake's Tyger and the 'Tygerish Multitude'

The 'beast in man' is a somewhat hackneyed phrase, applicable to all times and places. There is, it would appear, an element of the beast in all of us, a core of savagery, fanaticism and violence that may suddenly be released when the barriers of civilised life are broken. Hence the destructive, bestial frenzy of the female followers of Dionysus in Euripides' play *The Bacchae*, Heathcliff's animalism and violent pursuit of power in *Wuthering Heights*, Kurtz's abandonment of European culture and reversion to the 'unspeakable rites' of the natives in *Heart of Darkness*, and the shocking behaviour of Golding's public school products in *The Lord of the Flies*. On the other hand, what to some seems bestial and savage may, to others, be a way of life, or a revolt that is creative and liberating. The debate continues.

It ought to be possible, however, to cut through this Gordian knot by providing every manifestation of the literary 'beast-in-man' theme and its corollaries with a precise historical and ideological context. Thus long before Euripides and the city-state festivals, the Dionysian cult existed as a popular rural festival, combining both fertility and initiation rites; during the Peloponnesian War, in democratic Athens, the Dionysiac ritual acquired a potentially liberating, yet — when repressed — a more violent and tragic aspect, since it was the democratic masses themselves who sought to benefit from military conquests. Heathcliff's violence can be understood in the context of Chartism in the industrial north and Emily Bronte's response to it. Conrad's 'unspeakable rites' are the result of Eurocentric ignorance, culture shock, and a particularly unpleasant, late-Victorian experience of the colonial enterprise.

Golding's violent schoolchildren are ideological inventions, born out of an intellectual loss of faith in man in the epoch of imperialist decline. And so on.

Blake knew all about Dionysian forces, and he tried to ride them, as the children in one of his illustrations ride the phallic serpent. Yet of all the writers mentioned, he is the only one who shows a grasp of the social and political meanings of symbolic archetypes. Hence, in *The Marriage of Heaven and Hell*, Blake's Tory Angel sees the French Revolution — the accomplishment of real men and women — as a bestial monster:

> . . . and now we saw it was the head of Leviathan; his forehead was divided into streaks of green and purple like those on a tyger's forehead: soon we saw his mouth & red gills hang just above the raging foam, tinging the black deep with beams of blood, advancing toward us with all the fury of a spiritual existence.

To the Blakean Devil, however, this huge serpentine whale with tigerish streaks is merely a reactionary mental construct of the Tory Angel; the Angel's class bias conceives of a 'black deep' of lower-class life from whence these prodigies arise — a world depicted as a 'nether deep . . . black as a sea', rolling 'with a terrible noise'. (As Conrad may have heard an unspeakable rite in every sound of Congolese drumming, which to those who understand it is complex and beautiful music, so the Angel possibly hears only a monstrous, terrible noise in the cries and shouts of militant demonstrations.) For the 'Devils' who *inhabit* these nether regions of work, creativity and agitation, however, the life of the populace is neither monstrous nor terrible. On the contrary: Blake's Devil finds himself 'sitting on a pleasant bank beside a river by moon-light, hearing a harper, who sung to the harp'. All is humanised.

Nevertheless, the French Revolution *was* violent and bloody, and the creative artist in Blake had to come to terms with this. Hence the importance of *The Tyger.* In attempting a 'radical', historically-based reading of *The Tyger*, I shall to some extent follow Stanley Gardner, Martin K. Nurmi and David Erdman. I have rejected those interpretations that treat the poem as if it were a religious or metaphysical problem. Apart from reducing the poem to metaphysics, such interpretations cannot explain why the problem should have set itself when it did and in the form in which it appears. Nurmi and Erdman have interpreted the poem historically, but have not interpreted all the social and political meanings (that is, the *relative*, not *absolute* meanings) embedded in the poem's basic symbolism. The actual form and shape given to 'universal' symbols, and hence the *particular* meanings they possess, can only be explained historically and culturally. As we shall see, Blake's choice of the 'wild-beast-in-the-forest' symbol involves the same kind of political and ideological critique that is being made in the passage from *The Marriage of Heaven and Hell*, discussed above.

Like Yeats's *Easter 1916* and Alexander Blok's *The Twelve*, *The Tyger* is a response to the terrible, new-born beauty of violent revolution. The poet now confronts his own antinomian energies as an external creation, whose 'fearful symmetry' obeys no known laws, and yet has a manifest, organised (and ferocious) presence. Whether as subjective potentiality or as political upheaval, the Tyger cannot be ignored:

> Tyger! Tyger! burning bright
> In the forests of the night,
> What immortal hand or eye
> Could frame thy fearful symmetry?

Blake conveys violent, revolutionary energy by his use of a resonating poetic symbol (the wild beast in the forest) and the invention of a *persona*, whose thirteen unanswered questions, bound by the six hammered stanzas, give the poem its peculiarly compressed verbal power.

Blake's dual symbol had a history. More important, it had a political context. By examining both, the contextual meaning of the poem becomes clearer.

In the opening of Dante's *Inferno*, the poet is seen trying to leave the dark wood of Error, which is 'savage and harsh and dense', but he is turned back by wild animals — the leopard of incontinence, the lion of bestiality and the wolf of malice and fraud. Wild beasts symbolise the dehumanisation of man through sin: whereas unfallen man is noble and god-like, sinful man is bestial; wild beasts are the sign of his degradation. In Milton's *Comus*, the dark wood reappears as a 'close dungeon of unnumerable boughs', where Comus the enchanter and his 'rout of monsters' make their 'riotous and unruly noise'. Each has been changed

> Into some brutish form of wolf, or bear,
> Or ounce, or tiger, hog or bearded goat

— or, again, they prowl in the hideous wood 'Like stabled wolves, or tigers at their prey'. Placed in its social and political context, and mediated through Milton's puritan consciousness, this monstrous rout of bestial passions can be equated with the licentious rapacity of a depraved aristocracy; on the other hand, it might just as easily be the brutalised and intemperate mob. Comus' unruly train have the qualities of both.

Wild passions in dark woods inevitably carry social as well as psychological implications. The dark recesses of the soul can often be traced to their social locations. Bearing in mind, then, the traditional meanings of the dual symbol (fallen man, bestial passion, social depravity), what immediately strikes us about Blake's poem is not — as Kathleen Raine would have it — that the Tyger is 'a symbol of competitive, predatious selfhood',[1] but that this 'predatious selfhood' has acquired a new splendour. Moreover, the beast in question had leapt to the centre of consciousness in such a way that the speaker is unable to judge it or categorise it according to traditional schemas; the emblem has burst out of its religious frame. There is even the feeling that this old symbol of bestial passion may be the one point of purifying, if destructive brightness in the traditional forests of Error.

In an important essay,[2] Martin K. Nurmi argued that Blake's *The Tyger* was a direct response to events in France, and that the 'cruel excesses' of the August Rising and the September Massacres of 1792 provoked an initially horrified reaction (hence the 'horrid ribs' and 'sanguine woe' in the first draft), but that this was modified when the National Convention was formed (21 September) and the French Republic was announced (22 September). The final draft,

says Nurmi, was 'the result of hard thought, not of events';
the tiger's 'dreadfulness' could now be seen in perspective,
as part of 'the divine plan'.[3] This is convincing, but it is not
the only evidence for the poem's topicality. *The Tyger* is
a symbolist poem. By unearthing the currency of Blake's
symbol at the time he wrote the poem, we might gain a
further insight into its political meaning.

It can be argued, in fact, that Blake was not only consciously transforming a traditional symbolism, but that he
was criticising, through the speaker of *The Tyger*, a prevailing conservative ideology that viewed revolution merely as a
horrifying, dehumanising process. The 'framers' of the liberal,
1791 constitution had unleashed a force that was to prove,
for a time, unframeable. In their mass agitation for an egalitarian republic, the Parisian *sans-culottes* embarked upon a
course that would challenge bourgeois power itself. Hence
the reaction of at least one English anti-Jacobin, who wrote
in 1793 in response to the war being waged by revolutionary
France, that it 'is less against ranks and distinctions, than
against the accumultation of wealth'.[4] Challenging property
itself, the armed doctrine of Jacobinism was irredeemable; its
popular adherents, by tearing down morality, religion and the
law, were less than human; what were they but wild animals?
As early as 7 January 1792, *The Times* thought the French
people had become 'loose from all restraints, and, in many
instances, more ferocious than wolves and tigers'. Samuel
Romilly, after the September Massacres, poured scorn on the
idea of a French Republic, and wrote: 'One might as well
think of establishing a republic of tigers in some forest of
Africa.'[5] Even Wordsworth, recollecting in tranquillity, had
found Paris in 1792

> a place of fear
> Unfit for the repose which night requires,
> Defenceless as a wood where tigers roam.[6]

Here the tigers are clearly the enraged mob, seeking new prey.

Perhaps the clearest indication, however, that this tiger
symbolism had a particular currency in Blake's time is this
passage from the same anti-Jacobin pamphlet quoted above:

Exception has been taken at Mr. Burke's opprobrious term *Swinish* multitude. I am ready for one (if this expression does not apply to the tyrannicide mob of Paris, kept in a state of intoxication for three or four days together, and marched under the desperate leaders of the 10th of August, and the 3rd of September, to overturn Royalty, and to subvert the new Constitution they had sworn to defend) to change the epithet to tygerish multitude; the more so, as Voltaire, who knew his nation better than myself, has assured us, that it is a mixture of the Tyger and the Ape. The fact is, the Monkey-compound has disappeared with the Aristocratical part of the Community, and left the wanton cruelty of the Tyger to be claimed exclusively by the Democracy.[7]

Burke's swinish multitude, the lewd, ignorant and degraded populace, have undergone a sea change. They are now the 'tygerish multitude', though swinishness — their 'intoxication' when they marched to overturn monarchy — is not wholly absent. Mass supremacy has changed the character of the French nation: its aristocratic imitativeness has disappeared, to be replaced by the 'wanton cruelty' of democratic government. We should note here not only the class prejudice that attributes 'wanton cruelty' solely to the oppressed (who were certainly driven to acts of violence against their oppressors) but also the violence implicit in the terms being used: swine may be greedy, undiscriminating and only useful as 'pig's meat' (to quote one Radical response to Burke) but tigers are lawless, rampant beasts. If any public order is to be maintained, such beasts ought, we feel, to be either caught or shot. (After all, they are no longer *human*.)

However, despite the growing bellicosity of English conservative reaction, with its language of counter-revolution and counter-revolutionary war, it was difficult to see how a whole feral nation might be put down. Confident contempt for the mob gave way to a kind of blind, stunned horror at the fact that such a thing as a French Republic — worse, a *democratic* French Republic — could come about. When Marat, one of the chief instigators of this new 'tygerish' democracy, was assassinated on 13 July 1793, *The Times* lost no opportunity in describing him as the visual symbol of political violence and carnage:

> He was a little man, of a cadaverous complexion, and a countenance exceedingly expressive of the bloody disposition of his mind. To a painter of massacre, he would have afforded a fine portrait for the chief murderer. His head would be inestimable for such a subject.
>
> His eyes resembled those of the *tyger cat*, and there was a kind of ferociousness in his looks that corresponded with the savage fierceness of that animal.
>
> The only artifice he used in favour of those lineaments of the beast, was that of wearing a round hat, so far pulled down before, as to hide a great part of his countenance.[8]

Significantly, it is not the portrait of Marat as 'chief murderer', but David's homage to an idealised leader that has survived; likewise, it is not some anti-Jacobin's 'Tyger', but Blake's 'Tyger! Tyger! burning bright'; not some lurid picture of a 'tyger cat's' ferocious eyes, or *sans-culotte*'s 'flaming with rage',[9] but Blake's

> In what distant deeps or skies
> Burnt the fire of thine eyes?

that has survived. The difference is, of course, that Blake's poem is highly complex and ambiguous, and carries no obvious internal pointer to the relation it might bear to its specific historical moment — except, possibly, the mention of 'stars' in the fifth stanza, which is generally accepted as a reference to oppressive ruling powers. Nurmi has rightly said: 'Blake is not, to be sure, writing merely a revolutionary lyric. His tiger is not another Orc, another portrayal of the spirit of revolt, but something much more inclusive, a symbol showing the creative power of energy, even of wrathful energy, wherever it appears.'[10] Yet might one not argue that the unprecedented historical conjuncture of Blake's memorable lyric was such that nothing *could* be 'more inclusive' to the revolutionary imagination? That the fiery crucible of the poem's creation was *both* this unique conjuncture *and* a profoundly imaginative, critical insight? If it is true that 'One thought fills immensity', it is also true that 'Eternity is in

love with the productions of time'. By penetrating the con-
junctural as a particular crisis of consciousness, we may get
closer to the poem's inner life — a life that is too often
dissipated in metaphysical and speculative criticism of the
poem.

Firstly, the burning Tyger and the forests of the night are
bound together in strong opposition; this is conveyed not
only in the polarity of 'burning' and 'forests', but more
emphatically in the rhyme 'bright' and 'night'. Blake's dual
symbol is an active, living contradiction, a unity of opposites
(in contrast to the complementary unity of 'Lamb' and
'mead' in *The Lamb*). This burning Tyger is in eternal
conflict with its environment (an environment that is both
spiritual and material). If the forests (the plural is significant,
as is the construction '*of* the night', suggesting hegemonic
possession) are, on *one* level, oppressive and crowded cities
such as Paris and London, then it follows that it is urban
oppression and degradation, not some unfathomable Creator
in the sky, that have bred tigers in the forests of oppression.
If the rage and vengeance of the masses in France have been
engendered by centuries of despotism, erupting most forcefully in the urban centres, then the speaker's question:

> What immortal hand or eye
> Could frame thy fearful symmetry?

is both the wrong question and a question that has already
been answered. (To deepen the paradox, one might add that
there is a third question here, and that it is this question that
drives the poem forward.)

We have hinted that the question: Who made the Tyger?
presumes a single, undivided Author of Creation, whereas
what we see is a dialectical process arising from the birth of
'contraries', a contradictory existence that precedes its
rationalisable essence: in the Beginning, darkness gave rise
to its opposite (light) which, intensifying into a burning
brightness in response to the darkness, has led in turn to a
further intensification of the darkness. There is in this (as
well as in the flame-like stripes of the tiger) a fearful symmetry
that is at once recognisable: the fearful symmetry of *conflict*.
(But this is to anticipate the third question.) If we ask who

made the Tyger, we must also ask who made the forests, but this question the speaker omits. All he is interested in is the awesome Tyger, not the horror of nocturnal forests. On another level, the speaker's question has already been answered, for the first two lines are a powerful symbol, imaginatively evoked by the speaker himself. Thus, unbeknown to the speaker, the 'immortal hand or eye' is *his own*. The potentiality for imaginative creation exists in all of us. The 'immortal hand or eye' thus belongs to the speaker of the poem, to Blake, who wrote and engraved it, and to *us* when we are able to participate actively in the creation of the Tyger (or rather of *The Tyger*).

But the word 'frame' means to 'contain' as well as to 'make'. The question *then* becomes: 'Who could contain such violent energy?' (There is, of course, a sense in which the making of the Tyger is not merely 'revolt' or perpetual opposition, but has its own organised, yet ferocious purpose, its own 'fearful' logic.) The speaker's false consciousness has repressed, in this question, the truth he unconsciously reveals in the poem: that the Tyger's violent energy is the inevitable response to oppression. Logically, therefore, such energy can only be 'contained' when oppression ceases.

Yet, if the Tyger is the Democratic Revolution, it must have its *immediate* makers as well as a causal condition for its appearance (the forests of oppression). At this point 'revolt' modulates into *revolution*, a symptom into a consciously willed event. Burning with the wrath engendered by an oppressive system, the Tyger's makers (who are themselves 'tygers of wrath' — *vide* Marat in *The Times*' lurid description) pose anew the whole question of the Creation. Wrath is a product of spiritual division. The creation of the Tyger has thus shattered, not only the idea of a merciful, loving God, but the very notion of a single, undivided Creator from whom all things flow.

The relation between the Tyger and its immediate maker(s) — a relation complicated by the questioning speaker, who is patently not an immediate maker or producer — is presented to us through a hammered chain of urgent questions.

Tyger! Tyger! burning bright
In the forests of the night,
What immortal hand or eye
Could frame thy fearful symmetry?

In what distant deeps or skies
Burnt the fire of thine eyes?
On what wings dare he aspire?
What the hand dare seize the fire?

And what shoulder, & what art,
Could twist the sinews of thy heart?
And when thy heart began to beat,
What dread hand? & what dread feet?

What the hammer? What the chain?
In what furnace was thy brain?
What the anvil? What dread grasp
Dare its deadly terrors clasp?

When the stars threw down their spears,
And water'd heaven with their tears,
Did he smile his work to see?
Did he who made the Lamb make thee?

Tyger! Tyger! burning bright
In the forests of the night,
What immortal hand or eye
Dare frame thy fearful symmetry?

The poem's energy lies in its onward movement, breaking down the speaker's attempts to bind, frame and fix, through his questions, what he nevertheless knows is unfixable. The speaker's false consciousness lies not only in his alienation from what he has, in one sense, imaginatively created, but in his questioning mentality, suggesting undertones of anxiety and near-hysteria.[11] By asking questions in this way, he cannot see that rational consciousness provides no basis for understanding how energetic production is carried on. He remains, like Euripides' Pentheus, outside the process, interrogating its mysteries from afar. Yet the paradox — and this is Blake's real achievement — resides in the fact that the speaker's questions *do* succeed in imaginatively re-creating the process of making the Tyger, whereas a univocal narrative would perhaps have only reproduced an unproblematic linear flow, lacking in tension. The reason for this success is not merely an effect of imagery, rhythm and repetition, though these play a major part; the deeper reason, as I have hinted, is an ideological tension, an enacted crisis of consciousness, where the need to 'frame' is continually undermined by the unframeable laws of life. This crisis is dramatised in *The Book of Urizen*, when Urizen, 'sicken'd to see/His eternal creations appear', realises

> That no flesh nor spirit could keep
> His iron laws one moment.[12]

The word 'frame' connotes both those who frame laws and those who frame pictures; in other words, 'framers' in the realms of politics and art. But the Tyger obeys no previously given legal, moral or artistic codes and laws. Thus the answer to the 'third' question is: 'no-one'. The final question,

> What immortal hand or eye
> *Dare* frame thy fearful symmetry?

is more a direct challenge: any 'framer' who dares to institutionalise the revolutionary process risks being devoured by its ferocious logic — as the years 1792-4 amply testified. On the other hand, if we read 'frame' in its first sense as 'make' or 'conceive', the challenge is one that dares us to defy and overthrow the ruling powers as the makers of the Tyger have done. Both meanings are possible.

I have said 'makers' and not 'Maker'. In stanza two the 'makers' are Daedalus, the Cretan artificer, and Prometheus, stealer of heaven's fire, who brought culture to mankind and suffered for his deed. (Blake's poem shares the wisdom of the old myths: both are aware that the important steps in human advancement can never be obedient and peaceful, but invariably bring danger, violence and suffering.) In stanzas three and four the making of the Tyger is imagined in terms of manual skill, of 'art' in the old sense of the word. In stanza three the art is that of the rope-maker, who twists hemp into yarn. In stanza four the Tyger is completed by the blacksmith, whose muscular energy and 'dread grasp' are alone capable of handling this unprecedented creature's 'deadly terrors'. The dread work bears the spirit of its makers: the twisting of sinews, the forging and hammering of links of iron, issue in a terrible act of creation. In the various deeds and skills, the hand has been predominant: an 'immortal hand' frames the beast, seizes the fire, twists the sinews, is a 'dread hand', holds the hammer, strikes the anvil, and with 'dread grasp' dares to 'clasp' the Tyger's 'deadly terrors'. Not until stanza five has the process reached a stage when the maker — as envisaged by the speaker — stands back to contemplate his handiwork. The cumulative image, then, is of a creative, rebellious, muscular and somewhat awe-inspiring Artisan, fragmentarily perceived as the mysterious hands, eyes, shoulders and feet of One Man, or as bits of different men; whether one or many, the speaker can only grasp portions of the whole. (Thus the poem itself has proved too big to grasp; different readers grasp different portions of it.) Why artisans should be so awe-inspiring is perhaps a political and historical rather than a metaphysical question. In the years 1792-3 the *sans-culottes* in France and the radical artisans and craftsmen in England were, after all, daring to assert their own power. Blake may have shared a temporary horror at 'the wanton cruelty of the Tyger', but never would he, as a London craftsman, show establishment scorn and fear of 'the tyrannicide mob', for such a 'mob' would have included thousands of craftsmen such as himself. The artisanal creator in *The Tyger*, like Los in Blake's prophetic books, is an emergent archetype of those later creative artisans and heroic working men found in Radical and Chartist poetry and, still later (though in debased form), in the working men heroes of socialist realism.[13] This aspect of Blake's mythology has, as far as I know, never been examined.

The fire referred to in stanza two has been interpreted by some as the consuming fire of divine wrath. It is both more and less than that. Translated into historical terms, this fire is the revolutionary anger of the 'tygerish multitude', the essential raw material from which the Tyger of Democracy has to be made. Those middle-class leaders who dared to seize this fire unleashed a movement whose outcome none

could have foreseen, least of all its instigators. Hence the
question:

> Did he smile his work to see?
> Did he who made the Lamb make thee?

sounds a note of painful irony (closer to hysteria in the first
draft),[14] while a plaintive reminder of Innocent self-sacrifice
and love is sharply, if vainly introduced. The perplexity and
awe of the first four stanzas have given way here to a more
knowing reflection, in which the pace of the poem slackens;
but this is 'reculer pour mieux sauter': the incipient theological speculation is brutally cut short by the return of the
opening lines.

As a spiritual interpretation of its times, Blake's lyric is
laden with ambiguity. It is, in fact, a poem with two voices:
conservative doubt (the dominant *persona*) and celebratory,
revolutionary energy, the latter critical and subversive of the
former. Further evidence for this subversive critique may be
drawn from the engraved design. Jean H. Hagstrum has
complained that 'the magnificent verbal "Tyger" is unworthily
illustrated by a simpering animal'.[15] The design is hardly
stunning, but there seems to be a purpose behind it. The
scene is not night, but daytime (one version has blue sky and
a pink wash round the Tyger), while the Tyger's face has
become almost human. Why? My feeling is that the poem's
illustrator, unlike the awe-stricken speaker, has come to
accept the humanised Tyger (and hence revolution) as beneficent, seen from one point of view, when from another it is
simply destructive and 'devouring'. (Tigers are not 'cruel',
they kill only to feed themselves and their young.) We must
not forget, however, that the Tyger of Democracy, whether
in its French or in its English form, did not usher in the kind
of society Blake wanted. In 1797 he writes of lions and tigers
as 'dishumanised men' — a return to the traditional symbolism
outlined at the start of this chapter. On the British side of
the Channel the hammers of industry and the untamed
energy of capitalist enterprise were creating a society that
was indeed based on 'competitive, predatious selfhood'. After
Thermidor the same destiny awaited France. Yet the con-

juncture of Blake's poem is one in which creative energy, however terrifying, is still 'burning bright'. That complex affirmation is the one that remains with us.

6

Producers and Devourers

Blake's brilliant intellectual satire and revolutionary tract, *The Marriage of Heaven and Hell* (*c.* 1790-93) has attracted much critical commentary, but only a few interpretations have attempted to locate the work in its social context. One is Sabri-Tabrizi's *The 'Heaven' and 'Hell' of William Blake* (1973). Sabri-Tabrizi makes a number of important points, most of which seem to have been ignored by subsequent critics. The first is that 'Heaven' and 'Hell' 'represent social classes and conditions'.[1] 'Heaven' is the world of 'the rich and propertied or higher clerical class', 'Hell' is that of the poor and working class. This view is based on the discovery, through close reading, that Emmanuel Swedenborg's descriptions of Hell in his *Heaven and Hell* draw heavily, if unconsciously, on his knowledge of the coal mines he owned.[2] Swedenborg's Heaven, on the other hand, is an idealised picture of the spacious world of the leisured upper classes. Since Blake's *Marriage* is in large part a satire on the writings and teachings of the founder of the New Church, Sabri-Tabrizi argues that Blake has seen through its theology as the worldly, predestinarian argument for an unjust social order. Whereas Swedenborg justified the condemnation of his 'infernal spirits' (or workers) to a life in the 'Hell' of his mines, Blake's sympathies are with those same spirits (whom he calls Devils, or producers), whose class-biased presentation he has exposed by his critical reading of the Swedish theologian's work. Swedenborg's New Church remains a defence of the old order; the 'revival' of Blake's 'Eternal Hell' is a positive response to the revolutionary upsurge of the oppressed.

Sabri-Tabrizi's thesis provides the starting-point for a

critique of the usual run of idealist interpretations, according
to which *The Marriage* is simply a celebration of creative
energy and the active imagination in opposition to reason
and 'materialistic' philosophy. In his commentary on the
facsimile edition of *The Marriage* (Oxford University Press
and the Trianon Press, 1975), for example, Geoffrey Keynes
offers us the fully-rounded philosophy of an individual
working in a socio-political vacuum: 'To him [i.e. Blake]
passive acceptance was evil, active opposition was good. This
is the key to the meaning of the paradoxes and inversions of
which the whole work consists.' But *who* and *what* was
Blake, and for whom was he writing? Can he be seen as some
timeless, classless genius, ladling out universal prescriptions
for everyone to follow? If, as Keynes says, Blake held to the
principle that 'active opposition is good', he must surely
have welcomed the 'active opposition' of the *ancien regime*
to the Third Estate, the 'active opposition' of the Tories to
the movement for political reform, and the 'active opposition'
of Pitt to the French Republic in 1793 in the form of war
preparations. Torn from its social and political context,
Blake's *Marriage* is emptied of its living, revolutionary significance. The 'active/passive' dualism makes little sense if
we do not see that Blake was on the side of active, Republican-
minded citizens, not 'active' oppressors.

Reason and Energy, on the other hand, do have a universal
significance. With these terms, Blake anticipated Freud's
analysis of the ego and the id and their interrelations.
Blake's polarities, like Freud's, draw attention to the *inner
dynamics* of the psyche, overturning the mechanistic,
undialectical model of the mind as comprising only the
conscious and the pre-conscious, or latent memory. 'Energy
is the only life, and is from the Body; and Reason is the
bound or outward circumference of Energy' conforms
closely to Freud's topography, outlined in *The Ego and the
Id* (1923), of the id as passion, bodily instinct and unconscious drives, and the ego as reason and common sense, or
'that part of the id which has been modified by the direct
influence of the external world'. When Blake writes that
those 'who restrain desire, do so because theirs is weak enough
to be restrained', and that 'the restrainer or reason usurps

its place & governs the unwilling', he is putting forward a theory of repression, which for Freud is the essential mechanism whereby the unconscious, including the pleasure principle, or 'desire' (what Freud calls the libido) is governed and tamed by the reality principle. Blake asserts: 'The tygers of wrath are wiser than the horses of instruction', and: 'the chains are the cunning of weak and tame minds which have power to resist energy'. Freud confirms: 'in its relation to the id [the ego] is like a man on horseback, who has to hold in check the superior strength of the horse; with this difference, that the rider tries to do so with his own strength while the ego uses borrowed forces'. (Note that the Freudian id as instructed horse has been tamed; Blake's tigers have not.) Freud's categories are shorn of overt political meanings, though not of political implications; Blake's, however, are political through and through. Those who govern society and restrain the masses are the ones who, with their fiendish self-righteousness, have most effectively governed and restrained desire in themselves. This does not mean that they are therefore more rational, or that those who do not restrain desire in themselves are correspondingly less rational. If Reason is the outward circumference of Energy, then it may, by enclosing Energy in a narrower, more confined space, succeed in reducing it to 'the shadow of desire', but in doing so it also diminishes itself. Such a law applies to political and social as much as it does to psychological repression. The typical ruling-class personality may be very good indeed at governing, taming and repressing, but in all other respects (such as in the sexual act, practical work that involves the body as well as the brain, artistic creation and all feats of the imagination) it may well be worse than useless.

'The Argument' of *The Marriage* opens cryptically:

> Rintrah roars & shakes his fires in the burdened air;
> Hungry clouds swag on the deep.

Sabri-Tabrizi argues at length that 'Rintrah' is Urizenic, a reactionary force; Keynes, on the other hand, says: '"Rintrah" may be understood as "Wrath", the wrath of the poet-prophet, Blake himself.' In the poem *Tiriel* (1789), Tiriel, the blind tyrant, calls upon 'Thunder & fire & pestilence' to punish his rebellious sons:

> He ceast. The heavy clouds confusd rolld round the
>   lofty towers
> Discharging their enormous voices. At the fathers curse
> The earth trembled fires belched from the yawning
>   clefts
> And when the shaking ceast a fog possesst the accursed
>   clime
> The cry was great in Tiriels palace . . .

In 1788 there had been an 'aristocratic revolt' against Louis XVI, sparking off popular riots. In 1789 the political rift widened: it was not a dispute between the wealthy privileged orders and the King, but (as Rudé puts it) a *war* between the Third Estate and the two other orders.[3] As the economic and political crisis deepened, the voice of the people began to be heard. Encouraged by outside popular pressure, the Third Estate (in effect, the revolutionary bourgeoisie) arrogated to itself the title of the National Assembly. This revolutionary act brought the masses further into play: on July 14 the Bastille itself fell.

Just as Tiriel's thunderous, fiery and pestilential curse on his 'sons' makes the 'earth' tremble and fires belch 'from the yawning clefts' (echoed in the volcanic fires of the title-page to *The Marriage*), so the ideological and political conflicts between the minority ruling orders in France awakened deeper fires from 'the yawning clefts' in society as a whole. Dismissing Sabri-Tabrizi's interpretation of the opening lines of 'The Argument' as an allusion to the sulphurous, smoky air of Swedenborg's infernal coal mines, we can grasp the dialectical movement that the opening of Blake's *Marriage* enacts:

> Rintrah roars & shakes his fires in the burdened air:
> Hungry clouds swag on the deep.

> As a new heaven is begun, and it is now thirty-three
>   years since its advent, the Eternal Hell revives.

(Thirty-three years is the time that has elapsed since the date of the New Jerusalem as announced by Swedenborg — that is, 1757, the year of Blake's birth — and it is also the age of Christ when he died.) Rintrah roars and hungry clouds 'swag

on the deep'; 'a new heaven is begun' and 'the Eternal Hell
revives'.

The dialectic here is that of the class struggle. The 'above'
and 'below' of 'burdened air' and 'deep', 'new heaven' and
'Eternal Hell' indicate relationships of dominance, but the
unity of opposites is not only political, the dominance of
rulers overruled: it is based on the *appropriation* by the
ruling few of what the governed many create. The line:
'Hungry clouds swag on the deep' refers to an imminent
thunderstorm at sea, in which 'hungry' clouds, filled with
too much moisture absorbed from 'the deep', burden the
air and are about to burst. (The dialect word 'swag', meaning
to hang swaying like a 'bundle' or 'fat belly' (*C.O.D.*) and
from which is derived the noun 'swag', meaning booty, and
possibly 'swagger', meaning to strut, has a radical force that
the word 'sway' would have lacked.) Later on, in 'The voice
of the Devil' (plates 5-6), Blake gives us the 'history' of the
usurpation of power by 'Reason' from two ideological viewpoints, that of the rulers and that of the ruled: 'It indeed
appear'd to Reason as if Desire was cast out, but the Devil's
account is, that the Messiah fell, & formed a heaven of what
he stole from the Abyss'. Here 'the Governor, or Reason'
(Milton's 'Messiah') is the 'fallen' usurper; the 'Heaven' of
the rationalists (whom Blake the libertarian sees as ideologues
for an existing social order) was formed out of the *stolen*
products that those deep in the social 'Abyss' created. (It is
worth remembering at this point that Blake's 'diabolical' wit
and mode of argument defy logical or systematic analysis.
There is much in *The Marriage* that is comic, while Blake's
satiric 'Devil' persona delights in a disruptive presentation,
throwing off brilliantly memorable verbal sparks with that
subversive intellectual audacity that is typical of a certain
kind of anarchic individualism, or what Blake would have
called 'Poetic Genius', possessed only by those who follow
their 'Energies'.)

Plates 16-17 are a highly suggestive amalgam of related
ideas presented in extremely condensed form. Taken with
the passages so far discussed, they further illuminate the
Blakean dialectic:

The Giants who formed this world into its sensual existence and now seem to live in it in chains, are in truth the
causes of its life & the sources of all activity; but the
chains are the cunning of weak and tame minds which have
power to resist energy, according to the proverb, the weak
in courage is strong in cunning.

Thus one portion of being is the Prolific, the other the
Devouring: to the devourer it seems as if the producer was
in his chains; but it is not so, he only takes portions of
existence and fancies that the whole.

But the Prolific would cease to be Prolific unless the
Devourer, as a sea, received the excess of his delights . . .

These two classes of men are always upon earth, & they
should be enemies: whoever tries to reconcile them seeks
to destroy existence.

Religion is an endeavour to reconcile the two.

The deeper implications of this passage will be examined
later. The argument is as follows: the 'Giants who formed
this world into its sensual existence' and are 'the sources of
all activity' seem to live in it in chains. These chains 'are the
cunning of weak and tame minds' who have power to resist
the energy of prolific creators. But the chains, we are told,
are in fact illusory. It is only through the myopic, false
consciousness of the devourer that the producer seems to
be in his chains. Far from chaining him, this dependence on
the devourer releases the producer's prolific energies. The
unequal relationship turns out to be absolutely necessary,
since for the producer to produce to excess, he must have
devourers who can receive 'the excess of his delights'. (We shall
return to this paradox later.) Finally, we are told that producers and devourers are 'two classes of men' irreconcilably
opposed, and that it is the utopian mission of 'religion' to
achieve a reconciliation between them (that is, by blurring
or smoothing the class contradictions).

The question arises: Who are Blake's 'Giants' and prolific
producers? Are they, as Sabri-Tabrizi argues, the poor and
the working class? Before attempting an immediate answer,
let us set against Blake's radical historiography a more
consistent exposition by a writer with whom he is now

often (and often too loosely) compared — Gerrard Winstanley, the writer who has a prime claim to the title of the first English socialist. Winstanley's *The True Levellers' Standard Advanced* (1649) opens:

> In the beginning of time, the great creator Reason made the earth to be a common treasury, to preserve beasts, birds, fishes and man, the Lord that was to govern this creation . . .
>
> But since human flesh (that king of beasts) began to delight himself in the objects of the creation, more than in the spirit of reason and righteousness . . . he fell into blindness of mind and weakness of heart, and runs abroad for a teacher and ruler. And so selfish imagination . . . did set up one man to teach and rule over another . . .
>
> And hereupon the earth . . . was hedged into enclosures by the teachers and rulers, and the others were made servants and slaves: and the earth, that is within this creation made a common storehouse for all, is bought and sold and kept in the hands of a few, whereby the great creator is mightily dishonoured, as if he were a respecter of persons, delighting in the comfortable livelihood of some, and rejoicing in the miserable poverty and straits of others. From the beginning it was not so.

Winstanley presents an unambiguous and lucid account of how mankind came to be divided into classes: 'teachers and rulers' on the one hand, and 'servants and slaves' on the other, arose on the basis of private property in the means of production, which for Winstanley is always the land and the means for tilling it. A spokesman for the dispossessed landless labourers of the seventeenth century, Winstanley anticipates the method of modern historical materialism. His 'contraries' compare interestingly with Blake's: it is not Reason that usurps Desire, but 'selfish imagination' that usurps 'the great creator Reason', while instead of 'the Devouring' and 'the Prolific' we have 'teachers and rulers', 'servants and slaves' — explicit class categories.

The originality of Blake's terms shows that he is trying to describe a new historical phenomenon — in particular, the Radical, plebeian intellectual and self-educated artist or craftsman who is now emerging as a potent force for change. (The revival of 'the Eternal Hell' of Radicalism, dead since 1784, occurred in 1790 when Horne Tooke got 1,779 votes at the Westminster election. Westminster, where Blake lived, 'was one of the few "open" constituencies in the south of England, with a householder franchise which admitted many master-artisans and some journeymen to the vote'.)[4] In other words, the 'producer' whom *The Marriage* chiefly celebrates is not the dispossessed labourer, peasant or 'chained' servant, but the prolifically creative, Radical artist-craftsman or artisan who, as an 'active citizen' (at least in Westminster), struggles to free himself, his fellow-producers, and hence society as a whole, from the economic, political, moral and aesthetic constraints of the old aristocratic, monarchical system.

The poetic resonance of Blake's categories ('Giants', 'Prolific', 'Devouring') — that is, their lack of historical concreteness and social specificity (which are the hallmark of other radical writers from Winstanley through Rousseau to Paine) — is indicative of an individualistic and subjective desire for liberation. In the passage we have quoted, the deep structure of Blake's argument, with its idea of a usurpation giving rise to dialectical oppositions, is the same as Winstanley's. Like many 'liberation' texts, it offers an explanation of the present order in terms of a historical usurpation leading to a system that is the 'contrary' or polar inversion of an original human condition. Man's original creative energies have been usurped by rational scepticism, the dominance of 'Hell' by that of 'Heaven', the paramountcy of 'Giants' by the rule of 'weak and tame minds'. The rhetorical method, vocabulary and style of Blake's illuminated text, however, with its sudden breaks and transitions, its mixing of modes (such as poetry, philosophy and satire), and its proliferation of linearly related, 'contrary' categories (Reason/Energy → Soul/Body → Restraint/Desire → Angel/Devil → Devourer/Producer, etc.) enact an urgent, *subjective* need to break with the old forms, not only through a radical philosophy or radical politics, but through a radical aesthetic. The visual impact and originality of *The Marriage*, with its plentitude of pictorial and typographical meanings, the power of its language (where new associations, based on semantic transformations, are deliberately exploited), are as important to Blake as any 'objective', prosaic meaning. This is not simply a question of aesthetics, for politics and aesthetics are always intertwined. The aesthetics and style of *The Marriage* cannot, then, be excluded in the attempt to define its class viewpoint and the social conditions of its appearance: its readers must produce its meanings.

Our task has been made easier in one way by the self-consciousness of the text. The first 'Memorable Fancy', relating in travelogue style how the narrator has collected some 'Proverbs of Hell', is an ironic parody of Swedenborg's 'Memorable Relations'. This has led readers and critics into not taking the narrator seriously, that is, literally — the 'Blakean' Hell being thought of only metaphorically and not as a real place. In fact, Blake's Hell does have, and indeed *must* have, a real social location. (This is to read *The Marriage*, as Blake's Devil reads the Bible, in its 'infernal or diabolical sense'. There are too many 'Angelic' readers of Blake.) The text reads as follows:

> As I was walking among the fires of hell, delighted with the enjoyments of Genius, which to Angels look like Torment and insanity, I collected some of their Proverbs; thinking that as the sayings used in a nation mark its character, so the Proverbs of Hell show the nature of Infernal wisdom better than any description of buildings or garments.

The narrator (a mock-genteel persona) has discovered in this 'Infernal wisdom' a rich subculture (or what might be termed a 'counter-culture' or 'radical culture'). He is conveying to us some of the oral literature ('sayings') of a nation within a nation. In this sense, we are being asked to attribute the 'Proverbs of Hell' not to the genius of a single individual, but to the 'Infernal wisdom' of the creative majority. (It is interesting to note, incidentally, that Blake did not sign *The Marriage* with his usual 'The Author & Printer W Blake'.) The proverbs are meant to be taken as the varied living utterances of 'Devils' whose physical (and in this must be included sexual) energies (Energy being 'the only life' and 'from the

Body') are the inexhaustible wellsprings of infernal culture, a culture that is both Jacobin and antinomian. As Lindsay points out, 'English Jacobins called the Devil the first Jacobin' (1978, 60).

Infernal culture, expressing the energy of active producers, is, however, essentially individualistic, despite the solidarity the real, historical 'Devils' might have displayed as a class, their sense of community, or the interdependent nature of the productive process. Blake lived, in fact, in an extremely competitive environment. On 28 May 1804 he told Hayley: 'in London every calumny and falsehood utter'd against another of the same trade is thought fair play. Engravers, Painters, Statuaries, Printers, Poets, we are not in a field of battle, but a City of Assassinations'. The proverb: 'The most sublime act is to set another before you' suggests that for a Devil, taking a back seat requires some effort (though a Devil in the fifth 'Memorable Fancy' says that the worship of God is 'Honouring his gifts in other men, each according to his genius, and loving the greatest men best'). 'No bird soars too high, if he soars with his own wings' assumes that each man's gifts are *his own*, not God's or society's; 'The apple tree never asks the beech how he shall grow; nor the lion, the horse, how he shall take his prey' combines both the idea of the sovereign intellect's independence from 'the horses of instruction' and the principle that each man must follow his individual genius. Both A. L. Morton and Christopher Hill have emphasised Blake's connection with the 'left-wing' radicals of the seventeenth century. However, in *The Marriage* he is arguably closer to the anarchic individualism of the Ranters (whose support derived largely from freed migratory craftsmen, men who were 'unattached and prepared to break with tradition', according to Morton)[5] than he is to the Diggers' peasant collectivism, whose spirit still lives in the writings of Gerrard Winstanley, a man of profound socialist instincts.

The third 'Memorable Fancy' informs us that the culture of 'Hell' is not only oral, but includes technical means for spreading its 'Infernal wisdom' (something Pitt and the Tories, with their spies and censors, were eager to put an end to). The visit to a 'Printing house in hell' takes us through the process of the transmission of knowledge 'from generation to generation'. The printing house is, on one level, Blake's own workshop. But to argue (with one critic) that it is Blake's own 'cavernous skull that is being cleared of rubbish . . . [and] made infinite by imaginative labor'; that the 'books which result from this labor come from a printing house in a cave, but they also come out of a *head*',[6] while passing over the reference to the work of the type-founder (in the *melting* of '*metals* into living fluids' which are then *cast* 'into the expanse'), obscures the premise that creative labour, or Energy, 'is from the Body', and that such work cannot occur merely in the 'cave' of one's own skull, but is practical and social.

Behind Blake's account of how books are made, with its allegorical personifications (reminiscent of alchemical texts), lies an urban, radical culture, a world of political theorists, journalists and pamphleteers, also engaged in 'clearing away the rubbish' of dead ideas; a milieu of 'progressive' illustrators, decorative artists, poets, painters, engravers, type-founders, compositors, copper-plate printers, book-binders, book-sellers, antiquarians and librarians. Blake's own 'infernal method' of printing was a stereotype process he himself (soaring with 'his own wings') developed, though others had hit on the idea independently. (In this period, technical innovation and experiment were invariably carried out by practical men: apart from Watt's modifications to the steam engine, which were the result of formal scientific experiment, and industrial processes such as bleaching and dyeing, which were the result of advances in chemistry, none of the major inventions of the industrial revolution were the results of advances in theoretical science.) Blake deserves the appellation of Renaissance Artist, however, since he combined in his work the trades of copper-plate printer, book-binder, book-seller, print-seller, painter, engraver and philosopher, together with the unclassifiable pursuits of prophet and poet, though perhaps 'Poetic Genius', being the whole man, embraces all these activities.

Blake's 'Prolific' or 'Devils', then, are not producers of the means of subsistence, though most are practical men who use their hands; they are, in the main, producers of *art* and of *ideas*, men of 'Poetic Genius' who have allied themselves with the energy and the cause of the working masses. They are, in sum, the new petty-bourgeois and lower-class democratic intelligentsia. The printer and the book-seller (the latter often combining the functions of proprietor and publisher), were key figures in this radical milieu. Prolific book-sellers and publishers in Paternoster Road and St Paul's Church-yard — men such as Joseph Johnson, who published Wordsworth and Mary Wollstonecraft as well as Paine's *Rights of Man* — were of central importance to the whole cause of English Radicalism. 'It is to such men', wrote the author of *The Young Tradesman* in 1824, '[that] our men of genius take their productions for sale: and the success of works of genius very frequently depends upon their spirit, probity, and patronage . . . it is by the diffusion of knowledge by books that all species of tyranny and oppression can be most effectively resisted' (a view, of course, that ignores the role of newspapers, and also presumes a literate population). Blake's allegorical description of 'the method in which knowledge is transmitted from generation to generation' could be seen as supporting that view; however, after 1790 (when Johnson had printed, but did not publish, Blake's *French Revolution*) Blake was always his own printer and book-seller — not out of some Crusoe-like, do-it-yourself crankiness, but for important artistic and ideological reasons.

The role of the printer (whether copper-plate or using type) in artisan London (in which 'the chief trades', according to Sir John Clapham, were, apart from the building trades, the 'shoemaker, tailor, cabinet-maker, printer, clock-maker, jeweller, [and] baker')[7] was significant in various ways. W. H. Reid, truly one of Blake's Tory 'Angels', tells us that Swedenborgianism as an 'infidel' movement originated 'in a printer's job' in the parish of Clerkenwell. Its next appearance was 'in an alley in Little Eastcheap, partly in the modern and fashionable form of a debating society: but, instead of preachers collecting the people, these people were so hard run to collect preachers, that for a considerable time the office was generally confined to the printer alluded to, and one of his relatives'.[8] (*The Magazine of Heaven and Hell* was conventionally printed; Blake printed and coloured his copies of *The Marriage of Heaven and Hell* in a singularly unconventional 'printer's job'.)

We know that Blake attended an early London meeting of the Swedenborgian New Church in 1789, and that within a year he was satirising Swedenborg in *The Marriage of Heaven and Hell*. Two other men, one a carpenter called John Wright, the other a copper-plate printer called William Bryan, also recorded their disillusionment with the New Church. Wright tells us of his visit to the 'Jerusalem Church' in 1788, in Great Eastcheap:

> The Sunday following, so called, I went to the place, where I saw nothing but old *forms* of worship established by *man's will*, and not according to the will of GOD, although called by that blessed name of *New Jerusalem*, in which these old forms have neither part nor lot. I saw no one there, except the preacher, whom I knew; he had been a preacher among *John Wesley's* people.[9]

This compares closely with Blake's rejection of Swedenborg's 'old forms' in *The Marriage*: 'And lo! Swedenborg is the Angel sitting at the tomb: his writings are the linen clothes folded up'. In October 1788 Wright and Bryan felt the call for a radical change in their lives. As Wright puts it: 'a burning wind is spreading over the earth, and wouldest thou leave to its ravages those whom thou canst save?'[10] In 1789 the Holy Spirit told both men to visit 'a Society at *Avignon* who were favoured with divine communications'. Bryan records the event:

> The 23rd of the month called January, 1789, in the morning, having made all things ready for my work, which was then copper-plate printing, I found a stop in my mind to go on with it. Waiting a little, I took some paper to wet for another plate, but found the same stop: then I perceived that it was of the Lord. Retiring into my little room, I sat down, endeavouring to get my mind into perfect stillness, when a voice spoke in me, commanding me to prepare for my journey, that night.[11]

The humble copper-plate printer, who has to make prints from plates others have engraved, hears the voice of the Lord telling him to leave his work and embark on a journey. William Blake, an engraver who felt the same need for radical change, continued the ideological struggle (which, particularly in England, so often took a sectarian form) through his art, 'printing', as he says in *The Marriage*, 'in the infernal method, by corrosives, which in Hell are salutary and medicinal' — that is, exposing reactionary dogma with corrosive, burning acid in his new etching process. Instead of God's voice, it is 'The Voice of the Devil' that *he* hears. Blake's antinomian and immanentist rejection of a Lord who is above or without (he has learned from Swedenborg that the divine and the human are one, and hence that 'All deities reside in the human breast') was the first step in overcoming that mental self-division of those who saw their lives, minds and actions governed by 'the Lord', 'Angels', 'the Holy Spirit' and so forth.

Blake's increasing self-sufficiency as an artist-craftsman is mirrored in his philosophical independence and a conviction that the rule of kings and priests is ending, a conviction that has, of course, to be seen as part of the wider revolutionary movement. As Reid puts it, the 1790s were a new era in England 'because it delineates the first period in which the doctrines of Infidelity have been extensively circulated among the lower orders.'[12] Although Reid includes Swedenborg among the 'Infidels', Blake puts him with the religious conformists: 'He conversed with Angels who are all religious, & conversed not with Devils who all hate religion, for he was incapable thro' his conceited notions'. Blake corroborates Reid in one respect, however, for his Devils, like Reid's 'infidel' lower orders, 'all hate religion'.

William Sharp, a friend of Blake and a follower of the millenarian Richard Brothers and later of Joanna Southcott, was an engraver whose struggle for independence (not wholly achieved in terms of an original art, however) closely parallels that of Blake, and tells us something about the conflict between 'producers' and 'devourers' within the print trade itself. According to W. S. Baker, Sharp 'became dissatisfied with the remuneration he received from the print dealers'.[13] (Normally the engraver merely copied an artist's design, which was then printed on a press belonging to the copper-plate printer, after which the prints were sold to the print-dealer or print-shop owner.) Just as Blake was able to buy a printing press on the death of his father in 1784, so Sharp,

> becoming possessed of some property, by the decease of a brother, began to publish his own works. Soon afterwards, about the year 1787, that date appearing on his print of 'Zenobia', he moved to a larger house in Charles St., near the Middlesex hospital.[14]

Sharp, like Blake, had at least broken free of the chains of the print-dealers, who exerted a financial and aesthetic hold over artists and engravers. Catering for the tastes and fashions of middle-class print-buyers (part of the great consuming — that is, 'devouring' — public), the dealers, like the orthodox patrons and connoisseurs, took aesthetic 'portions of existence' and fancied those the whole. Sharp, like Blake, showed — once a degree of independence as a creative 'producer' had been achieved — that the interests of the producers were quite different from those of the devourers. Instead of picturesque scenes, copies of paintings by Reynolds, West and the like, he could engrave portraits of the people's heroes, such as Richard Brothers, Tom Paine and Horne Tooke, and publish prints from his own drawings. Such a career brought with it, of course, the threat of punishment in a very real, earthly 'dungeon'. Like Blake later, Sharp was arrested, being brought before members of the privy council in 1794-5 on suspicion of having 'revolutionary principles'.

Unless the artist-craftsman could free himself from the dictates of Tory patrons and the tastes of the buyers (however lucrative that subservience might prove), there could be no cleansed perception, no overflowing fountain of 'infernal' culture. Yet at this point the Romantic paradox appears: to whom could the revolutionary artist convey his 'infinite' perceptions if not to a 'devouring' public? With astonishing far-sightedness, anticipating Marx, Blake is able to perceive the dilemma in terms of an *irreconcilable* enmity between 'two classes of men'. Historically, this enmity can be explained by the fact that the producer became divorced from an abstract, impersonal and unknown public by the mechanism of the market. The Blakean free artist, the man *inhumanity of capitalism*

who had freed himself from the oppressor's law and from spiritual repression, and who exercised his Poetic Genius without restraint, had become locked in a 'marriage' of enmity with those passive 'devourers' on whom, as an artist, he had to depend for a living. The contradiction was insoluble: 'These two classes of men are always upon earth.' Whereas Keats, Shelley and Wordsworth showed a certain élitist disdain as poets for 'the foolish crowd' and the 'unthinking' Public, Blake's class position enabled him to see this relationship dialectically. (Yet the Romantic disdain for his readers is there when his 'Devil' says: 'I have also The Bible of Hell, which the world shall have whether they will or no.')

Blake articulates in *The Marriage* and 'A Song of Liberty' the same kind of revolutionary spirit that inspired the actions of the citizens of Paris in 1789. Writing at around the same time as Blake, Paine recalled how the masses armed themselves prior to the assault on the Bastille:

> . . . the night was spent in providing themselves with every sort of weapon they could make or procure: Guns, swords, blacksmiths' hammers, carpenters' axes, iron crows, pikes, halberts, pitchforks, spits, clubs, &c. &c. The incredible numbers in which they assembled the next morning, and the still more incredible resolution they exhibited, embarrassed and astonished their enemies. Little did the new ministry expect such a salute. Accustomed to slavery themselves, they had no idea that Liberty was capable of such inspiration, or that a body of unarmed citizens would dare to face the military force of thirty thousand men.[15]

Just as the creatively inspired, revolutionary artisans of Paris had used blacksmiths' hammers, carpenters' axes and iron crows as weapons, so Blake turned his own art into a weapon. It came to possess the same qualities of imaginative daring, skill, energy, resolution, and capacity for seizing the moment that were shown by the revolutionaries in France. All it lacked (and this was Blake's predicament as an artist) was the mass readership that Paine was able to reach. Yet, imaginatively inspired as the citizens of Paris were inspired, Blake was even able to see his own alienation from the art-buying and poetry-reading public as a dialectical contradiction, part of a wider class struggle.

Blake's *Marriage* reflects a new awareness that social existence is riven by 'yawning clefts', and hence into two opposed ways of seeing, two ideological camps. To the revolutionary artist, for whom sharply distinct outlines are an aesthetic imperative, whoever tries to reconcile these viewpoints 'seeks to destroy existence'. It is with this *ideological* split that Blake's *Marriage* is chiefly concerned. Just as a 'fool sees not the same tree that a wise man sees', so devouring Angels and prolific Devils perceive the world in wholly different ways. Blake's Angel sees the French Revolution as a terrifying monster rising from the depths of society, a Leviathan whose 'mouth & red gills' hang 'just above the raging foam, tinging the black deep with beams of blood'. (The 'Hungry clouds' that 'swag on the deep' in the opening free-verse 'Argument' have now burst: 'the deep', from which those devouring clouds absorbed their moisture, and from which the upper-class Anglican clergy stole in order to form their 'Heaven', has now turned into a 'raging foam'.) The Angel hears and sees in the Revolution 'a terrible noise' and a huge monster; but Blake finds himself 'sitting on a pleasant bank beside a river by moonlight, hearing a harper, who sung to the harp'. What to conservative Angels is a cacophony of noise (the noise of the 'rabble') is to him pleasant music. Blake's preoccupation with ideology and modes of perception, reflecting his class position, also informs his account of the origin of priesthood:

> The ancient Poets animated all sensible objects with Gods or Geniuses, calling them by the names and adorning them with the properties of woods, rivers, mountains, lakes, cities, nations, and whatever their enlarged & numerous senses could perceive . . .
>
> Till a system was formed, which some took advantage of, & enslav'd the vulgar by attempting to realise or abstract the mental deities from their objects: thus began Priesthood:
>
> Choosing forms of worship from poetic tales.
>
> And at length they pronounc'd that the Gods had order'd such things.

Thus men forgot that All deities reside in the human breast.

The original-state-*versus*-usurpation idea is in line with previous 'radical' explanations of the origin of priesthood. But for writers such as Winstanley, Diderot and Rousseau, those priests who 'enslav'd the vulgar' by using religion to defend an unjust social order were — in the words of the English radicals of the seventeenth century — pre-eminently '*tithing* priests', whose reliance on rent, tithes, and feudal dues made them obvious targets for class hatred. Blake's explanation: 'thus began Priesthood', is, of course, an idealist one: ideology (the abstraction of 'mental deities from their objects') precedes class formation ('Priesthood'). Nevertheless, Blake anticipates Marx by showing how a 'fantastical realm' of institutionalised ideas is directly linked to the rise of an unproductive class.

The antinomy of producer and devourer in *The Marriage* contains an important ambiguity, which has so far only been touched upon. That is, it can be read either as producer/consumer or as producer/*exploiter*. Both meanings are present. The ambiguity exists for us, where it did not exist for Blake, because the historical distinction between wage worker and capitalist — particularly in London, that vast hive of small workshops — had not yet sufficiently hardened. In Blake's later work, the ambiguity is partly resolved.

The ideological moment of *The Marriage* can also be felt in Blake's doctrine of 'contraries' and in his notion of 'excess'. Blake's dialectic, which owes more to the spiritual 'contraries' of Jacob Boehme than it does to the alchemical (and hence, more 'materialist') contraries of Paracelsus, is both radical and conservative. Underlying the whole satiric purpose of *The Marriage* is the semantic transformation of terms such as 'good' and 'evil', 'Heaven' and 'Hell'. But does the transformation (the 'Evil' of Energy becoming 'Eternal Delight') leave us with a new set of eternally fixed oppositions, such that idealist readings of *The Marriage* appear as the most 'natural' ones to take? If the 'contraries' of Heaven and Hell, Reason and Energy, are eternally 'married', locked together for all time, then does this not also apply to those 'social classes and conditions' which, as Sabri-Tabrizi has argued, they represent? This surely turns Blake into a Swedenborgian. 'A Song of Liberty' clearly calls for the *ending* of tyranny, Empire, and the rule of 'the lion & wolf'. Yet the ambiguity (Is *class* society, though perceived from the 'abyss' up and not from the top down, nevertheless reaffirmed, when the class struggle is seen as eternal?) remains. Given its historical and political context, *The Marriage* could not have gone as far in its critique as Winstanley did almost 150 years before.[16]

Finally, the notion of 'excess', that well-known agent of social disorder, needs to be set in its ideological context. At one level, 'excess' is going 'beyond' or transcending one-self; a kind of Dionysiac ecstacy or surplus energy that cannot be contained or rationalised, a feeling of being at one with prolific creation. This has nothing in common with hedonism or libertinism, the moralist's idea of excess as intemperance or over-indulgence. The proverb: 'The road of excess leads to the palace of wisdom' contains at one level the Dionysian belief that another, higher order of 'wisdom', of spiritual knowledge and perception, can be attained through libidinal 'excess' or ecstatic self-abandon. Excess is, of course, fundamental to the spirit of Romanticism. Yet instead of viewing it as part of the universal human need for transcendental experiences (which can only be realised outside the work process), the principle of excess, looked at from a more 'earthly' angle, might be seen to have an *immanent*, work-oriented side to it.

In *The Marriage*, Blake says: 'the Prolific would cease to be the Prolific unless the Devourer, as a sea, received the excess of his delights' (where 'as a sea' has an ironic twist). A. S. Vasquez points out that under the new, 'freed' conditions of artistic production, the Romantic artist 'had to produce a number of works that exceeded, in quantity and economic value, what he needed in order to survive'.[17] Blake's notion of creative excess, either as a productive surplus ('the excess of his delights'), or as a prolific, bountiful giving, in the sense in which God and nature are prolific and bountiful (hence: 'The lust of the goat is the bounty of God') can be connected with an important shift in eighteenth-century economic thought, as the dominance of mercantile gave way to industrial capital.

Mercantilist theories had derived the source of profit (or excess wealth) from the circulation sphere, that is, exchange of commodities (buying cheap and selling dear). Profit (always a definite, measurable quantity of money) owed its existence to the laws of the market and to the business skills of the merchant. The Physiocrats, on the other hand, saw that mercantile profit could not involve the creation of *new* wealth, since it was simply a redistribution of wealth already created, and therefore, as Blake might have put it, 'unable to do other than repeat the same dull round over again'. The source of society's wealth, and hence of the social surplus, thus lies in the sphere, not of *exchange*, but of *production*. It is through the agricultural producers, those who tap the inexhaustible bounties of nature, that a marketable surplus is created, and *this* surplus is not merely monetary profit; it is the living and essential foundation upon which the whole of civilised life — in other words, the aristocracy, the clergy, commerce, the professions, and the whole of urban life — depends.

In Physiocratic theory (so-called because of the importance it attached to nature, *phusis* in Greek), the farmer is only able to create a surplus (i.e. what is surplus to his needs) through the bounty of nature. It is not labour but nature itself that is prolific. Man only intervenes; he taps the vital source. He becomes prolific by virtue of his closeness to nature. The natural process of germination, growth, flowering and bearing fruit, made possible by the combined action of nutrients in the soil, heat from the sun and moisture from the rain, is the basis of life and hence of all wealth; it is the overflowing fountain in the human economy. The Rousseauesque 'natural man', simple, free and spontaneous; the Romantic cult of nature; the quasi-mystical notion of prolific nature working through man (as opposed to man working on nature); even Wordworth's characterisation of poetry as 'the spontaneous overflow of powerful feelings' (where the 'feelings' are 'nature's') — all these can be connected with the Physiocrats' discovery that prolific nature and the farmer are the source of the social surplus.

Physiocratic theory emerged at a time when the bourgeoisie, not yet a class acting for itself, was incapable of carrying through a major political change, yet the theory contained a systematic and far-reaching critique of existing society, which could now be seen to be divided into productive and unproductive classes. Those who were productive produced in excess of their requirements. The unproductive classes merely consumed, distributed or changed the form of the surplus produced by the productive classes. For the representatives of the bourgeoisie and petty-bourgeoisie, however, such a theory was in need of drastic modification, since it made all the non-agricultural classes dependent and even parasitic upon the bounties of nature, made serviceable by the investment and labour of the farmer. Adam Smith extended the Physiocrats' categories to every sphere in which *productive capital* was employed, these spheres being agriculture, trade and manufacture. (Here it is *capital*, not simply labour itself, that is productive.) The concept of productive labour was held to mean any labour that was *put to work by capital* (since capital involves an increased return on investment).

The position of the Physiocrats and followers of Rousseau might be summed up in the maxim: 'Where nature is not, man is barren'. Blake's 'proverb of Hell' is a reversal of this: 'Where *man* is not, *nature* is barren'. In a craft and artisan environment, the emphasis shifts from the fertility of nature to human productivity, from prolific nature to prolific work. The craftsman does not rely on the bounties of nature in order to be prolific or productive, but on his own *human* energies. (The Physiocrats would retort: Then how does he eat? To which Adam Smith would reply that any commodity, even a book, has an economic value.)

In Blake's mythological epics, the most 'progressive' figures are Los, a blacksmith-prophet, and his female 'Emanation', Enitharmon, who weaves at her loom. In *Milton* it is Los who must first 'forge the instruments/Of Harvest' (the plough and harrow) for Palamabron the ploughman — a nice reversal of the Physiocratic order. It is not the ploughman — who is also Blake the engraver, ploughing 'furrows' on a copper plate with his graving tool — who is the guiding creative force in Blake's scheme of things, but Los, struggling to create 'Definite Form' with 'Hammer & Tongs' as he labours 'at his resolute Anvil'. Los, not Palamabron, is the archetype of the creative producer. (There is an interesting parallel here with the Nigerian dramatist, novelist and poet Wole Soyinka. Ogun, the Yoruba god of iron and of all those who work with iron, is the poet's guiding inspiration and source of creative energy. See, for example, the long poem *Idanre*, where Ogun is celebrated as divine creator and destroyer.)

In Blake's poetic myth Adam Smith is rebutted along with the Physiocrats, since labour that is unwilling or is carried out in the service of some master can never be creative, just as any artistic work that is the slave of 'fashionable Fools' or a particular, ready-made market will be on the side of that 'Class of Men whose whole delight is in Destroying'. Nor is art quantifiable. It is (to use Marx's terms) a use-value, not an exchange value. Thus what Blake means by being 'prolific' is not producing a merely *quantitative* excess, but striving for a better world through genuine works of art, combinations of words, sounds and images that awaken a new, enlarged perception of reality, and whose creation springs from a deep physical and emotional need, which is also a *social* need.

Blake's class affinities and his own work process — preparing the copper plate, seeing his reflection as a 'mighty Devil' in its mirror-like surface (Erdman, 1975), applying the 'corrosive fires' of acid or ploughing its surface with his burin, making the imprint by turning the wheel of his press, mixing his colours — all this called up a poetic reverie that, while it actively participated in and urged on the work, also evoked other kinds of work, and at the same time inspired certain archetypal images and symbols. As Gaston Bachelard has shown, this kind of reverie or day-dreaming has a phenomenological aspect, in that, while he is freely associating, the 'dreamer' is physically working with actual material substances. By getting to know their inner life, their secret virtues and mysterious habits (such as the extent of metallic resistance to the pressure of the cutting edge, the quantity of water and pigment needed to get the right viscosity, etc.) the 'mystical' artist-craftsman sees them obeying his will, which to him is spiritual and not governed by mechanical laws. His spiritual will enters these substances, and they in turn enter him. Thus a dialectic unfolds. His artistic will is akin to that of a creator-god, yet a god who is *in* his creation: the artist engages, at an imaginative level, in the work of cosmic creation and the cosmic process itself, in which he is both maker and made. In his cosmic mythology, he comes to see that the creation — which includes himself — is only kept going by his own kind of imaginative labour. Without it, the sun would not rise, or give off spear-like rays like those from a blacksmith's hammer when it sets.[18] Thus the Paracelsan, hermetic view that man's reason alone cannot penetrate nature's mysteries. Their unveiling must bring into play deeper levels of the psyche. In the alchemical work of imaginative creation, 'matter' is infused with 'spirit', including that of the divine artist himself. His energetic will fashions, animates and gives inner meaning to his creation, which appears infinite to all those who give themselves, as Los gives himself, through inspired, imaginative labour. This process — especially when fire and considerable energy are required — is one of conflict and struggle, as Bachelard says:

> If, passively, as an idle visitor, you find yourself in the stifling atmosphere surrounding a china kiln, then the *anguish of heat* [cf. Blake's 'furnaces of affliction'] takes hold of you. You retreat. You do not want to look any longer. You are afraid of the sparks. You think it is hell.
> Nevertheless, move closer. Take on in your imagination the work of the artisan. Imagine yourself putting the wood into the oven: cram the oven with shovels-full of coal, challenge the oven to a duel of energy. In short, be ardent and the ardor of the hearth will shoot its arrows in vain against your chest; you will be invigorated by the struggle. The fire can only return your blows. The psychology of *opposition* invigorates the worker . . .
> Take away dreams and you stultify the worker. Leave out the oneiric force of work and you diminish, you annihilate the artisan. Each labor has its oneirism, each material worked on contributes its inner reveries . . . The

oneirism of work is the very condition of the worker's mental integrity.[19]

Under conditions of capitalist production, with its increasing division of labour, where labour is *abstract* labour, 'creative labour' becomes less and less possible. (One of the characteristically 'Urizenic' features of bourgeois economic science is the way it turns human needs into dehumanising constraints, the whole man's creative excess into calculable 'portions' called profit margins.) On the other hand, the 'craft' viewpoint tends to belittle the working class (not fully born as an organised movement in Blake's time) as an agent of its own liberation; dehumanised by the new work discipline, with its reduction of factory worker into 'hands', the exploited labourers have to rely on the visions of the inspired few. Yet Blake's viewpoint as a direct producer allowed him to see with 'prophetic' insight that labour (one of the most frequently used words in his longer poems), though enslaving under conditions of enforced drudgery, is at the same time the key to man's liberation — *labour*, not merely 'imagination', and certainly not *nature*.

In 1794 Blake engraved *The Book of Urizen*. The war with France, which had begun the previous year, had brought a stiffening of political reaction, the defection of erstwhile 'Reformers' among the Whigs, and increasing polarisation. In response to the rapid growth of English Jacobinism, English *anti*-Jacobinism reared its head. Already, in November 1792, an 'Association for Preserving Liberty and Property against Republicans and Levellers' had been formed. The London Corresponding Society, with its bold policy of universal suffrage and annual parliaments, took the place of the middle-class Society for Constitutional Information as the spearhead of reform. A predominantly artisan organisation, the LCS had over 5,000 active members by early 1794, and could organise mass demonstrations the like of which would not be seen again until the great Chartist demonstrations of the 1840s. In August 1793 Muir and Palmer, two leaders of the Scottish 'Friends of the People', were transported for long terms by a reactionary Scottish judiciary. Savage sentences were also passed by English courts. On 14 April

1794, a resolution was passed at a large LCS meeting on Chalk Farm Green, which declared that the tyrannical laws and actions of the courts in Scotland and England 'ought to be considered as dissolving entirely the social compact between the English nation and their governors'. The wealthy landowners, monopolists and elected representatives of 'rotten boroughs' who made up the government responded vigorously. Pitt got from the Commons a Committee of Secresy, set up to monitor and pursue all 'traitors'. Convinced that a 'traitorous conspiracy' was afoot, he called for the suspension of Habeas Corpus, making the most of lurid reports from the Committee that an armed Jacobin uprising was being planned. While the Thermidorian reaction took place in France, government agents raided LCS leaders' houses, 'seditious' material was seized, and Pitt's spy system was set in motion. In October 1794 the famous London Treason Trials began.

Blake's *Book of Urizen*, which is richly illuminated, marks the first appearance of Blake's famous Urizen myth. Parodying the biblical Creation and *Paradise Lost*, it is a bitter, ironic account of the Creation in the light of a usurpation by 'the Governor or Reason', and suggests a response both to the bourgeois dictatorship in France and to the counter-revolutionary nature of Pitt's Tory government. The Creation itself is the Fall, the restriction of Energy by circumscribing Reason. The prime mover of the Committee of Secresy was himself an epitome of Urizenic calculation, a believer in statistics, privacy (few could unlock the heart of this passionless bachelor), and the rule of Law, whose desire to 'crush and destroy' the new revolutionary principles rapidly became an obsession; this, it seems, was rich mythopoeic material for Blake.

> Lo, a shadow of horror is risen
> In Eternity! Unknown, unprolific!
> Self-closed, all-repelling: what Demon
> Hath form'd this abominable void,
> This soul-shudd'ring vacuum? — Some said
> 'It is Urizen', but unknown, abstracted,
> Brooding secret, the dark power hid.

Times on times he divided & measur'd
Space by space in his ninefold darkness
Unseen, unknown! changes appeard
In his desolate mountains rifted furious
By the black winds of perturbation.

For he strove in battles dire,
In unseen conflictions with shapes
Bred from his forsaken wilderness
Of beast, bird, fish, serpent & element,
Combustion, blast, vapour and cloud.

Dark, revolving in silent activity:
Unseen in tormenting passions;
An activity unknown and horrible;
A self-contemplating shadow,
In enormous labours occupied.

Urizen's 'enormous labours' are not *creative* at all, but are the unprolific, unproductive mental activity of a detached intellect, the horror of a purely *mental* consciousness as the mind revolves upon itself. Urizen also represents a catastrophic separation of the *super-ego* from the rest of the psyche, a psychic split occasioned by the social separation of the ruling 'thinkers' (Reason) from the ruled 'doers' (Energy), of thought from action, intellectual labour from concrete practice. In 1794 the political polarisation that had occurred made this psychic split all the more glaring in the eyes of a Jacobin craftsman, whose own intellectual abstractions were by no means always held in check. (Thus Blake is also battling with the Urizenic tendencies in himself.) The third stanza suggests, given the political context, that reaction's lurid pictures of 'traitorous conspiracies' are sick mental fantasies (later we find Urizen 'In dark secresy hiding in Surgeing/Sulphureous fluid his phantasies'), while the associative clustering of rhythmically weighted adjectives and participles, and the absence of any definite, concrete images, indicates the ponderous, vague, detached world of abstracted mental consciousness.

Urizen emerges from his 'holy', undemocratic solitude in order to speak:

> From the depths of dark solitude, from
> The eternal abode in my holiness,
> Hidden set apart in my stern counsels
> Reserv'd for the days of futurity,
> I have sought for a joy without pain,
> For a solid without fluctuation . . .

The world-view beginning to unfold is Newtonian; a world of fixed solids with voids in between is one from which all spontaneous energy must be expelled:

> First I fought with the fire, consum'd
> Inwards into a deep world within:
> A void immense, wild dark & deep,
> Where nothing was; Natures wide womb
> And self balanc'd stretch'd o'er the void
> I alone, even I! the winds merciless
> Bound . . .

Establishing order out of chaos is the theme of many creation myths, from the Babylonian creation myth to the Book of Genesis. Yet the egoistic creator here is a reactionary disciplinarian, one of Winstanley's 'teachers and rulers'. What they 'create' is never something living and renewing, but always a book of law:

> Lo! I unfold my darkness: and on
> This rock, place with strong hand the Book
> Of eternal brass, written in my solitude.

> Laws of peace, of love, of unity:
> Of pity, compassion, forgiveness.
> Let each chuse one habitation:
> His ancient infinite mansion:
> One command, one joy, one desire,
> One curse, one weight, one measure,
> One King, one God, one Law.

A modern equivalent of Mosaic monotheism, the authority of Pitt's 'efficient' new centralised state, was binding on all. As Pitt said in a speech in February, 1793: 'It is the boast of the Laws of England, that it affords equal security and protection to the high and the low, to the rich and the poor' —

in other words, it ensures that the rich remain rich and the poor poor. Yet 'One Law for the Lion & Ox is oppression' when it sanctions the royal Lion's right to prey on the poor labouring Ox.

The Urizenic rift cannot be countered except through a dialectical process in which the labour of Los (who is rent from Urizen's side) provides Urizen with a definite human shape. Blake's art, which harnesses the polar 'contraries' of physical energy and conceptual thought, dispels vague abstraction by giving the oppressor a definite form, or what Blake calls 'determinate outline'. History, not Desire, now imposes its demands on the revolutionary artist.

The 'self-contemplating shadow' of the abstracting intellect is given determinate outline in the famous 1795 colour print *Newton*. The design is austerely simple, the picture being divided diagonally from top left to bottom right into a dark upper void and an indefinite, 'physico-vegetative' lower world. The naked, linear, 'spiritual form' of Newton is compositionally on the dividing line between void and solid, half in one and half in the other, the upper outline of the texturally indefinite, lichen-covered rock on which he sits (and which seems to be in a cave) making an angle with Newton's bent spine. The triangular shape of Newton's body, which seems to grow out of the rock, culminates in the drawn triangle on the scroll. The figure's cool, abstract concentration is emphasised — with a cartoonist's wit — by the fact that Newton's Grecian nose, eye, feet, hands and fingers all form themselves into triangles. There is a beautiful completeness and symmetry in the way the figure bends from his sitting position and coolly measures what he has drawn with his compasses. Yet here we see the mind revolving on itself, 'Self-closed, all-repelling', a mind enclosed in a false self, shut off from the true, inner self that embraces, rather than repels, others. The geometrical figure on the scroll (a circle's segment in an isosceles triangle) is the ultimate abstraction, a mathematical formula within which Newton seeks to rationalise the universe.

Blake's visual symbolism here (as elsewhere) concentrates on the human body itself, of which Newton's solitary mental labour is the life-spurning negation. His muscles are like parallelograms, or a snake's scales; the whole body curves in upon itself, hunching itself into an embryo-like ball (the characteristic position of all intellectuals), a movement echoed in the polyp-like plant on the rock behind Newton's left foot. Newton's body has itself become polyp-like: the limbs are like a squid's tentacles, the haunches and posterior forming a new 'head', as if transcending reality through mental abstraction were ironically turning the thinker into a lower form of life. The effect is strange and disturbing. However, in one sense Newton *does* transcend material nature: the validity of philosophic concentration is by no means denied. There is beauty as well as horror in Newton's 'mathematisation' of the world. The beauty lies in man's powers of conceptualisation (and Blake's art is a highly *conceptualised* art); the horror lies in the way conceptual thought usurps and tries to cut itself off from bodily energy and physical work, thus dividing man himself.

The other, social side of abstract mental consciousness is degrading physical labour. Though the artist-craftsman may suffer in periods of dearth and high prices (as Blake suffered during the years of economic blockade), as long as he remains self-employed, owns his instruments of labour (engraving tools and materials, printing press, etc.), is in control of his own labour process, and has some freedom in deciding the nature of his work, he retains a measure of human dignity that the dispossessed wage labourers lack. Blake's poetry of protest and concern establishes a particular kind of relationship between the independent producer and those who have no other choice but to work for Urizen:

> And Vala like a shadow oft appeared to Urizen.
> The King of Light beheld her mourning among the
>   Brick kilns, compelld
> To labour night & day among the fires, her lamenting
>   voice
> Is heard when silent night returns & the labourers
>   take their rest.

'O Lord wilt thou not look upon our sore afflictions
Among these flames incessant labouring, our hard
                                        masters laugh
At all our sorrow. We are made to turn the wheel
                                        for water,
To carry the heavy basket on our scorched shoulders,
                                        to sift
The sand & ashes, & to mix the clay with tears &
                                        repentence.
I see not Luvah as of old, I only see his feet
Like pillars of fire travelling thro darkness & non-
                                        entity.
The times are now returnd upon us, we have given
                                        ourselves
To scorn and now are scorned by the slaves of our
                                        enemies;
Our beauty is covered over with clay & ashes, & our
                                        backs
Furrowd with whips, & our flesh bruised with the
                                        heavy basket.
Forgive us O thou piteous one whom we have
                                        offended, forgive
The weak remaining shadow of Vala that returns in
                                        sorrow to thee.'

These are the uncreative, alienated producers, ideologically as
well as physically bound to the devourer. Every motion is
'*compelld*'; it is not just intrinsic to the nature of the work.
These female labourers on London's building sites cannot
spiritually rise above their condition. Forgetting, in time of
war, the example of revolutionary France ('Luvah as of old'),
they can only appeal to the pity and forgiveness of the same
Urizenic master who whips them. Their suffering turns
inwards with that self-lacerating sense of guilt that Methodism so often exploited.

   Some critics may object that Blake's poetry is much
'more' than social criticism or social protest. That is true.
In *Vala, or The Four Zoas*, however, it is usually the passages
of direct social relevance that carry most emotive force:

What is the price of Experience? Do men buy it for
                                                      a song?
Or wisdom for a dance in the street? No, it is bought
                                                      with the price
Of all that a man hath, his house, his wife, his
                                                      children.
Wisdom is sold in the desolate market where none
                                                      come to buy,
And in the witherd field where the farmer ploughs for
                                                      bread in vain.

It is an easy thing to triumph in the summers sun
And in the vintage & to sing on the waggon loaded
                                                      with corn.
It is an easy thing to talk of patience to the afflicted,
To speak the laws of prudence to the houseless
                                                      wanderer,
To listen to the hungry ravens cry in wintry season
When the red blood is filld with wine & with the
                                                      marrow of lambs . . .

It is an easy thing to rejoice in the tents of prosperity:
Thus could I sing & thus rejoice, but it is not so with
                                                      me.

The deeper emphasis on economic and social realities in
Blake's poetry first appears in *Visions of the Daughters of
Albion* (1793) and *Songs of Experience* (1794), and reflects
the fact that after 1792-3 the bourgeois-democratic struggle
acquired a less constitutional, more economic and social
character as the grievances of the unrepresented masses began
to be heard. During the years of hardship after 1795-6,
when Blake began writing *The Four Zoas*, this social concern
intensified. Yet the passages of explicit social comment in
Blake's longer works go with a negative development: as 'the
Jacobin current went into more hidden underground
channels, so his own prophecies became more mysterious
and private'.[20]
   The passage from Enion's Lamentation just quoted refers
to the effects of the enclosures. A contemporary wrote in
1795:

The rich farmer . . . out of the profits of *several farms*, makes an ample provision for *one family*. Thus thousands of families, which formerly gained an independent livelihood on those separate farms, have been gradually reduced to the class of day-labourers . . . The depriving the peasantry of all landed property has beggared multitudes.[21]

Hastened by the drive to produce more food as a result of the war, the enclosures created a vast new rural and urban proletariat; these 'houseless wanderers', who exposed the hollowness of bourgeois morality with its talk of 'patience and its laws of prudence', were used as farm or factory fodder, or wandered the streets, part of the growing reserve army of labour.

Blake's position as an artist-craftsman during the industrial revolution has already been discussed in Chapter One. The gearing of industry to the needs of war, the violence of the capitalist class in destroying craft skills and ensuring that a plentiful supply of unskilled, cheap labour became available, and the human consequences of all this, are nowhere more forcefully conveyed than in this classic passage from *The Four Zoas*:

> Then left the Sons of Urizen the plow & harrow, the
>   loom,
> The hammer & the chisel & the rule & compass;
> They forg'd the sword, the chariot of war, the
>   battle ax,
> The trumpet fitted to the battle & the flute of summer
> And all the arts of life they chang'd into the arts
>   of death.
> The hour glass contemn'd because its simple
>   workmanship
> Was as the workmanship of the plowman & the water
>   wheel
> That raises water into Cisterns, broken & burn'd
>   in fire
> Because its workmanship was like the workmanship
>   of the Shepherd,
> And in their stead intricate wheels invented, Wheel
>   without wheel,

To perplex youth in their outgoings & to bind labours
Of day & night the myriads of Eternity, that they
might file
And polish brass & iron hour after hour, laborious
workmanship,
Kept ignorant of the use that they might spend the
days of wisdom
In sorrowful drudgery to obtain a scanty pittance
of bread,
In ignorance to view a small portion & think that All,
And call it Demonstration, blind to all the simple
rules of life.

This is a human catastrophe on a vast scale. In *The Marriage* it is the devourer who 'takes portions of existence and fancies that the whole'. Here the factory worker, whose skills have been replaced by machinery, and whose only reason for working is his wage, cannot see how his labour-power is being used, is indoctrinated into believing that 'a scanty pittance of bread' is all his work is worth, and so is kept 'In ignorance to view a small portion & think that All'. The disastrous division of human beings into 'hands' and 'brains', into those who conceive and those who merely execute, conspires against creativity by narrowing human perception in two opposite yet mutually reinforcing directions: that of 'Urizenic' abstraction and calculation on the one hand, and that of ignorant, 'sorrowful drudgery' on the other. Blake's 'insights' come from his consistent class viewpoint as an independent producer: his emphasis on the *human* is also an emphasis on the human unity involved, or at least implied, in the creative act.

That unity implied in Blake's own creative work was seriously undermined when he began working on commissions for the Sussex patron William Hayley. The story of Blake's 'three years' slumber' on the Sussex coast is not merely one of Genius curbed by Mediocrity; it is also the story of how conception and execution become separated in the patron-protégé relationship. On the other hand, nothing aroused Blake's resentment more than the charge that he could not 'execute' properly. The charge was particularly wounding when the dominant class confused skill with dexterity, and treated engravers as people who simply executed the designs and followed the wishes of others. (Blake's poorest designs and engravings, such as his illustrations to Hayley's *Fables* — surely the nadir of his art — are usually the result of a lack of sympathy with another's ideas, rather than a deficiency on his own part.)

With Hayley and his circle Blake came once more into contact with the middle-class gentry. (The previous occasion was when he visited the Rev. A. S. Mathew and his wife in 1782-3.) His artistic style had been developed in a conscious struggle against aristocratic and genteel taste, which proscribed hard outlines, expressive distortion, aesthetic honesty and a too blatant (especially male) nudity, since this frequently embarrassed the 'ladies'. Conflicts were therefore inevitable. Genteel taste applauded 'sentiment', grace, exquisiteness and sublimity, and decried anything that made it feel socially uncomfortable. To the Hayley circle Blake presented the image of an industrious artist who, in his harmless and lovable way, saw fairies and visions and spoke with Angels. In material terms Blake's position improved, but his art suffered as commissions unworthy of his talents were asked for. The old radical honesty kept surfacing. In a miniature he did of Cowper, Blake dared to show the poet's madness by giving him tired, watery eyes and a thin drooping mouth. Lady Hesketh was appalled. *'Dreadful! Shocking!'* was her comment. 'I intreat you on my knees not to suffer so horrible a representation of our angelic friend to be presented to the publick,' she wrote to Hayley in 1801. Blake probably sympathised with Cowper more than anyone, but Lady Hesketh knew her 'publick' better. Artistic truth gave way to decent lies: in the engraving, Cowper's eyes are brighter and sharper, the mouth firmer.

The Hayley episode is mythologised in Book I of *Milton*, which Blake completed in 1804. The poem's thought, language and structure are not easy to follow. Its encyclopaedic scope (typical of Blake's desire to embrace everything), its passages of undiluted philosophy, its obscure transitions and reliance on 'stock-effect' words (such as 'thunder'd', 'fires' and 'cold pale horror'), are enough to tire the capacity of any reader. Yet there are several passages of great beauty, such as the 'Wine-press' (I, Plate 27), the 'Choir of the Day' and the flower passage (II, Plate 31). In Book I the predominant role of *labour*, suggested by the imagery of work and of different work processes, together with the problem of how the vast variety of human skills, functions and responsibilities ought to be employed and shared out, are important themes. Yet too often they are treated by critics as secondary to a philosophic or autobiographical scheme, whose meaning lies above or outside the social process. Instead, we should see Blake's narrative as a kind of allegory of the whole social order: what it is, how it has been upset and how it can be restored, as well as the artist's place within it.

Blake's 'Eternal Prophet' is Los the blacksmith, whose function is to create 'Definite Form' as he labours among 'indefinite Druid rocks & snows of doubt & reasoning'. In Blake's narrative, it is Los who forges the plough and harrow for Palamabron (Blake). The plough and harrow are the engraver's burins or graving tools, whose function is to prepare the field (the copper plate) for new life, removing and burying the old. (The burin 'engraves', makes a grave and buries, as in the proverb of Hell: 'Drive your cart and your plow over the bones of the dead'.) Satan (Hayley), the 'Miller of Eternity made subservient to the Great Harvest', tries to usurp the artist's *métier* by mildly entreating Palamabron to give him his horses and 'fiery Harrow', the artist's instruments of labour. Palamabron, as one of the 'Redeemed', is, however, saved from Satan's law, whose 'Work is Eternal Death, with Mills & Ovens & Cauldrons'. The dispossessed Palamabron's horses are 'madden'd' under Satan's usurpation, and the result is confusion. Satan accuses Palamabron of ingratitude before a democratic Assembly of Eternals, his bosom 'Opake against the Divine Vision'. Leutha (female allure and sexual charm) confesses her guilt before the Assembly. Los and Milton — who descends from Heaven and 'enters' the poet — act as redeemers, and Los calls his 'Fellow Labourers' to the work of the 'Great Vintage & Harvest' of the Last Judgment, telling them:

> . . . you must bind the Sheaves not by Nations or
>   Families;
>   You shall bind them in Three Classes; according to
>   their Classes
>   So shall you bind them.

The Last Judgment becomes for Blake the final great event for which the artist's work is a symbolic preparation. The three classes, fixed by Los, are the Elect (who 'cannot Believe in Eternal Life'), the Reprobate ('who never cease to believe') and the Redeemed ('who live in doubts & fears perpetually tormented by the Elect'). After the harvest comes the vintage; the wine-press is 'the Printing-Press/Of Los': present labour is far from meaningless when it is performed with future judgment and redemption in mind.

The emphasis has largely shifted from the Eternal Now to the anticipation of a future state. The poet's vision of a regenerated social order in *Milton* might be contrasted with *The Marriage*'s vision of a world turned upside down. In *Milton* Los warns: 'Let each his own station/Keep', telling Satan: 'Get to thy Labours at the Mills & leave me to my wrath.' The plea: 'leave me to my wrath' is hardly a call to revolution, but acknowledges a divison of labour in which the creative artist has his own mission (one might almost say his own niche), to which Satan (who grinds the corn that others have sown, reaped and harvested) must play a subservient, mechanical role. The mechanical drudge, 'the Slave at the Mill', is now to be *pitied*. Eleven years before, when to pity was to 'make somebody Poor', his liberation was joyously acclaimed:

> Let the slave grinding at the mill, run out into the
>   field:
> Let him look up into the heavens & laugh in the
>   bright air . . .

But Blake looked to mercy and pity when he saw that Albion's 'machines are woven with his life'. Hence 'Nothing but mercy can save him' (*Jerusalem*, Chapter 2, Plate 40). Albion had become a mechanised nation, whose mill-bound slaves were increasing.

Yet *Milton* imagines, or rather perceives, a world made and continuously sustained by *labour*. (Even Blake's use of the word 'Eternal' is not unconnected with his knowledge of the 'eternal' need for work.)[22] The work of eating and digesting, for example, is wittily described in terms of the blacksmith's forge, with the teeth as 'dentant Hammers' and the stomach as a furnace. Blake's working hero is the creative smith whose hammers and bellows are heard all over London, forging the instruments of a millennial harvest:

> The Surrey hills glow like the clinkers of the furnace:
> Lambeths Vale
> Where Jerusalem's foundations began . . .

Enitharmon at her loom weaves the web of life, the body's tissues; Palamabron ploughs his furrow; Los's labourers gather in the sheaves and tread the grapes; Los's Sons are ornamental craftsmen (like the Huguenot-descended craftsmen in Soho with whom Blake grew up) who 'surround the Passions with porches of iron & silver/Creating form & beauty around the dark regions of sorrow'; they 'labour incessant, with many tears & afflictions', while others fabricate cabinets 'of gold & ivory'. Even the sky and time are 'built' by the Sons of Los; temporal units are 'wondrous buildings', and every moment 'a Couch of gold for soft repose'. But the poet's work is done in 'less than a pulsation of the artery'. Creative labour is not performed in any measurable time.

Los, whose 'unfallen' name is Urthona or 'earth-owner', is an archetype of the creator who is also a producer of tools, weapons, representations and ideas, a figure who epitomises imaginative power, strength of will and heroic labour; his work embodies fiery energy and a shaping purpose, forging 'Definite Form' out of a chaos of intractable 'abstract horrors'. In the revolutionary years the blacksmith's raw material was the people's anger. Later, it is their suffering: 'I took the sighs & tears, & bitter groans:/I lifted them into my Furnaces to form the spiritual sword/That lays open the hidden heart' (*Jerusalem*, Chapter 1, Plate 9). Los is also the Romantic archetype of the Promethean artist, the heroic individual who denies Self in order to serve the needs of Man. His rebellion against a rationalistic modern chaos confirms the values of a more 'ancient', organic social order while at the same time pointing irresistibly into the future.

Blake's mythical smith has many qualities that lie not in the poet's head but in those social and historical realities of which the poet felt himself intuitively to be a part: the smith is of ancient origin (being the first true master-craftsman in early agricultural society); he is therefore indispensable to society; he is a fierce rebel (as were the Jacobin blacksmiths of Paris); his role as a kind of founder of industrial and economic progress connects him with the progressive energies of the industrial revolution; and his 'eternal' nature has a connection with real life to the extent that the blacksmith's skills were some of the last to be extinguished by the industrial revolution.

On the other side, the 'dark Satanic Mills' belonging to the Satanic Miller are usually associated with the textile mills of the industrial north. In so far as the phrase in the hymn connects with the experience of industrialism, and continues to have a meaning in that context, it would be blind pedantry to 'explain' it in any other way. (Blake's true meaning *does* however need explication when the hymn is used for jingoistic purposes.) More generally, Blake's mills are places where any mechanical or repetitive work takes place: schools, universities, building sites, or real mills of any kind. (Well-known flour mills in London included 'Albion Mills' near Blackfriars bridge; John Rennie's large Wandsworth mills, which produced 60,000 sacks of flour a year with fifty men and forty work-horses, and operated on both steam and water power, and the lines of wind-mills silhouetted on the bleak, marshy promontory otherwise known as the Isle of Dogs.)

The original mills of God grind slow but exceeding small: together with ploughing, sowing the good seed, harvesting the sheaves and threshing the grain, they symbolise a process of divine justice born out of the peasants' age-old hopes for a better world and a more just society, hopes upon which early Christianity, as a predominantly peasant and slave movement, largely drew. In Matthew 3:12, John the Baptist announces that Christ will 'thoroughly purge his floor, and gather his wheat into the garner; but he will burn up the chaff with unquenchable fire'. In *Vala, or The Four Zoas*, Blake's Urizen, now regenerated, reaps the corn, binds the sheaves and stores them in his barns:

> Then Dark Urthona took the Corn out of the Stoves
> of Urizen
> He ground it in his rumbling Mills, Terrible the
> distress
> Of all the Nations of Earth ground in the Mills
> of Urthona . . .

But in *Milton*, the milling part of this process is missing, due to Satan's usurpation. It is as if a new social reality had forced Blake to modify his biblical sources. Divine justice now works mainly through the *non-mechanical* binding of human sheaves and the crushing of human grapes in the wine-press (which in Revelation 14:19 is 'the great winepress of the wrath of God', and in *Milton* is Blake's printing press), from which are prepared the bread and the wine of a humanity reborn in the body of the risen Christ.

Of Chaucer's Miller, Blake wrote in *A Descriptive Catalogue* (1809) that he is the 'spectrous shadow' of the Plowman, 'a terrible fellow, such as exists in all times and places for the trial of men, to astonish every neighbourhood with brutal strength and courage, to get rich and powerful . . .' Why should the Miller become such a Satanic, 'spectrous' figure? To begin with, the work of the miller as a distinct, separate occupation did not have the blacksmith's ancient pedigree. In a subsistence economy milling, grinding or pounding grain is done by all who work in the fields. But when grain is *sold*, it is the miller (who may be an outsider) who buys it and then sells it again. He is therefore a commercial middleman rather than a direct producer. Secondly, mills are historically associated with the use of mechanical power: medieval windmills and water mills, ancestors of the 'Mills of resistless wheels', which Blake associates with mechanistic philosophy (the 'Water-Wheels of Newton'), were already places where much of the work was done by machines rather than human hands. Blake's idea of mechanised labour is one in which the not-human, far from relieving man of the burden of work, only further enslaves him:

> I also stood in Satans bosom & beheld its desolations!
> A ruin'd Man: a ruin'd building of God not made
> with hands . . .
> Its furnaces of affliction in which his Angels &
> Emanations
> Labour with blacken'd visages among its stupendous
> ruins . . .

Thus Satan is associated with the pitiless exploitation of human labour power.

A fourth — perhaps the most crucial — reason for the Satanic nature of Blake's miller is connected with the miller's status as a middleman. The 1790s and early years of the nineteenth century were years of food scarcity and hence, according to the law of supply and demand, of extremely high bread prices. Blake's deepest instincts rebelled against the inhuman laws of those — their hearts 'harder than the nether millstone' — who 'Compell the poor to live upon a Crust of bread by soft mild arts'. (Pitt in 1800 actually advised the poor and hungry to eat less.) Just so did the common people refuse to recognise the so-called 'laws' of supply and demand. Edward Thompson quotes the Mayor of Gloucester, writing in 1795:

> I have great reason to be apprehensive of a visit from the Colliers in the Forest of Dean, who have for some days been going round to the Townes in their Neighbourhood, & selling the Flour, Wheat, & Bread belonging to the Millers & Bakers, at a reduced price.[23]

The core of the people's grievance is contained in a 1795 handbill, also quoted by Thompson:

> Those Cruall Villians [villains] the Millers Bakers etc Flower Sellers rases Flowe under a Combination to what price they please on purpose to make an Artificall Famine in a Land of plenty.[24]

The bread rioters knew their enemy: a large flour mill in Birmingham was attacked in 1795, and the great Albion Flour Mills near Blackfriars were burned down twice in 1787, and again in 1811, to much popular rejoicing. Blake's 'Satanic' Miller is, in a real historical sense, the people's enemy.

Our key phrase here ought to be that of the 1795 handbill: 'an Artificall Famine in a Land of plenty'. Blake's art celebrates, as it recognises — often with horror — that the world we live in is *man-made.* (Mainstream Romanticism departed from this man-centred vision in its imaginative depiction of cosmic, natural forces.) Just as man's enhanced power over nature has made all famines seem artificial — a result of faulty human institutions — so man's enhanced powers of thought and creation make cultural poverty seem increasingly absurd and unnecessary. The driving vision here is the possibility of achieving a world of *abundance.* Behind the Blakean notion of creative labour is the belief that man has a limitless potentiality for achieving physical and spiritual happiness: the road of human excess climbs to infinite heights. This is the revolutionary spirit of the bourgeois-democratic epoch, the spirit that leaves the moralist, the cynic and the broken-willed among the detritus of history.

Blake's Los can be seen as a mythic prototype of the revolutionary leader whose thunderous words, like hammer blows, overcome the restraining powers of darkness and release the English people (Blake's 'Albion') from sick slumber and narrow, servile perceptions. Such is the message of the Romantic artist as 'active citizen' and republican artisan, who was to remain an active political force into the era of Chartism and beyond. The republican, artisanal viewpoint, whose roots lay in the struggles of the 1790s, can still be felt in the nineteenth-century working-class literary tradition. W. J. Linton (1812-1897) was a wood engraver, journalist and poet who knew and was to some extent influenced by Blake's art. His newspaper for working men, *The English Republic* (1851-5) followed the older, petty-bourgeois radical tradition in proposing an ideal republican form of society. John Bedford Leno (1826-1895) took part in the Chartist agitation of the 1840s and the Socialist movement of the 1880s and 1890s. Self-dubbed 'pieman, pastry-cook, printer, publisher, politician and poetaster', he was a printer by trade, and with Gerald Massey began a newspaper called *Spirit of Freedom, or Working Man's Vindicator* (which a 'witty baker' travestied as 'Spirit of Mischief, or Working Man's Window Breaker'). As Leno later admitted, he had 'possibly formed the idea that the effectiveness of an article was dependent upon the amount of treason it contained'. Author of several volumes of verse, his *King Labour's Song Book* (1861) pays tribute to the energy of the working class and envisages its future emancipation. Between his view of labour and Blake's there is, as I shall try to show, a certain connection. The writings and lyrics of the collier-poet Joseph Skipsey show a more direct Blakean influence. His shorter poems are evidence that *Songs of Innocence and of Experience* had a steady, if little publicised, influence among working men.

It seems that no-one has connected Blake with this working-class literary tradition. Since a reliable, cheap, one volume edition of Blake's complete works did not become available until 1927, this is not surprising. As far as the working-class movement went, Shelley and Byron among poets (not Wordsworth and Keats) were the important figures. Shelley in particular set the tone, style and imagery for much of the verse printed in the Unstamped and Chartist press, and for poets such as Ernest Jones and Gerald Massey. It is one of the ironies of literary history that Blake should have been taken up, not by the working-class movement, but by the Pre-Raphaelites, Swinburne and Yeats. Those who had most to gain from the liberation of Albion might have perceived more clearly the materialist kernel contained in the mystical shell.

It could, for example, be argued that the view of labour expressed in Blake's imagery and symbolism lies somewhere between an older, Christian-apocalyptic tradition and the modern, historical-materialist outlook. In the older tradition, utopian prophecies are addressed to, and to some extent are voiced by, the working poor as the recurrent utopian hope of salvation and redemption, a vision of a regained paradise that is part earthly, part heavenly. The modern standpoint is that of historical progress, in which the role of labour *itself* as a force for change comes increasingly to the fore. In 'Night the Ninth' of *Vala, or The Four Zoas* a regenerated, labouring Urizen sows, ploughs and harrows the seeds of men, from whom a kingless humanity arises:

> Then he began to sow the seed; he girded round his
> loins
> With a bright girdle & his skirt fill'd with immortal
> souls.
> Howling & Wailing fly the souls from Urizen's strong
> hand
>
> For from the hand of Urizen the myriads fall like stars
> Into their own appointed places driven back by the
> winds . . .
> The Kings & Princes of the Earth cry with a feeble
> cry
> Driven on the unproducing sands & on the harden'd
> rocks . . .
> The daughters of Urizen stand with Cups & measures
> of foaming wine
> Immense upon the heavens with bread & delicate
> repasts . . .

The archetypal sower's 'strong hand' contrasts in our mind with the vision of 'Kings & Princes of the Earth' driven with a 'feeble cry' on the *'unproducing* sands', implying that this is where unproductive kings belong. There follows an image of abundance, as the daughters of Urizen 'stand with Cups & measures of foaming wine/Immense upon the heavens with bread & delicate repasts'. Between the image of the gigantic and sturdy peasant, who throws kings onto 'unproducing sands', and the vision of abundance ('foaming wine . . . bread & delicate repasts') there is, of course, a real connection, but the modern political meaning remains encapsulated in the biblical form of the Last Judgment and the parable of the sower.

Despite all the obvious literary differences, there is a certain continuity between Blake's vision of the sower who brings about a kingless plenitude and the image of 'King

Labour' we find in J. B. Leno:

> The wizard, King Labour, walked over the land,
>   And the spade for a sceptre he bore;
> And each step he took left an Eden behind,
>   While the desert untamed frowned before.
> He levelled huge mountains, and blasted the rock,
>   Where for ages vast treasures lay hid,
> And shewed Heaven the coffer where Earth stored
>   her wealth,
>   And laughed loud as he shattered the lid.
> Then shout, toilers, shout, we need no king on earth,
>   But the king whose large, generous hand
> Has scattered bright gold over mountain and plain,
>   And whose taxes are wrung from the land.

When the regenerated Urizen sows the seed with his 'strong hand', the 'Kings & Princes of the Earth cry with a feeble cry/Driven on the unproducing sands'. When Leno's King Labour walks over the land, taming deserts and levelling mountains, we again see that there is no need for parasitic, 'unproducing' kings: 'Then shout, toilers, shout, we need no king on earth.' Despite the obvious differences of form, style, versification and general accessibility, in both passages man's future state is seen from the viewpoint of productive labour.

But there is a crucial difference. Unlike Leno with his popular *King Labour's Song Book*, Blake had next to no audience for his prophetic books; they are difficult, frequently obscure and therefore hardly designed for a mass, popular audience. As Blake told one Dr Trusler on 23 August 1799: 'You say that I want somebody to Elucidate my Ideas. But you ought to know that what is Grand is necessarily obscure to Weak men. That which can be made Explicit to the Idiot is not worth my care.' Poetic form and language could therefore be said to work against the overt political attitude of much of Blake's art, an art which, as we have seen, implies a democratic, non-élitist society, a world of abundance in which there are no more kings or exploiters. Historically, of course, the class which Blake represented was incapable of bringing about such a society. This historic task was left to the modern industrial working class, its parties and allies. Thus literary form has its own political, class content.

Blake's craftist and intellectual superiority ('what is Grand is necessarily obscure to Weak men'), his hostility to mechanised work and the mass market, and his emphasis on the role of creative labour in bringing about the New Jerusalem, are part of a single contradictory whole. Blake's *Jerusalem* opens with an address 'To the Public' in which the 'Reader! Lover of books! Lover of heaven!' is told: 'Poetry Fetter'd Fetters the Human Race'. Yet the printed copies of this illuminated work were being sold (or offered for sale) at a prohibitive cost. (Only one coloured copy of the poem exists.) How is it possible to mentally free 'the Human Race' through the creation of expensive luxury items? This is the contradiction of petty craft production in a developed capitalist economy, the same contradiction that was encountered by William Morris. The general tendency of expanding industrial capitalism, with its increasing mechanisation of the labour process, is towards the *cheapening* of commodities due to the incorporation of less and less labour in each commodity. Noncapitalist craft production, however, is labour-intensive, and therefore becomes more a matter of producing high-priced goods for the few who can afford them — that is, when craft production itself is being supplanted by factory production. Blake's revolt against mechanical printing and his reversion to the 'illuminated' books of medieval tradition, and Morris's revolt against shoddy mediocrity with his arts and crafts movement, were genuine revolts, both against the capitalist art market, with its demotion of works of art to the level of marketable commodities purchased by unknown consumers, and against alienated work, the 'laborious workmanship' that is kept ignorant of the use to which it is put and has no pleasure in it. Yet the immediate beneficiaries of this artistic revolt tended to be those who had the money to buy, not those with whom the artist's deepest sympathies lay.

The ideal recipient was perhaps the spiritual inhabitant of some visionary 'Jerusalem' or of William Morris's 'Nowhere'. If there is ever a world where poverty, war, exploitation and scarcity have been overcome, however, it will presumably have no need for the creative artist as a special individual, producing for a mass of non-creative and, by implication, passive consumers. That distinction will have been consigned to the era Marxists term the pre-history of man, which is the old era of class struggles. The artist as individual creator will himself have to be abolished, along with the distinction between 'useful work' and 'useless toil' (the terms are Morris's), creative and non-creative labour, art as aesthetic embellishment and work as a non-aesthetic, functional necessity. In the society of the future, 'the wall between art and industry' will have to come down — in the words of Trotsky. Moreover, there will be 'a gigantic expansion of the scope and artistic quality of industry' itself.[25] In *human*, as opposed to *class* society, the impersonal and alienating market, together with 'producers' and 'consumers' as distinct, separate roles (in itself a false, market concept, since every producer is also a consumer) will have disappeared.

ARISTOCRATIC SENSIBILITY AND RADICAL EXPRESSIONISM

H. Fuseli, *The Nightmare*, 1783. Exploring 'the interior psyche' and 'the soul in nightmare'. Jean H. Hagstrum, *William Blake: Poet and Painter*, p. 68-9

T. Gainsborough, *The Morning Walk*, 1785. 'These are celestial beings, devoid of the grosser qualities of human personality.' Ellis Waterhouse, *Painting in Britain 1530 to 1790*, Penguin 1953, p. 188

'REPUBLICAN ART' AND VISIONARY ART: EXPRESSIVE INTENSITY AND
CONCENTRATION, SHARP CONTRASTS, STRONG LINEAR RHYTHMS AND
BOLD USE OF DIAGONALS

J. L. David, *Oath of the
Horatii*, 1784-5

Blake, *Satan, Sin and
Death*

J. Barry, *King Lear Weeping over the Dead Body of Cordelia*, 1785

Blake, *God Creating Adam*, 1795

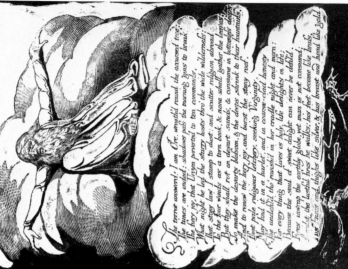

America, plate 10

America, 1793, plate 8

The Blossom, Songs of Innocence, 1789

The Angel Michael binding Satan

The Ancient of Days, 1794

TWO VISIONS OF THE FEMALE WILL. FUSELI'S DOMINEERING, COIFFURED DAMES BELONG TO
A SOCIAL CLASS; BLAKE'S DAUGHTERS OF ALBION ARE MORE UNIVERSAL

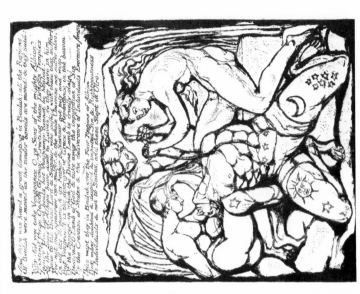

H. Fuseli, *The Debutante*

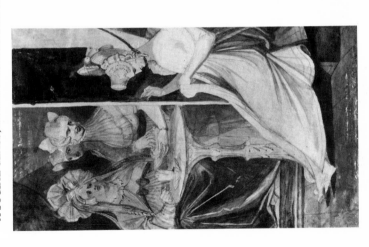

Blake, *Jerusalem*, plate 25

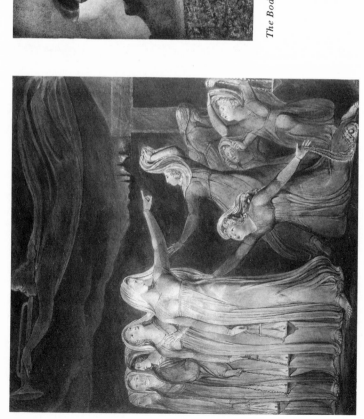

The Body of Abel found by Adam and Eve

The Wise and Foolish Virgins

Unique Style or Visual Ideology?

Blake's visual art, much of which 'illuminates' his own poetry, is said to be unique. It is an art that is *sui generis*. Despite his kinship with artists such as Fuseli, Flaxman, Romney and Carstens, Blake is on his own. The problem, in the words of one critic, is 'defining Blake's uniqueness' or clarifying 'the nature of the unique whole into which he absorbed the many disparate traditions available in his artistic milieu.' The question we must ask therefore is 'why Blake's style is so, and not otherwise'. Once we have shown why he preferred certain influences and rejected others, 'we will be closer to understanding, not just the uniqueness of Blake's style, but the whole search for new artistic conventions in late eighteenth-century art.'[1]

Other critics seem to think that by reproducing Blake's personal ideology (whether philosophic, political, religious or aesthetic) — an ideology that is also, of course, a 'unique whole' — they have thereby adequately explained the artist's work. Thus David Bindman, introducing the 1978 Tate exhibition of Blake's work, says:

> His paintings and books are, therefore, 'Visions of Eternity', images not of the world we live in but of the cosmos seen in the light of Eternity . . .

> Blake is very much a man of his time, trying to learn as much as he can from other artists and writers. But the occasion of a major exhibition of his work is also an opportunity to savour its uniqueness.[2]

The idea that a unique style can be developed by a single artist rests on the bourgeois-Romantic belief in the individual as creative centre of his own work. The more we discover about the individual and his philosophy, the closer we get to the heart of his work. There are three basic methodological errors here. First, no artist has such a degree of control over his/her artistic creativity that he/she can remain the creative centre of his/her work. The idea that individuals are their own centres arose with the historic appearance of 'free' individuals in a 'free' market economy. Bourgeois ideology starts from the individual's putative make-up, needs and desires as the reason for the existence of the capitalist market. Marxism begins instead with the *social contradictions* mirrored in the historic appearance of the capitalist market and the 'free' individual. The same approach applies to art and to artists. Art is a social activity.

The depiction of visual ideas involves the manipulation of visual signs and techniques that have a definite aesthetic value when selected and combined in a certain way. This is what is meant by 'style'. Yet even the most individualistic artist is produced by the manifold social and historical contradictions of which he is part. Since all aesthetic signs and techniques are created and developed out of these social and historical contradictions, no artist is ever the creative 'centre' of his/her work: the uniqueness of a style, if and when it exists, is not the unique essence of an individual person, but the 'uniqueness' of a historical moment that can never be repeated.

Secondly, by reconstituting and re-interpreting the world vision of the individual artist, the art historian does not thereby discover the real meaning of the artist's works, since 'the personal overall' ideology of an artist is not analogous to that of one of his works.'[3] It is not what an artist intended or *thinks* — even about his art or his own works — that is important, but what he has *presented*. In order to 'know' his work fully, an artist must know all the material, social and aesthetic contradictions that have produced it — which is a near-impossibility for any artist at any time.

Thirdly, there is and can be no such thing as an artist's own individual 'style'. There are only collective 'styles' (such as rococo, neoclassicism, impressionism, abstract expressionism, etc.), and what Nicos Hadjinicolaou has called the 'visual ideologies' of certain social classes and sections of of social classes.[4] Within these visual ideologies, of course, there is plenty of room for individuality, but to say that an artist can create his own visual style is as much as saying that he can determine how the world appears to him. To show *why* an artist cannot create his own world vision, and hence visual style, requires an argument that challenges the usual idealist, bourgeois-individualist assumptions.

Since what we are dealing with here are visual *signs*, the place to begin is with the sign itself. The study of signs is called semiology or semiotics. There are in fact two schools of semiotics, a rationalist school, associated with Ferdinand de Saussure, Roland Barthes and French structuralism, and a Marxist school, associated with Bakhtin, Vološinov, and Soviet sociolinguistics.

Anything can be a sign, and there need be no necessary connection between a 'signifier' and a 'signified'. For example, an inkbottle can stand for a car, an elephant, or an army commander for the sake of demonstration or argument, while there is no *necessary* connection between the *word* 'horse' as signifier and the *concept* 'horse' as signified. Anything may serve as semiotic material, and there is nothing in the signifiers themselves that gives them their meaning when these signifiers (such as written letters and words) are purely arbitrary.[5] A conventional sign is therefore a *relation* between a signifier and a signified that is socially agreed; meaning is generated by combinations of conventional signs, also socially agreed (i.e. grammar and syntax).

Since the conventional sign (whether verbal or visual) is the socially-agreed *relation* between a concrete signifier and a conceptual signified devised for the purposes of communication, it follows — in the words of Vološinov — that signs 'can arise only on interindividual territory'.[6] All linguistic signs, as 'semiotic-ideological material', are socially, not individually, determined; and since the individual human consciousness is largely comprised of combinations of such linguistic signs (it being impossible for thought to exist without language), individual consciousness is a 'social-ideological fact'.

When we come to *visual* as opposed to linguistic signs, it

might appear that their conventionality or arbitrariness is negligible. For example, Magritte has to write under his picture of a pipe, *Ceci n'est pas une pipe*, telling us that it is *only a picture*, a visual *sign* comprising a signifier (paint on canvas) and a signified (the generalised concept 'pipe'). Nevertheless, Magritte's two-dimensional visual represent-ation is *iconically tied* to the object we know and perceive as a pipe in the way that the *oral* or *written* sign 'pipe' is not. Here, however, a distinction has to be made, following Barthes, between a *denotative* and a *connotative* visual sign. The denotative merely designates: e.g. 'This picture, called *Albion rose*, is a picture of a naked young man with arms outstretched, the sun behind him, etc.' The connotative implies something in *addition* to the primary representation: e.g. '*Albion rose* is Blake's vision of a regenerated, freed humanity'. It is, of course, with connotative signs that we are mainly concerned.

If signs and combinations of signs are relations, not things, and 'arise only on interindividual territory', the question then is: What is their objective, social, and material basis? This is important for any historical-materialist approach, which must always keep in mind the material — that is, socioeconomic — foundations upon which ideological superstructures are built.

Idealist semiology, particularly in the later writings of Barthes, tends to see *everything* as 'semiotic-ideological material'. If everything is ideological, there can be no real, causative link between social class and ideology; neither can there be any production of new scientific knowledge, since the objective material world no longer exists independently of human consciousness, having been absorbed into the 'ideological'. At this point it becomes impossible to dis-tinguish truth from fiction, what really exists from what exists only in people's heads (or as combinations of signs), since 'truth', 'fiction' and 'what *really* exists' are themselves ideological categories. We thus return, with Berkeley and Plato, into a womb-like World-as-Idea, and finally into solipsism.

The primal cause of this infantile regression might lie in the original Saussurean definition of the sign. By drawing an oval round it, as follows:

we may discover that we have made it autonomous, and have thereby successfully excluded objective reality. Although *real* trees and *real* horses are acknowledged as really existing, the signifier itself has no necessary connection with such concrete objects, only with a signified, as the *concept* 'tree', 'horse', etc. Thus the positivist fallacy is avoided. What, then, is the material basis of this sign?

At this point our idealist turns into a rigorous materialist. If the material world is ideological, then the ideological must be material. The sign itself is material. 'Signifying practice' (the articulation of verbal utterances, the production of written signs and combinations of signs, or the editing of picture frames in strips of celluloid) is given the status of material production. Signifying practitioners do not *reflect* reality, but *construct* it (a variant of the Romantic artist-as-creator). 'Theoretical practice' (thinking, talking and writing) and 'signifying practice' (e.g. making films) are put on an equal footing with other forms of practical work. The division of labour and the unequal distribution of rewards *within*, say, the 'consciousness industry' — between editors, TV producers and advertising executives on one hand, and compositors, lighting men and film processors on the other — are ignored.

To elide 'signifying practices' with the material base is to ignore these social realities and contradictions. Hence, without an analysis of the *objective class context* within which different 'signifying practices' occur, the relation between these various practices and the socioeconomic base is obscured.

In any 'signifying practice', such as visual art, the nature and range of semiotic items that may be selected from a given repertoire; the way these items are transformed; the adoption of new signifying techniques, and the process of sign formation itself, are all determined by the class struggle. The need for each contending class to become conscious of itself in the course of history, and thus to impose its view of the world on other classes in society, determines both the myriad 'signifying practices' that human beings engage in, and the nature of the 'semiotic-ideological material' that arises at any historical moment. As Vološinov puts it:

> Each stage in the development of a society has its own special and restricted circle of [semiotic] items which alone have access to that society's attention and which are endowed with evaluative accentuation by that attention. Only items within that circle will achieve sign formation and become objects in semiotic communication.[7]

Taking signs in their broadest sense, 'to enter the social purview of the group and elicit ideological semiotic reaction, [signs] must be associated with the vital socioeconomic prerequisites of the particular group's existence.'[8] In other words, these signs and combinations of signs must make contact with the bases of the group's material life. In this way, says Vološinov, signs become an arena of class struggle. When signs wear out, become 'allegorical' and old-fashioned, they are no longer serving as an arena for the clash of 'live social accents'.[9]

Having established the social and class nature of all 'signifying practices', we can now turn to the question of visual style. Nicos Hadjinicolaou, in *Art History and Class Struggle*, substitutes the term 'visual ideology' for 'style'. He defines it as 'the way in which the formal and thematic elements of a picture are combined on each specific occasion. This combination is a particular form of the overall ideology of a social class.'[10] A visual representation is a specific combination of visual signs that invites the viewer to perceive the world and grasp reality in a particular way. Instead of responding to each representation merely as the manifestation of a collective style on one hand, or as an individual artist's world vision on the other, we should rather, says Hadjinicolaou, connect it with a way of seeing specific to a social class or section of a social class at a particular moment in history. In this way the visual artefact is restored to its social context. Each painting or sculpture enacts a class viewpoint. Visual ideology is therefore the consciousness a class has of itself, of the world, and of its relationship to other social classes, realised through the medium of visual representation. By helping to develop a visual style, an artist is in fact developing the visual ideology of a social class. Artistic perception in this sense can never be neutral, but always reflects a particular class viewpoint. While there is a danger in such an approach of reducing art to ideology, of seeing art as one manifestation of a class ideology and not as something that is capable of *transcending* ideology, Hadjinicolaou has provided a starting point for a Marxist study of art history.

In periods of intense class struggle, ideological and artistic weapons play an important role. The more directly contact is made with a particular class's vital material interests, the more immediate the significance of ideological signs, and hence of artistic signs, becomes. Periods of revolutionary change, such as the 1790s, show how the rise of revolutionary social classes can be accompanied by the emergence of 'visual ideologies' that may not have existed before. As Hadjinicolaou says,

> From an abstract point of view each class or layer or section of a class 'ought' to have at each historical 'moment' its own visual ideology, given the particular vision each has of itself, of other classes and of society in general. In reality however things are a great deal more complex, for in the first place some classes have never historically had a developed visual ideology of their own. In some cases they did not produce a certain type of picture, for example paintings, at all. This comes from the fact that the need to produce some types of image pre-supposes a specific ideology, and a particular social position. In the second place, the visual ideology of the dominant classes strongly permeates the visual ideologies of the dominated classes, to the point where the latter may be totally distorted. It has a kind of monopoly over the whole of society.[11]

This fits exactly the case of Blake, in whom, as I shall argue, there emerged the visual ideology of the radicalised petty bourgeoisie and small, independent producers (artisans and craftsmen), classes which, despite their accumulated oral and literary culture and tradition of politico-religious dissent, had previously had no coherent 'visual ideology' of their own.

Turning now to Blake, we can see that his visual art has, by the 1780s, become clearly *oppositional*. Certain formal tendencies already present in the art of the time are re-combined, pushed to their extreme, then combined with other, hitherto suppressed traditions. The movement is towards an important artistic revolution that history and the history of art both denied; a revolution in which reality is visualised in conceptual rather than empirical or naturalistic terms, since any copying of empirical reality is now deemed to be on the side of an oppressive *status quo*. Blake's visual art after the 1790s is characterised by four main features: an uncompromising linearity and emphasis on 'spiritualised' human forms, deriving both from Gothic art and from the idealised human anatomies of neoclassicism; the use of expressive postures, involving distortion, together with an emotional and dramatic intensity of gesture, deriving from late mannerism; a diagrammatic concentration and use of *symbolic* gesture, deriving from Christian iconographic, emblematic and possibly Oriental tradition; and a strong anti-illusionism, deriving from the non-naturalistic tradition of medieval graphic design and illustration and again, possibly, from Oriental tradition.

Any combination of these formal elements — I have not mentioned thematic elements or other significant features such as picture size, printing techniques and the non-use of oil paint — has to be understood in its social context, that is, in terms of the visual ideology or ideologies of particular social classes which these formal elements, in their different combinations, articulate. Before the impression is gained that I am arguing for a 'Blakean' visual ideology (a contradiction in terms), it needs to be stressed that Blake's mature visual art, which was produced over a period of nearly fifty years, passes through several different styles and therefore visual ideologies. This again disproves the notion of a 'unique' Blakean style, since the artist adopted several styles during his long life. To say that one particular style is 'essentially

Blakean' is to assert something that is unknowable.

There is, then, 'no such thing as "an artist's style"; pictures produced by one person are not to be centred on him. The fact that they have been produced by the same artist does not link them together.'[12] If we are to understand the different styles in Blake, therefore, we must reject the bourgeois obsession with ego-centred, individual wholeness and continuity — the fact that this engraving and that colour print, this original illuminated book and that commissioned illustration, all happen to have been done by the same person. A common Romantic archetype is the 'unique' individual who, from his own inner centre, and from some inner compulsion, struggles with form to create unique works of art, a unique style, and a unique sensibility, without prior regard for, or sense of responsibility towards, a viewing or reading public — thus, 'the work antedates its future consumer'.[13] (Mary Shelley's *Frankenstein*, in which the 'filthy creation' — the monster — issues from Frankenstein's antisocial, solitary labour in a closed room, can be seen as a critique of irresponsible, egoistic creation.) In reality, no artist exists in a vacuum, but works under definite social constraints and historical conditions. He is urged and inspired — whether he is conscious of this fact or not — by what Mayakovsky calls a 'social command'. In the field of visual art, the 'social command' (embedded in the patron-client, producer-market-consumer, or some other relationship) is always implied in, or refracted through, the particular combination of aesthetic signs — that is, the formal and thematic elements — that make up the final picture.

By following these methodological principles, we shall be able to set Blake's visual art in its proper context, and demystify the almost universal assumption that Blake 'formed a distinctly personal style'.[14] But first, it is necessary to take a broad historical view.

8

Republican Art

The period spanning Blake's life coincides with the formation
of a so-called 'English School' of painting and fine art. This
term is a convenient art gallery or library classification,
under which Gainsborough, Reynolds, Stubbs, Fuseli, Blake,
Turner and Constable might, say, be grouped together as
'major' figures, with Wilson, West, Barry, Wright of Derby,
Morland, Romney, Flaxman, Crome and Linnell as 'lesser'
ones. This list does not, of course, encompass the range of
visual expression in the period, in which the popular caricat-
ure prints of Gillray and Rowlandson were equally important.
Nor does the so-called 'English School' denote a single
national style or visual ideology. The groupings are based on
a posited national artistic identity that tends to reflect the
dominant (that is, class-dominant) visual ideologies of the
time. Artists who evolved quite opposing visual ideologies,
yet between whom there appear to be relevant connections
(such as a common influence — Michelangelo in Reynolds
and Blake, for example) are often brought together in a fairly
arbitrary way by art historians. Stylistic groupings have been
made, of course, and a tendency towards abstraction, or what
Rosenblum has called 'the tabula rasa', has been observed.[1]
But a purely stylistic basis of classification is unsatisfactory
for various reasons, while the *explanation* of this tendency
towards abstraction in late eighteenth-century art remains
at present a fairly partial and subjective one. The only objective basis for classification, I shall argue, is historical materialism, which allows us to study the development of visual
ideologies as they actually arise in the course of the class
struggle.

The rise of an 'English School' nevertheless has *some*

validity in that an indigenous tradition of English painting barely existed before the 1750s. When it did emerge, it tended to be at first derivative, allusive, eclectic and 'literary'. This is the famous 'backwardness' of English art. Peter Fuller has argued that an indigenous medieval tradition in English art was 'erased' during the Reformation, and that after this English art never really got back on its feet. After the seventeenth century, 'visual practice was suspended in a vacuum between aristocratic patronage and an open market', and 'no real social, political, or cultural revolution [was] associated with the coming into being of an industrial bourgeoisie.'[2] As a result of the early nineteenth-century political compromise between the aristocracy and the bourgeoisie, England could produce no Courbet, only the Pre-Raphaelites. (Fuller does not mention Turner.)

Nearly three centuries after the flowering of Renaissance art in Italy, a 'native' tradition of English art still needed to be developed. Aristocratic patronage in the eighteenth century had favoured French or Italian artists, thereby stifling the development of an indigenous tradition. Such a tradition could therefore only be initiated by the artistic representatives of that class whose involvement in trade, commerce and manufacture helped to form a new national awareness and an understanding of the internal mechanics of English social life. Hence, at a time when the hundred and fifty great English country houses built between 1710 and 1740 were becoming the main focus of artistic production – mainly foreign-inspired and foreign-dominated – the academy at St Martin's Lane, founded by the engraver William Hogarth, began to form an independent, bourgeois tradition in English art. The parallel between the rise of the novel and the work of Hogarth is summed up in Fuller's statement that Hogarth's real subject was 'English society in its totality.'[3]

This middle-class tradition, with its realism, didacticism, and moralising aims, encountered a royalist-conservative reaction in the 1760s, culminating in the founding of a Royal Academy in 1768, which can be seen as the attempt to institutionalise a national visual ideology under royal patronage. Yet George III's assumption of royal prerogative through his minister Lord Bute had sparked off a Wilkesite opposition, which in turn transformed the earlier middle-class tradition. A new radical, republican tendency in art, whose leading collective style was the neoclassical, and whose main generic vehicle was history painting, took over from the older tradition begun by Hogarth, Highmore, Gravelot and Hayman. This radical, neoclassical and 'romantic-classical' tradition, established by the Wilkesite history painters J. H. Mortimer and John Edge Pine, was continued through the work of such artists as Hamilton, Barry, Fuseli, Romney, Flaxman and Blake, and is inseparable from the development of a bourgeois and, later, petty-bourgeois opposition to the monarchy and its parliamentary representatives. Whereas the aims, values and ideals of the French constitutional monarchists and bourgeois nationalists were reflected in the neoclassical, politically-allusive treatment of themes and subjects from Graeco-Roman history, English bourgeois nationalists turned, with more 'Gothic', mannerist and 'Romantic' emphasis, to English history, Shakespeare, Milton and the Bible. (Flaxman remained the most severely purist of the English neoclassicists, with his Homer illustrations and classical designs for Wedgwood.) It must be understood, of course, that this bourgeois-radical tradition, as a *visual ideology*, exists independently of the political or aesthetic views and stylistic vacillations of individual artists.

In his annotations to Reynolds's *Discourses*, written about 1808, Blake wrote:

> Having spent the Vigour of my Youth & Genius under the Oppression of Sr Joshua & his Gang of Cunning Hired Knaves Without Employment & as much as could possibly be Without Bread, The Reader must Expect to Read in all my Remarks on these Books Nothing but Indignation & Resentment. While Sr Joshua was rolling in Riches, Barry was Poor and Unemploy'd except by his own Energy; Mortimer was call'd a Madman, & only Portrait Painting applauded & rewarded by the Rich & Great. Reynolds & Gainsborough Blotted and Blurred one against the other & Divided all the English World between them. Fuseli, Indignant, almost hid himself. I am hid.

Blake had entered as a student of drawing at the Royal Academy's Schools of Design in 1779, and probably left after a few months. The labelling of the Council of the Royal Academy as a 'Gang of Cunning Hired Knaves' is usually set down as the embittered reaction of neglected genius. The image of the Romantic artist as lonely outsider, representing nothing except himself, is thus perpetuated. Yet Blake not only thought of himself as 'a direct continuer of the ethical and historical tradition of Mortimer and Barry',[4] as Erdman says, but sees himself here as belonging to a group of related victims of the Reynolds-Gainsborough tyranny. Barry's unrewarded 'Energy', Mortimer's 'Madman' stigma, Fuseli's indignation and near fate as one of the 'hid', and Blake's own memories of neglect and hunger, were the shared experiences of those artists who, refusing to 'paint for the King', as Gillray put it, took an 'independent' line, and through their work (whether they were conscious of it or not) allied themselves with the progressive, bourgeois-democratic forces in society. Though lacking the patronage and status of Reynolds and Gainsborough, artists such as Mortimer, Barry, Fuseli and Blake had, in social terms, the potential *majority* behind them. Why they should suffer such neglect and abuse can only be explained if we examine the social, historical and ideological roots of 'the Oppression of Sr Joshua & his Gang of Cunning Hired Knaves' — and the struggle against it.

Royal patronage of art and political repression went hand in hand during the eleven years of absolute rule under Charles I (that is, between 1629 and 1640). While Rubens and Van Dyck were painting for the English court, merchants were being made to pay for unpopular wars and lavish entertainments, and political opponents of the regime were being persecuted. The Revolution of 1642 suppressed royalist and court culture, such as masques and 'decadent' plays (the theatres having been closed), and a new visual ideology of Dutch-inspired, realistic portraits (the so-called 'warts-and-all' tradition) was promoted, reflecting the values and outlook of the Puritan bourgeoisie. After the Restoration, art once more revolved around the court, but with the 'Revolution

Settlement' (i.e. class compromise) of 1688, the new dominant Whig aristocracy and mercantile bourgeoisie ensured that no exclusive, court-aristocratic visual ideology would be able to rule in England as it was to do in France, where a court rococo style flourished under the patronage of Louis XV's mistress, Madame de Pompadour.

Between 1715 and 1760, in fact, royal patronage of art in England was non-existent. No 'Hired Knaves' of the court could sue for royal favours under England's Protestant, pro-Whig monarchs. (George II's philistinism was expressed in a positive *hatred* of poetry and painting.) Instead, painters and sculptors were largely enlisted in the decoration of English country houses. As far as the public sphere was concerned, however, private patronage had left an artistic desert: before the 1760s there was no formally recognised art academy, no public facilities for the training of artists, no art schools, no art galleries and no public exhibitions. Parliament, though called upon to do so, never became an independent patron of the arts: its leading members (who were, of course, patrons in their own right) saw no need; after 1760, those members who did see the need could not act through parliament independently of the king and his ministers; all MPs were in any case elected on a limited, undemocratic franchise, and by the time the call was made it was too late.

It was therefore left to independent, primarily City-sponsored, private institutions and their artists to develop an alternative, bourgeois visual ideology. Hogarth's St Martin's Lane Academy (whose member-participants enjoyed equal rights), and The Society of Arts in the Strand, founded in 1754 'for the encouragement of arts, manufactures and commerce', incorporated the aims of this 'independent' tradition, with its strongly moralistic, critical and realistic outlook. The link with 'manufactures and commerce' also tended to rein in any non-utilitarian, élitist approaches to painting as a 'fine art'. Not until the artistic and political divisions of the 1760s did the distinction between painting as a craft or trade and painting as a 'fine art' become established: all painters, whatever their particular specialism, still belonged to the Painter-Stainers Company.

On 5 November 1759, at the annual dinner held in the

Foundling Hospital, 157 painters, sculptors, engravers, metal-workers and other artists agreed to organise the first public exhibition in England. At this thoroughly Whig gathering (5 November commemorated the landing of William III at Torbay in 1688), patronage of art was combined with charitable purposes. The chairman and treasurer was John Wilkes. He suggested the founding of 'a museum all our own' ('our' in effect being the City's) and signed the proposal calling for the establishment of an Arts Academy. (Later, in 1777, Wilkes was to raise a motion in the Commons calling for a National Gallery, saying that the government should also support the growing school of engravers and workers in the industrial arts.) The Society for the Encouragement of Arts, Manufactures and Commerce to which most of the artists at this dinner belonged, was a predominantly middle-class institution, winning popular support through its democratic organisation, the charitable use of funds, public exhibitions and, in due course, paintings with politically radical themes.

The public exhibition, held at the Society's room in the Strand in April-May 1760, attracted an average of well over a thousand visitors per day. It included works by Reynolds, Paul Sandby, the sculptor Roubiliac, and the landscape artist Richard Wilson. With profits from the sale of catalogues, £100 Consols (Bank of England shares) were purchased. An added source of revenue had been found. Yet internal differences became immediately apparent, heralding a three-way split that was to reflect wider political and class divisions. To begin with, no aspiring, respectable 'society' painter such as Reynolds or Sandby could live long in an institution that had such democratic rules and relied on a mass public for its revenue. The most prestigious exhibitors (and Hogarth was now one of them) were unhappy with 'the mode of admitting the spectators, for every member of the society [i.e. the Society of Arts] had the discretionary privilege of introducing as many persons as he chose, by means of gratuitous tickets; and consequently the company was far from being select, or suited to the wishes of the exhibitors.'[5] In 1761 these artists broke away to form The Society of Artists of Great Britain, exhibiting at Spring Gardens, Charing Cross. An admission fee of one shilling was charged, in addition to the cost of the catalogue, thus effectively excluding wage-earners.

The remaining artists, who objected to the fact that profits from the 1760 exhibition had been used to purchase Bank shares instead of going into an artists' and artists' widows' charitable fund (according to the 1759 agreement), called themselves The Free Society of Artists. Although Romney, Mortimer and Pine were among its exhibitors, it mainly comprised humbler artists such as seal engravers, needle-workers, metal-workers, wax modellers, miniature painters and copperplate engravers. It continued exhibiting until 1783.

Hostility to the 'meaner sort' was the hallmark of the 'fashionable' painters. Constables were, admittedly, brought in to keep order at some of the public exhibitions held in the Strand, yet if the 'meanly clad' and 'less select' were untrained in the critical appreciation of oil painting, they could see the topical relevance and republican message of a painting such as Pine's *Canute the Great reproving his courtiers for their impious flattery*, exhibited at the Strand in 1763. It was in that year that Wilkes's famous *North Briton* Number 45 attacked George III's ministers for 'misleading' the king over his powers of prerogative. As chief defender of English liberty against monarchical tyranny, Wilkes was able to rouse popular support among thousands of East End artisans and wage-earners. The man whom reaction was to dub 'that Devil Wilkes' had helped to stir 'the "lower orders" from a century-long slumber.'[6] Radical opposition found its reflection in the republican history paintings of Mortimer and Pine, and in the activities of republicans such as Thomas Hollis, an antiquarian who was deeply involved in the affairs of the Society of Arts.[7]

If the Society of Arts and the Free Society were dominated by City Radicals and republicans, then the Society of Artists was hardly pro-king. A split within the Society of Artists itself soon became inevitable. By re-asserting the monarch's control over parliament, George III, like Canute, was resisting the tide of history. And George III was keen on patronising art. Art was therefore to be of great service in a new royalist 'restoration' based on the support of a few landed and monied oligarchs, whose wealth came from the American colonies, the East India trade, the slave trade and a domestic peasantry, and whose political power rested on a system of rotten boroughs, bribes and places.

In 1765 the Society of Artists was granted a Royal Charter. By 1767 secret negotiations were going on between the king and a group of directors, led by the architect William Chambers, for the possible establishment of a Royal Academy. In 1768 dissensions within the Society came to a head, coinciding with a sharp turn in what had now become a struggle for parliamentary reform. Having 'illegally' returned to England, Wilkes won the 1768 Middlesex election, and was immediately arrested and imprisoned. This sparked off an unprecedented strike wave. On 10 May soldiers of the Scotch regiment (no doubt loyal to the King's Scottish favourite) killed several demonstrators in St George's Fields. The political struggle found its reflection in the sphere of art. In October 1768 the Society of Artists elected as its President Joshua Kirby, a former coach-painter. In the words of one historian, he was backed by 'a crowd of nobodies, the rank and file of the absurdly large number of Fellows'.[8] Three weeks later eight directors, whose spokesman, William Chambers, had been secretly approaching the king with a prospect of rich rewards, resigned. From these eight — West, Wilson, Penny, Newton, Wilton, Moser, Sandby and Chambers — the Royal Academy was launched.

The significance of the 1768 split has been obscured by those who try to present the Royal Academy as a logical culmination of previous efforts to raise the status of art and artists in England — in other words, to create an 'English School' of painting and fine art. In reality, the Academy was the result of of an élitist, pro-royalist reaction against middle-class independence, artisan traditions, liberal values, democratic organisation, the reliance on popular support, a genuine concern for the public domain, and the growth of the middle-class art market (in which the public exhibition became the artist's market place). As an élitist reaction, it eventually aimed (having crushed the opposition) at *institutionalising* and *incorporating* different tendencies under one King, one Academy, and one President. John Berger has said:

Academies were and are formed as instruments of the State. Their function is to direct art according to a State policy . . . by codifying a system of artistic rules which ensure the continuation of a traditional, homogeneous art reflecting the State ideology . . .

When art is an activity of artisans, the rules are intrinsic to the *practice* of working from prototypes. These vary from place to place: as does also the skill of the copiers and the judgement of the masters . . .

By contrast the Academy centralises all artistic activity and regularises all standards and judgements . . .

Academicism is an attempt to make art conformist and uniform at a time when, for both social and artistic reasons, it has a natural tendency to be centrifugal and diverse.[9]

Now we can see more clearly the context of Blake's opposition to the dominant class and its political ideology, and — as we shall show — its visual ideology.

The instruments of foundation of the Royal Academy, signed by the king, show it to be in essence an exclusive club mirroring the interests of the monarchy and landed oligarchy. There were to be no more than forty members 'of fair moral character', who were to be called Academicians. The ruling Council, comprising a President and eight Academicians, had complete control over the Academy's affairs. The Treasurer was to be a royal appointment, the accounts being audited by the Keeper of His Majesty's Privy Purse. Most important, those who had been considered 'artists' in the Society of Artists (such as engravers, wax modellers, metalworkers, etc.) were excluded from membership.

The London engravers treated this exclusion as a hostile act, and came to constitute, as Erdman has suggested, 'one element in the artisan radicalism of London'.[10] (Blake was an apprentice engraver between 1772 and 1779.) In 1770, in response to pressure, the Academy decided to allow in a number of engravers as Associates, that is, members without voting rights. The engravers indignantly rejected this sop, and demanded full acceptance as artists on a par with other artists. In 1775, the engraver Robert Strange published his *Inquiry into the Rise and Establishment of the Royal*

Academy of Arts, of which the pro-king *Morning Post* wrote: 'It . . . appears from this valuable performance that the Royal Academy was instituted with no other view than to oppress him.'[11] Strange (who, however, later went over to the king) was not alone in his delusion.

The election of two Radical MPs for Westminster in 1807 was accompanied by renewed agitation on the part of the majority of engravers for academic recognition, and in 1808 they once again petitioned the Royal Academy for full membership. In 1809 (the year of Blake's exhibition) the Prince of Wales canvassed unsuccessfully on their behalf, and in 1812 thirteen engravers sent a firmly-worded memorial to the king protesting about their status as 'copyists'. Their bitterness and resentment can still be felt in John Pye's *Patronage of British Art*, first published in 1845, which confirms Blake's characterisation of the first Royal Academicians as self-seekers won over to the king by the promise of rich rewards. Pye (himself an engraver) describes the rise of royal patronage and the resultant demise of the independent societies as a net loss to British art.

The Royal Academy not only excluded engravers as Academicians, but denied academic honours to any artist who exhibited elsewhere. This, it seems, was intended to crush the Society of Artists, which nevertheless continued exhibiting until 1791. Truly, between the Tory 'King's men' and the 'true Whig' independent societies, it became a question of 'destroy or be destroyed'. Reynolds's opening lecture as President of the Royal Academy shows his bias against the independent societies and his determination to foster an art and an aesthetics that are untainted by mercantile and manufacturing interests:

> An institution like this has often been recommended upon considerations merely mercantile; but an Academy founded upon such principles can never effect even its own narrow purposes. If it has an origin no higher, no taste can ever be formed in manufactures; but, if the higher arts of design flourish, their inferior ends will be answered, of course.[12]

Reynolds typically implies both social and artistic hierarchies:

'the higher arts of design' can only be pursued by setting fine arts above mechanical arts, 'arts' above 'crafts', taste above 'merely mercantile' considerations, and, implicitly, the court and aristocracy above merchants and manufacturers.

Yet, so powerful and persuasive did this kind of defence of 'the higher arts' against the 'merely mercantile' (or the 'merely mechanical' or 'merely manufactured', etc.) become — particularly when the whole organicist, Romantic revolt was against the 'manufactured' and the 'mechanical' in art — that we find something of the same aristocratic disdain in Blake. While he said of Reynolds that 'Such Artists . . . are at all times Hired by the Satans for the Depression of Art', he was equally prone to mix artistic with social contempt (being, in a sense, an aristocrat among labouring artisans). The following are examples, drawn from the *Notebook* (*c.* 1808-11) of this master-craftsman's — or rather artist-craftsman's — viewpoint (the italics are mine):

> Gainsborough told a Gentleman of Rank & Fortune that the Worst Painters always chose the Grandest Subjects. I desired the Gentleman to Set Gainsborough about one of Rafael's Grandest Subjects, Namely Christ delivering the Keys to St Peter, & he would find that in Gainsborough's hand it would be *a Vulgar Subject of Poor Fishermen & a Journeyman Carpenter*.

> All Rubens' Pictures are Painted by Journeymen . . .

> > You must agree that Rubens was a Fool,
> > And yet you make him master of your School
> > And give more money for his *slobberings*
> > Than you will give for Rafael's finest Things.
> > I understood Christ was a *Carpenter*
> > *And not a Brewer's Servant*, my good Sir.

(Here, 'Carpenter' means *master* carpenter, which is a grander subject than 'Journeyman Carpenter'. Blake's prejudice against 'slobbering brewer's servants' can perhaps be explained: after 1800 many of the once respectable houses in Broad Street — where several master-carpenters had once lived — were sub-divided into lodging rooms and apartments. The one-room tenants were mostly labourers, some of whom

were employed in the large brewery (called Lion Brewery)
built on the south side of the street in 1801.)

> Anglus can never see Perfection
> But in *the Journeyman's Labour.*

> Woolett's & Strange's works are like
> those of Titian & Correggio: the
> *Life's Labour of Ignorant Journeymen,*
> Suited to the Purposes of Commerce no
> doubt, for Commerce Cannot endure Individual
> > Merit . . .

> . . . the Monopolizing Trader who *Manufactures Art*
> by the Hands of *Ignorant Journeymen* . . .

At these moments, the viewpoint of the radical artist-
craftsman and that of the Tory 'King's man' seem almost
to coincide.

We should not, however, confuse a servant of the real
aristocracy with a genius from the labouring aristocracy.
Reynolds's aim had been to keep art in the hands of the few.
Did this enhance the development of British art? Or lead to
genuine innovation? One need only compare — though the
comparison will doubtless be resented — the ingenious
eclecticism of Reynolds, the coyness and smoothness of
Lawrence, or the empty heroics of Benjamin West (of whom
Hazlitt said that 'he is only great by the acre'), with the
work of those who made urgent appeals to the 'public'
for the advancement of art in England: with an artist such
as George Stubbs (Treasurer of the Society of Artists from
1768 to 1772, and a Director from 1765 to 1774), whose
revolutionary naturalism was to remain largely unapprec-
iated until the 1930s; with Mortimer (President of the
Society of Artists from 1768 to 1779), who has had to wait
even longer for his originality to be recognised; with Joseph
Wright of Derby (another member of the Society, and a
regular exhibitor at Spring Gardens), whose daring depiction
of scientific and industrial themes was not applauded until
this century; with James Barry (expelled from the Royal
Academy in 1799), whose powerful, still insufficiently
understood masterpiece, *King Lear Weeping over the Dead*

Body of Cordelia (1786-8), was in one important respect fifty years ahead of its time; with Fuseli, whose *Nightmare* (1782) is one of the most astonishing paintings of the eighteenth century; or with Blake. I am not arguing here that 'progressive' means 'better', or that liberal, republican sentiments produce better paintings than royalist or aristocratic ones. It is not a question here of political or aesthetic prejudice, but of objective historical analysis. In other words, we need to examine objectively the nature of the 'visual ideologies' themselves. Only in this way can we begin to forestall normative assumptions as to what constitutes an explanation of, or judgment on, a particular artist's work.

Before I define what is meant by the term 'republican art', let me repeat what was said in the last chapter.

All 'semiotic-ideological material' arises on interindividual territory; that is, in the process of class formation. Every class in history, in becoming conscious of itself as a class, develops an ideology. This is a particular class's view of the world, both in cognitive and perceptual terms; its view of itself in relation to that world; its view of itself in relation to other classes, and to society as a whole. Visual ideology is visual 'signifying practice', the production of visual-ideological signs that, if they are to serve as an arena for living ideological conflict, must find suitable form and so make contact with the bases of a particular class's material life, i.e. its particular relationship to the means of production.

In order to understand the context of Blake's own struggle, it is necessary to begin first with the dominant visual ideology — that is, with the visual ideology of the oligarchy and landed gentry.

Here, the artist's main function was to represent, in large-scale family, group or individual portraits, the wealth, power and fitness to rule of his royal or landed patrons. Patronage thus exerted a direct control over visual ideology. A haughty carriage, noble mien and elevated status could be greatly enhanced in equestrian portraits (the 'horse of instruction' obediently bearing the weight of its owner) or in the absurd, semi-mythological celestial compositions of the baroque tradition (the visual ideology of the absolutist court), which

Blake summed up with satiric brevity:

> Bloated Gods, Mercury, Juno, Venus, and the rattle traps of Mythology and the lumber of an awkward French Palace are thrown together around Clumsy and Ricketty Princes and Princesses higgledy piggledy.[13]

In England, portraiture was more restrained (England being a constitutional monarchy), though the wealth and power of earls, dukes and admirals, and the genteel grace or charm of countesses and duchesses, continued to be the theme of painting after painting well into the nineteenth century. The inherited right to wield economic and political power was the premise upon which the great eighteenth-century landed families, living in their country houses and London mansions, based the vision they had of themselves. This class vision determined the visual ideology of the art they patronised — of those large, often huge, canvasses destined to hang on the walls of spacious halls, staircases, libraries, dining-rooms and drawing-rooms of the rich. (Not until the 'English School' of Gainsborough and Reynolds were native British artists entrusted with this task.)

There is always, in the eighteenth-century English portrait, a direct correspondence between social position and facial expression, between the political, military or ecclesiastical authority wielded by the subject and his depicted stance or gesture. Such paintings had, of course, to be life-like, with proper use of perspective and chiaroscuro. A verisimilitude that faithfully reproduced what the subject was wearing (such as velvet, satin, silk, lace, and jewels) through colour and surface texture was, in effect, symbolically endorsing that subject's wealth and status, composing it as a solid material 'fact' — that is, as something 'natural'. Yet surface detail had to collaborate, in later eighteenth-century portraiture, with flattering generalisation and a smooth, harmonious composition. Thus in Gainsborough's portraits 'nature' is subordinate to 'Nature', individual details to the ordered, harmonious whole, symbolic of the social harmony landed patrons bestow upon the world and over which they preside. In his later portraits, this symbolic harmony appears as a merging of the human (hair, posture, folds of a dress, etc.)

and the natural (clouds, leaves, trees, etc.). Speaking of the increasingly blurred effects in these later paintings, Reynolds said, 'this chaos . . . by a kind of magick, at a certain distance assumes form, and all the parts seem to drop into their proper places'.[14] The visual sign depicts a social ideal that can be empirically observed: 'at a certain distance' all 'drop into their proper places'. General Nature wishes away conflict and resolves contradictions 'by a kind of magick'. As in Pope's *Windsor-Forest*, the chaos and strife of the world are 'harmoniously confus'd'; this world is a place

> Where order in variety we see,
> And where, tho' all things differ, all agree.

The 'general masses' and soft tints of this particular visual ideology, whose oily 'blots' and 'blurs' Blake repeatedly attacked, combined, therefore, with what one might call a 'proper distance', requiring the spectator to *stand back* from the canvas and, as he does so, to appreciate at a proper distance the human subjects and the formal unity of which they are a part. This spatial propriety, which the spectator must experience phenomenologically, is of course common to all large frescoes and canvasses, whatever their visual ideology. In the formal aristocratic portrait, however, it goes with a formal distance inherent in the visual ideology of the genre itself. The superior gaze, cool stance and proprietary air of Gainsborough's, Reynolds's and Lawrence's subjects rarely hint of an *inner* life, or reveal the personality behind the mask as Goya's portraits do. Such 'proper' representations of the human subject could never betray the feelings, passions and psychic turmoil that Mortimer, Barry, Fuseli and Blake unveiled. Imprisoned in the rules of an aristocratic — albeit partly bourgeoisified — genre, the ruling ideology of English art in the eighteenth century could not escape the formality and artificiality that lay, as John Berger puts it, 'deep within its own terms of seeing'.[15] This way of seeing was the way in which the eighteenth-century aristocracy and landed gentry perceived the world, a world that had themselves as its 'natural' rulers. Gainsborough's genius lay in providing this ideological sense of what is 'natural' with a *visual* naturalness; thus formal rules and artifice can be made to appear free, easy and informal, as 'those move easiest who have learned to dance'.[16]

The art of Reynolds, according to Antal, kept 'close to an unbroken baroque tradition'.[17] We shall not understand Blake's visual art, therefore, unless we see the *oppositional* elements within it. Almost point for point (if we take, say, the 1795 colour prints) it opposes the visual ideology I have just described. Being oppositional, it is also *bound* to the ruling visual ideology in a special way; it is locked in eternal combat with a mortal enemy, just as Michael in Blake's watercolour is bound to the Dragon he tries to bind. The points of radical opposition can be summed up as follows: a positive artistic enhancement of the *print*, and therefore a progressive desire to raise the level of popular taste rather than any catering for, or desire to reform, the tastes of the rich; consequent smallness of picture size — hence, pictures that are suitable for the walls of middle-class or plebeian homes rather than those of the upper class, and hence, too, a close contemplation by the viewer of symbolic 'minute particulars' rather than a 'proper' gaze at general masses; an almost reductive, 'essentialist' schematisation rather than elaboration or verisimilitude; the depiction of 'naked states of the human soul' rather than actual personages — hence 'spiritualisation' rather than 'materialisation'; the rejection of illusionistic three-dimensionality, of perspective and chiaroscuro modelling; mannerist and expressionist distortion; the use of the pen, pencil or graver instead of the brush — hence an emphasis on draughtsmanship rather than 'painterly' qualities, and an active hostility to the use of oils; the heightening of 'contraries' or visual opposites *within* the picture, either texturally (as in *Newton*), or thematically, through definite form and determinate outline, instead of harmonious resolution through a colouristic use of 'blots' and 'blurs'; instantaneous exposure and immediate revelation instead of subtle or decent disguise and decorous 'covering up'; direct, often shock assaults on the viewer rather than pleasurable enticements to the eye, and so forth. This kind of *oppositional* visual ideology, which really grows out of the petty-bourgeois opposition to the monarchy and to the landed and mercantile oligarchy, first began with the opposition to monarchical absolutism in France, and to George III in England. The difference between the two movements will help to explain the origin of Blake's kind of art, and the precise visual ideology to which it belongs.

The Enlightenment, rationalist opposition to the *ancien régime* found its initial reflection in the neoclassical reaction against the hedonism and licentiousness of rococo, which had become the visual ideology of the French court. In the same year that the Foundling Hospital gathering took place in England, d'Alembert wrote of the new philosophy of rationalism:

> A most remarkable change in our ideas is taking place, one of such rapidity that it seems to promise a greater change still to come. It will be for the future to decide the aim, the nature and the limits of this revolution . . .

The 'revolution' was an ideological one. In art, the 'noble simplicity and calm grandeur' that Winckelmann praised in the art of the Greeks, together with the new, bourgeois-rationalist outlook, transformed visual ideology. The neo-classical art that swept the Paris salons reflected the beginnings of bourgeois patronage and hence of bourgeois-inspired attacks on the luxury, decadence and parasitism of court life and the ostentatious consumption of the rich. The very terms in which this art is usually described are saturated with middle-class, reformist values and attitudes:

> an equally *severe* and *chastened* style was required for the expression of these *noble* and *edifying* themes: an *honest, straightforward* anti-illusionist style capable of *blunt uncompromising* statements — of *sober clarity* and archaic *purity* . . .
>
> Powdery pastel hues were replaced by *clear* though often *sombre* colours which tended towards the primary and eventually, in the interests of *truth and honesty*, to the elimination of colour altogether in favour of the most rudimentary linear techniques. There could be no visual deception with *pure unshaded* outline.[18] (my italics)

Here, the moralistic approach that we noted with Hogarth

and Highmore is allied to an *idealising and abstracting* rather than *realistic* tendency, though the representational technique is naturalistic; the aim is not a realistic critique of society so much as a distillation of bourgeois-reformist values through the assimilation of classical styles, themes and subjects into a living visual ideology, one that becomes increasingly abstract and linear. A pure, uncompromising and unhesitating linearity is the predominant feature of what Blake calls 'Republican Art' in a letter to his republican friend George Cumberland (12 April 1827):

I know too well that a great majority of Englishmen are fond of the Indefinite which they measure by Newton's Doctrine of the Fluxions of an Atom, A Thing that does not exist. These are Politicians & think that Republican Art is Inimical to their Atom. For a Line or Lineament is not formed by Chance: a Line is a Line in its Minutest Subdivisions: Strait or Crooked It is itself & Not Intermeasurable with or by any Thing Else.

As I shall argue, this firm, indivisible line is the semiotic equivalent of a firm moral, philosophical and political line. (The over-used metaphor of 'hard-liners' and 'waverers' still shows the connection.)

The most important element in neoclassical — and 'Republican' — art is the human body. Yet whereas in Blake the human body is spiritualised and eternalised, in Vien, Greuze and David it is earth-bound and architecturally framed. The human figure, overdressed and over-apotheosised in so much baroque and rococo art, is brought down to an earthly and mundane yet more honestly dignified plane. Flat-sandalled feet are firmly planted on tiled or paved floors, and frieze-like groupings are formed by the architectural spaces of classical buildings. Rigid verticals, calm horizontals and Roman arches conform to rational laws and the rules of linear perspective; even the pictorial space within which the various edifying moral dramas and death scenes take place seems to argue for a more earth-bound, rational world and social order, within which the human subjects are held and framed. Simple Graeco-Roman costumes have replaced abundant draperies. The athletic, muscular and scrupulously rendered anatomies of these neoclassical human forms, in their various attitudes of noble grief, stoical virtue or heroic determination, are the formal and thematic components of a reformist, constitutionalist and republican visual ideology. At a certain point there is a return to the male nude — which is, of course, historicised and/or mythologised. The agonised striving of the *Laocoon* and the republican grandeur, dignity and nobility of Michelangelo's *David* are seen as the visible realisations of an aesthetic and humanist ideal, morally and intellectually far superior to the fleshy female nudes and overdressed aristocrats of rococo and aristocratic portraiture. Moreover, the new relationship between viewer and picture implied in every neoclassical painting also implies altered *social* relationships, a change in social relations. This is a most important aspect of visual ideology. Rococo art controls the spectator through a stage-managed, often subtly impressive orchestration of visual enticements by means of a decorative use of colour and richness of texture; Enlightenment, rationalist, visual ideology, on the other hand, speaks plainly and deliberately to the rational observer through regulated compositions and unambiguously linear forms, appealing to a *moral* rather than aesthetic sensibility through the very nature of the subject.

The exemplary figure here is Jacques-Louis David. Since Blake's early visual art (if we discount the copies from the Gothic monuments in Westminster Abbey) begins within a neoclassical aesthetic, I shall take David as the primary and most influential exemplar of this pre-revolutionary visual ideology.

The one painting that has been singled out as a kind of watershed or culminating point is David's *Oath or the Horatii*, exhibited in Rome in 1784 and at the Paris Salon in 1785. In fact, it implies a possible break *within* neoclassicism, a transition from the cult of sensibility that had previously dominated neoclassical paintings, to a new, masculine, unsentimental — indeed, *anti*-sentimental — spirit, a change from the *appeal* to moral virtue through the *exemplum virtutis* to a harder and more uncompromising assertion of moral qualities in action. Instead of depicting the past, art is now geared to the problems of the present. This change might be paralleled with the change that was to occur inside the opposition to the *ancien régime*, which can be characterised (if over-simplified) as a change of strategy from appeals and petitions, and calls upon the old order to reform itself, to independent, revolutionary action. David's *Oath of the Horatii* is, in fact, an unambiguous call to action.

The cult of sensibility had appealed to moral virtues through 'affecting' scenes, such as the death-bed scene and scenes of mourning, where weeping figures (usually females and tragic heroines drawn from Graeco-Roman history and legend) could suggest, in a Rousseauesque way, a lost world of antique virtues and noble feelings. Gavin Hamilton's *Achilles mourning over Patroclus* (1763) — in which, however, the agonised grief of Achilles, rather than female pity, is predominant; Angelica Kauffman's *Cleopatra mourning at Mark Antony's tomb* (1769), with its mood of quiet piety; David's *Andromache mourning Hector* (1783), and Flaxman's illustration to Homer, *Achilles lamenting the death of Patroclus* (1793), might be cited as examples. Blake's choice of similarly 'affecting' and morally edifying scenes — this time from English history — has a clear anti-monarchical bias. His *Edward and Eleanor* (1779), a subject also treated by Angelica Kauffman and John Deare, and *The Penance of Jane Shore* (1779), show female virtue in favourable contrast to the power of kings. One painting — again a death scene — that combines republican sentiment with masculine assertion, thereby anticipating David's *Oath of the Horatii*, is Hamilton's *Brutus swearing to avenge Lucretia's death* (1763), in which the three male oath-takers (two with weapons) take precedence over the figures of the dead Lucretia and the weeping figure above her. Fuseli's thematically republican *Oath on the Rütli* (1779) is another anticipation of David's theme, but its inflated theatricality has nothing in common with David's hard, naturalistic objectivity.

Argument has raged over whether David's painting is 'republican' at all. 'The painting is no more a celebration of Republicanism than David's *Death of Socrates* is a condemnation of demagogy', argues Hugh Honour in his *Neo-Classicism*.[19] His reasons are: the painting was commissioned by the Crown; it does not represent a Roman Republican

scene; there were no Republicans in France in 1784; it suggests no 'general criticism of society'; contemporary
comments on the painting contained no allusions to politics,
and if the Horatii swear to 'shed their blood to the last drop
for their *patrie*', then 'in France at this date patriotism
still implied loyalty to the King'.[20] The first point can be
countered by the fact that David was not a free agent, but
worked under definite constraints, while the last point has
been answered by Hadjinicolaou: — far from implying 'loyalty
to the King', the word *patrie* was associated (in the words of
Diderot) 'with a free state of which we are members and
whose laws ensure our freedom and happiness. There is
no such thing [says Diderot] as a fatherland under the yoke
of despotism'.[21] David's *Oath of the Horatii* has thus become
a battleground, a test case for the validity, not only of what
(following Blake and Erdman) I have called 'Republican
Art', but of the whole concept, elaborated by Hadjinicolaou,
of visual ideology itself.

Although Hadjinicolaou states that the *Oath of the Horatii*
belongs to the 'visual ideology of the rising bourgeoisie at the
end of the Old Regime',[22] he does not undertake a rigorous
analysis of its formal and thematic elements. What, then,
are these elements, and how are they combined? As I shall
try to show, David's painting was an excellent model for
'republican' visual ideology. It is thus a valid starting point
for understanding *one* side of Blake's visual art, taking each
element — or, in the language of semiotics, each visual 'sign'
— in turn.

To begin with, the painting is not merely an assemblage of
images, but is itself a single, unified image (as David's *Marat*
and Blake's *Newton* are unified images). Nothing is admitted,
as Barry put it in 1775, which does not cooperate. In other
words, it strikes the viewer as a single, forceful statement — a
kind of 'vision' — long before we know what it is about or
how it has been achieved. (Here, I suggest, is a contradiction
within rationalist visual ideology, a contradiction that anti-
rationalists such as Blake and Fuseli vigorously exploited:
the visual image strikes us at a *psychic* level long before the
conscious mind has taken it in.) The first element or 'sign'
is the subject. Three brothers swear an oath before their

father to kill the Curiatii and to assert Roman power over the Albanii. Although this is not a Roman Republican scene, the civic virtue and military valour here extolled are certainly something that was traditionally associated with the Roman Republic. The second element is the contrast between the frieze-like arrangement of the standing male figures, all with arms outstretched, and the three sitting, weeping females. The female group belongs, one might almost say, to a sentimental past that has now been decisively, even brutally, rejected. The third element is another contrast, this time between the sharp, criss-crossing diagonals made by the swords, arms and legs of the Horatii, and the static verticals of the columns and horizontals of the paved stone floor. (An enclosing, architectural pictorial space is the semiotic 'sign' for the social and political order: here, it has been reduced to bare essentials.) These two sets of contrasts heighten the sense of *conflict*, of formal elements that contradict or *cut across* other elements in the picture. The fourth element is linearity — incisive outlines which, in this case, are rectilinear. This connotes two things: implacable firmness and rectitude, suggesting a decision that cannot be revoked, and a sudden break or transition, in this case, from one tone or plane to another; thus the indefinite, vacant gloom of the background and the flashing swords and highlights on the arms and hands of the foregrounded Horatii are sharply contrasted. The three swords are the main organising component in the picture, the dominant visual sign (they are on the golden section), and connote battle, violence and a hard discipline that transforms men not merely into wielders of weapons, but into *human weapons*: the brothers' outstretched arms and hands (in a gesture similar to the modern Nazi salute) repeat exactly, in this highly-charged, ritualistic scene, the configuration of the swords themselves. The three Horatii are a solid, united vanguard, the symbolic spearhead of a new movement.

Other visual elements in the picture are light, and the setting. The 'pristine purity of colour' and the 'primitive Doric columns'[23] — the architect William Chambers, spokesman for the élitist group that founded the Royal Academy in 1768, was appalled by the threat of a Doric stylistic invasion' in 1793 — connote a world of primal, elemental

feelings and simple ways, a world from which the decadence
and luxury of courts (with which Winckelmann's followers
had associated the 'decadence' of baroque and rococo) have
been ejected. *Light* is always an important visual sign (and
in Blake, as we shall see, its 'spiritual' meaning is crucial).
Here, the clear, bold, early morning light, which strikes the
figures at a low angle from left to right, unambiguously
picking out those nearest the picture plane (roughly at an
angle of 45 degrees to the transverse), connotes, it seems to
me, both the bold, 'plain' light of truth, and a new dawn.
Taken together, all these visual signs constitute a powerful
new visual ideology.

In 1789 Carmontelle wrote: 'If revolutions contribute
towards the development of noble sentiments among artists,
it is these noble sentiments of the artists themselves that have
prepared these revolutions . . . genius therefore only seems
to follow Liberty when, in a real sense, it has disposed
everything for its triumph.'[24] Doubts as to the political
significance of David's *Oath of the Horatii* have nevertheless
been raised, based on the fact that comments made when the
picture was first exhibited were purely stylistic ones, and that
not until six years later, with the gift of hindsight, was its
'republicanism' seen. Hadjinicolaou argues that the painting
was praised by conservatives and progressives alike at the
time because its visual ideology is 'positive', not 'critical'.
As Hadjinicolaou puts it:

> Every collective visual ideology is positive. This derives
> from the fact that, being *in origin* necessarily the visual
> ideology of a single social class or section of a class, it
> represents the way in which that class sees itself and the
> world. A class can only see itself and the world positively:
> that is to say, it defines itself in relation to, and by means
> of, the 'values' which belong to it.[25]

Because the visual ideology of *Oath of the Horatii* is positive,
not critical, it allowed the aristocracy to praise it, or, at least
when the criticised it, to '*shelter behind a façade of criticising the form of the Horatii*'.[26] In other words, the painting
could be endowed with 'contradictory aesthetic ideologies'
because the positive visual ideology of a work is of necessity
'polyvocal' or 'polyvalent'.[27]

There are puzzling contradictions in Hadjinicolaou's argument, or at least possibilities of confusion. Surely, if every
collective visual ideology is positive, and is 'the visual
ideology of a single social class or section of a class', it must
in the nature of things appear 'critical' of the visual ideologies
of those classes to which it is opposed (unless we conceive
of a class society in which different classes live together
harmoniously). In fact, although conservatives praised 'the
sublime execution' of *Oath of the Horatii*, they also found
something in it they feared and disliked. The *Mercure de
France* (10 October 1785), for example, was afraid that
David would be taken as a model for others to follow:

> There is no doubt that this picture, which has been widely
> and rightly admired, will persuade a great many of our
> young painters to take Monsieur David as a model; it is
> therefore relevant to point out that the *severity of his style
> and the forceful expression* which are apparent in it are
> here virtues which suit the subject but which are *open to
> extremely dangerous abuse*. A skilled artist is permitted
> certain austerities [*hardiesses*] that are forbidden to
> others, because genius knows its own powers and aims,
> and marches to its goal with a firm step, and because it is
> to genius alone that the opening and following of new
> paths belongs.

As Thomas Crow has said, this writer 'entertains the hope
that, whatever it is the *Horatii* represents, it will go away'.[28]
Other critics, worried by the enthusiasm of the reception to
the painting, found fault in the painting's clear, cold and
rigid forms and 'crude' colours, saying that 'the tones are
not sufficiently graduated' and that 'the outlines are too
sharp'.[29] This is not 'sheltering' behind a 'façade' of formal
criticism: if our definition of visual ideology is correct, it
includes *all* the thematic and formal elements that make up
a picture. Austerity, 'crudity', clarity, sudden tonal contrasts,
visual conflicts and sharp outlines were essential components
of a new, *revolutionary* bourgeois visual ideology. The purified,
visual language of unadorned truth was bound to disturb
those who had become used to pleasing variety, grace, supple-
ness, and mellowing atmospheric effects.

In England, as Antal has pointed out, there was no tradition of 'straightforward, rational and realistic classicism, comparable to the consistent development in France of David's progressive middle class art'.[30] Instead, the very early anticipations of classicism in the 1760s were already marked by certain 'irrational' and mannerist elements, in the work of Mortimer, for example. The 'straightforward, rational and realistic classicism' of Benjamin West, Angelica Kauffman, and some of Gavin Hamilton's works, finds a less fruitful soil in England than it does in France. The reason Antal gives for this relative absence in England of a 'realistic' (i.e. naturalistic) classicism, a consistent, rational middle-class art, and the rise instead of irrational, mannerist, expressionist and 'romantic-classical' tendencies (in Mortimer, Fuseli and Blake), is 'the fundamentally unrevolutionary character and the ideological vacillations of the English middle class'.[31] Yet the parallel absence of this naturalistic, rational classicism in Germany and Switzerland is blamed on the *backwardness* of the German and Swiss middle class (and 'backward' the English middle class was certainly not):

> The German middle class, which, like the Swiss, was retarded in its development, had no real possibility of evolving at this moment and no means of achieving political reforms. Consequently Germany was the appropriate field for the rise of the emotional movement of Storm and Stress with its uprooted intellectuals, isolated even within the middle class, its doctrine of the aristocracy of genius and its vague, inarticulate political ideas. The more rational, democratic and sober movement of the Enlightenment needed different soil.[32]

Antal concedes that the English middle class had had its 'heroic', self-confident period in the early eighteenth century; the onset of an emotional, pre-romantic tendency in art — the subjective emphasis on *inner* liberation, similar to that in Germany — 'was due to the entry of the English middle class upon a period less politically conscious. So well established themselves, they felt little sympathy with the Revolution of the French middle class, particularly after their violent swing to the left'.[33] Thus Fuseli and Blake are associated with early romantic expressionism and the *Sturm und Drang* (Storm and Stress) movement, and hence a European visual ideology, aspects or phases of which are to be seen in the Dane Abildgaard (1743-1809), the Germans 'Maler' Müller (1749-1825) and Runge (1777-1810), the Italian Giani (1758-1823) and the Frenchman Girodet (1767-1824). Blake, says Antal, carried 'this new style to further, more subjective, more emotional, more mystical extremes'.[34] It became a rarefied and precarious style, adopted by only a relatively small number of artists.

Antal, it seems, has not admitted the possibility that a visual ideology could have developed towards the end of the eighteenth century that went outside or beyond the aristocracy and 'middle class'. Yet in England, from the 1760s on, the most revolutionary class was not the bourgeoisie but those plebeian, skilled artisans, craftsmen and small traders who made up the bulk of the movement for parliamentary reform after 1792. In other words, the urban masses in England were by no means politically inarticulate: the absence of a revolutionary bourgeoisie such as that which emerged in France, and which still had its political revolution to accomplish — a political revolution that the English bourgeoisie had carried out in the seventeenth century — did not leave a political vacuum, and hence only room, within visual ideology, for 'uprooted intellectuals' with 'vague, inarticulate political ideas'.

If, as Antal says, Blake was 'living in an emotional world of his own',[35] then this must apply to hundreds of thousands of independent and semi-independent producers, whose lives were drastically affected by the agrarian and industrial revolutions, the stranglehold of the chartered monopolies, the war, inflation and the slump of the late 1790s. It is just possible that Antal has confused the backward bourgeoisie in Germany with the radicalised petty bourgeoisie and small producers in England.

Within neoclassicism there is a strong tendency towards simplicity and primitivism, both in technique and in subject matter. Rosenblum has identified this as a kind of teleological movement towards formal abstraction similar to that seen in modern art.[36] Yet this tendency can be given objective historical substance if we see it in terms of *visual ideology* — that is, if we refuse to separate visual form and political or social content in any analysis of such a tendency. The critique of luxury and courtly excess ended, with an apparently similar teleological determinism, with the ruthless purging of all 'enemies of the people' and the ideal vision of a popular republic. In the sphere of visual art, what began with Vien as a neoclassical *subduing* of rococo tendencies, 'ended' with the bare, factual simplicity or David's idealised *Dead Marat* (1793) and the unshaded outlines of Flaxman and Carstens. We should not, however, artificially abstract this tendency from other, equally important tendencies. Depending on how we select our evidence, the period can be seen *either* as a movement towards linear, geometrical abstraction, *or* as a movement in the opposite direction, that is, towards realism, naturalism and the sensuous re-creation of the visible world. The presence in any period of such 'contrary' tendencies, which are all part of a single, dialectical whole, evinces the contradictory development of social classes in history.

The primitivising tendency in English art has social and political implications, and goes with the mannerist, expressionist and pre-romantic features of English neoclassicism observed by Antal. I shall now analyse these tendencies, showing how the absence in England of a 'straightforward, rational and realistic classicism' comparable to that in France had deep historical and ideological causes.

Orthodox neoclassicism implies an analogy between Greek or Roman antiquity and modern times. English republican thought (in writers such as Milton, Harrington, Moyle and the eighteenth-century Commonwealthmen) had favoured the establishment of a 'free', 'virtuous' English Republic on the Greek or Roman model. Yet in the second half of the eighteenth century this Graeco-Roman republicanism, with its view of antiquity as *classical* antiquity, began to give way to indigenous historical examples, and research into *British*, 'Gothic' and Celtic antiquity. This indigenous emphasis was not, in fact, a new phenomenon. The English revolutionaries of the seventeenth century had fought not so much in the shadow of classical antiquity as in the cause of the 'ancient rights and liberties' of the English people; not in the name of Reason, but in the cause of God. English history, moreover, contained enough examples of native freedom and 'free subjects' defending their rights against arbitrary rule to make possible a genre of radical history paintings that looked to English and ancient British history rather than to classical Greece and Rome as historical precedents. (John Copley's *Charles I Demanding the Surrender of the Five Impeached M.P.s* caused a sensation in 1785: the queen thought it 'a most unfortunate subject'.) Furthermore, by the second half of the eighteenth century, classical antiquity had become associated with the landed interest and the political dominance of a small, powerful class of mercantilists and landed oligarchs. Thirdly, England had already experienced a republican form of government with the Cromwellian dictatorship of 1649; the French bourgeoisie, with its abortive *Fronde* as the only precedent for its resistance to absolutism, and the pathetic weakness of its *parlement* (in effect a rubber stamp for the monarchy), had yet to achieve such a dictatorship. Lastly, while the French bourgeoisie had yet to create any kind of represent-ative body at the political level (and rapidly discovered that it needed the power of the masses to accomplish this historic task), the English House of Commons was seen by the radical bourgeoisie as the corrupted form of an institution that had once been healthy, and one in need of reform. The class coalition that sheltered under the English constitutional monarchy, and had benefitted handsomely from the slave trade, the American plantations and the East India trade, was opposed by three generations of radical reform movements, embodying a free-trade interest with its own petty-bourgeois, libertarian wing. In 1792 the by now moderate middle-class reform movements were overtaken by an artisan, democratic organisation, the London Corresponding Society, and by 1819 the industrial working class itself entered the picture. Even from the time of Wilkes, the radical movement had had its popular, extraparliamentary wing, and this perhaps helps to explain the more *libertarian* emphasis within the progressive movement in England, reflected in the mannerist, 'romantic-classical' tendencies in artists such as Hamilton, Mortimer, Barry, Fuseli and Blake.

Thus the 'Gothicising', mannerist and primitivist tendencies in English neoclassical painting; the preoccupation with English history (as well as with subjects from Milton, Shakespeare and the Bible); the presence of a libertarian, pre-romantic element from the early 1760s; and the fact that a 'straightforward, rational and realistic classicism' was prone to be weak, conservative and flaccid, have, as I have indicated, deep historical and ideological causes. As positive examples we might cite, respectively, Hamilton's *Achilles mourning over Patroclus* (1763), Mortimer's tendentiously anti-royalist *The discovery of Prince Arthur's Tomb by the inscription on the leaden cross*, and the work of Fuseli and Blake, and, as a negative example, a painting such as West's *The Departure of Regulus*. The pose and drapery of the soldier on the extreme right of Hamilton's painting show a Gothic rather than classical linearity, while the absence of any framing architectural space connotes a world even more 'primitive' than the 'crude' Doric columns of David's *Oath of the Horatii*. The English 'love of wildness' is not a national characteristic, but stems from the historical formation of the English middle class. Its vacillations between the conservative oligarchy and the libertarian petty bourgeoisie and artisan classes reveal its peculiar internal contradictions, which were further complicated by the emergence of a new, factory-owning capitalist class during the 1770s and 1780s.

In Mortimer, Barry and Blake a new primitivist republicanism is evident, carrying with it new thematic motifs. A new connotative human type emerges, a hero who wears the garb, not of Hamilton's Brutus, with his classical toga, nor of David's helmeted Horatii, but (martial or otherwise) that of the ancient Briton, Celt and 'bard', and finally — in Blake — no garb at all, only the expressionist nudity of a newly-unveiled inner humanity. This, then, is the new Rousseauesque man, the indigenous, muscular republican hero, who in Blake is the essential, original Man. He is also a *bard*. As Erdman has said, 'what the history painter of Barry's or Blake's sort does it to assert the moral and social power of the inspired bard, a power to overwhelm evil rulers and summon together patriots.'[37] There is, in fact, a progressive continuity between the figure of the exemplary, prophetic hero in Mortimer (as in the series *The Progress of Virtue* in the Tate Gallery, where the qualities of hardy Michelangelesque masculinity are stressed); in Barry (the tall soldier in *King Lear Weeping over the Dead Body of Cordelia*), and in Blake (the repeated 'young man' stereotype, and, one imagines, the figures in Blake's lost fresco, *The Ancient Britons*). Blake's muscular hero, of course (whether as Albion, Orc, Adam, Adam Kadmon or Ancient Briton) is stripped of the social dress that might locate him in any temporal context: here, the republican hero, with all the vacillations, strivings and oppressions that he undergoes, has become an eternal archetype.

Another, no less important, but hardly 'republican' archetype in this primitivist movement within visual art is the Rousseauesque 'natural man' as noble savage. The classic Rousseauesque natural man is the stoical man of virtue who expresses the General Will of the people, guided both by an adherence to the simple life and by 'right reason' (*recta ratio*). When all men are equals in a genuine community, it is then that the General Will is purest. The natural man and the noble savage belong to a purified social community, conceptualised and poetically imagined as an ideal contrary to a depraved modern social order. Rousseau asks: 'whence proceeds all evil?' and answers:

> From our social order, which, in every respect contrary to nature whom nothing can destroy, tyrannizes over her without cease and compels her without cease to reclaim her rights . . . It alone explains all the vices of men and all the evils of society.[38]

Whereas Rousseau's natural man as revolutionary hero is closely linked to the republican heroes I have described, the noble savage tends to be sentimentally idealised and depoliticised. Examples of this noble savage in paintings are to be found in Joseph Wright's *Indian Girl mourning her dead warrior lover*, in West's *The Death of Wolfe* (1770), with its

pensively watching Red Indian, and the savages (unintention-
ally ennobled) in Zoffany's *The Death of Captain Cook*
(1789), which are based on classical nudes. Not far away is
the feeling — and possibly the fear — that 'savage' or 'primitive' man, living a life close to nature, and inured to a warlike
existence, is morally superior to, and physically stronger
than, those living in 'civilised', decadent societies. In Wright
and West this stereotype is sentimentalised and rendered
harmless. In Blake's engraved illustrations to Stedman's
*Narrative of a five Years' expedition against the Revolted
Negroes of Surinam*, however, the humanity and physical
beauty (albeit Europeanised) of the 'savage' negro are positiv-
ely asserted.

Barry's *King Lear Weeping over the Dead Body of Cordelia*
(1786-88) in the Tate Gallery is one of the finest examples of
'primitivist' classicism in English art. An impressive, moving,
and very *public* painting (it measures 106" x 144½"), it
contains many of the formal and thematic elements of a
republican visual ideology. Barry (according to Erdman)
championed the republicans not only of America but of
Ireland, was a democrat on African slavery, supported the
rights of women, knew Wilkes, was in an eating club with
Price and Priestley, dined with Thomas Holcroft, was a friend
of the Hollises, and was one of Godwin's intimates as early
as 1783.[39] We may assume that this painting reflects the
democratic republicanism of the artist who painted it. To
begin with, the subject itself runs directly counter to
eighteenth-century taste: *King Lear* continued to be performed until the 1830s in an altered version, in which Cordelia
does not die. The play's original ending was far too painful
and tragic to be acceptable to eighteenth-century audiences.
Thus Barry has restored a Shakespearean original, and in
doing so is considerably ahead of his time.

The figure of Lear himself is massive, almost gross, and it
is here that the mannerist element enters: with his massive
head, white wind-blown hair and beard, hand on forehead,
and heavy, frowning brows, he is the powerful symbol of
final collapse — a decayed monarch sent mad by his own grief
and the realisation of his folly: that hand on the forehead,
and the significantly accusing look of the figure in shadow

just behind the soldier who compositionally dominates the picture, convey the idea that it is *Lear* who is to blame for Cordelia's death and the carnage all around, which he, a king, has been helpless to prevent, as he cannot prevent his own madness and death. The kneeling Kent's loyal and tearful compassion is certainly not the dominant mood of the picture. The outstretched right arm of the helmeted, plumed soldier nearest the viewer (whose simple buskins, leather thongs and youthful masculinity suggests the moral type of the 'new man'), together with the sharp tonal contrast between his illuminated arm and the shadow behind, even the angle of the pike held by the middle figure in the group of three, are compositional echoes of the *Oath of the Horatii*. Barry's picture even contains a similar Davidian contrast between upright masculinity and 'feminine' weeping. It is as if, just as in David's picture, there is one group of three (Kent, Lear and the dead Cordelia) which belongs to the past, while another (the three figures in the centre) belongs to the future. Yet the tragedy is not minimised: the suffering is not played down in any way. Uncomplicated, well-defined linear rhythms and straightforward repetitions (the limp, hanging right arm of the dead Edmund and of the dead Cordelia), lend a simple, almost crude power to this ancient scene, with its simple battle tent and, on the wild, denuded rocky hill behind, the massive stone trilithons of an ancient henge. This is Ancient Britain, a world whose elemental yet subdued austerity is suggested not only by the costumes and the setting, but by the sombre, earth-bound colours, which range from dark brown to light brown to russet, with some grey, blue and white. The emotional force of the whole painting is considerable, yet its classical restraint still holds it within a 'romantic-classical' rather than romantic visual ideology.

Conservative, eighteenth-century visual ideology is invariably 'tasteful' in that it resolves, and in some cases dissolves, conflict and contradiction through formal means. There is an attempt to *compose* life rather than to express it, to pictorialise the world rather than to explore it or see it afresh. There is the general preference for soft gradations and 'pleasing' rhythms over striking contrasts and dynamic or astringent rhythms. Pain has been shut out. At worst, life is merely prettified or aestheticised. The movement towards 'Republican Art' (in Mortimer, David, Barry and Blake) is the attempt to make art reflect a new social reality. Here, pain, suffering, striving, conflict and the power struggle are not kept out; it is now the artist's *responsibility* to express them as truthfully, simply and forcefully as he can. Distortion, strange or grotesque effects, may be necessary in order to strike the deeper truths that orthodox artistic conventions do not allow. Hence the return to Michelangelesque, mannerist effects. David's *Horatii*, Barry's *Lear*, Fuseli's *Nightmare* and Blake's *Good and Evil Angels* are therefore not intended as 'pleasing compositions', but as forceful *arguments*. They express, in turn, an irrevocable, military decision, the implacable will of fate, orgasmic submission, and the 'marriage' of irreconcilable opposites. This new art is a tremendous release of energy dammed up by academic flaccidity and ideological censorship. Instead of drawing on rhetorical formulae, sublimating conflict into a 'higher order' of reflective emotion, it makes a direct assault on the viewer's capacity to respond, not in a partial way, but as a total human being, so that he too can *feel* the suffering, passion, striving and submission of other human beings. Commitment to such an art necessarily entailed an inner and outer struggle for the artist himself. It was not just a matter of competing to see who could be most 'sublime' and striking, though this, with the new bourgeois individualism, certainly came into it. It was a question of *expressing*, through the medium of visual representation, new feelings, mental states and ideas.

The division between those artists who served the landed classes and the monarchy and those who strove as individuals to serve the English 'people' became an aesthetic, political and social cleavage whose bitterness increased between the 1760s and 1790s. To be a fashionable 'society' painter was the lot of a tiny few, bringing rich rewards and imposing a conformity to certain social codes. Reynolds, for example, sedulously cultivated a wide circle of rich friends and acquaintances (all potential patrons), gradually increasing his prices as his reputation grew (thus further enhancing his reputation). In 1764 he made £6,000. Replying to a query from a provincial gentleman in 1777, he wrote, with business-like brevity: 'As far as the Knees seventy [guineas] '.[40] Knowing where his money came from, Reynolds certainly knew the money value of his paintings. Once his reputation was established, royal favours, sinecures, a pension and a knighthood came his way. The aristocratic visual ideology of Reynolds's *Self-portrait* (1773) and *Sarah Siddons as the Tragic Muse* (1784) is one of opportunistic eclecticism and accomplished technicism. In the first, the painter stands in legal robes by a bust of Michelangelo. It is a visual cheat: 'Reynolds' looks like Rembrandt! The second painting, in which the celebrated actress's pose recalls Michelangelo's Isaiah on the Sistine ceiling, is designed to appeal to the cultivated connoisseur by its ingenious allusiveness. To serve, nurture and refine 'taste' was Reynolds's whole endeavour. As he told students at the Royal Academy: 'You must have no dependence on your own genius'.[41]

Gainsborough, though conforming to the visual ideology his patrons required, at least chafed at the bit. In a famous letter he confessed a distaste for portraiture and the kind of people he had to paint, saying how he wished he could take his viola de gamba to the country and paint 'land-skips'.[42] Bourgeois-individualistic impulses — the desire for greater artistic 'freedom' — are present here, but freedom came with a new clientèle (the middle class) and the emergence of an art market, which implied a far bigger change than simply giving up portraits for landscapes.

George Romney is an example of an artist who, dissatis-fied with fashionable portrait painting, tried to break with the dominant visual ideology of the aristocracy by taking the path of artists such as Barry, Fuseli, Flaxman and Blake, yet who never quite succeeded in the attempt. His work passes through at least five distinct genres or styles (i.e. visual ideologies): the 'aristocratic-formal', as seen in the large, fully-robed figure of Lord Thurlow (Blake's 'Guardian of the secret codes' at Westminster who, with 'his furr'd robes and false locks' was 'Driven out by the flames of Orc');[43]

the 'aristocratic-informal', as seen in the well-known Lady Hamilton series; the sober, middle-class portrait, as seen in the portrait of Richard Cumberland (author of popularly sentimental comedies), which is in the naturalistic, 'warts-and-all' tradition of bourgeois realism; the 'neoclassic-abstract', as seen in the bare, stark geometry of *The Death of Cordelia* (1789), a drawing which Rosenblum connects with Blake's 1797 title page to *Songs of Experience*; and what could be called English romantic-classic or 'visionary art', as seen in *The Spirit of God Floating Over Chaos*, in which the floating figure of God, arms outstretched, is a stereotype to be found in Fuseli and Blake. By the 1790s Romney was approaching the position of Blake, the most uncompromising exponent of 'spiritual' art — an art for whom patrons were very few. Romney believed that Blake rivalled Michelangelo;[44] he also supported the French Revolution (as a Foxite rather than a Painite). A series of paintings based on scenes from Milton and the Bible, planned in 1794, included such titles as *The Visions of Adam with the Angel* — a far cry from the large, fully-robed portrait of Lord Thurlow.

Having once earned £4,000 as a portrait painter in 1775, Romney had, it seems, finally arrived at a spiritual-revolutionary conception of art, which implied a far deeper commitment than any fashionable portrait painter could reasonably sustain. Radical intentions could not be carried through into aesthetic practice. The libertarian impulse, as with Gainsborough, remained stifled (though Gainsborough *was* able to indulge himself in landscapes — a far less radical genre than 'visionary' painting — more than Romney could indulge in his 'visions'). The fashionable portrait painter of Cavendish Square could only be 'revolutionary' in his pencil and pen-and-wash drawings, not on canvas — and drawings were never lucrative. On the other hand, the linear purity of Blake's and Flaxman's visual technique implied a *rejection* of easel painting in oils, a fact that Romney may not have fully grasped. As it was, a politico-religious conscience was not matched by a strong artistic will. Fear, vacillation and foreboding began to take hold, and Romney became a victim of an artistic crisis that history and the class struggle, not he himself, had precipitated. In 1794, speaking of his projected biblical series, he wrote to William Hayley: 'Alas! I cannot begin them for a year or two, and if my name was mentioned, I should have nothing but abuse, and that I cannot bear. Fear has always been my enemy: my nerves are too weak for supporting anything in public.'[45] Compromised by his rich patrons and fashionable connections, Romney was unable to bear the potential 'abuse' (and perhaps worse) that a Jacobin visionary such as Blake came to expect. (Yet Blake too felt the strain, experienced by all radicals in these dangerous times. In June 1793 he wrote: 'I say I shan't live five years, And if I live one it will be a Wonder.') In 1799, broken in health, and afflicted with the melancholy shared by other radicals at the time (Blake spoke in 1800 of emerging from a 'Deep pit of Melancholy'), Romney returned to his native Kendal, dying there in 1802.

If spiritual and artistic collapse was the price Romney paid for artistic unpreparedness and a fear of public abuse, stemming from his habitual reliance on wealthy private patrons, then the Cork-born James Barry put himself beyond the pale (and out of the Royal Academy) by his principled independence, his belief in the artist's *public* role and the need for a *national* (not élitist) art, and his commitment to the progress of art. Barry's dedication to history painting left him virtually without patrons, while class bias was to mark him down as a wild Irishman, a man whose 'perverse and ungovernable disposition'[46] placed him outside the realm of taste, which also applied, at that time, to the required social decorum of the artist. It condemned him to isolation and, after 1799, to a life of neglect, squalor and poverty until his death in 1806. The years 1777-1783 were also hard times, when he was labouring gratis on his epic series *The Progress of Human Culture* at the Adelphi Rooms for the Society of Arts. Barry was denigrated in his own time, and much of the mud seems to have stuck. According to a recent account, Barry was 'self-centred', and had an 'inflated ego'.[47] His 'bad temper led him to insult the president [of the Royal Academy]',[48] and his expulsion from the Academy in 1799 (one year after the rising of Wolfe Tone's United Irishmen, with which Barry sympathised), is blamed on 'insult and libel against his fellow Academicians'[49] — itself a libel against this champion in England of the neoclassic 'grand style', who also strove to democratise the Academy's proceedings. A contemporary described Barry as 'a little ordinary man, not in the most graceful dishabilée, [with] a dirty shirt without any cravat, his neck open and a tolerable length of beard, his stockings not of the purest white in the world'.[50] Adding these comments together, Barry emerges not only as a plebeian and a radical, but as a new kind of artist, one that by the late nineteenth century, with its aesthetes and Bohemians, had become a cliché: the Romantic artist.

Henry Fuseli showed a similar disregard for convention, the hallmark of Rousseauesque individualism. His openness in conversation and his habit of swearing (in a Swiss accent) went with the liberated yet strangely displaced quality of the visual ideology to which his art primarily belonged. Fuseli was not interested in politics *per se*, so much as in *sexual* politics, and in its exploration through dream material, vertiginous viewpoints, phallic symbols and exaggeratedly submissive or dominant postures, suggesting an excited, *psychic* response to political and social changes and upheavals. Such a response is bound, in some respects, to be ambiguous: dominance and submission (whether in the male or in the female) have an equal appeal to the irrational, unconscious mind. Blake's loyalty to Fuseli, who was sixteen years his senior, was unswerving, but Fuseli moved in quite different circles from the visionary engraver: it was a world of bankers (Fuseli's principal patrons), of businessmen, scholars and art collectors, a world of dinner parties, heated drawing-room discussions, and frequent visits to the theatre. Fuseli was a keen theatre-goer, and the *theatricality* of his art — one might even say, its 'staginess' — is one of its persistent characteristics.

Fuseli's use of the human figure to express particular emotional and psychological states is, of course, extremely 'radical' and very close to Blake, but the radicalism is politically ambiguous. (It is perhaps no accident that a 'Fuseli touch' has been noticed in Gillray, who could, in mercenary fashion, serve both the political radicals and the Association for Preserving Liberty and Property against Republicans and Levellers.) I suspect that at one level the radical content of Fuseli's art is the radicalism of the élite rather than that of

the shops and taverns in which the works of Paine were reac
By this I mean that the 'liberation' is somehow socially
contained: it is the liberation of the comfortable few — who
could, perhaps, delight in shocking themselves and their more
staid and conventional colleagues — rather than the social
and political liberation of the many. The *mind*, as it were,
may be allowed to run riot, but not the masses. There are,
I would argue, social and political limits to the radicalism
of Fuseli's eroticism, and his emphasis on the irrational just
beneath the surface of 'civilised' society. The overbearing
ladies with their disturbingly elaborate hair-dos, the huge,
often nude, repeatedly attenuated figures from Nordic
mythology, Milton and Shakespeare, with their dagger-like
feet and bony knees, who either step with giant strides or
stand, colossus-like, pointing, reaching out, and holding
daggers in a repertoire of highly stylised, melodramatised
gestures (usually seen from below, as if from a theatre pit),
form a visual ideology based on Gothic and mannerist
exaggeration rather than a Davidean or Blakean revolutionary
hardness and intensity.

Gillray wrote to Fuseli in 1790: 'There are but two ways
of working successfully, that is, lastingly, in this country, for
an artist — the one is, to paint for the King; the other, to
meditate a scheme of your own.'[51] As a Royal Academician
from 1790 and as Professor of Painting from 1799 (taking
the place of the expelled Barry) Fuseli served an institution
that was patronised by the king and voted £500 for the
war against France in 1798. But he also declared that 'Every
artist has, or ought to have, a character or system of his
own.'[52] Blake's assertion, 'I must Create a System or be
enslav'd by another Man's', is stronger, since it precludes
any possibility of compromise.

The struggle to create a system of one's own involved a
battle with strong material forces. Blake's battle is well
known: first, the apprentice, then the poor student at the
Academy's Schools of Design; next, a short-lived attempt
at establishing a print-shop business; earning a living by
engraving book illustrations for booksellers; a period
(1790-95) of relative independence and even wealth (in
1793 he took in pupils of 'high rank' and the theft of £60

worth of plate and £40 worth of clothes shows that the
Blakes were by no means badly off in Lambeth); then, after
1796, the reliance on patronage, first that of Cumberland
and Butts, and then that of Hayley; later, the humiliating
dependence, with the drawings for Blair's poem *The Grave*,
on men like Cromek, who told him: 'I had to battle with a
man who had predetermined not to be served. What public
reputation you have, the reputation of eccentricity excepted,
I have acquired for you'; then: 'Tuesday, Janry 20, 1807,
between Two & Seven in the Evening — Despair'; after this,
years of isolation, neglect, failure and poverty, until the last
years and the almost adulatory friendship of the young
painters who called themselves 'The Ancients'.

Between 1789 and 1795, Blake completed over two
hundred engravings and etchings on his own account, including his 'illuminated books', and eighty-seven for other
publishers, some designed by other artists. From 1796 to
1827 — a period five times as long as the earlier period —
he completed only 172 engravings and works on his own
account (though this includes *Milton*, the *Job* engravings,
Jerusalem and the Dante illustrations), and over 250 for
other publishers and for patrons. Blake's career was a
perpetual struggle to become independent of entrepreneurs,
booksellers and patrons, with brief moments in which he
could create his 'own' system. For the republican artist,
artistic 'freedom' was not an abstraction, but an active, day-
to-day struggle, in which the prison and the workhouse
could, at times, seem dangerously near. The difference
between working for the king and 'working for oneself' was a
cleavage between two ways of life, two opposed ways of
looking at the world, and two fundamentally opposed visual
ideologies. Blake wrote in his copy of Reynolds's *Discourses:*

The Enquiry in England is not whether a Man has Talents
& Genius, But whether he is Passive & Polite & a Virtuous
Ass & obedient to Noblemen's Opinions in Art & Science.
If he is, he is a Good Man. If Not, he must be Starved.

'Republican Art', by definition, cannot collaborate with this
system: it has to struggle against it.

The ideal petty-bourgeois republic is a world without kings, noblemen, rich merchants, monopolists, priests, landowners and capitalists; it is a world purified of luxury and corruption, and is hence an egalitarian, democratic society, one in which no single group, such as chartered corporations, can usurp political power or corner large markets. Here, ideal market conditions — that is, from the point of view of the small producers — prevail; exchanges are not only *equal*, but are carried out *between* equals. Indeed, equal exchange is only possible between equals, because where on the one side a Boydell, say,[53] or a Cromek can dictate the price and cheat the small engraver, on the other side inequality persists. Yet, paradoxically, imaginative creation is only possible when the 'devourer' absorbs the fruits of the 'prolific', of those who create to excess: not everyone can be a prolific producer. Moreover, even the small traders and producers must make profits.

When Reynolds wrote: 'To give advice to those who are contending for royal liberality, has been for some years the duty of my station in the Academy', Blake replied: 'Liberality! we want not Liberality. We want a Fair Price & Proportionate Value & a General Demand for Art.' Competing against powerful commercial interests and those who in the artistic sphere had made the fashionable exhibition their lucrative market place, Blake (who mounted an abortive one-man exhibition in 1809) could only protest: 'The Rich Men of England form themselves into a Society to Sell & Not to Buy Pictures. The Artist who does not throw his Contempt on such Trading Exhibitions, does not know either his own Interest or his Duty.' Petty-bourgeois 'Republican Art' serves an ideal, not monopolistic interests.

Yet the actual republics that had emerged between the fifteenth and late eighteenth centuries had all been of relatively short duration, and within these, the power of the petty bourgeoisie had been even more transient and precarious. Examples are the Florentine Republic of 1494 (of which Michelangelo's *David* is the lasting symbol), the Dutch Republic of the early seventeenth century, the period of Leveller supremacy followed by Cromwell's dictatorship at the end of the Civil War in England, and the Jacobin

Republic in France (1792-94). All four found their reflection in artistic production. In the Netherlands, a new visual genre arose: the realistic, naturalistic landscape. Since this seems to go against the conception of 'Republican Art' held by Blake and others, it is to this that we shall now turn.

The question that needs to be settled is the status of the naturalistic landscape as a genre expressing the visual ideology of a patriotic, and, in the Netherlands, republican bourgeoisie. Blake showed little or no interest in landscape painting: his only 'landscapes' are his woodcut illustrations to Thornton's *Virgil* (which inspired Samuel Palmer), and a few pencil sketches done during his stay at Felpham, while the landscape that forms the background to his Bible illustration, *The Christ Child Asleep on the Cross*, done in tempera, is deliberately barred from view by a strange wooden construction. Why was there this apparent split within contemporary English art — that is, between the anthropocentric or neoclassic, and the topographical? And why should the realist landscape, from its relatively humble position in the eighteenth century, become the dominant genre in England?

One clue, I think, lies in the development of the Dutch realist landscape in the seventeenth century. Having waged a long struggle to free their land from Hapsburg domination, the republican stadtholders and bourgeoisie of the Low Countries found in landscapes and coastal seascapes the perfect expression for the patriotic possession of their land: 'land' thus becomes the semiotic sign for 'nation'. Secondly, the viewpoint is always earth-bound: what is depicted on the two-dimensional canvas is how the landscape *actually appears* to an individual, independent observer. The discovery of linear perspective and of vanishing points is utilised to create the illusion of an outdoor world perceived by an individual observer standing on *terra firma*. (Dutch indoor scenes do not have the same *patriotic* significance, but bourgeois interiors are a perfect complement to landscapes: the latter show us how the bourgeoisie perceived the external world, the former show us how they perceived *themselves*.) In these small Dutch landscapes, designed for sober bourgeois homes, distant objects — a ship, a tree, or a figure on the horizon — may be indicated by the merest flick of the brush, which the connoisseur could appreciate and admire. This introduces the third element: the connoisseur, without whom such a development in picture production could not have taken place. (The 'cunning sure' was an important figure, too, in the late eighteenth-century London print market — where *landscape* was one of the main genres.) The fourth element is the existence of the art market itself. Pictures had become exchangeable commodities, appraised by connoisseurs, designed for the homes of the Dutch bourgeoisie, reflecting its individualistic viewpoint, and re-creating, through illusionistic naturalism, a three-dimensional world of which the bourgeois individual is himself the master.

The English landscape — in Gainsborough, for example — had one function similar to that of the Dutch landscape, in that it connoted *land-ownership* through skilful visual appropriation, and the political dominance of a certain class. This class was the aristocracy and landed gentry, who could be depicted as proud possessors of their landed estates, as in *Mr and Mrs Andrews* (1748). Later, however, landed property became more and more that of the capitalist farmer, who had enclosed his fields and employed agricultural wage labourers to do the work of tilling, planting and harvesting. The expropriation of the small farmer as a result of the enclosures, his reduction to the level of tenant farmer and then to that of agricultural labourer with the consequent decay of village life and transformation of the traditional English countryside was a process too well known (cf. Goldsmith's *The Deserted Village*, Crabbe and Clare) to make landscape a genre with those overtones of patriotic liberation and bourgeois republicanism which it had had for the Dutch realists of the seventeenth century. Hence the almost total lack of interest in real (i.e. *contemporary* and *topographical*) landscapes on the part of radical, republican artists such as Mortimer, Barry and Blake. Landscape, as a genre, was, it seems, too loaded, too much the property of an exploiting class, and thus provided scant opportunity for the development of suitable semiotic-ideological material. What, then, of Stubbs, Joseph Wright, Turner and Constable?

There is at least one painting by Stubbs that suggests a 'critical visual ideology'. This is *The Reapers* (1783), where the black-coated farmer-overseer on his solid shire horse earns an expression of resentful yet contained antagonism from one of his labourers, while the sheaf-bearing woman keeps to a tight-lipped non-involvement. Morland's rural scenes have a certain amount of critical realism in them, as well as sentimental idealisation. A landscape such as Wright's *Arkwright's Cotton Mills at Night* (1783) is the fascinating and sympathetic record of a changed landscape brought about by the new industrial manufacturers. Arkwright's mill *belongs* in this Derbyshire landscape: the factory has become an integral feature of the English countryside. Through a peculiar and complex series of interactions, landscape becomes the genre *par excellence* that expresses the *class compromise between the industrial bourgeoisie and the traditional landed gentry*. This, in a nutshell, is its 'Englishness'. It thus carries with it a far greater consensus than any other genre. The contradictions it contains are manifold, yet all these seem capable of being worked out within the genre itself. If there is a point at which landscapes cease to express an idea of 'England', it is in those lonely, special places — 'landscapes of the soul' — where the painter has tried to escape from 'man' altogether, or, of course, in non-English or exotic landscapes. This, frequently, is where the socially alienated, subjective element (which is also seen in the stylistic transformations of late Turner and Constable) predominates over the objective, to the extent that any idea of the land as 'nation' or 'country' has almost disappeared. (*Sea*scapes, it should be noted, are as typical of an island nation as landscapes.) Nevertheless, such is the strength of the genre, that even isolated, empty, or geographically 'marginal' scenes, such as deserted coastlines, moors and the like, which serve to express, perhaps, the artist's mood of meditative gloom and personal alienation, also become 'English' through a kind of ideological — or rather visual-ideological — recuperation.

The importance of Wright (1739-97) and Stubbs (1724-1806) lies in a scrupulous concern for objective, scientific truth, an empirical rigour that binds them ideologically to the

Birmingham Lunar Society and to industrial patrons such as Arkwright and Wedgwood. Both painters were 'natural philosophers': Stubbs, the son of a tanner, carried out anatomical studies of horses, while the problem of light was, for Wright, the subject of ceaseless experiment. Experimental enquiry into the exact forms, structures and behaviour of natural phenomena links Wright and Stubbs not only to the empirical, scientific outlook of the new industrial bourgeoisie, but to Turner and Constable. The artist who dissected horses in his house in Lincolnshire, and was concerned to 'look into Nature for himself and consult and *study her only*',[54] had something in common with the painter who (so runs the story) tied himself to a ship's mast in a storm, the better to record his experience on canvas; likewise, the painstaking researches into the precise effects of artificial light made by Wright came from that same desire to *know, grasp* and *re-create* the external visible world that made Constable take his easel outdoors in order to capture, on canvas, and for the first time, the airy brightness and freshness of an English summer's day.

Blake, as we know, found that natural objects deadened inspiration in him, and hated (perhaps from his Royal Academy days) the idea of dissecting or anatomising anything. His art remained that of the engraver's desk and the printing press. 'The nature of my work,' he wrote in *A Vision of the Last Judgement* (1810), 'is Visionary or Imaginative; it is an Endeavour to Restore what the Ancients call'd the Golden Age'. Whereas Wright, Stubbs, Turner and Constable — whose work chronologically overlaps that of Blake — fastened themselves to an external, empirical reality, Blake could not. His art looked 'within', or fed on symbolic archetypes and artistic precedent. How far Blake departed from an empiricist outlook can be seen in this letter to Butts (11 September 1801):

I labour incessantly to accomplish not one half of what I intend, because my Abstract folly hurries me often away while I am at work, carrying me over Mountains & Valleys, which are not Real, in a Land of Abstraction where Spectres of the Dead wander. This I endeavour to prevent

& with my whole might chain my feet to the world of Duty & Reality; but in vain! the faster I bind, the better is the Ballast, for I, so far from being bound down, take the world with me in my flights, & often it seems lighter than a ball of wool rolled by the wind.

This seems to have been a recurrent experience. It is not just 'daydreaming'; nowhere in Blake are 'Mountains & Valleys' ever real. The world he inhabits is, to some extent, the world of the uprooted and the dispossessed, a world of dreams and visions, of lost inheritances, ideal republics and New Jerusalems. While the complacent, empiricist bourgeois mocked (and mocks) such art as 'madness', it shows us the other side of capitalist 'progress', which, as I have argued, found its expression (in some ways, paradoxically) in the development of English landscape. And — we must never forget — it was no less positive, and involved just as much of a struggle with form and content, as did 'empirical' art.

The particular ideology characteristic of the English bourgeoisie is empiricism: that is, knowledge of the world based on evidence provided by the sense impressions, where reality is seen from the viewpoint of the individual, analytical observer — of the analyst who, having concretely analysed, then synthesises. Within the field of picture production, landscape became the genre most successfully developed in England in the late eighteenth and early nineteenth centuries, both because it mirrored the historic class compromise referred to, and because it allowed for the rigorous exploration of individual empirical experience in a way that no other genre could. In Wright and Stubbs, there is a careful, analytical control over what is being observed and how it is represented. In Turner and Constable, however, there is a greater preparedness to take *risks*, to *experience* rather than simply observe, conveying the emotional depth of that experience in a wider variety of brushstrokes and ways of applying pigment, from the generous and the heavily built-up, to the sweeping and poignantly flickering. Wright and Stubbs belong to an age of improving farmers and first-generation manufacturers, whose mills and factories were still rural landmarks; Turner and Constable belong to the era of rapid urban-industrial expansion. The former reveal a more embryonic vision, whereas the elemental seascapes, sunsets, stormy skies, clouds and rocky landscapes of Turner, though dwarfing man and threatening to engulf him, show a *greater* confidence in man's ability to survive, master, and understand nature, since nature's elemental power has, after all, been successfully caught by the artist on his vast two-dimensional canvas. Thus with Turner the capacity to transcend our limitations incites us, *dares* us even, to become participants in a wider drama, to explore and experience the world to the full. The viewpoint here is that of the progressive liberal bourgeoisie, conquering new worlds. Turner's implied viewer is perhaps not so much the spectator who nostalgically reflects on transient glories, or passively watches the world go by, as an active, sensitive participant-observer who hunts out new areas of experience, and experiences life as a complex, shifting totality.

In the somewhat more claustrophobic world of the radical, republican history painters I have examined in this chapter, 'history' is always *political* or *moral* history. Yet in a sense *all* painters are 'history painters', and it is often not political or moral history, but *social* history — that is, social and economic change — that gives us a deeper sense of what history is all about. Wright's historical vision reveals the bourgeois subject newly emerging from the shell of aristocratic paternalism, as in *A Blacksmith's Shop*, where this new subject is hammering the future on the anvil of the present inside a dark neoclassical ruin that seems to symbolise the old society. In Turner, the old world is a distant castle or an old sailing ship being tugged to her last berth. An acute consciousness of history as the rich meeting of past and future in a momentary, complex present becomes the peculiar vision of the nineteenth-century intelligentsia as a whole. Neoclassical, romantic-classical and 'visionary' art were in a sense incapable of this rich, complex vision. (Those who argue that Turner is just as much a 'visionary' as Blake should not forget that Turner, the colourist and early impressionist 'poet', began as a copier of *nature*, not of Gothic tombs.) Using ideal forms (or ideal forms susceptible to mannerist or expressionist distortion), basing itself on a man-centred view of the world, and holding to an ideal solution to the complex problems posed by history, 'Republican', 'visionary' art was incapable of the kind of development shown by the empirico-scientific, realistic, naturalistic tradition in visual art — in particular, that of English landscape painting. (The *strength* of this landscape tradition is seen in two of Blake's immediate followers, Samuel Palmer and Edward Calvert — the latter an engraver. In both, imaginative visions assumed the form of ideal, visionary landscapes.) The modernist reaction against realism and representational art, the return to non-naturalistic modes, and hence the rediscovery of artists such as Blake, should not blind us as to where, in the period we have been discussing, the dominant tendencies lay.

9

Blake's Visual Art

In discussing the work of any artist, there is always a need to distinguish between artistic achievement and ideological outlook. Art, in other words, is not the same as ideology. If by 'visual ideology' is meant simply the mechanical, visual 'filling in' of a space already cleared by previously existing ideas, then art is nothing more than the humble follower of ideology. Rather, we should recognise that visual ideas have their own life and concreteness, a life and concreteness that can never be predicted in advance of their artistic realisation. Blake's art has *transcended* the historical conditions within which it was produced. If the artistic 'vision' was based on an illusion, there remains an essential element of truth and necessity in the illusion.

The transcendent power of art − its power to move and excite those who are far removed from the original artist both in time and space − might, on the face of it, seem a strong argument against a historical-materialist approach, supporting the view that the only way to account for art's transcendent qualities is to speak in terms of an unhistorical World of Art, of creative works that are expressions not of this or that moment in historical development, but of some transcendent Human Spirit. Unfortunately, these resounding phrases are rarely applied to humbler human artefacts such as the wheel and the pulley. Yet these have just as surely 'transcended' the functions they served for their original inventors and creators as have Homer's *Odyssey* and the sculptures of Praxiteles. Any work of art that trancends its original context does, of course, eventually belong to humanity as a whole, just as any invention or scientific discovery comes to belong to mankind in general rather than to the inventor or discoverer, or the society or nation that produced it.

Yet art, because it is *more* particularised, *more* concrete, and *more* specific to a particular culture than a scientific law or an invention, is much *less* universal, and therefore more local than science. Many would dispute this, of course, and argue that certain archetypal themes, narratives, myths, symbols, etc. are found in a wide variety of cultures and at different epochs. Yet if we regard art forms as *specific combinations* of formal and thematic elements, all of which are necessary to that particular art form — whether this be an Elizabethan tragedy, an Indian temple relief, or the Beni and Mganda dances of East and Central Africa — then the particularised, cultural-specific nature of all art forms is borne out. Art is limited by language, by cultural and religious values, beliefs and customs, and by the specific codes it uses and manipulates. Works of art are therefore *bearers of their implied social contexts*, transmitting these to future or other contexts as something qualitative and difficult to define, as one mark of their uniqueness, individuality, and sensuous life. ('Social context' can imply one of two things: implicit *support* for existing social relations, or a desire to transform them.) But uniqueness, individuality and sensuous life do not belong to the work of art as an unchangeable inner essence, though this might appear to be the case to those who reify works of art as discrete, observable objects. On the contrary, these qualities come to life in the active *relation* between text and reader, picture and viewer, musical sound and listener, a relation that is not fixed, but is always subject to historical change.

If, as I have suggested, the particularised, the sensuous and the 'universal-in-the-local' are at one level the way a work of art carries within itself the implied reproduction of certain social relations or a struggle to transform those relations (i.e. the 'implied social context') then at another level these qualities are the concretely realised, artistic shape which specific, 'practical-sensuous activity' has made in the effort to master nature and understand the world. As Brecht puts it: 'What the spectator . . . enjoys about art is the making of art, the active creative element. In art we view nature herself as if she were an artist'.[1] Where existing forms need to be transcended, as in the case of Romantic art, artistic creation requires the discovery of *new*, unprecedented yet intelligible coherences. The artist must apply skill and knowledge — including 'scientific' knowledge — in engaging with his 'raw materials' — namely, emotions and feelings, human behaviour, memories etc. as well as images, sounds and language. A work of art thus has two sides: it both implies the social and cultural context in which (and class or classes *for* which) it was produced, and it also embodies the human struggle to create and revolutionise *form*, to give an intelligible shape to reality.

How is this discussion relevant to an objective evaluation of Blake's visual art? It should prevent us from classifying Blake's art as 'visionary', 'mystical', 'idealist', 'other-worldly', etc. if this implies that his 'visionary art' did not require just as much knowledge, skill and effort to master the visual medium as an art based on naturalist or realist principles. Naturalism copies the empirically observable, then composes it. Visionary or conceptual art looks for *essential structures*, thereby de-familiarising what the habituated eye perceives as an observable reality.

Secondly, Blake is one of the most notable *technical innovators* in the history of art. His technical innovations were part of a rebellion against the artistic dominance of the aristocracy and commercial bourgeoisie. It involved a struggle to transform the relations of artistic production in favour of the creative artisan. Blake's invention of the 'illuminated book' (where text and illustration are etched together on the same plate), and the colour print, were technical innovations whose real driving force was the historic need to transform the conditions within which art was produced. This is part of the revolutionary nature of Blake's art. It goes beyond that art which, while showing 'commitment' to revolutionary or progressive causes, as with Romney's 'visionary' art, fails to show how the existing production apparatus can itself be transformed. Walter Benjamin's remarks on Brecht are relevant here:

Brecht has coined the phrase 'functional transformation' (*Umfunktionierung*) to describe the transformation of forms and instruments of production by a progressive intelligentsia — all intelligentsia interested in liberating the means of production and hence active in the class struggle. He was the first to address to the intellectuals the far-reaching demand that they should not supply the production apparatus without, at the same time, within the limits of the possible, changing that apparatus in the direction of Socialism. 'The publication of the *Versuche*', we read in the author's introduction to the series of texts published under that title, 'marks a point at which certain works are not so much intended to represent individual experiences (i.e. to have the character of finished works) as they are aimed at using (transforming) certain existing institutes and institutions.' It is not spiritual renewal, as the fascists proclaim it, that is desirable; what is proposed is technical innovation.[2]

The core of Benjamin's argument — that literary and artistic production, if it is to challenge the material basis of capitalist society, must visibly challenge the dominant production relations by advancing the *techniques* and *forces* of artistic production — is foreshadowed in the way Blake, as an artist, worked. Blake anticipates in his own way the level of revolutionary transformation demanded by Benjamin — even if his mission was utopian.

One rare attempt at an honest, *critical* evaluation of Blake's visual art has been made by J. R. Harvey in *The Cambridge Quarterly* for March 1977 (Vol. VII, No. 2). Arguing the need for a 'decisive critique', Harvey proceeds to characterise Blake as a reproducer of hard, linear stereotypes. Harvey's bias is extremely illuminating: Blake's relentless concentration and tight grip are *'incapable* of relaxation' (my emphasis); his belief that 'the senses, in so far as they met the real world, were evil', is deemed 'incredible in an artist'; 'his immovable Cordelia-like recusancy' and 'set pertinacity' in adhering to Basire's 'hard and dry' school of line engraving is put down to the 'strain of blinkered dogmatizing of a craftsman who in his apprenticeship was taught by a master to do the manipulations in a certain way, who has found them good,

and who will consider no others (unless he invents them)'.
Blake's 'whole campaign against oils is blind with exagger-
ated bigotry', while the 'stale repeated anatomy' of the
stereotyped figures (patriarch, young man, female) is associated with Blake's 'dogged self-confinement' rather than
expansiveness of vision. Finally, there is a hostility to Blake's
kind of clarity, which is altogether too hard, bare and thin.
Harvey deprecates the absence of shadows and 'atmosphere',
the lack of any 'fig-leaves' and hence of 'velvet pleasures'.
The parallel with the contemporary criticisms made of
David's *Oath of the Horatii*, referred to in the previous
chapter, is surely no accident. Blake's art, for Harvey, is *too*
linear, *too* clear, *too* austere and *too* 'dogmatic' to be com-
fortably accepted: on the contrary, there is something in
it — despite its occasional greatness — that the art-critical
stomach involuntarily throws up (if one is honest about it).
Could this be a sign of this art's continued power to provoke
a consciously intended reaction, and if so what reaction?

Blake's visual art (if we take the 1795 colour prints as our
main point of reference) is *oppositional*; it is a rebellious
art. It is not easily discussed in the standard terms of art
criticism, selecting from the palette of art-critical vocabulary
in order to describe its various effects. With Blake, 'critical
appreciation' of individual pictures often seems irrelevant,
even perverse. So many of his pictures are *saying* or *arguing*
something; they address us, not as passive consumers of
aesthetic objects, but as thinking, responsive, human beings.
As with a Brecht play, a Blake print seems to have been
intended, not for quiet reflection and silent absorption, but
for discussion and argument. (For example, it would seem
that the colour print *Good and Evil Angels* is provoking the
viewer to take sides.) It is frequently a polemical art, melting
down certain issues to their bare essentials, challenging the
viewer to be honest about his responses, and to state clearly
where he stands. So saturated is modern art criticism with
commodity fetishism and the values of the art market, that
this quality of Blake's art is usually missed or misunderstood:
it is assumed that, if all art is 'presenting' something to a
viewer, it won't at the same time hit him with a hammer.
The urgency, intensity and polemical directness of Blake's

visual art is thus usually passed over in favour of something more amenable to academic discourse and 'critical appreciation'.

One problem is the frequent failure to relate the supposed meaning of Blake's pictures to the visual images themselves. Take this, for example, as a 'reading' of an illustration to *The Book of Urizen*, in which three serpent-coiled figures are seen falling headlong down the page: 'Immortals falling into the abyss of time and space created by the materialist philosophy of Bacon, Newton and Locke'.[3] We look again at the illustration, but look in vain. How is it possible to visualise, let alone depict, such an abstract philosophical concept? Although it may be conceded that Blake's art is for the most part illustrative, and thus heavily dependent on his poetry and philosophy, I want to make a case for it as an art that succeeds on its own (i.e. visual) terms. The way visual images (or 'signs') are combined, makes up the primary meaning of any picture. Ideas and concepts in pictures, if they are to be successfully communicated, must be present as *visual* ideas. There has to be a fusion of image and idea. Both should be conveyed simultaneously and, ideally, instantaneously. Otherwise the artist has failed, and the viewer is left with the tedious task of hunting out possible meanings, none of which seem to fit, or which rely on evidence drawn from everywhere except the picture itself.

Blake's illuminated art has been researched by numerous scholars, the most thorough being David Erdman, whose *Illuminated Blake* is a scrupulous revelation of the many meanings and previously unnoticed details to be found in even the smallest corners of Blake's richly varied 'illuminations'. Erdman's microscopic examination and painstaking exegesis warn us against treating Blake's poetry merely as written words on the page: even the etched words themselves, with their varied calligraphy, decorative motifs, coils, tendrils, etc. have a precise visual meaning. Yet while the ingenious explication of symbols and visual puns may have the excitement of a Chinese puzzle or a detective story, and tell us much about the allusively fertile, ever-fluid, symbolist imagination of the artist, in the final analysis it is doubtful whether, after going through the scholarly exegesis, Blake's

visual images really carry all Erdman's meanings, tha
independently of the exegesis — though it is true that
tell their own story rather than serve as mere decoration and
playful illustration.[4] Erdman, and Erdman's Blake, become
almost *too* dependent on each other, like text and image —
or rather like the vine and the tree (symbolic of the loving
child-parent relationship) in *Songs of Innocence.*

It is, then, the free-standing pictures that will mainly
occupy our attention. Yet even those pictures that are
unaccompanied by a written text frequently rely on some
written source, such as some of the 1795 colour prints, the
Dante illustrations and the illustrations to the Bible. That
Blake is not simply an 'illustrator', however, is testified by
the fact that he always re-interprets, and sometimes even
subverts, the meaning of his original text.

What, then, are the main formal and thematic components
of Blake's visual art, and what distinct style or 'visual
ideology' do these comprise? (We must, of course, bear in
mind the limitations of these terms and the fact that Blake's
art passes through more than one style or 'visual ideology'.)
We have been told, for example, that Blake's paintings are
'images not of the world we live in but of the cosmos seen in
the light of Eternity',[5] and again, that his visual art grappled
with the paradox of 'the human form divine', where infinite
energy and radiance are necessarily confined in the bounding
line of Urizenic creation.[6] Such formulae would be justified
if they related, in a *specific* and *concrete* way, to the visual
images and techniques themselves, so that as we perceive
the images, we also 'see' the concepts they embody. That,
at any rate, is our first task. If an idea — however much it
attracts us — is not already 'there' in the image we perceive,
then it remains still unrealised, either in the mind of the artist
or in the mind of the critic, in which case either an artistic
or a critical failure has occurred.

The Human Form Divine

Blake's mature visual art of the 1790s grew out of two
traditions: neoclassicism and Gothic art. In both these
traditions, the human figure occupies a central place, and it

is the one endlessly-repeated, endlessly-explored subject in Blake's art. Whatever else gets into his pictures — a barren landscape, trees, entwining branches, clouds, birds, flames, sheep, or the trilithons of an ancient henge — it is subordinate to, and even imitative of, a central, recurrent image: the human body. Yet despite this often intense preoccupation with the human form, Blake's treatment is non-individualised and stereotyped, deriving from the ideal forms of classical sculpture, Michelangelo and Gothic art. No attempt is made at realistic or individualised characterisation. The human form is treated as a *concrete universal,* through which spiritual meanings can be expressed, using a repertoire of symbolic and expressive postures, gestures, attitudes, hand and foot positions, physiognomies and facial expressions, with additional elements such as scaly skin, serpent-entwined limbs, etc., symbolic spatial relationships between figures (who may be flying, falling, etc.) and a symbolic location (such as under water or under the ground, in clouds, on a rocky seashore, among lambs, in fire, etc.). These basic images and thematic contrasts are boldly delineated (going against the current demands of 'taste' in painting and engraving) but are by no means confined in a series of 'stale' repetitions, as Harvey alleges. On the contrary, it is the small variations — Blake's 'minute particulars' — that acquire particular importance within this symbolic code. Precedents for this code are to be found in the 'body language' and symbolic hand and finger positions of the deities represented in Indian and Tibetan art, in Christian iconography, medieval illuminated manuscripts, alchemical texts and traditional emblem books. Lack of individual characterisation, stereotyping and emphasis on nudity force our attention on — in other words, *foreground* — the basic symbolism and symbolic variations.

The young, energetic male nude is one familiar Blakean stereotype. Freed of clothing (symbolic of temporal and social constraints), he becomes the *idée fixe* of republican humanism, yet only once — in the colour print *Albion Rose* — does this 'young man' stereotype exhibit complete fulfilment and acceptance, the result of total liberation. In *America, a Prophecy* (1793) the young man (now Orc) is seen chained and spread-eagled on a rock (Plate 1); then striving with both arms to raise himself out of the root-filled, furrowed earth (Plate 2); or risen, with his chains broken yet still trailing (Plate 3); then sitting, legs wide apart, on a skeletal corpse (which, Erdman suggests, is the young man's 'dead self')[7] and looking up into the sky (Plate 6), and again, rising on one leg (the left foot flexed) with arms outstretched, among rebellious flames (Plate 10).

The 'contrary' of this stereotype is Orc's aged adversary, Urizen, a bearded, cloaked patriarch (deriving in part from Michelangelo's God on the Sistine ceiling, Romney's hovering divinity in *The Spirit of God Floating Over Chaos*, and Barry's Lear in *King Lear Weeping over the Dead Body of Cordelia*). In *America* Urizen is George III. He appears in Plate 8, with arms extended, kneeling, with one leg raised, in a posture very similar to that of Orc in flames two plates later. The similarity stresses an antithetical unity of opposites, so that our attention is forced on the significant differences: whereas Urizen is clothed, Orc is naked; Urizen is up above in vague, oppressive, heavy clouds (symbolising doubt and reason), Orc is down below in spear-like, swirling, revolutionary flames: Orc's left foot is posed for ascent, Urizen's sandalled right foot is flat on the 'ground'. But the most telling difference, and it is a clue to Blake's whole method, lies in the hands (after the face, the most expressive part of the human body). Urizen's hands, the fingers closed, rest on the top edge of his cloudy domain, and suggest, when seen with his calm, impassive expression, a kind of dead, uncreative *possession*. Orc's hands, however, have the expressive beauty and life of a pianist's or potter's hands; they are alive, taut and muscular. They do not hold on, like Urizen's, but *feel*. Orc has to climb, rise, create; Urizen simply wishes to remain where he is, and things to remain as they are.

The positions of arms, hands and feet, therefore, carry an abundance of dramatic and symbolic meanings. The slightest difference or variation implies a change of meaning, in which character, actions and intentions are minutely discriminated:

> I intreat, then, that the Spectator will attend to the Hands & Feet, to the Lineaments of the Countenances; they are

all descriptive of Character, & not a line is drawn without intention, & that most discriminate & particular.[8]

Such an art, like Brecht's 'epic theatre' is, in Benjamin's phrase, essentially *gestural*. The gesture reveals its meanings at the instant of capture; when the instant is frozen, the meaning is preserved.

One recurrent motif is arms horizontally outstretched. When the palms face outwards (one 'east', one 'west'), and closed fingers are pointing up, it may signify pushing away or resisting, an attempt to free oneself, or keep things or people apart. If the fingers, one or two slightly bent, are horizontally extended, with palms facing down, this may mean searching or groping: thus the manacled Evil Angel in *Good and Evil Angels* (1795) blindly gropes his way out of the flames into the Good Angel's domain. But if the fingers incline down, are firmly closed, and belong to Blake's hovering, bearded patriarch, then this signifies an ironic, oppressive 'protection', counselling suffering mankind to remain obedient, as in *The Lazar House*, where Death's punitive arrows dart from the apparently blind divinity's hands:

> And over them triumphant Death his Dart
> Shook, but delaid to strike, though oft invok't
> With vows, as their chief good, and final hope.
>
> *Paradise Lost*, Bk XI, 11. 491-3

Thel's outstretched arms (her back is turned to the viewer) in *Thel and the Worm* (from *The Book of Thel*, Plate 4) obviously signify astonishment, but a very similar gesture, seen frontally, in *Christ the Mediator* (one of the biblical series for Butts), signifies moderation, loving peace and protection, and is, of course, the archetypal gesture of Christian forgiveness and sacrifice.[9] When the fingers are pointing down (palms still facing outwards or 'east-west'), this signifies acceptance, either generous, fully conscious and fulfilling as in *Albion Rose* (where the thumb position is anatomically impossible), selfhood-annihilating and traumatic, as in Plate 32 of *Milton*, where the divine imagination, as Milton's falling star, now enters Blake (whose head and torso are bent right back), or worshipping, as in Plate 76 of *Jerusalem*, where Albion looks up at the crucified Jesus in the same posture as Albion in *Albion Rose*, only reversed.

A series of 'minutely discriminated', stylised gestures and postures, showing dramatic moments, power relationships, spiritual 'states', and 'character', forms, therefore, the basis of Blake's expressive and symbolic visual code. This reliance on symbolic gestures and postures is by no means peculiar to Blake. It is, in fact, easy to read once the basic 'alphabet' and 'syntax' have been mastered; it draws on rich sources, and is also a key element in popular forms such as mime and the mimetic dance, ritualistic and popular theatre, and melodrama. The depiction of stylised postures, gestures and facial expressions is in fact a very *dramatic* form of visual representation. It serves to show different feelings, states, actions and responses – from cowed horror, prostrate helplessness and 'folded up' despair, to shame, grief, ecstasy or hope, from begging and imploring to groping and tenderly pitying, from the loving embrace to the possessive grip, from rebellion and defiance to tyrannical repression, from the misery of long imprisonment to the delight of swift release. Such a technique should, in fact, be part of any actor's 'tool kit'. Remove some of its 'strangeness' (such as deliberate anatomical and facial distortion, flying and hovering figures, symbolic seascapes and landscapes, etc.) and Blake's 'postural', 'gestural' code suddenly becomes very familiar. (Thus defamiliarisation may bring us back to what we already know, yet were not fully conscious of.)

Nudity is an integral component of Blake's vision of the human form, but his interest is not anatomical (as it was for Renaissance artists), but rather philosophic. Nudity represents, at one level, the *essential Man* that is revealed once perception has been 'cleansed'. However, when the senses have been dulled by routine, the familiar and the everyday, it is not the 'visionary imagination' of itself that is the greatest cleanser, but its stimulant – revolutionary change. The revolutionary movement in the late eighteenth century, by seeking to 'cleanse' society of corrupt, obsolete and reactionary institutions – both political and social – offered the possibility of a freed, 'cleansed' humanity, an essential, undisguised human dignity. Humanity's *worst* sides, however, were also exposed as never before. Hence Burke's complaint in his *Reflections*:

> All the pleasing illusions, which made power gentle and obedience liberal, which harmonised the different shades of life, and which, by a bland assimilation incorporated into politics the sentiments which beautify and soften private society, are to be dissolved by this new conquering empire of light and reason. All the decent drapery of life is to be rudely torn off. All the superadded ideas, furnished from the wardrobe of a moral imagination, which the heart owns and the understanding ratifies as necessary to cover the defects of our naked, shivering human nature, and to raise it to dignity in our own estimation, are to be exploded as ridiculous, absurd, and antiquated fashion.

Pleasing illusions that harmonise the 'different shades of life' are preferred to the raking light of reason. Sinful man needs 'decent drapery' to cover his nakedness; that is, the 'super-added' idea of a mythical social harmony that idealises inequalities and covers class contradictions. The visual aesthetic implied here is the antithesis of Blake's. The male nudes of Praxiteles and Michelangelo suddenly find themselves supporting the French Third Estate. The naked human form in Blake is not a fixed ideal, divorced from reality, but contains its own contraries, whose dialectical opposition is conveyed through the variations and 'minute particulars' of Blake's visual code.

Nudity in Blake is hence not one thing, but different things. According to Christian tradition, there were in fact four kinds of nudity: *nuditas naturalis*, man's natural state (which, in pictures of the Virgin and child, the Son of Man has entered); *nuditas temporalis*, signifying lack of worldly goods and possessions (symbolised in pictures of St Jerome); *nuditas virtualis*, symbolic of purity and innocence (see in Adam and Eve before the Fall); and a fourth kind, *nuditas criminalis*, symbolic of criminal guilt (seen in Adam and Eve after the Fall, when they try to cover their nakedness).

Nuditas criminalis is seen in Blake's colour print *Nebuchadnezzar* (Plate 24 of *The Marriage of Heaven and*

Hell, and subsequently a colour print), where the naked tyrant's descent to the level of a crawling animal with claws is dramatically exposed, as if by a spotlight. Criminal guilt is also the subject of *The Body of Abel*, in which Cain holds his head in guilty horror as he tries to flee the place of murder. Blake has lengthened Cain's right leg, which cannot, it seems, free itself from a newly-dug grave, beside which there lies a spade. (Cain already has 'one foot in the grave'.) Behind the grave are Adam and Eve, Adam horror-struck, holding his arms in an earth-spurning (palms down) gesture, Eve with her head exaggeratedly bent, exposing her long neck, her arms limp and her hair falling, in a stylised posture very similar to that in one of Fuseli's drawings. The dark clouds, the huge sun and the black mountains contribute to the surreal, psychic quality of this picture. When Blake wrote in later life that 'Art can never exist without Naked Beauty displayed', he should have remembered that one of his aims had been to *expose* as well as to 'display'.

The Light of Eternity

If, as David Bindman says, Blake's paintings are not 'images of the world we live in', but constitute 'Visions of Eternity', then they must still employ an appropriate visual language, one which we, as humble inhabitants of 'this' world, must be able to read. How are 'Eternal', 'visionary' concepts made concretely visible? To answer this question is not simply to dabble in misty rhetoric, but involves the whole question of visual ideology and visual technique.

Any art that relies for its effects not on verisimilitude — that is, on an adherence to physical likenesses — but on 'spiritual' meanings and symbolic truths, must somehow guide the viewer towards those spiritual meanings and symbolic truths by stressing the 'spiritual' and symbolic nature of what it is we actually see. The art of the Pre-Raphaelites, despite its frequent religiosity, and sometimes elaborate spiritual symbolism (e.g. Rossetti), notoriously fails in this respect: 'the world we live in', glamorised in gaudy, sickly colours and rich, super-naturalistic detail, is all too luxuriously and sensuously present. How then did Blake translate his 'eternal visions' into concrete, visual images? The answer, in a phrase, is by trying to overturn a 400-year-old tradition in Western art. More than a hundred years before the modernist reaction against classical (i.e. Euclidian/Newtonian) concepts of space and empiricist views of reality (i.e. the systematic perception of external phenomena from a single perspectival viewpoint), Blake consciously reacted against naturalistic illusionism.

As a producer of visual signs, working in a particular social and historical context, Blake came to develop a visual language that addressed the needs and reflected the outlook of the radicalised petty bourgeoisie and artisan classes. This led to a rejection of the whole illusionistic tradition, which was seen to sanction the *status quo* by creating 'natural-seeming', solid masses and spatial volumes, and thus mirroring a material reality that was acceptable to the dominant classes. There is, of course, a historical reason for this — that the historical crisis precipitated an artistic one — but for the moment, we shall examine the problem in artistic terms.

For 'reality' to be seen at all, there must be a light or light of some kind. Any realistic representation of external reality must, therefore, imply or demonstrate illumination from a known physical source, such as sunlight, moonlight, fire, or artificial light. A 'spiritual' representation, on the other hand, is the representation of a reality perceived by the light of eternal or divine truth, or by some inner light. Religious radicals in Blake's London, who believed that the light of divine truth was immanent and therefore within man, hence radiant and omnipresent (rather than simply sent from above) — a light that one could perceive directly, here and now, without the help of some interfering priesthood — would have been impressed by a pictorial language that could translate such an idea into a concrete image, which would then take on its *own* life as a *visual idea*. Success or failure in translating the metaphor of 'eternal light' (that is, eternal *truth*) into concrete visual terms would be judged, at one level, by the artist's handling of light.

Blake does not entirely abandon chiaroscuro (i.e. light and shade) as Flaxman does in his drawings, but his handling of light subverts the whole post-Renaissance tradition of plastic modelling and perspectival depth. Instead of indicating a recessional, three-dimensional space (as for example in a Vermeer interior, where daylight floods in through a side window), Blake's lighting is nearly always *frontal*. This, together with the elimination of a receding background, helps to *foreground* everything in the picture, reducing physical volume, distance and depth, and bringing everything up close to the viewer's eyes. (J. R. Harvey's view that Blake is 'incapable of relaxation' and that his art denies us 'velvet pleasures' may be connected to the fact that frontal illumination is often hard and intense, and emphasises the flat picture surface.) Instead of giving weight and solidity to his figures, Blake's frontal lighting 'spiritualises' them; it simply lays them across a flat surface, just as a camera flashlight, by suddenly catching a naked figure, say, in a flood of illumination, reduces the figure's visible mass and volume by eliminating shadows caused by vertical or side lighting, and leaves the barest elements of shading as the outline itself. a bold frontal illumination (even accounting for internal, muscular lines and shading) not only flattens the surfaces of the body, face and limbs, but also fixes the figure as an outline.

The 'flashlight' effect creates a 'thisness' or permanence, a kind of instantaneous, eternal *present* — what Blake called a 'vision of the Eternal Now'. The effect of a single, instantaneous image is also conveyed by Blake's use of colour. Unlike oils, water colours run. Not only is the possible range of pigment smaller, but the resultant surface texture is thinner, has less body, and is more evenly spread. Blake frequently exploits a restricted number, or a narrow prismatic range, of colours — for example, from whitish yellow, to yellowish brown, to sombre russet, to subtle touches of rust red (sometimes like dried blood) — in order to fix each composition as a single, homogeneous vision. Subtlety of colour and texture, and the use of strong frontal illumination, produce an effect of feathery, at times ethereal lightness, anchored down by the firm outlines and linear rhythms. The flesh of Blake's figures often has a limpid pallor, done with a light wash, as in *Death on a Pale Horse*, where the upper horse and the angel with the scroll — both frontally lit — are identically coloured, so that the eye moves automatically, without adjustment, from one to the other. This reinforces the impression that they belong to the same frontal picture plane. The dark areas serve mainly as a tonal contrast, since there are no points of reference to indicate a receding background. Thus foreground is all. Such pictures have, in a sense, no temporal dimension, since they lack depth and distance (space and time always being associated in our minds). Because there is so little spatial depth for the viewer to look into or withdraw from, we are forced to take in everything at once. Where there is no hierarchy of 'large, distinct and close to', and 'small, indistinct, and far away', the eye is unable to rest, relax, or focus at leisure. We are locked into a reciprocal gaze as the picture stares back at us with its own light, its own truth.

'Representation' thus turns into assertive argument. We cannot 'enter' the picture space, but are confronted with its entire surface. All parts of the picture surface are not, of course, equally *illuminated*, since there is always *some* depth and *some* chiaroscuro; but those parts that are most brightly lit may leap out at us with a light that has no visible natural source. Hence the light that is not merely reflected, but seems to *radiate* from the muscular torso of the sacrificial victim being stoned to death by the brown-cloaked, Mosaic executioners in *The Stoning of Achan* (*c*. 1800), shines back at the viewer with an accusatory challenge, forcing him to acknowledge the human body's divine light which, as a naked 'human form divine', the viewer himself sends out (perhaps illuminating the world), yet too often tries to subdue or turn away from when that light returns.

In the 1795 colour print *Nebuchadnezzar* the lighting has another function. The Babylonian king is shown crawling on all fours before a thatched byre, his finger-nails and toe-nails having turned into claws, and his arms looking more like an animal's forelegs. With furrowed brow, wild-eyed stare, terrified fleshy nostrils and square, open mouth, he looks round at the viewer aghast, in sudden terror, like some guilty creature caught in dazzling headlights. The light source in this picture defies a simple naturalistic explanation:

at first, it seems to come from above, falling on Nebuchad-nezzar's back, shoulder and the top of his right leg, leaving the lower half of his body in shadow, as if God's all-judging, heavenly light had flashed into the moral darkness below. However, strong highlights on Nebuchadnezzar's face and right arm (which should be partly in the shade) indicate another light source — from the direction of the viewer. It is *this* light that has caused the degraded monarch to turn round, thus making the viewer, in effect, the cause of the king's surprise and fear. It is *we* who have surprised the earth-bound king, as he crawls by night on his bestial, furtive mission.

In contrast to the antinomian radicalism of the 1795 colour prints, the watercolour illustrations to the Bible done for Thomas Butts between 1800 and 1809 belong to a more orthodox, Christian visual ideology, marked by a greater use of illusionistic effects. The eight illustrations done around 1805 depicting the crucifixion, entombment and resurrec-tion of Christ, evoke religious mystery and holiness, and suggest a 'passive attitude towards life with devotional con-templation and abandonment of the will' (OED) characteristic of quietism. Seven of these pictures are night scenes, and make use of strong chiaroscuro effects, a somewhat static symmetry and subdued facial expressions. As night scenes (in one a candle is actually a source of illumination) they can be compared to previous examples of the genre, notably those paintings belonging to the so-called 'candlelight' tradition.

Pious devotion and contemplation — though of an earthly rather than mystical kind — is expressed in the candlelight scenes of the seventeenth-century painter Georges de La Tour, which are precisely observed studies of the effect of a single light source on a human face or faces, such as the repentant Magdalen, Joseph, or the madonna-like mother in *The Newborn Child*. The dominant mood in La Tour is one of meditative introspection, private reverie and nocturnal intimacy. The visual ideology is essentially a progressive, early bourgeois naturalism.

In his 1805 series Blake exploits some of the chiaroscuro effects of the 'night scene' and the candlelight tradition for non-naturalistic ends. The most dramatic example is *The Angel Rolling the Stone away from the Sepulchre*, where the body of the retreating angel is itself a mysterious, glowing source of light. The non-naturalistic intention is demonstrated by the fact that whereas the angel's back is illuminated, the backs of his wings are in the shade. The faces of the two symmetrically-placed angels on either side are lit as if by candlelight, except that there is no candle, only the rising figure of Christ beneath them. In *The Entombment*, Mary holds a candle (which is in the dead centre of a symmetrical composition); thus her face, which looks down, is suitably lit. But so, non-naturalistically, are the faces of all the other figures. In another night scene, *The Soldiers Casting Lots for Christ's Garments*, light glows symbolically from Christ on the cross, which we see from behind. The back of the cross is in shade, but the dice-playing soldiers in the foreground are frontally illuminated in the typical Blakean manner. Another pen and watercolour done for Butts in 1805, *The Parable of the Wise and Foolish Virgins*, likewise cheats the eye accustomed to naturalistic lighting. In the distance, dawn is breaking over black hills, but the figures in the foreground are frontally illuminated. The five lit lamps of the wise virgins seem, at first glance, to be responsible for their glowing garments and serenely bright faces, but this cannot be so, according to empirical laws. By defying naturalistic explanations, the spiritual meaning of the parable is emphasised: the oiled lamps symbolise a glowing inner faith and preparedness for heaven.

Determinate Outline

A Spirit and a Vision are not, as the modern philosophy supposes, a cloudy vapour, or a nothing: they are organised and minutely articulated beyond all that the mortal and perishing nature can produce. He who does not imagine in stronger and better lineaments, and in stronger and better light than his perishing and mortal eye can see, does not imagine at all. (*A Descriptive Catalogue*, 1809)

Such art of losing the outlines is the art of Venice and Flanders: it loses all character, and leaves what some people call expression; but this is a false notion of expression; expression cannot exist without character as its stamina; and neither character nor expression can exist without firm and determinate outline . . . The great and golden rule of art, as well as of life, is this: That the more distinct, sharp, and wirey the bounding line, the more perfect the work of art; and the less keen and sharp, the greater is the evidence of weak imitation, plagiarism, and bungling. (*A Descriptive Catalogue*)

Every line is the Line of Beauty; it is only fumble & Bungle which cannot draw a Line; this only is Ugliness. That is not a Line which doubts & Hesitates in the Midst of its Course. (*Public Address*, 1810)

I know too well that a great majority of Englishmen are fond of The Indefinite which they Measure by Newton's Doctrine of the Fluxions of an Atom, A Thing that does not Exist. These are Politicians & think that Republican Art is Inimical to their Atom. For a Line or Lineament is not formed by Chance: a Line is a Line in its Minutest Subdivisions: Strait or Crooked It is Itself & Not Intermeasurable with or by any Thing Else.

(To George Cumberland, 12 April 1827)

Blake's art, which is a *linearist* art in the tradition of Dürer, Raphael, Michelangelo, Hogarth and David, was forged in the revolutionary years 1788-1795. Its distinct character, therefore, was formed under the pressure of revolutionary events.

Every genuine revolutionary development, whether in art or in politics, has two sides: it makes a sharp break with one past, and it re-affirms its unbroken continuity with another. (In Blake's case, this was with the linearist tradition itself.) The revolutionary break, without which human development is impossible, is thus always the affirmation of an *independent line*, a continuity and solidarity with a hitherto repressed tradition. Moreover, the revolutionary 'line' requires repeated delineation, refinement, and bold assertion in order to keep its sharpness and distinctness: any relaxation, hesitation or uncertainty, vagueness or vacillation, threatens

its existence at every point. Since it expresses the revolutionary *independence* of an oppressed class, nation or culture,
which the oppressing class continually seeks to annul through
ideological absorption (and, when that fails, physical liquid-
ation), the 'bounding line' must be repeatedly emphasised,
developed, and refined.

Linear distinctness, in the words of Blake, becomes the
'great and golden rule' not only of art, but of life. The need
to distinguish clearly between one thing and another is, in
fact, where all human knowledge and science begin: once
man detaches himself from nature through hunting, the
use of fire, and agriculture, he is able not only to demarcate
between the natural and the human, or the animal and the
human, but to draw further distinctions *within* the natural
and the human, as greater control over nature is accompanied
by further divisions in social organisation. For Blake, 'the
bounding outline' became an all-embracing principle of art,
life, cognition, and existence itself:

> How do we distinguish the oak from the beech, the horse
> from the ox, but by the bounding outline? How do we
> distinguish one face or countenance from another, but by
> the bounding line and its infinite inflexions and move-
> ments? What is it that builds a house and plants a garden,
> but the definite and determinate? What is it that distin-
> guishes honesty from knavery, but the hard and wiry
> line of rectitude and certainty in the actions and intentions?
> Leave out this line, and you leave out life itself; all is chaos
> again, and the line of the almighty must be drawn out
> upon it before man or beast can exist.
>
> (*A Descriptive Catalogue*)

Reference to the 'hard and wiry line of rectitude and
certainty in the actions and intentions' shows us that Blake's
theory of outline is not only an aesthetic principle, but a
principle of moral and social action. The same might be said
for David in his *Oath of the Horatii*. This cannot be put down
to the 'strain of blinkered dogmatizing of a craftsman who in
his apprecticeship was taught by a master to do the manipulations in a certain way, who has found them good, and who
will consider no others'. The reasons why Blake, as a trained

draughtsman, 'found them good', have an important historical and artistic significance, and contain a deep, eloquently-
defended commitment to certain values.

Blake's principle of linearity, in life as in art, is a principle
of conscious loyalty and certainty, of clarity, firmness and
continuity. If for Blake a line could not be subdivided by
doubting reason — that is, broken down into individual
'atoms' — then for a modern African poet, torn from his
peasant roots, yet wishing for a continuity with those roots,
the same moral principle (though in a different context) still
applies:

> We must be what we are mother,
> Life is not a perpetual absurdity.
> Through a spiritual life-line
> Defying the pin point of
> An intellectual definition
> We are conjoined in an
> Inviolable bond each to each.[10]

On another level, Blake says of Reynolds and Gainsborough
that they 'Blotted & Blurred one against the other'. He then
adds: 'The Arts & Sciences are the Destruction of Tyrannies
or Bad Governments.'[11] Whereas 'Blots and Blurs' are
associated with 'Tyrannies', 'Bad Governments' and corruption, 'Fine Forms' and determinate outlines deserve the
title of 'Republican Art'. Blake may have been re-asserting
a connection that was already there, if only as a metaphor.
The King of Brobdingnag, for example, tells Gulliver:

> I observe among you some lines of an institution, which in
> its original might have been tolerable, but these half
> erased, and the rest wholly blurred and blotted by corrup-
> tions.[12]

In his defence of outline Blake owed much to George
Cumberland, whose *Thoughts on Outline* (1796) showed
a passionate commitment to linearist principles. The contest
in England between 'linearists' and 'colourists' was a fierce
one. Blake, when he came to articulate his own position in
public, was only taking sides in a battle that had started long
before, but he made its 'lines' clearer, ideologically as well

as artistically. Nor did the battle fade. In Isaac Babel's short story *Line and Colour*, a friend of Alexander Kerensky, surprised when Kerensky fails to recognise someone at a watering place, asks why he does not wear glasses. Kerensky replies that an unfocused vision has made him more aware of colours, which he now prefers to hard outlines. The story concludes with Kerensky speaking at a public meeting, unaware of the crowd's growing hostility, only to be followed by the be-spectacled Trotsky who, sensing the mood of the crowd, mounts the platform, and begins: 'Comrades!' The modern linearist, 'hard-edge' approach has nevertheless tended to lose the kind of political (even human) content it has in the art of Blake and David, acquiring instead the austere, purely *geometrical* formalism of so much modern abstract art — the kind of abstract formalism with which eighteenth-century neoclassicism and the linearist art of Blake must on no account be confused.

Blake's designs are based on linear rhythms, but he is less happy with the parallel, statuesque folds of Gothic drapery than he is with naked human contours. Though 'Every Line is the Line of Beauty', he prefers unbroken, flowing lines to 'fumble & Bungle'. As Anne Kostelanetz Mellor has observed, Blake's handling of outline in Cumberland's *Thoughts on Outline* 'de-emphasizes Cumberland's flesh bulges and awkward attempts at muscular definition and stresses instead the flow of outline along an entire torso or limb'.[13] Blake's line is 'firm, clear and smooth; his musculature delicately indicated; and his contours a single, harmonious, flowing line' in his illustrations to Stuart and Revett's *Antiquities of Athens* (1794, 3rd ed.).[14] This unbroken flowing line is superbly demonstrated in *Michael Binding Satan*, where it sweeps unimpeded from Michael's right foot, up his whole leg and thigh, round his back and shoulders in a single confident curve. The similar, reversed posture of the right-hand flying figure in *Europe*, Plate 9, is likewise a testimony of Blake's exuberant and unhesitating draughtsmanship.

In *Blake's Human Form Divine* (University of California Press, 1974) Mellor associates Blake's 'bounding line' with a constricting rationality, such that Blake's philosophy and aesthetic are at odds:

Blake's poetic denunciation of both the physical human body and of the bounding line or enclosed form as the work of an oppressive reason thus conflicted directly with his artistic reliance upon strong outlines and the human figure. (p. xvii)

Blake's 'denunciation' of the bounding line seems to be based on a single quotation from *The Marriage of Heaven and Hell*: 'Reason is the bound or outward circumference of Energy'. This does not, in itself, suggest a blanket denunciation of bounding lines, since the visual depiction of Energy without linear form is for Blake not Energy at all, but merely blots and blurs and chaotic formlessness. If Blake philosophically denounced the human form and the bounding line, why did he so strongly adhere to both as a matter of artistic principle throughout his working life?

Mellor's whole thesis is an attempt to generalise the dialectic of Blake's thought, visual art and poetry in terms of all-embracing dualities such as 'closed' and 'open' minds, 'closed' and 'open' forms, and 'closed' and 'open' syntax. The result is an unhappy confusion, since Blake's 'poetic attacks upon the limitations of a closed intellectual or social system' have nothing whatsoever to do with the supposedly 'closed' nature of his linearist technique. Further confusions arise when the focus of the argument shifts, unannounced, from the 'closed' nature of linear forms as such (*because* they are outlines) to the 'closed' or 'open' nature of a particular *design*, according to the limits set by the picture frame. Such a loose, generalising approach, which interprets 'the bounding line *or enclosed form* as the work of an oppressive reason', fails to appreciate the fact that meaning, execution and design in Blake are subtly and *necessarily* interwoven. A new artistic whole emerges with each new creative fusion of form and content. To suggest that Blake was somehow tied, in spite of himself, to a technique (linearism) that he came to reject philosophically (only to reconcile himself to it later), shows a serious misunderstanding of Blake's art — and his philosophy.

Mellor is on safer ground when she begins to distinguish between the different *kinds* of outlines, linear forms and their functions in Blake's art. Some outlines do, it is true, indicate 'an oppressive reason' — when this is the meaning intended; other outlines (though equally 'determinate') may suggest infinite energy, such as leaping flames, spiralling vegetation, or Blake's joyous flying forms. (Here the lines *bound* in the sense of *leaping*.) Form and function, meaning and design, are thus inseparable. Blake's linearism is capable of expressing many things, depending on the specific nature of the outlines and the rhythms they set up: whether, for example, they are rectilinear or rectangular, spiralling, coiling or circular, flowing and sinuous or rigid and static; whether they are human, geometric, or based on natural forms. But to interpret the 'bounding line' *per se* as evil because it binds or sets a limit to the potentially infinite, radiant energy that Blake perceived in 'the human form divine' leads us, surely, into a philosophic-aesthetic quagmire. Thus, if human divinity, according to Blake, is radiant and expansive, 'the divine image (argues Mellor) must preserve its integrity by widening its borders, overwhelming all lesser images of man and accepting only those ultimate limits necessary to maintain its identity as an image'.[15] How the divine (which is infinite) can preserve its identity as an image by 'widening its borders' is unclear: in this case divinity, if it is worthy of the name, should surely have *no* borders, however wide? As Blake said: 'More! More! is the cry of a mistaken soul; less than All cannot satisfy Man.' Or is Mellor arguing that huge, balloon-like human forms are more spiritual and divine than small, thin ones? In fact, as I have argued, it is *determinate outline itself*, enhanced by strong frontal illumination, that 'spiritualises' — hence, makes 'divine'; nor does the 'divine image' have to contend with outline by pushing it to visually ungraspable 'utlimate limits', but finds expression in and through it, according to the specific nature of the outlines themselves.

Fearful Symmetry and Harmonious Balance

Blake's pictures are frequently symmetrical, or nearly so, the picture usually being divided down the middle, giving a bilateral symmetry. Symmetry and near-symmetry can suggest a tension or conflict between polar opposites, emphasise difference-in-likeness, or, when perfect, reconcile all linear rhythms in a static, harmonious balance.

Tension and conflict may be conveyed through various means, for example, through human posture. The *contra-posto*, almost anatomically impossible, striding-and-binding, walking-and-bending posture of Michael in *Michael Binding Satan* depicts a struggle whose endless, cyclic nature is suggested by the symmetrical opposition of the two heads and the circular, revolving linear rhythms of the whole design. The bilateral design of the title page of *The Marriage of Heaven and Hell*, the colour print *Good and Evil Angels*, and the watercolour illustration *Satan, Sin and Death*, with its derivative Davidian diagonals, also serve to generate internal, bilateral opposition.

Symmetry or near-symmetry is a dangerous tool, however, in that it can so easily be dull and boring. The gradations between harmonious balance and wooden immobility, between a visually strong, purposive rigidity and an unintentional, weak rigidity are notoriously slippery. On the whole, the simpler the design, the more effective the symmetry (as in the Rouault-like, bold illustrations to *The Book of Urizen*). *When the Morning Stars Sang Together* (one of the watercolour series done for Butts) has a symmetry that is joyous, dance-like and beautifully con-ceived. Its fine, linear sensitivity, limpid colours and utterly radiant clarity belong to a quite different mood from the pious, light-amid-the-gloom religiosity of the frequently symmetrical crucifixion, entombment and resurrection series. The symmetry in Plate 11 of *Europe*, on the other hand, has a critical and ironic function. Two angels, symmetrically placed, cross sceptres in the centre of an almost perfectly symmetrical composition. Up above is 'Albion's Angel' (George III, with bat's wings) holding his 'brazen Book' of codified laws. The symmetry here is intentionally frozen, static and unproductive, and hence critical of the frozen nature of authoritarian law. Here again pictorial form acts as a vehicle for rhetorical argument. The perfect symmetry of *The Holy Family, or Christ in the Lap of Truth* is praised by Anne Kostelanetz Mellor for the sublime calm and feeling of quiescent inner peace it expresses, where all conflicts have been consummately reconciled. Yet my own impression here is that of a weak, derivative, and nerveless Byzantine stasis. The symmetry is all too worked out, too overdone: the eye flags when faced with such predictable reconciliations. (Blake, as a champion of 'Republican' art, is on the whole better at conflicts than he is at reconciliations.) Such failures show the risks involved in symmetrical compositions.

J. R. Harvey implies that Blake was himself responsible for his artistic failures. Such a view ignores the hazards of patronage as well as other external factors. Blake's most catastrophic artistic lapses (such as the absurd *As if an Angel Dropped Down from the Clouds*, done for a Rev. Joseph Thomas in 1809) seem to occur when oppositional energy and the 'corrosive fires' of independent criticism have been suppressed by an obedience to, or a dependence on, others; hence, the negative presence of conservative visual ideology in Blake's art: a need for harmonious reconciliations. Thus Harvey praises Blake's *Paradise Lost* illustrations for a rather 'Satanic' reason: their sensuousness, harmony and balance. These illustrations, however, are *ideologically* as well as visually weak when compared, say, to the 1795 colour prints. There is little activity or visual tension in the majority of these illustrations. Despite frontal illumination, everything seems to have happened *before*, not *when*, the viewer's eye meets the picture surface. The lapidary finish, highly-worked textures and rich decorative detail in *Raphael Warns Adam and Eve* emphasise this point: whatever meanings this picture originally intended are weakened, in my opinion, by its arabesque, oriental superfluity, betraying a sense of pictorial space having been merely filled in. Hard, determinate outline, which had been developed in opposition to the soft and sensuous 'Blotted & Blurred' art of the ruling class, is somehow 'betrayed' — robbed of its strong, critical force — by being made to enclose relaxed, sculptural figures whose unaccentuated gestures, normalised postures and inexpressive faces made their linear muscularity seem redundant. One feels that everything is now complete, over and done with. When the intellectual eye has to *work*, or when, as sometimes occurs, Blake's pale, delicate watercolours and firmly-drawn outlines combine in a wholly different kind of sensuousness — a sort of coupling (not merging) of 'feminine' and 'masculine' qualities at the level of visual technique — then the picture succeeds as an 'ever-present' vision. This cannot, in my view, be said for the *Paradise Lost* illustrations.

Anti-Illusionism and Conceptual Art

In illusionist art, the illusion of linear perspective and of three-dimensional spaces and volumes invites us to make a silent and natural transition from the physical, three-dimensional world in which we ourselves, as viewers, are, to the imaginary world depicted in the painting. The painting asks us to suspend our disbelief that it is 'merely' oil or water pigment on a flat surface. It positions us at a definite physical point in a physical universe (for example, in the corner of a room, on a hill, in a street, or by the seashore), so that the flat board, paper or canvas becomes a transparent surface or 'window' through which the viewer looks into, or out upon, a 'real world' that is a 'natural', physical extension of *this* one. Illusionism gives the viewer an unquestionable, physical point of view, then invites him to enter the picture space and move around inside it. An exact imitation of the relative size of persons and objects — of people in a street, or cattle in a field — cheats the eye into believing that it is adjusting focus as it moves over the picture surface, just as it would have to were the objects *really* nearer and *really* further away. We momentarily forget that this relative distance is an illusion: in reality the picture is only an arrangement of lines and colours across a flat surface.

Illusionist, perspectival art does not merely create illusory *effects*, but is founded on mathematical and scientific observation. Its Renaissance founders, such as Brunelleschi and Ucello, carried out repeated measurements — involving the use of devices such as spy-holes and mirrors — in order to arrive at precise, objective representations based on a single perspectival viewpoint. In its origins, linear perspective is also connected with the habit of precise, objective measurement that arose in the accounting, money economy of mercantile Florence.

When it is assumed that 'reality' is always an *empirical* reality, and that the visual artist has to follow certain rules in 'mirroring' this empirical reality, any breaking of these rules (the rules of perspective, with its vanishing point, and of chiaroscuro) is acceptable in so far as this aids expression or is necessary to convey certain meanings *within* the illusionist framework, but becomes unacceptable — even a sign of 'madness' — when the framework itself is challenged. The late eighteenth-century revolt against the Enlightenment brought such a challenge in the non-illusionist art of Blake, Runge, Carstens, Flaxman and others, and its articulate ideological justification in Blake's rejection of the rationalist, empiricist philosophy of 'Bacon, Newton, & Locke'.

Blake's anti-illusionism and anti-empiricism might be seen as the spontaneous result of historical forces, but it was also a *conscious* revolt. In 1788 he wrote: 'Man's perceptions are not bounded by organs of perception; he perceives more than sense (tho' ever so acute) can discover'. This is similar to Kant, who in 1783 argued that anyone 'who retains his long habit of taking experience for a merely empirical synthesis of perceptions . . . never thinks of the fact that it goes much further than perception's reach.'[16] Knowledge is not merely the accumulation and subsequent association of what Locke called 'ideas' — ideas acquired first of all through the senses — but involves the *active penetration* of reality, a conscious *structuring* of experience according to non-empirical, *a priori* categories. Both Kant and Blake had arrived at the view that 'reality' is not the objective world as it 'really is', as observed through the senses, but is always a *mental picture*, a paradigmatic structuring of reality. In other words, reality is only empirical to an empiricist.

Blake however came to defend a Neoplatonic, *pre*-Lockean belief in innate ideas and non-empirical, elemental forms and structures, and his aesthetic, consciously formulated, was founded on Gestalt principles: 'Knowledge of Ideal Beauty is Not to be Acquired. It is Born with us.' Ideal, 'primitive', *a priori* forms are eternal, permanent and real: 'There Exist in the Eternal World the Permanent Realities of Every Thing which we see reflected in this Vegetable Glass of Nature'. 'Perception' becomes 'Vision': 'All that we See is Vision, from Generated Organs gone as soon as come, Permanent in The Imagination, Consider'd as Nothing by the Natural Man'. Thus an innate knowledge of ideal forms is asserted against a continuing study of natural forms and processes in the material world.

Yet Blake's own ideal of beauty — such as his perfectly-proportioned, muscular male nude — was not born with him, but was learned and acquired. It went back to Michelangelo and the art of the Greeks. It was therefore culturally inherited. Nor were any of his ideal forms and 'Permanent Realities' the product of non-empirical, innate thought, since

> the concept of form is derived exclusively from the external world and does not arise in the mind as a product of pure thought. There must have been things which had shape and whose shapes were compared before anyone could arrive at the concept of form.[17]

The illusion of a transparently objective reality is hence replaced by another illusion: that of a world of universal, permanent and ideal forms, whose eternal validity is proclaimed only because they have been *abstracted* from the external world.

There are parallels here in the work of other artists, especially those in search of new religious systems, such as Asmus Jakob Carstens (b. 1754), who, according to Rosenblum, saw himself as a universal artist and thinker, working in 'some supranational realm of idea and spirit'.[18] Carstens also found oils repugnant, and, like Blake, held a private exhibition (in 1795). Karl Runge's medievalist designs parallel Blake's in their elemental, left-right symmetry and their sense of 'a fixed, immutable order'.[19] Yet Blake's own 'Permanent Realities' are in fact mutable, alive and powerfully expressive. They are not dead, rigid and fixed at all. As so often happens, artistic practice undermines, or belies, a stated ideological position when that position is based not on the artistic practice itself but on some pre-formulated, cast-iron theory.

However, when Blake says: 'from Generated Organs gone as soon as come, Permanent in the Imagination', he is describing a paradox in artistic creation. Blake's 'Permanent

Realities', like those of other artists, have been fashioned from the temporal flux of existence; they only work as *instants of vision*, not as stale, lifeless copies of some 'external', prefabricated ideal. Blake's whole method of working was, in a way, closer to 'classicism' than to 'romanticism' (hence the term 'romantic classicism'). In the painstaking execution of his often geometric, schematic designs, he left nothing to chance. His was not the art of the colourist who creates momentary impressions and fleeting moods with a few brush strokes, but that of the 'definite and determinate' linearist, delineating clear, bold forms and outlines that, however carefully executed, still manage to be fresh, instantaneous and alive.

In its conscious anti-illusionism, Blake's art can be described as a *conceptual* art. Referring to the rise of modernism, Hans Hess argues that the increasing competitiveness of the art market led to a more intensely subjective and symbolist, rather than realistic content in paintings:

> The modern picture moves away from the world and encloses its content, so to say, behind closed windows. We can still see what happens, but can no longer see the things themselves, only their signs and symbols which we can rethink and reconstitute. What we see is not any more a mirror of life and thought, but something less visual, less tangible and more conceptual.[20]

The alienation of the artist under capitalism forces him, eventually, to create his 'own world', to express a 'unique inner vision' (which, in the modern art market, can become a highly saleable commodity). As more and more of these unique inner visions proliferate, the greater need there is for originality, since each artist must compete against every other artist in order to sell his own, 'original' product — i.e. himself — to the potential buying public. A restlessly innovative and experimentalist, 'conceptual' and fashion-conscious art — the art of the *avant garde* — emerges.

Does this *avant-garde* modernism begin with Blake? It would surely be highly anachronistic to think so, yet it has been persuasively argued. In his *Transformations in Late Eighteenth Century Art* Robert Rosenblum sees a continuity

between modern art and the art of the late eighteenth century, with its search for a visual *tabula rasa*, its 'technical
regression to the linear and planar origins of art'.[21] A teleological movement towards the linear and planar abstractions
of modernism is thus being argued. (As one piece of evidence,
Blake's small sepia drawing, called *A Vision*, is placed next
to Braque's cubist *Houses at L'Estaque* for comparison.)

This, as I suggested in the last chapter, is a too formalist
and one-sided approach, since it abstracts or isolates certain
formal tendencies within the period and proceeds to explain
the movement of art in that period in terms of these formal
tendencies. Although there is a parallel between the anti-
illusionist, primitivist and purist art of Blake, Carstens,
Flaxman and others on the one hand, and the modernist
reaction against realism and the whole perspectival tradition
on the other, the differences are equally important. Firstly,
neoclassicism and 'romantic classicism' did not lead
towards 'pure abstraction', but remained bound, at least
in paintings and drawings, by the representation of the
human figure. An art that does not dispense with the classic-
ally inherited human form as an integral outline can only
subject that form to a limited amount of distortion; to do
what Braque or Picasso did to it is not a further stage in the
process, but arises out of new historical conditions. Secondly,
the purism of late eighteenth-century art was inspired by a
democratic-humanist ideal. Blake's art certainly transcends
the dominant *bourgeois* perspectives of its epoch, but it
does not free itself of the ideal — an ideal to which modernist
art is no longer tied. Thirdly (following on from this),
whereas Blake's art arose out of the bourgeois-democratic
revolution, the modernist rejection of empiricist illusionism
is the result of a much later stage in historical development,
when liberal democracy (with its realist heritage) entered its
final crisis. Fourthly, this modern crisis, with its extremes
of alienation, has spawned an entirely new phenomenon:
technicism, or technical innovation for innovation's sake,
regardless of its human aims and consequences. In the early
bourgeois-democratic epoch, when all revolutions in technique led to an expansion of the productive forces, such a
widespread technicist aberration was impossible, though the

alienation of the artist under conditions of a new, capitalist division of labour could at times create something that was closely akin to it.

Blake's anti-illusionism, therefore, transcends the bourgeois perspectives of its epoch without in any way — through some mysterious mode of travel known only to 'prophets' and 'geniuses' — leaping into a modernist aesthetic. An analysis of Blake's most famous design — the etching and colour print known as *The Ancient of Days* (1794) — will help to concretise some of the points made here.

The design has been reproduced so many times and is so familiar that further detailed analysis may seem superfluous. But various elements in this design have passed unnoticed (they probably operate on the viewer at an unconscious level), while some viewers continue to misinterpret it as a naïve, 'primitive' and 'crude', yet strangely powerful vision of the moment of Creation.

The design works not only as an original variation on an iconographical theme, but as an unresolved set of tensions and polarities. Like *The Tyger*, with its two voices (one celebrating revolutionary energy, the other articulating conservative fear and doubt), the picture is its own antithesis. What Blake has done is to depict a calculated, rational act (dividing and circumscribing the world with a pair of compasses) by means of an equally calculated, anti-rational, and therefore ironic visual language. The rational and the irrational conflict. To such a conflict there can be no end: such is the eternal dialectic of Blake's 'Permanent Realities'.

The design reveals a fleeting instant during a storm, when the sun shines through a momentary break in the clouds. The visionary artist depicts a powerful sun-god stretching his arm down through the clouds into the dark abyss with lightning-like compasses: beneficent creation is also a kind of punishment. The sombre colours and use of a blue-red polarity almost 'bruise' the eye. God is light. But this God is Urizen: his circumscribed disc-world blocks out the real sun, whose rays come from behind, as in a total eclipse. Circumscribing the world, seeking to 'bind the infinite', Urizen has circumscribed himself. He 'creates' with his *left* (sinister) arm, not right (which is strangely invisible, either behind him or missing). This left arm at first glance seems to be full of phallic-like potency, suggesting, perhaps, an Oedipal image of patriarchal power. It is considerably elongated, in one of Blake's most daring anatomical distortions. Yet it is strangely shoulder-less and hanging, like a limp elephant's trunk, as if *pulled* down rather than voluntarily reaching, hence stretched beyond its normal length by the force of gravity whose laws Urizen has himself created. When we look at the hand itself, further irrationalities appear. The hold is an exceptionally difficult one to maintain, contributing to the visual impact of the overall posture, which, forced and painfully contorted, could be partly responsible for Urizen's tears! Instead of firmly grasping the meeting point of the compass's two arms, Urizen's hand — and thus Urizen himself — seem to have been divided by them. The left arm of the compass pulls the forefinger one way, the right pulls the other three fingers the other way, forming a right angle, while the thumb remains hidden. It is not its user who controls, but the instrument.

As in *Newton* the bunched, calculating geometrician is being satirised: human form has been painfully forced into geometric form by the act of measuring, yet the impossibility of a complete conversion thwarts the tyrannical laws of science as it adds to the feeling of tension. *The Ancient of Days* design is based on a concentrated schematism: Urizen's body forms a triangle within a circle, whose centre is Urizen's brain (to be precise, his neo-cortex, where the will is located), while his fixed right foot forms the centre of another, horizontal circle, leaving his rigid, pillar-like left leg 'free to do some turning'.[22] There is some tension too in the leftward pull of Urizen's wind-blown hair and the downward pull of his arm. The design consists of horizontals, verticals, parallel diagonals, and two concentric circles, which can be diagrammatised as shown on page 272. By giving the human such a geometrical form, Blake intends us to see the irony of the whole composition.

Finally, the picture defies rational explanation through its conscious anti-illusionism. All of Urizen's left arm is frontally highlighted. Why then is the inside of his right thigh in the shade? Indeed, if Urizen's back is to the sun,

where does this frontal light come from — or does Urizen (in spite of himself) radiate light like Albion in *Albion Rose?* The dark shading above Urizen's back (clearly seen in Copy K) suggests that the disc is convex, but the fact that Urizen is inside it shows that it is concave. And where are those lower clouds? Urizen's forearm seems to be spatially in front of them; in which case they must be in some narrow space between his arm and the disc, for otherwise they would not be lit from behind. (This is supported by the fact that Urizen's hair passes *in front* of clouds that in turn pass in front of the disc.) The shading lends a tantalising appearance of three-dimensionality to what is in fact an 'irrational' and *conceptualised* two-dimensional world.

The function of Blake's visual language here, then, is ironic and satiric. The first impression conveyed by *The Ancient of Days* is one of divine creative power, but this is negated by the 'minute particulars' and underlying irony of the whole design. Urizen is not 'God' at all, nor is he creative. He is merely the 'Supreme Being' of rational theology who resides in the breasts of the dominant class. Blake's visual language opposes as well as exposes the profound *ir*rationality of a governing Reason that tries to make the infinite finite, binds what cannot be bound, and with terrible compulsion keeps on measuring what cannot be measured.

The 1795 Colour Prints

In 1795 the class struggle in England reached a point where peaceful compromise was no longer possible — where victory or defeat for the reform movement had become the issue. The LCS resolution passed on 14 April 1794 had, we remember, declared that 'the social compact between the English nation and their governors' had been entirely dissolved. The reform movement, which was now also an antiwar movement, presented a decisive challenge to the continued rule of the governing class, and this class responded with all the powers at its disposal: suspension of Habeas Corpus, Pitt's Committee of Secresy (with its battery of spies and informers), press-gangs, provocations, house-searches, arrests, trials, imprisonments, and deportations. The results of the

Treason Trials proved to be merely a temporary setback for the ruling class. 1795 was the crisis year.

The war itself and the victories of the French revolutionary armies brought about severe economic distress, due to the policies of a now isolated, counter-revolutionary regime: food scarcity and high prices led to mass riots, and the LCS won new members, enlarging the number of its branches. Government recruiting offices were attacked, and the situation was pregnant with 'grave popular disorders'. On 26 October 1795, the LCS resolved on a great popular demostration. On 29 October this huge demostration, numbering 200,000 (nearly a quarter of the population of London — the equivalent today would be around three million!) filled the streets of London. The occasion was the opening of parliament. Anti-royalist, republican feelings ran high, and the king's coach was attacked. A Royal Proclamation against seditious meetings was made on 4 November, and on 27 November the Seditious Meetings Bill was passed, the Opposition raising 73 votes against the government's 273. Mass support for the LCS increased, and another large meeting was held in December. But resolutions, meetings, speeches and demonstrations seemed to be leading nowhere. The issue had in effect become one of political *power*, and the way to achieving that power was beyond the grasp of the LCS leaders. The artisans and craftsmen who had formed the backbone of this democratic organisation began to fall away, some leaders resigned, the 'Two Acts' began to bite, and the reform movement went into a decline from which it would not recover for another two decades.

In France itself a bourgeois dictatorship was strengthening its hold, against the 'left' as well as the 'right'. As Saint-Just complained during the reign of 'Virtue': 'La Révolution est glacée'. The inspiration of 1792-93 was absent at a time when the mass democratic current in England was reaching its flood-tide — a time when that inspiration was, perhaps, most greatly needed. The moment for the conjuncture of two revolutions had long since passed. Hence the peculiar suddenness with which the movement fell away after 1795. Perhaps the only thing that could have saved it was invasion by a French revolutionary army, but the Channel and Albion's rocky shores precluded such a possibility. Moreover, the English bourgeoisie was politically flaccid and spineless compared to the French (one reason why the leadership of the reform movement passed into the hands of radical artisans). A political revolution in England would have had to succeed *against a bourgeois opposition* — and only *proletarian* revolutions have achieved this. The situation was an impasse.

The mass reform movement, though its energies had been harnessed by the organising discipline of the LCS leaders and committees, was never wholly unified in terms of strategy and tactics. The leaders themselves, such as Thelwall and Place, were neither ideologically nor politically equipped for the taking of power through violent insurrection (though Godwin dissociated himself from Thelwall's *practical* radicalism), while radical sentiments of an insurrectionary, violent kind often assumed the form of conspiracies and riots on the one hand, and millenarian protest and prophecy on the other. The tone of Brothers's pamphlets is frequently violent: God's anger and the wrath of the Lamb are directed specifically at the wickedness of contemporary tyranny, at political persecution and social injustice. As Nathaniel Halhed, one of Brothers's parliamentary supporters, put it: 'times of calamity are peculiarly fertile in visions and prognostications, predictions and prophecies.'[23] 1795 was an exceptionally fertile year.

In this historical context, when the Bible was being read for its specific usefulness to the popular cause, Blake produced a series of colour prints on mainly biblical and religious themes. Failure to see these colour prints as one manifestation of the politico-religious ferment current at the time surely blinds us to their social and political content.

There is a comment by Gareth Wilkinson (1838) on Blake's lost fresco, *The Ancient Britons* (1809), that is relevant here. Wilkinson says that Blake's pictorial imagery is 'unutterable and abominable' yet has a 'terrific tremendous power', giving 'the impression that his whole inner man must have been in a monstrous and deformed condition — for it teemed with monstrous and horrid productions'.[24] Some of the 1795 colour prints, such as *God Creating Adam, God*

Judging Adam, Good and Evil Angels, Nebuchadnezzar, Hecate and *The House of Death*, are elemental, primordial visions whose strangeness disturbs and alienates at the same time as it holds and fascinates. Strangeness and deformity might at first appear to be the result of a 'monstrous and deformed' inner condition (a conclusion that reconciles us to social norms), but it is also possible that they are intended to expose, through a particular alienation technique, a monstrous and deformed *social* condition. The visions of a Bunyan, a Swift, a Blake, a Kafka or a Tutuola arrest and disturb precisely because they cannot simply be put down to some peculiar experience or eccentricity in the personality that mediates them: there is surely some profound dislocation in the social mechanism, some traumatic *historic* experience, that has gone into their making.

Taking this as our point of departure, what is it that connects these colour prints thematically? One view is that they reflect Blake's new Gnostic pessimism, his apparent belief, deduced from a reading of *The Book of Urizen*, that the Creation was itself the Fall, a disastrous separation of the material and spiritual worlds. The creation of the material world, and hence of man, is evil because it has created finitude, a world of 'fallen' matter from which infinite, divine energy has withdrawn itself. It marks the loss of Eternity which can never be regained in the material realm. The 1795 colour prints are, therefore, according to this view, a kind of 'anti-utopian nightmare, systematically imprisoning man within the stifling forms of the human body and rational categories', since the 'creation of man' is now seen as 'a denial of human divinity'.[25] On the other hand, this view of a cosmic split and closure could be a philosophical, mythopoeic response to a historic crisis which brought its own social and political splits and closures, where 'man' = *society*. The loss of Eternity and the sense of systematic imprisonment might, therefore, be translated as the receding vision of revolutionary transformation and a growing sense of oppression in the period of Thermidor, the war, and mounting political reaction, a period when the dissolution of 'the social compact between the English nation and their governors' could neither be healed and reconciled nor resolve itself in some new, revolutionary synthesis. English social and political life hardened into its familiar form of a continuing and drawn-out conflict between alienated, 'self-closed', yet 'married' social classes who, while inflicting certain defeats on each other, waged wars of position rather than wars of movement, and tended to draw back from decisive, revolutionary confrontations. As after 1795 for Blake, so in the 1850s for Dickens, the apartheid-like impasse of English social life felt more and more like a prison.

Taken as a whole, the 1795 colour prints convey claustro-phobic oppression, spiritual degeneration and frozen antagonisms, which are relieved only by momentary love, compassion, and Christian forgiveness. They make use of an austere, restricted pictorial language: either a horizontal (above-below) and vertical (left-right) visual polarity, or the concentration on a single figure.

'Above and below' in paintings can simply represent sky and earth, or they can have a symbolic meaning as 'Heaven and Earth'. (In the title page of *The Marriage of Heaven and Hell* 'above and below' represent Earth and Hell.) Implicit in this Heaven-Earth, God-Man visual symbolism, however, is the idea of *rulers* and *ruled*, which Blake exploits with compelling, 'primitive' force in *God Creating Adam* and *The House of Death*. In the former design, a Urizenic creator fashions the human form of Adam out of terrestrial clay. The repeated, emphatic horizontality of the whole, the oppressive heaviness of the creator (as 'governor') with his elaborate wings, heavy brows, white hair and beard and white robe; the prostrate, earth-bound form of Adam, whose legs, tapering indefinitely, are in the grip of a large, red, coiling worm; the proximity of the two heads, Adam's turning away in soulful dismay, the governing creator's similarly lacking in the joy of creation as he places his uncreative hands on Adam's bony brow, all suggest something quite different from what we would normally conceive as an act of creation. Instead of bringing man to joyous life, this creator only brings pain, misery and suffering; ostensibly helping Adam to rise, the oppressive weight of this creator is also *keeping him down*. This is the vision of God not as creative force, but as ruling tyrant, and it owes its origins to the fact that the plebeian artist is himself struggling against an oppressive social order ruled by this same God. It is a view of reality seen from the viewpoint of a struggling plebeian visionary. Towards the bottom of the picture, we can make out waves, foam, a rocky shoreline and green grass. Is this not an image of England?

In *Pity*, the above-below, ruler-ruled polarity is temporarily relieved by a gesture of extraordinarily tender compassion that extends for an instant into a lower world of suffering. Striding the blast, the 'new-born babe' — a *homunculus*, rescued from a prostrate female who has died in child-birth — is taken up in the gentle maternal hands of a female who bends down from one of the 'sightless couriers of the air' on which she is riding. The arrow-like flight of the elongated horses is broken for a moment by vertical stillness, as if an instant of humane calm, a moment of Eternity, is all that is possible in the sweep and rush of time.

Left-right polarity is seen in *Good and Evil Angels* and in *God Judging Adam*. In the latter, Adam stands, head bowed, before his rod-wielding judge, who sits in a sun-chariot drawn by two 'horses of instruction', the chariot's flames bound (in one version) in a perfect circle. The greyish pigment of God's (Urizen's?) body is stone-like. The similar physique of both judge and judged suggests a mutual 'fall' and interpenetration of opposites. Both are bound in a relationship that negates human potentiality. Obedience to Urizenic law turns the one who submits into a frozen mirror-image of the one who rules and judges.

In *Nebuchadnezzar, Hecate* and *Newton* the human has become degraded, through association with, or descent into, the less-than-human: the punished tyrant has grown claws, the witch is surrounded by an owl, an ass feeding on vegetation and other weird creatures, while Newton's hunched body has become polyp-like. Nowhere does Blake 'denounce' the physical human body as such, though he sometimes shows it degraded. Using a visual language in which the human form remains the central symbol, he portrays a degenerate condition, not as the loss of 'eternity' or of 'divinity', but as the fall from a *human* ideal.

Such an anthropocentric, humanist visual ideology has, of course, its limitations (though it is these limitations that make it ideologically coherent). Because Blake's human form has to carry so many meanings within a fairly restricted symbolic repertoire, it is the individual variations and 'minute particulars' which give elasticity to the symbolism, thus avoiding the stale repetitions that Harvey criticises. This is not to say that Blake's visual art does not have frequent lapses — the failures are many. In eschewing 'nature' (which 'deadens' inspiration), it does not, as a rule, depict any specific social or economic realities, since these require the type of sociological realism that is precluded by Blake's visionary art. What it can do is convey, in an extremely powerful and often unsettling manner, certain *essential* images and structures in their most distilled and concentrated form. These, as I have tried to show, are rooted in a new kind of social experience; they articulate an oppositional, radical and lower-class viewpoint, and they mark a revolutionary break with dominant forms and styles. These visions of striving, liberation, claustrophobic oppression, and beatific joy, with their ironic perception of 'eternal contraries' — perhaps the hallmark of Blake's art — could never have been encompassed by an illusionist visual ideology.

10

Jerusalem and Albion

He warmly declared that all he knew was in the Bible, but then he understands by the Bible the spiritual sense. For as to the natural sense, that Voltaire was commanded by God to expose.[1]

I know of no other Christianity and of no other Gospel than the Liberty both of body & mind to exercise the Divine Arts of Imagination . . . What is the Divine Spirit? is the Holy Ghost any other than an Intellectual Fountain? . . . Can you think at all & not pronounce heartily! That to Labour in Knowledge, is to Build up Jerusalem: and to Despise Knowledge, is to Despise Jerusalem & her Builders.[2]

Without Unceasing Practice nothing can be done. Practise is Art. If you leave off you are Lost.
The unproductive Man is not a Christian, much less the Destroyer.[3]

The standpoint of life, of practice, should be first and fundamental in the theory of knowledge. (Lenin, *Materialism and Empirio-Criticism.*)

Ideology is a process accomplished by the so-called thinker consciously, indeed, but with a false consciousness. The real motives impelling him remain unknown to him . . . (Marx, Letter to Mehring, 14 July 1893.)

Much damage has been done to our understanding of Blake's visual and poetic art by the systematisers and literary source-hunters. An ideological and artistic struggle, waged under conditions of insecurity, fear of persecution and frequent poverty, whose inner life was dynamic and contradictory, is frozen into a theological system, a set of cosmological ideas, or a catalogue of symbolic explanations. Kathleen Raine's view is that Blake was steeped in a body of occult knowledge with its own symbolic language:

> It is therefore necessary at this time to relearn both traditional doctrine and its symbolic language, before poetry like that of Dante or of Blake can be more than superficially understood. At least we may be encouraged to discover that the same key unlocks all.[4]

D. G. Gillham's comment is apt:

> The suggestion is that Blake discovered how to interpret symbols in terms of a traditional body of knowledge, but the best poets do not work in this way; their images are flexible, change significance in various contexts and discover new directions on different occasions. The Neoplatonists and alchemists ascribed a fixed significance to their symbols, and to assume that Blake was prepared to accept such limitations is to rob him of his poetic function.[5]

On the same side as Gillham, F. R. Leavis said of Raine's approach that it

> generates blindness, and perpetuates a cult that, whatever it serves, doesn't serve Blake or humanity. The notion that by a devout study of Blake's symbolism a key can be found that will open to a supreme esoteric wisdom is absurd: and to emphasize in that spirit the part played in his life's work by Swedenborg, Boehme, Paracelsus, Orphic tradition, Gnosticism, and a 'perennial philosophy' is to deny what makes him important.[6]

All this is true if we ignore the social, historical and ideological context. As soon, however, as we restore Gnosticism, Boehme and Swedenborg to their proper context, their relevance becomes clear. A. L. Morton, Christopher Hill, E. P. Thompson and Jack Lindsay have, meanwhile, emphasised another tradition important for an understanding of Blake: antinomianism, a tendency, if not a movement, among dissenting artisans and tradesmen, whose roots lay in the 'left wing' of the anti-feudal struggle. When we return to these class roots, we find them giving flower to those very ideas that make up Raine's timeless, 'esoteric wisdom'. Neoplatonism, animism and magic, for example, came together in a whole set of popular beliefs (the cosmos as 'an organic unity in which every part bore a sympathetic relationship to the rest';[7] the symbolic unity of the inner and outer worlds; man as microcosm; the influence of the imagination in a world seen as 'a pulsating mass of vital influences',[8] etc.). The key word here is *popular*:

> Magic may have been unfashionable with the scientists whose meetings in London and Oxford gave rise to the Royal Society, but it gained new converts among the radical sects thrown up by the Civil War, many of whose members pressed for the introduction of the occult sciences into the educational curriculum.[9]

We are brought, as always, back to the same historical process.

The survival, albeit tenuous, of religious and mystical radicalism in England after 1660 was mainly due to the failure of the democratic revolution, which 1642 had set in motion. The English Revolution was fought out in religious as well as political terms. Political content was often clothed in a religious form. The doctrine of free grace, the universal forgiveness of sins, and the belief in an inner light, accompanied the demands for freedom, equality and democracy that spread among the plebeian ranks of the New Model Army, which had fought for *its* kind of society, not the reformed social hierarchy of the Grandees. In the eighteenth century, tiny radical sects and tendencies, like sealed vessels, became the repository of democratic, anarchist and communist ideas, ideas which, until Paine, Godwin and Spence, tended to be cast in religious and hermetic language. The return of the king in 1660 also meant the return of an episcopal hierarchy. Without the Anglican Church, religious radicalism would have lacked the fuel on which to fire its memories of past struggles, its dreams of the future and, not infrequently, its fantasies.

The central fact about the Church of England in the eighteenth century was its complete identification with the state and the ruling class, whose 'natural religion' was a reaction against the religious 'fanaticism' of the Civil War era. The thirty-nine articles were simply a test of loyalty to the regime. Archbishops and bishops came from the landed nobility and aristocracy, some living off tithes from areas which they rarely, if ever visited. Bishop Watson of Llandaff, a defender of Antichrist in Blake's eyes, never lived in his diocese during the thirty-four years he was its spiritual pastor, and probably earned thirty or forty times as much as Blake. (In 1815 the Bishop of Durham was getting £19,000 a year.) Watson's tract on *The Wisdom and Goodness of God, in having made both Rich and Poor* drew Blake's comment: 'God made Man happy & Rich, but the Subtil made the innocent, Poor. This must be a most wicked & blasphemous book.' The higher Anglican clergy were quite cynical in their defence of the system that maintained them. Here is Archdeacon Paley, in his *Principles of Moral and Political Philosophy* (1785), inquiring how 'weak and tame minds . . . have power to resist energy':

> In what manner opinion thus prevails over strength, or how power, which naturally belongs to superior force, is maintained in opposition to it; in other words, *by what motives the many are induced to submit to the few*, becomes an inquiry which lies at the root of almost every practical speculation. (my italics)

One can almost see the reverend gentleman, shaded by his enrooting Tree of Mystery, writing in his book of brass moral speculations on how to reduce 'all to our will, as spaniels are taught with art' (*The Four Zoas*, Night VII). In fact, 'opinion' could not rule without force, as Pitt well knew and Castlereagh proved.

When Blake wrote that spiritual cleansing 'will come to pass by an improvement of sensual enjoyment' and that 'every thing that lives is holy', he was following antinomian tradition.[10] The banner of unfettered desire and libidinal revolt was raised against a moral law that was being strengthened to curb lower-class 'immorality', 'sedition' and 'infidelity'. Self-appointed policemen included Tory Evangelicals such as William Wilberforce, with his Society for the

Suppression of Vice and Encouragement of Religion, who in 1792 considered proposing to the Archbishop of Canterbury 'a day of fasting and humiliation' to quell the spread of Jacobin and Painite ideas;[11] and John Bowdler, who, when he was not 'bowdlerising' books and persecuting nude sea bathers, was campaigning to have adultery made a capital offence. After 1794, a Gnostic element entered Blake's work.[12] Gnosticism, the earliest anticlerical heresy, renounced the flesh as evil and equated the 'evil being who is the creator of the visible world . . . with Jehovah, the God of the Jews'.[13] By 1810 Blake was convinced that 'the Creator of this World is a very Cruel Being' and that 'Man is born a Spectre or Satan & is altogether an Evil'. Although Blake is more Gnostic in his later work (with the exception of *The Everlasting Gospel*, which is as antinomian as *The Marriage*), and although Gnosticism and antinomianism may seem diametrically opposed, it was possible for a thirteenth-century Gnostic, who regarded the flesh as evil, to adopt an antinomian position, declaring that the faithful or elect, as recipients of divine grace, were beyond sin and hence were freed from moral law.[14]

In the writings of John Saltmarsh, the most eloquent antinomian preacher of the 1640s, an anti-élitist, democratic impulse prevails. No longer condemned as unredeemed sinners and reprobates, the common people are as much recipients of divine grace and wisdom as the educated few: 'Let not one despise another for gifts, parts, learning. Let the Spirit be heard in the meanest; let not the scribe or disputer of the law despise the fisherman, nor they despise them because scribes and disputers. The Spirit is in Paul as well as in Peter, in both as well as one.'[15] This is echoed in Blake: 'He who despises & mocks a Mental Gift in another, calling it pride & selfishness and sin, mocks Jesus the giver of every Mental Gift.'[16] Saltmarsh, who had once taken tithes, was righteously upbraided by Ley in *Light for Smoke*, who duly pronounced: 'The sinne is not remitted, unless the goods that be unlawfully taken be restored'.[17] Saltmarsh retorted: 'take heed how you put forgiveness of sin upon restitution; for that is not only *Popery* but like the Pope you would sell *pardons* onely to the rich, and none to the *poor*;

and you would put more upon *Sacrifice* than upon *Mercy*'.[18]
Likewise, the central theme of Blake's *Jerusalem* is the
unconditional forgiveness of sins:

> . . . Doth Jehovah Forgive a Debt only on condition
> > that it shall
> Be Payed? Doth he Forgive Pollution only on
> > conditions of Purity?
> That Debt is not Forgiven! That Pollution is not
> > Forgiven!
> Such is the Forgiveness of the Gods, the Moral
> > Virtues of the
> Heathen whose tender Mercies are Cruelty. But
> > Jehovah's Salvation
> Is without Money & without Price, in the Continual
> > Forgiveness of Sins . . .

A political activist, Saltmarsh criticised the Seekers for their
passive attitude, just as the Zealots, the revolutionary party
in Jerusalem, had criticised the Pharisees for clinging to
Mosaic law and waiting on divine aid, instead of actively
opposing Roman rule. To 'wait in any such way of Seeking
or expectations, is Anti-christian,' wrote Saltmarsh. 'Christ
is already in all *his* in *Spirit* and *truth*'.[19] When, in Chapter
2 of *Jerusalem*, the four Zoas fall into 'pitying & weeping
as at a tragic scene', Los grows furious, raging: 'Why stand we
here trembling around/Calling on God for help; and not
ourselves in whom God dwells. . .?'

Antinomianism was an ideology that liberated ordinary
people from the crippling burden of inherited guilt, impotence and fear of eternal damnation (hell was not a place
but a mental state), but its known practical consequences,
such as the Anabaptist commune at Münster, made it even
more feared by Tories such as Wesley, who kept meeting
antinomians between the 1730s and 1750s. He condemned
them as 'the first born children of Satan'.[20] Ironically,
George Lavington, Bishop of Exeter, was not the only one
to brand the field-preaching Methodists themselves as arro-
gant enthusiasts who, like the antinomians, claimed 'absolute
freedom from corruption' through inner faith.[21] William
Hurd in 1811 was still writing of antinomian groups in London:

As morality is an unnecessary thing, and as holiness, they say, can be no evidence of faith, so some of them meet in a room in a public house every Sunday evening, having before them that much despised book the Bible. Each member pays for a pot of beer, which is drunk by the company in a social manner.[22]

Lindsay thinks it can hardly be doubted that Blake attended such meetings or talked with some of their members.[23]

The Ranter tradition is also continued in Blake. Ranters, according to John Holland, believed that 'man cannot either know God, or believe in God, or pray to God, but it is God in man that knoweth himself'.[24] Blake wrote: 'God is Man & exists in us & we in him', and: 'All deities reside in the human breast'. The Swedenborgian Robert Hindmarsh met a man from Shoreditch in the 1780s who said that 'there was no God in the universe but man'.[25] Abiezer Coppe, the most violently apocalyptic and poetically inspired of the seventeenth-century Ranters, wrote of his 'plaguy holiness' being 'confounded' and 'thrown into the lake of brimstone';[26] in Chapter 2 of *Jerusalem* Blake wrote: 'Each Man is in his Spectre's power/Until the arrival of that hour,/When his Humanity awake/And cast his Spectre into the Lake'. Coppe's giving himself over to the oppressed and the outcast after the execution of the king; to all those beggars, wanderers, thieves and prostitutes he passionately championed — without, however, forming any coherent programme or party (much as modern anarchists champion the lumpenproletariat but disdain any centralised organisation) — brought immense psychological strains, then ecstatic release. We read of him lying 'trembling, sweating', full of 'terrour and amazement', seeing a 'great body of light' and hearing a 'thunderclap' with 'exceeding trembling and amazement, joy unspeakable'.[27] These, one imagines, are not mere metaphors. The Ranter Joseph Salmon experienced a similar spiritual ecstasy:

I saw heaven opened unto me and the new Jerusalem (in its divine brightness and corruscant beauty) greeting my Soule by its humble and gentle discensions . . . I appeared to my selfe as one confounded into the abyss of eternitie, nonentitized into the being of beings; my Soule split, and emptied into the fountains and ocean of divine fulness: expired into the aspires of pure life.[28]

This kind of experience, and the language used to describe it ('abyss of eternitie', 'nonentitized', 'my Soule split') are found again in Blake, whose Milton is compelled to 'go down to self annihilation' before discovering his true humanity. *Jerusalem* itself is like a series of 'trembling' confessions, ending in Albion's act of commitment and self-sacrifice, with his vision of a new, divine reality:

> So Albion spoke & threw himself into the Furnaces
> of affliction.
> All was a Vision, all a Dream: the Furnaces became
> Fountains of Living Waters flowing from the Humanity
> Divine.

New sects, mass confessions and conversions are usually the product of extreme social change, crisis and upheaval. Revolution in France, then war, high taxation, inflation and famine, the dispossession of small tenant farmers and their families, urban alienation, and the proletarianisation of independent artisans such as the handloom weavers, pushed capitalism's new victims either towards violent protest and insurrection, political agitation or, in periods of defeat, towards what E. P. Thompson has called the 'chiliasm of despair'.[29] Groans and tears, sighs and trembling, weeping and self-division, howls and shudderings, terror and astonishment, as well as joy, peace and bliss, fill the pages of *The Four Zoas, Milton* and *Jerusalem*. Blake was responding to his immediate spiritual-religious environment. Indeed, he was part of it. As always, its two most recurrent, abiding images of hope and salvation were the millennium and the New Jerusalem.

Early Christianity had arisen when itinerant craftsmen, impoverished free men, slaves from the *latifundia* and small peasants looked for a 'common road to emancipation' where none in practice existed.[30] Yet it 'had to be found if a single great revolutionary movement was to embrace them all'. The New Jerusalem would only descend 'after arduous struggles with the powers of hell'.[31] In Revelation John of Patmos wrote: 'He which testifieth these things saith, Surely I come quickly.' One thousand two hundred years later, and still waiting, Joachim da Fiore prophesied the Second Coming and an Age of the Holy Spirit, shortly expected. In 1650 Winstanley said: 'This is the fulness of the Beast's time, it is his last period.'[32] The 1790s were also the last days. One millenarian sect in the London of the 1790s whose roots lay in the seventeenth century was the Muggletonians (Reid's 'Mystics, Muggletonians, Millenaries'). The sect's founders, Lodowick Muggleton (1609-98) and his cousin John Reeve (1608-58), both tailors, had claimed to be the two witnesses in Revelation 11:3. They held to the Joachimite conception of history as three ages (Father, Son and Holy Spirit), a doctrine known as the Everlasting Gospel — hence the title of Blake's poem — which is illustrated in the line: 'The dark Religions are departed & sweet Science reigns'.[33] Muggleton's works were published four times between 1755 and 1760, and collected in one volume in 1820. Muggletonians associated the devil with ice-cold reason, an idea that probably influenced Blake. Thompson has characterised this conscious anti-rationalism as 'an esoteric tradition capable of nourishing a highly intellectual anti-intellectualism'.[34]

The Swedenborgian New Jerusalem Church was not authentically millenarian, yet it lit the path for those who passed through it, such as Blake, William Sharp, the carpenter John Wright and the copper-plate printer William Bryan, the last three later followers of Richard Brothers. Sharp had been a member of the Society for Constitutional Information since 1780, and joined the New Church in 1787. Flaxman, another friend of Blake, had been attached to the Swedenborgians since 1783, when meetings took place in Jacob Duché's chapel at the orphan asylum in St George's Fields, Lambeth.[35] 'It is, indeed, Swedenborg and the Muggletonians who complete the living chain connecting the age of Joachim of Flora with that of Blake', says A. L. Morton.[36]

Like Milton, Blake interpreted the times in which he lived in the light of Judaeo-Christian tradition, as, indeed, did thousands of his contemporaries. Isaiah, Ezekiel, Daniel and the Book of Revelation were once more excitedly thumbed through as revelations of a divine providence working through contemporary history, thousands of years after their authors had died. A modern prophet such as Richard Brothers read an apocalyptic significance into Pitt's desperate war against France, and in doing so gained numerous followers. Yet that was not all. Alongside his apocalyptic visions and megalomaniac fantasies (London, the modern Babylon, was going to be destroyed; Brothers made an appeal, and the Lord God told him: 'I pardon London and all the people in it, for your sake: there is no other man on earth that could stand before me to ask for so great a thing'[37]). Brothers made certain specific predictions, all naturally given firm support by the Lord God, Daniel and the Book of Revelation. (His literalism and belief in an ultimate higher authority showing his own self-alienation − are quite different from Blake's archetypal approach and assertion of the divine *in* the human.) In 1794 he prophesied England's war with the U.S.A. (which seemed imminent at the time, but only broke out twenty years later); 'the general fall of *European monarchy*' (more or less true by 1806, when Napoleon was master of all Europe west of Russia); various French victories and countries who would be forced to make peace, and the fact that France, whose people had 'the judgement of God in their favour' (comparable to Blake's characterisation of Luvah, who becomes Christ), would emerge the '*Queen among Nations*', while England would be 'left alone, deserted by all her Allies'[38] − which was indeed the case in 1797, three years later. Few, least of all Pitt and his government, could see that far in 1794. For all his compensatory fantasies and delusions of grandeur,[39] Brothers's reputation as a potential leader quickly spread among certain middle-class and artisan circles,[40] despite his total lack of real leadership qualities. When he prophesied in 1795 that George III would deliver up his crown to him, the authorities saw fit to have this Nephew of the Almighty and member of the tribe of Judah confined in a private madhouse in Islington − the same in which Charles Lamb's sister Mary was confined in 1796 after murdering her mother.

The apostles of revelation and the apostles of reason and progress were, of course, at this time split into irreconcilable camps, yet the cut was not clean. Joseph Priestley, a man reviled by the Church for his philosophical materialism, baffled his scientific colleagues by his religious and biblical preoccupations. This radical Unitarian and discoverer of oxygen, whose *History of the Corruptions of Christianity* (1782) was burned by the public hangman, was advised by Gibbon to stick to 'those sciences in which real and useful improvements *can* be made'. In 1796, having propagated the view that what others call 'soul' was simply an activity of the brain and the nervous system, Priestley, now in American exile, was trying to apply the Book of Daniel to contemporary affairs in England. One is reminded of Newton, who spent many hours reading Hebrew history, trying to fix the dates of biblical events back to the Creation. Like Priestley's, Blake's attachment to the Bible, whether deviant and rebellious or poetic and inspirational, generates a number of tensions and contradictions in his work, tensions that can only be understood in their historical context.

The seventeenth-century radical sects were all agreed on one thing when it came to the Bible: there could be no single authority now that each man was his own authority. (Protestant freedom thus anticipates Romantic individualism.) Few were interested in the Bible as history. Some, such as Winstanley, used it allegorically, others read its stories as myths, others again made selective, modern interpretations for political purposes. No one knew that the beast in Revelation referred to the Emperor Nero, so the Beast and the Antichrist became whatever king, emperor or pope happened to be on the throne at the time. Samuel Fisher's textual critiques showed the Bible to be merely a book like any other; Collins's *Discourse of the Grounds and Reasons of the Christian Religion* (1724) did the same, condemning allegorical interpretation of the Bible on rational, empirical grounds. Twisting the knife, Voltaire summarised its contents as the unenlightening record of a small nation of uncultured desert nomads and bloodthirsty peasants, replete with incoherent maxims, improbable stories and childish absurdities. Blake was strongly influenced by the demolition work the Enlightenment had carried out on the Bible, linked as this was to the attack on the clergy and state religion.[41] He respected neither the literal truth of the scriptures nor their moral content: 'That the Jews assumed a right Exclusively to the benefits of God will be a lasting witness against them & the same will it be against Christians.' To defend 'the Wickedness of the Israelites in murdering so many thousands under pretence of command from God' was, he felt, 'altogether Abominable & Blasphemous'.[42] Blake, clearly, was incapable of Voltaire's dry, cynical wit on such matters. The Bible was like a wayward parent whose faults and weaknesses stirred deep emotions. Thus Blake's 'Bible of Hell', of which *The Book of Urizen* and *The Book of Ahania* are his Genesis and Exodus, and which is probably the seed of *The Four Zoas*, turns out to be something far less negative and reductive than the de-mystifications of the rationalists. It is a subversive and imaginative *re-writing* of biblical myth and narrative, an ironic, bitter, yet creative re-casting and revision — not a mere allegorisation — in the light of modern history and personal experience. (By the time we get to *Jerusalem*, with its elaborate scheme of biblical correspondences, the radical irony has disappeared.)

Blake's positive attachment to the Bible was as a poet and visionary artist: 'The Whole Bible is fill'd with Imagination & Visions from End to End & not with Moral Virtues'; 'The Old & New Testaments are the Great Code of Art'. In 1788 he wrote:

> The Religions of all Nations are derived from each Nation's different reception of the Poetic Genius, which is every where call'd the Spirit of Prophecy . . . The Jewish & Christian Testaments are An original derivation from the Poetic Genius . . .[43]

Robert Lowth's *Lectures on the Sacred Poetry of the Hebrews* had revived an appreciation of the Bible as literature. In a Hebrew context, 'the Spirit of Prophecy' and 'the Poetic Genius' were one:

> . . . it is sufficiently evident, that the prophetic office had a most strict connexion with the poetic art. They had one common name, one common origin, one common author, the Holy Spirit. Those in particular were called to the exercise of the prophetic office, who were previously conversant with the sacred poetry.[44]

Lowth's *Lectures*, which explained the principles of Hebrew prosody, had an important influence on the Romantic movement, and possibly on Blake. Oliver Elton said that Blake's mind 'was nearer than Milton's to the spirit of Hebrew lyric, working as it does Orientally, through figures, apostrophes, and passionate separate affirmations, and not by the chainwork of reasoned Western oratory'.[45] (One might add, following Derrida, that the Hebraic exemplifies an 'unhappy', divided consciousness, whose reintegration is the main theme of *The Four Zoas*.) In Blake, the poet's role becomes a prophetic one: not merely to warn and castigate,[46] but to rouse and awaken, urging his fellow countrymen to build Jerusalem 'In England's green & pleasant Land'. In his longer works, the prophetic and apocalyptic modes[47] were combined with post-Miltonic epic form. The result is a unique product of its time.

An epic is originally an oral form, passed down from generation to generation as a collection of stories and episodes clustering around a central hero. It is thus a shared and collective, rather than individual utterance. The literary epic, however, has an 'author'. By the time we reach the Romantic period, the epic becomes an expression or projection of its author (*The Four Zoas, The Revolt of Islam, Don Juan*).[48] Romantic alienation, whether in Blake, Wordsworth, Goethe or Byron, militates against the classic epic spirit. Deserted by the masses, like Hölderlin's Empedocles, the Romantic artist finds himself confronting an increasingly alien reality, clinging to a lonely, heroic egotism, whether bardic and prophetic, introspective and self-searching, or cynical and ironic.

In *The Odyssey, The Aeneid, Paradise Lost*, and Exodus, which is the Israelite epic, the heroes are representatives of a whole people. As such, Odysseus, Aeneas, Adam and Moses have a special relationship with an immortal power or powers who intervene on man's behalf, either guiding in partisan fashion towards victory and salvation, or punishing for wrongs committed. In Blake's epics, this god-hero-people division disappears, and with it epic 'machinery' such as divine intervention and prolonged debates in heaven. *The Four Zoas* has familiar epic episodes, such as Urizen's Satan-like journey, his descent into the underworld and encounter with wild beasts and monsters, and the final epic contest of Nights VIII and IX.[49] But Urizen is a god, a human hero and a people all rolled into one. He is the god of reason, yet he is also England, the Prince of the Enlightenment, Newton, Pitt, Satan and the new class of industrial capitalists. Los, immortal prophet and god of the creative imagination, is also 'Blake' — the real hero of the poem. Luvah is the god of passion, he is the 'dying god', Christ, France, and is manifested in his political struggles with Urizen as Orc, who is the god of revolution and libidinous desire, the armed might of revolutionary France, and Napoleon. The nature of the Zoas is known only to 'the Heav'nly Father'; 'No individual knoweth'.[50] However, they cannot mediate between a supreme god and human individuals, as Athene mediates between Zeus and Odysseus, or as Gabriel and Raphael intercede on Adam's behalf, since empirically real individuals have no place within the poem's narrative. The Zoas are more like archetypes of the collective unconscious, forces in the 'Universal Man' that come together in 'a Perfect Unity' only in 'the Universal Brotherhood of Eden' — Blake's ideal democratic republic. Moreover, Blake's mythological archetypes keep changing. From poem to poem, within a single poem, and even in a single passage, they undergo a bewildering variety of transformations.

Alice Ostriker introduces *The Four Zoas* as follows:

> Its theme is a cosmic history of Mankind and his universe, from initial collapse and division among his primal energies, to final regeneration.[51]

Short of bringing in creatures from other planets, it is difficult to imagine a much grander theme than the 'cosmic history of Mankind and his universe'. We recognise, however, its ancestry in Christian historiography and eschatology:

> The Christians were perhaps the first to suspect a real grandeur in history, for to them it became a divine epic, stretching far back to the creation of man and forward to the final separation of good and evil in a last magnificent and decisive crisis.[52]

Myth and history, divine acts and human acts, the natural
and the supernatural, literal facts and allegorical truths,
the subjective world of the 'soul' and the objective world
of events, are equally real in this Christian tradition. For the
medieval Christian historian, any history was good history
as long as it adhered to the Bible, conformed to Church
orthodoxy, and showed the eventual victory of Christ over
Satan:

> Men were everywhere more inclined to believe than to
> examine, everywhere imagination had the upper hand of
> reason. No distinction was made between ideal and real,
> between poetical and historical truth. Heroic poems were
> considered a true and lofty form of history and history
> was everywhere displaced by epics, legends or poetical
> fiction of some kind.[53]

In Milton's *Paradise Lost*, the 'divine epic' is everywhere
assumed: it stretches from the Creation and the Fall, through
Christ's redemptive mission, to the end of the world and the
Day of Judgment, thereby embracing the whole of human
history. At the same time, Milton felt the need, especially
when hopes of establishing a republican commonwealth had
failed, to 'assert Eternal Providence,/And justify the ways of
God to men'. The leaders of the English Revolution were
men, but men whose calling had been divinely inspired. God
did not autocratically determine history, since men were
free to choose, but he could directly intervene in history
through his chosen people (this was where the 'British
Israelite' tradition came in)[54] and their chosen leaders. The
failure of the leaders of God's people, guided by divine
providence, to establish a lasting paradise on earth, was
explained by recourse to biblical myth, so reanimating the
myth itself. Yet the myth was expanded, adapted and made
contemporary in all sorts of ways. Much political and historical allusion can be read into the poem. At certain points,
we can see Satan as the deposed royal tyrant, Adam as the
Puritan magistrate, the war in heaven as the Civil War, the
fruit of the forbidden tree as a royal crown, the expulsion
of Adam and Eve as the Restoration, and so forth. Denying
the importance of these allusions on the grounds that Milton

is engaged with universals, not with the realities of contemporary history, is disingenuous. *Paradise Lost* is an
intensely *political* poem, whose politics are palpably present
in its narrative structure and ironic strategies, its language,
style and versification and, most important, in the author's
own profound involvement in the events he describes, events
whose full meaning it was his duty to draw out for the
benefit of those readers he was addressing: 'audience fit,
though few'. This imposed a dual responsibility that led
to a tension between what the poem *presents* and what the
narrator tells us to think, a tension between Milton's conscious and unconscious intentions that Blake, with his
antinomian allegiances, pounced on when he remarked:
'The reason Milton wrote in fetters when he wrote of
Angels & God, and at liberty when of Devils & Hell, is
because he was a true Poet and of the Devil's party without
knowing it.' Milton's unconscious sympathy with left-wing,
antinomian devils clashed with his conscious intentions. 'The
contradictions in Milton', says Christopher Hill, 'are
fascinating historical evidence: we must not arbitrarily
resolve them one way or another.'[55]

In Milton's divine epic, there is the fusion of biblical myth
and contemporary politics, 'poetical and historical truth',
yet Milton was aware of the distinction between the ideal
and the real; so far as his grasp of political and historical
realities is concerned, it cannot be said that 'everywhere
imagination had the upper hand of reason'. In *The Four
Zoas*, there is a much more ambitious kind of fusion.
Individual psychology, events in the natural world, politics
and ideology are barely distinguished as separate processes.
The Neoplatonic doctrine of the microcosm and the macro-
cosm (and hence the Swedenborgian doctrine of correspondences) is here sanctioned by the epic mode itself, where
the macrocosmic process — culminating in the final
apocalypse — works itself through all things, however small.
It is felt even in the fall of a sparrow, dying 'in the foodless
winter',[56] since this connects with 'the wither'd field where
the farmer plows for bread in vain' in Enion's lament,
referring to the famines and poor harvests of 1795 and after,
but recalling the third, black horse of Revelation 6:5-6, the

bringer of famine. In *Auguries of Innocence* Blake declares: 'A Robin Red breast in a Cage/Puts all Heaven in a Rage', and: 'The Harlot's cry from Street to Street/Shall weave Old England's winding Sheet'. If the apocalypse is the revolution, and if the revolution only comes when the limits of contraction and opacity (bringing war, famine, poverty and oppression) have been reached, then a sparrow's fall or a harlot's cry are a perfectly valid, prophetic fusion of 'poetical and historical truth'. Yet seen another way, this unity of the small world and the great world, type and archetype, the particular and the universal, go with what can only be called wish-fulfilment, compensatory fantasies and delusions of grandeur. Milton, composing *Paradise Lost* and *Samson Agonistes* in his blindness, was soberly objective about his true situation in Restoration England.

Blake, who had taken no direct part in any political activity as far as one can see, nevertheless bestowed on himself and his wife Catherine, during the period of war and political reaction, a central role in bringing about the new order of peace, justice, redemption, and the reign of Christ. In Nights VII-VIII of *The Four Zoas*, we see the couple as Los and Enitharmon (there are also echoes of Adam and Eve) coming together in harmonious collaboration after much conjugal turmoil and torments of love and jealousy, he drawing lines on heaven's walls, she colouring the spaces 'with beams of blushing love'. They build Golgonooza, a city of art, love and the imagination, while the spectres of those killed in the war enter Enitharmon's bosom. As she weaves and sings, Los loves them 'With a parental love'. The 'Divine Countenance' shines in Golgonooza: it is the Second Coming. Urizen, despite his counter-revolutionary armies and enslaving machines, is perplexed and terrified to see 'the Lamb of God clothed in Luvah's robes'. (Luvah, we remember, is also France.) While Los (Blake) works at his furnaces, Enitharmon (Catherine) continues to weave bodies for the spectres, who suddenly appear as a single female. Enitharmon calls her Jerusalem, and at this vision 'the sons of Eden round the Lamb of God' cry 'Glory, Glory, Glory . . . Now we behold redemption . . . We behold with wonder Enitharmon's Looms & Los's Forges'.

However beautiful all this may be as poetic truth, a personal fantasy has been woven onto outer reality. Blake's private sufferings and anxieties ('I have indeed fought thro' a Hell of terrors and horrors ... in a divided existence'; 'O the distress I have undergone, and my poor wife with me')[57] could only be resolved by the assertion — not always, however, wholly unjustified — of the imaginary self as universal hero and inspired prophet, compensating for the 'accumulating loss of confirmation of his being-in-the-world'.[58] Like Richard Brothers, who 'always had a presentiment of being sometime or other very great',[59] he was prey to delusions of grandeur when personal problems, unfair treatment (real or imagined), and the world's failure to recognise his merits posed a threat to his identity. In October 1801, while peace negotiations were going on — negotiations that were successfully concluded in the Treaty of Amiens the following year — Blake wrote to Flaxman:

> I rejoice to hear that your Great Work is accomplish'd. Peace opens the way to greater still. The Kingdoms of this World are now become the Kingdoms of God & his Christ, & we shall reign with him for ever & ever. The Reign of Literature & the Arts Commences.

Lindsay comments:

> He hopes that France and England will now become one country, with united arts. Such an idealisation of the situation is ludicrous. With all his deep insights he is quite unable to make a realistic evaluation of the historical forces in his world.[60]

Blake's 'divine epic' at times sadly confused the ideal and the real.

Yet there is one sense in which the Blakean epic is ideologically an 'advance' on Milton's: namely, in its fusion of the divine and the human. Politically as well as poetically, Milton's God was something of a blunder. Sitting 'High throned above all highth', from where he views his works and their works, he speaks like a cantankerous, irritable high court judge, blaming his human creations for failing the test he has set them.[61] The mechanical deists kicked God even further upstairs and made him invisible, thereby preventing similar blunders in future, while materialists such as La Mettrie and d'Holbach got rid of him altogether. For them, man was now on his own. It is not surprising, then, that God does not feature in Blake's epics, except as the briefly mentioned 'Council of God', a sort of democratic assembly, and the 'Seven Eyes of God', which is a succession of stages in history. This is because for Blake, 'God only Acts & Is, in existing beings or Men'. More than that: the cosmos is also human. In *The Four Zoas*, Urizen builds his Mundane Shell in the sky, but he also builds it in the porches of the brain of the Eternal Man, or Albion, who remains in a deathly, sickly sleep for most of the poem and does not stir until Night VIII — a pattern repeated and further developed in *Jerusalem*. Luvah's seizure of Urizen's horses is the conquest of intellect by passion, which is almost as harmful as Urizen's own takeover, and in a peculiar way collaborates with it. Guilty of 'reasoning from the loins', Luvah is finally told to return, with Vala, 'Into your place, the place of seed, not in the brain or heart'. Each Zoa has his allotted place and function within the Eternal Man. War is war within Man: 'O war within my members!' he cries. When Los with his hammer forges chains to bind Urizen in Night IV, he is also binding the 'Eternal Mind' which, after rolling in 'eddies of wrath', settles into 'a Lake bright & shining clear, White as the snow' — the passively reflecting mind of Lockean empiricism. Nature is seen in human terms, like 'The indignant Thistle whose bitterness is bred in his milk/And who lives on the contempt of his neighbour'. The lions, tigers and scorpions whom Urizen encounters during his unfortunate inspection tour of his 'dens' are, of course, specific human types. Blake's anthropomorphism is boldly announced in *Jerusalem*, Chapter 2: 'for Cities/are Men, fathers of multitudes, and Rivers & Mountains/Are also Men; every thing is Human, mighty! sublime!' And in Chapter 3 we read: 'All Things Exist in the Human Imagination'.

The fusions that occur in Blake's epics are an attempt to overcome the dissociation between subject and object, the earthly and the heavenly. The result — in some ways a paranoid-schizoid reaction to those 'physical and biological sciences of it-processes'[62] that have contributed to feelings of depersonalisation — occasionally tumbles into solipsism. There is, of course, a sense in which Blake is groping towards a world view which, at that time, could only be expressed in religious, symbolic and mythological terms. Yet it is arguable whether, in trying to fuse the psychic and the social, the human and the natural, into an impossible, albeit heroic kind of unity, Blake's 'ultimate kinship' is 'with the Marx of the 1844 Manuscripts', as Lindsay says,[63] or with Neoplatonic mysticism. Maybe we should not try to resolve the contradiction either way, but rather accept the fact that Blake's vision points in both directions.

Blake began writing his first long epic poem around 1796. Its writing, evolution, posthumous history and subsequent interpretation by critics is itself an epic. At the end of *The Marriage*, Blake warned his readers: 'I have also The Bible of Hell, which the world shall have whether they will or no.' Whether he had it or not, a title found on the back of one of Blake's drawings reads: 'The Bible of Hell, in Nocturnal Visions collected. Vol. I. Lambeth'. In 1794 Blake was commissioned to illustrate Young's *Night Thoughts* — for a 'despicably low sum', according to J. T. Smith. The edition was duly trumpeted and published in 1797, but was not a success. Blake used the spare sheets of drawing paper for his epic entitled: *Vala Or The Death and Judgement of the Ancient Man a DREAM of Nine Nights*. The division into 'Nights' was a borrowing from Young. The poem continued to be written, with marginal drawings, until *c.* 1803, re-titled *The Four Zoas* in 1804, then revised and added to until 1808. The poem was never engraved, though 31 lines were incorporated into *Milton* and 147 into *Jerusalem*. Before his death Blake gave the manuscript to John Linnell, one of whose descendants sold it at Christie's in 1918. Some of its more erotic drawings had been erased, probably by Linnell's son. The manuscript was donated to the British Museum, and is now in the British Library's Department of Manuscripts.

The poem is in a sense a twentieth-century work, since the first reliable text was not published until 1925. Indeed, it is as twentieth-century as Joyce's *Ulysses*, for it continues,

and will ever continue, to resist the brand of critical interpretation which treats the text as if it were an object of
literary consumption. Consumptionist criticism is even more
insensitive here, where the text is uncertain: what would have
remained, and in what order, had Blake decided to engrave
his epic, we shall never know. There must have been good
reasons why he allowed it to remain in manuscript. There is
much evidence in the poem of a heroic, therapeutic struggle
to reintegrate the dissociated personality, not merely of the
Eternal Man or Albion, but *of its author*. Not to see this is to
be guilty of complacent blindness. Martin K. Nurmi, for
example, writes:

> Blake's characters must be taken seriously as real person-
> ages in a strange phantasmagoric drama if one is to enter
> into this work in a way that leads to an understanding of
> the kind Blake wanted to communicate ... One must, that
> is, first enter the work as one would any other imaginative
> work by an appropriate suspension of disbelief despite
> its strangeness and simply accept what happens as actually
> happening even when it is altogether fantastic.[64]

Admission into such a work is not gained by presenting a
ticket marked 'disbelief suspended' — however 'appropriate'
the suspension — since what it asks of us is an enormous
effort of self-deconstruction as readers for which few of us
are prepared. One cannot read *The Four Zoas* as one reads
The Lord of the Rings. To presume to know the 'understanding of the kind Blake wanted to communicate' is to
ignore two things: first, that much of the poem is the work,
not of a firmly centred, authoritative ego, but of a de-centred,
fluid and divided one, in which the unconscious plays a major
role; secondly, that as far as we know, Blake did not want to
communicate his poem to anybody: the printed text is *our*
creation, not his.

The Four Zoas, Milton and *Jerusalem* are all attempts to
grapple with a recurrent psychological crisis, foreseen by
Blake when he wrote: 'He who desires but acts not, breeds
pestilence', and 'Sooner murder an infant in its cradle than
nurse unacted desires'.[65] After *The Book of Los* (1795)
Blake did not print an original illuminated work for thirteen

years. To use Mayakovsky's phrase, he trod on the throat of his song, hiding his radicalism from public view. Anyone who does that, after a period of intensely creative involvement, is likely to experience a large measure of frustration and guilt. For Blake, there was also a deep political guilt, to which were added a 'Nervous Fear'[66] and inhibiting persecution fantasies, particularly after Pitt's repressive measures of 1794-5 and 1799-1800.[67] The continued existence of an outside world external to Blake could, however, be merciful when some of its kinder inhabitants prevented his fall into the 'Ulro' of madness and despair. To his new-found patron George Cumberland, civil servant in the victualling department at the War Office, Blake, now aged 42, wrote in July 1800: 'I began to emerge from a Deep pit of Melancholy, Melancholy without real reason for it, a Disease which God keep you from & all good men.'[68] The move to Sussex in September 1800 was also salutary, removing Blake for the first time from 'the terrible desart of London', with a wife whom Hayley spoke of as 'an invaluable Helpmate, perhaps the only woman on Earth, who could have suited him as a wife', referring to Blake as 'this singularly Endangered mortal, unfit in truth to take care of Himself in a world like this'.[69] To Flaxman, who helped to arrange the move to Sussex, Blake wrote in euphoric style on 12 September: 'I bless thee, O Father of Heaven & Earth, that ever I saw Flaxman's face.' One can only speculate about what would have happened without Flaxman and Felpham.

The scheme of *The Four Zoas* is a refinement of Hippocratic, medieval and Elizabethan psychology, which explained all mental illness as an imbalance of the body's four humours. These humours are: black bile or melancholy, which is cold and wet (Tharmas: water); blood, which is hot, the seat of passion (Luvah/Orc: fire); mucus, or phlegm, the cold humour of rational self-possession (Urizen: air); and yellow bile or choler, which is dry, the seat of choler or wrath (Urthona/Los: earth). Blake modifies and adds to this traditional scheme of correspondences in various ways. Urthona, for example, is the 'eternal' name for Los, and Los represents, not merely choler, but imagination and creativity. Attempts by each of the four Zoas to usurp power results in war, division and sickness within the Eternal Man. This parallels exactly a schizophrenic psychosis, where the 'system of functions . . . is shattered into a multiplicity of warring functions . . . the various parts of the system function in relative independence, and are apt to come perpetually in conflict with one another'.[70] The Zoas are also divided from their female 'emanations', and some even undergo division in themselves. Only in Night IX, when the regenerated Zoas cooperate in the 'rural work' — and work is also therapeutic — of the apocalyptic vintage and harvest, is an idyllic unity restored, following the Man's command:

> In enmity & war first weaken'd, then in stern
> > repentance
> They must renew their brightness, & their disorganiz'd
> > functions
> Again reorganize, till they resume the image of the
> > human . . .

A fourfold unity is then 'reorganized'. Historically, this fourfold scheme has a primeval origin. Agricultural Stone Age settlements, according to Bernal, were divided into four exogamous sub-clans,[71] each with its appropriate sign and totem, to which correspond the four points of the compass, the four elements, and the square itself. The perfect square, which is the plan for the restored temple city of Jerusalem in Ezekiel 40:5-47; in Revelation — where, however, the temple is significantly omitted; in Richard Brothers's *A Description of Jerusalem* (1801);[72] in Blake's fourfold City of Golgonooza in Chapter 1 of *Jerusalem*, and in Robert Owen's ideal community (illustrated on every title page of *The New Moral World*), thus symbolising the return to a human ideal that existed before private property and class divisions arose. The deeply buried, collective memory of an original, 'fourfold' human community, with the possibility of its restoration, inspired generations of peasants and artisans in their struggle against each new manifestation of the Beast, the Antichrist and the Whore, in which a revolutionary Messiah comes to bring not peace, but the sword.[73]

The stresses and contradictions in *Paradise Lost* result from an attempt to explain the success and failure of a

revolution, and the poet's own view of it and involvement
in it. Blake experienced no such revolution. He only read
and heard of events across the Channel, while the Irish
rebellion of 1798 and the naval mutinies of 1797, although
major threats to British power, were not enough to bring
down the Beast. Albion lay cold like a corpse on his rocks,
with Urizenic snows cooling his brain and a disorganised sea —
symbol of division and separateness — all around washing
his limbs. Milton's epic is, in the end, a magnificent monu-
ment to the English Revolution. Blake's epics reflect the fact
that the reform societies of the 1790s never got off the
ground as a revolutionary possibility. However much we
would like it not to have been the case, once L.C.S. leaders
fell away, were imprisoned or transported, and new repressive legislation — the product of 'a new sort of conservatism'[74]
— was on the statute books, the political fire died down or
went underground, and no effective leadership or mass
support for unconstitutional, violent roads to democracy
emerged. The only hope was a French invasion. Apart from
that, the government ruled as it liked, opposed by the
feeblest of parliamentary oppositions.

All the division, sterile conflict, atomisation, disorganis-
ation, and sense of retrogression we find in *The Four Zoas*
clearly reflect the period after 1795, when the L.C.S. began
to disintegrate as a movement once mass meetings and demo-
strations were effectively outlawed. Bukharin once said
that 'the psychology of a class is not always identical with
the material interests of that class'.[75] Perhaps we should see
The Four Zoas, and to some extent *Jerusalem*, as the psychological 'inside story' of a movement that turned in on itself,
having proved incapable of riding the reaction after the
attack on the king's coach in 1795. The movement's
pamphleteers, its press, even its poets and artists, were
muzzled, censored and intimidated; its remaining leaders
became liable to house-searches and detention without trial;
its meetings were frequently banned, and the infiltration of
spies and informers bred an atmosphere of mutual suspicion,
fear and mistrust. Repression did, of course, have a radicalising effect (the United Britons are an example), yet the mass
reform movement as a whole began to break up: 'all the

Giants of Albion are become/Weak, wither'd, darken'd, &
Jerusalem is cast forth from Albion'. The disintegration of
the popular reform movement at this time was unexpectedly
rapid, and this evidently hit some — particularly a withdrawn,
sensitive and emotional enthusiast such as William Blake —
harder than others.[76] Blake's guilt, anxiety and confusion
arose from his self-imposed censorship in not openly pub-
lishing his works, the fear of dire repercussions if he were
to do so, and his self-disguise behind the obscurity of myths
and symbols. The 'Gate of the Tongue' (represented by
Tharmas) is closed in Night I of the poem; Enion's plea for
'some shadowy semblance' to be hidden probably refers to
a strategic, 'whispered' radicalism or literary disguise ensuring safety.[77] In Night V, Los repents that he has chained Orc
on the mountain, but knows that to release him could
result in 'his own death'. Such were Blake's fears. It is when
people are cowed, confused, and give up the struggle — when,
that is, the organising spirit is broken — that guilt, fear,
mutual   recrimination,   self-division   and   disorientation
result.[78] Blake shows us the mutually infectious, *psychic*
reaction to political repression. When the passion for political
liberty is branded sedition and treason, an anxious guilt for
being in love with something 'sinful' begins to poison those
who are most intimidated, and the disease spreads. Jerusalem,
'called Liberty among the Children of Albion', once idealised
as the purest of women, the ideal mother, wife and sister,
is branded a harlot (there can be no middle position between
these two extremes), and the tyrant's false image is internalised by the former lover of liberty, who now cowers, shrinks
and folds up into himself, a pathetic, bewildered victim of
political cowardice, inertia and misplaced guilt. Like the
sick Albion in *Jerusalem*, the victim of shame casts out his
former emanations as harlots — in Blake's case this would
apply to his own writings — and regards the comradely
fellowship and bonds of love established when he was in his
former state as 'unnatural consanguinities'. Spiritual degeneration and collapse do not stop there. To the 'fallen' man,
whose nerves are ragged and exposed, not only former
friends, but even sexual partners become enemies. Induced
by political reaction and fear of persecution, paranoid-

schizoid delusions take over, marking the victim's descent into a spiritual hell.

Blake is able to describe this process intimately; yet he did so, as R. D. Laing says, without actually going insane.[79] It is not, of course, a simple descent, but a complex inner conflict. Out of it the poet himself emerged, not as his former radical self, but as a 'New Jerusalemite', a Christian millenarian, at a time when millenarianism, communitarianism and utopianism were spreading among working people. (The debt of Owenite socialism to millenarianism has been examined by J. F. C. Harrison.)[80] In *Jerusalem*, Albion rouses himself from his spiritual sleep when he meets Jesus face to face, and it is at this point that universal brotherhood is restored. Blake's mind and art were formed, at each stage, by the time in which he lived.

In Night I of *The Four Zoas*, Enion tells Tharmas:

> Thy fear has made me tremble, thy terrors have
> > surrounded me.
> All Love is lost: Terror succeeds, & Hatred instead
> > of Love,[81]
> And stern demands of Right & Duty instead of
> > Liberty.
> Once thou wast to Me the loveliest son of heaven —
> > But now
> Why art thou Terrible? and yet I love thee in thy
> > terror till
> I am almost Extinct & soon shall be a shadow
> > in Oblivion,
> Unless some way can be found that I may look upon
> > thee & live.

Have Tharmas's 'terrors', and Enion's terror of Tharmas, who is now 'Terrible', been induced by Pitt's Terror? The very absence of any 'objective correlatives' for the disembodied emotional states expressed in the poem indicates, perhaps, an environment of political and social repression so severe in its effects that, in the case of Tharmas and Enion, it is involuntarily introjected as a spiritual nightmare. Once caught, the psychosis spreads, each victim infecting others, especially intimate partners, just as Tharmas infects Enion

with his 'terrors'. When Urizen explores the 'Abyss' in Night
VI, he encounters, not the vigorous counter-culture we saw
in *The Marriage*, but 'ruin'd spirits' who are 'Scar'd at the
sound of their own sigh' (one can't get more paranoid than
that), their senses unable to penetrate 'Beyond the bounds of
their own self'. Underneath the rational upper crust lies an
abyss of de-sensitised individuals:

> His voice to them was but an inarticulate thunder, for
> their Ears
> Were heavy & dull, & their eyes & nostrils closed up.
> Oft he stood by a howling victim Questioning in words
> Soothing or Furious; no one answered; every one
> wrap'd up
> In his own sorrow howl'd regardless of his words,
> nor voice
> Of sweet response could he obtain, tho' oft assay'd
> with tears.
> He knew they were his Children ruin'd in his ruin'd
> world.

Cursed beyond Urizen's curse, these belong not just to the
world of the downtrodden and oppressed, whom the educated establishment cannot reach, and whom the intellectual
radicals have abandoned. It is an outside view of an *inner
condition* of spiritual defeat and schizoid withdrawal, of
which other passages in the poem are a starkly eloquent
testimony.[82]

Tharmas's 'trembling' complaint to Enion, for example —

> Why wilt thou Examine every little fibre of my soul,
> Spreading them out before the sun like stalks of flax
> to dry?
> The infant joy is beautiful, but its anatomy
> Horrible, Ghast & Deadly; nought shalt thou find in it
> But Death, Despair & Everlasting brooding Melancholy.
> Thou wilt go mad with horror if thou dost Examine
> thus
> Every moment of my secret hours

— suggests a characteristic feature of schizophrenia, the loss
of ego boundaries. Its sufferers complain, like Tharmas, 'that

people know their thoughts, that their ideas are not safely enclosed in their own heads but enter into the minds of other people';[83] hence their inner selves become vulnerable, resulting in what Laing calls an 'ontological insecurity'.[84] Trying to cope with a cruel, de-personalising world, the victim's very sense of self is endangered: 'I am like an atom,/A Nothing, left in darkness; yet I am an identity:/I wish & feel & weep & groan. Ah, terrible! terrible!' We cannot believe, meanwhile, that Enion as the probing spy can go mad unless she is at the same time probing into herself. The two seem to be mirror-images of each other, and therefore divided parts of one self speaking as separate selves. This hypothesis is borne out later when Enion confesses:

> Examining the sins of Tharmas I soon found my
> own . . .
> I thought Tharmas a sinner & murder'd his
> Emanations,
> His secret loves & Graces. Ah me wretched! What
> have I done?
> For now I find that all those Emanations were my
> Children's souls,
> And I have murder'd these with Cruelty above
> atonement.

In other words, Tharmas's previous 'Thou wilt go mad' was really *an address to himself*. The idea that *he* has been cruel, with the consequent guilt, sense of persecution and dread this brings, has been projected onto Enion. Murdering one's own emanations is to bring 'self-murder' on one's soul — the ultimate crime. Enion, or Tharmas's image of Enion, is thus a projective identification of Tharmas's 'bad' self.[85] But this paranoid guilt over being cruel, once it is reintrojected ('I have murder'd these with *Cruelty above atonement*') must create a new panic, threatening a complete breakdown, which actually occurs.

One defence against a persecution anxiety is to remove that part of the ego containing the persecuting (and persecuted) self from the rest of the ego, thus dividing the ego into a false 'outer' self and a real 'inner' self. This false outer self forms part of what Blake calls the 'Spectre'.

Tharmas's Spectre is painfully drawn out, nerve by nerve, by the image of the cruel, dreaded Enion he once loved, who is herself terrified by the 'woven shadow' she has created. Since what we perceive in others exists in ourselves, and what we do to others we do to ourselves, in this terrifying — innocent? — world of uncontrollable subjective fantasies, Enion in turn begins to lose her sense of identity, crying: 'What am I?' The Spectre of Tharmas, whose 'scaly armour' is a psychotic defence, is alone capable of coupling sexually with Enion, and their act is a nightmarish trauma ('Twisting in fearful forms & howling, howling, harsh shrieking,/Howling, harsh shrieking; mingling, their bodies join in burning anguish'); but by this time Tharmas has already become a chaotic, formless sea.[86]

The opening Tharmas-Enion episode is thus a series of fractures. First, the superego cuts itself off from libidinous drives that appear to the superego as unbearably sinful. This 'polluted' libido is projected onto Enion, who is suitably rebuked by the Spectre:

> I scorn & yet I love.
> If thou hast sinn'd & art polluted, know that I am
> pure
> And unpolluted, & will bring to rigid strict account
> All thy past deeds . . .'

Secondly, there is a rift between the self and outer reality, caused by paranoid fear, leading to a self-destructive split within the ego itself. The split is also sexual: alienated from his spectrous masculinity, Tharmas becomes feminine and submissive. Drawing out the Spectre is like a painful birth, with Enion as the midwife. Yet she has woven it: 'Nine days she labour'd at her work, & nine dark sleepless nights'. The recurrence of the number nine (the poem itself is in nine Nights) suggests the period of gestation. It is as if Tharmas were Enion's own womb! Blake's concept of the Spectre seems, in fact, to have two sides: it is both the male's superego (which Freud defined as the internalised father, representing the moral conscience), and the removed part of the ego in schizoid states. As the former, the Spectre — for example, in Los's case — may be 'ravening' and persecutory

('Hung'ring & thirsting for Los's life' in *Jerusalem*, Chapter 1), but as part of the ego it is probably far more dangerous. To combat an externally-imposed, 'reasoning' guilt that impedes artistic creativity is, in fact, a positive struggle.

In Kleinian psychology, schizophrenia originates in the first year of infancy, when the ego is not yet formed, and a love-hate relationship develops towards the mother's breast: love when it is there, hate when it is not. (The mother is not yet perceived as a person.) According to Rosenfeld, 'the schizophrenic has never completely outgrown the earliest phase of development to which this object relationship belongs, and in the acute schizophrenic state he regresses to this early level.'[87] Before his final, remarkable transformation as revolutionary orator and winnower of Mystery — the chaff of 'Kings & Councellors & Giant Warriors' — from the grain of enslaved humanity, Tharmas regresses to an infantile stage. (His 'sign' is the tongue, which is used for feeding and sucking as well as for speaking.) Unable to transcend his melancholic, Narcissus-like state, he is metamorphosed with Enion, who has remained Echo-like, into an infant playing round the house of Vala, now a consoling mother-shepherdess: 'henceforth in Vala's bosom thou shalt find sweet peace', Vala tells him. Tharmas and Enion have become infant brother and sister, yet strangely enough, a sexual relationship between them still exists. Tharmas complains to his mother: 'in the night on the couch of Enion/I drink new life . . . But in the morning she arises to avoid my Eyes,/Then my loins fade . . .' Vala then tells Tharmas to bring Enion to her. If censorship and displacement are operating here, one would like to know what has been censored and displaced.

Los has similar problems with Enitharmon, who keeps evading his embraces:

> Alternate Love & Hate his breast: here Scorn &
> Jealousy
> In embryon passions; they kiss'd not nor embrac'd
> for shame & fear.

This shyness, seeing that they are brother and sister, is not entirely surprising. The name Enitharmon links Enion and

Tharmas, and is also a near-anagram of Catherine — Blake's wife, certainly, but not exclusively. Blake's sister was called Catherine, and so was his mother, whose maiden name was *Arm*itage. The Los and Enitharmon of *The Four Zoas* represent a potentially creative relationship hampered by fruitless conflicts and brooding introspection. In Night IV, after hammering out the form of Urizen, Los becomes Urizenic, a truly dialectical development: 'he became what he beheld'. His Urizenic side comes out in the coercive binding of his son Orc, an explicitly Oedipal episode, where the complex is more the father's than the son's:

> . . . Los beheld the ruddy boy
> Embracing his bright mother, & beheld malignant
>> fires
> In his young eyes, discerning plain that Orc plotted
>> his death.

(If Los becomes what he beholds, we can assume that he is also repressing his younger, rebellious, Oedipal self; in other words, the war between Urizen and Orc takes place within Los himself.) Enchained by time ('days & years, in chains of iron round the limbs of Urizen'), then by sorrow ('link by link the chains of sorrow'), Los forges the 'Links of fate' and the human spine, until he becomes enchained by marriage ('a marriage chain') and then paternal jealousy. It is this chain (formed out of girdles that 'secret sobs' of pity have burst in twain) that Los uses to chain Orc to the rock. Few poets have managed to condense so much meaning into a single image. Los becomes Urizenic in another way in Night VII, as the couple sit beneath the Tree of Mystery:

> Los sat in showers of Urizen watching cold
>> Enitharmon.
> His broodings rush down to his feet, producing
>> Eggs that hatching
> Burst forth upon the winds above the tree of
>> Mystery.

This weird procreation fantasy (female 'hatching' overtaking male creativity, where the 'producing' is purely biological)[88] first occurs in *The Book of Ahania*, where Fuzon, Urizen's son, symbolically castrates his father, whose 'dire Contemplations' rush down 'like floods from his mountains,/ In torrents of mud settling thick,/With Eggs of unnatural production'. One hatches into 'an enormous dread Serpent' which, with phallic insistency, furiously pushes its horns at Urizen until the latter smites it; later, Urizen throws a rock into Fuzon's bosom: having repressed his own libido, he now depersonalises his libidinous enemy.[89] More psychic events occur in the Los-Enitharmon narrative, such as Enitharmon's Freudian forgetfulness of who her parents are, and a mind-body split in both parties — where the Spectre of Urthona has intercourse with the 'shadow' of Enitharmon — before a progressive, creative partnership can be restored.

The artistic power, political relevance and critical force of *The Four Zoas* rest mainly on the Urizen episodes. The building of the vast Mundane Shell in Night II is both magnificent and terrible, inspiring and appalling, re-creating the response a class-conscious worker might have when viewing the Great Pyramid of Cheops or the Palace of Versailles. There is splendour in Urizenic creation, or Blake could not have fashioned such a line as

Travelling in silent majesty along their order'd ways

which is a fine tribute to the rationalist vision of an ordered universe. But the palace-cum-temple in the sky is merely a heavenly superstructure, its builders coerced by Urizen. What of life here on earth? (At times, Blake's critique seems more applicable to Ptolemaic cosmology than to Cartesian and Newtonian science, though Swift's satire on the *furor mathematicus* of the Laputans and their floating island make a similar point about abstract science and political tyranny.) The answer comes in Enion's lament at the end of Night II, as she sings of

> . . . the slave grinding at the mill,
> And the captive in chains, & the poor in prison, & the
> soldier in the field,
> When the shatter'd bone hath laid him groaning among
> the happier dead.

These are the real foundations of exploitation, misery and repression upon which the whole Urizenic superstructure rests.

Urizen ignores his emanation's advice not to look into the future and casts her out, with the result that all his wise men leave him, his 'wondrous' kingdom collapses, and he falls. Having handed over his steeds to Luvah, he has failed to guide Tharmas, who in Night IV assumes control. In Night V Orc is born, so the woeful Urizen decides to explore his 'horrid' dens (an ironic parallel with Satan's journey, provoked by the creation of man in *Paradise Lost*), inquiring into the misery, ruin and rebellious discontent he himself has largely caused. (There is something of the irony of *King Oedipus* and *King Lear* here.) Urizen, once Prince of the Enlightenment, is now little more than self-preserving, conservative reaction — a Blakean transformation that is, perhaps, neither fair nor historically justified. Blake's viewpoint, however, is from the abyss, where incessant conflict, 'grizly fears', 'howlings, gnashings, groanings, shriekings, shudderings, sobbings, burstings/Mingle together to create a world for Los'. Urizen takes his protective metal books with him wherever he goes, writing in them age after age with his iron pen, 'fixing many a Science in the deep', yet never solving the real problem: why the majority suffer. For all his compulsive dogmatising, Urizen finds neither peace nor repose. The welcome he gets from the underworld, with its lions and scorpions, is roughly what a Tory election canvasser might expect from the unemployed in Glasgow. 'Can I not leave this world of Cumbrous wheels . . .?' is Urizen's plea for detached, Lockean observation and objectivity ('Where self-sustaining I may view all things beneath my feet' — i.e. like Milton's God). But this is now impossible. He is trapped in the recurrent cycle of history that impels the futile 'regulation' of dead books, and he is unable to control the elements, because he himself is 'subject'. He is part of the world he has created.

Finally, Urizen meets Orc in Night VII. Snow-bound, he cannot understand the revolutionary optimism of this fiery individual: how can Orc, feeding on 'visions of sweet bliss far other than this burning clime', bathe in such 'visions of delight' in this 'horrible place'? — visions

> . . . so lovely that they urge thy rage
> Tenfold with fierce desire to rend thy chain & howl
> > in fury
> And dim oblivion of all woe, & desperate repose.
> Or is thy joy founded on torment which others bear
> > for thee?

Urizen's perplexity is like the Tory Angel's in *The Marriage*. His idea of Orc's optimism reminds one of the Girondin mathematician Antoine Nicolas Condorcet who, while in hiding in 1794, and condemned to death by the Jacobins, wrote of a future humanity freed of chains, a picture resembling 'an asylum'

> in which, living in imagination with mankind re-established in its rights and in its true nature [the philosopher] can forget mankind corrupted and tormented by greed, fear, envy. It is in this asylum that he lives with his fellows, in a heaven which his reason has created, and which his love of humanity embellishes with the purest joys.[90]

Orc's forceful reply suddenly jolts the poem into vivid and dramatic life:

> Curse thy hoary brown! What dost thou in this deep?
> Thy Pity I condemn. Scatter thy snows elsewhere . . .
> Tho' rocks roll o'er thee, tho' floods pour, tho' winds
> > black as the sea
> Cut thee in gashes, tho' the blood pours down around
> > thy ankles,
> Freezing thy feet to the hard rock, still thy pen
> > obdurate
> Traces the wonders of Futurity in horrible fear of
> > the future.

If Urizen believes that the Jacobin Orc can remain oblivious 'of all woe' or forget the worst, like Condorcet, he is grossly mistaken. Orc, his feet and hands nailed, Christ-like and Prometheus-like, to the hard rock, is all passion and sensitivity, wholly incapable, like Enion, of insensitive indifference to the suffering around him. Urizen's reply is breath-taking in its unyielding, unhearing obtuseness: 'Read my books, explore my Constellations . . .' *Read my books!* — Presumably to anaesthetise empathy. Orc curses Urizen a second time, but he is already beginning to weaken: 'I well remember how I stole thy light & it became fire/Consuming' is the revolution's acknowledgment of its debt to the Enlightenment; later in the poem, when Orc is a serpent coiled round the Tree of Mystery, we have entered the Napoleonic era.[91]

In Night VIII the epic changes gear, and the earlier apocalyptic hints burst forth in a powerful millenarian vision, though Blake's apocalypse is almost mild compared to that of John of Patmos.[92] History gives way to the divine epic, and at one point in Night VIII a confessional surfeit of biblical names and references takes over. The failure of a revolution has become spiritual food for a Christian solution. Luvah/Orc becomes Christ, Urizen degenerates into the dragon form of Satan, and the old battle is fought out once again. The Urizen-Orc dialectic simply peters out, and a magico-religious fantasy takes its place. In the visionary imagination the right words (or mental pictures) can always create the necessary reality. But the emphasis on work, brotherhood and cooperation in Night IX links up with the rise of utopian socialism during this period, and hence with more practical, if no less utopian attempts at making such millenarian visions a reality.

With *Jerusalem* (1804-20) the utopianism is more urgent and explicit. Between *The Four Zoas* and *Jerusalem*, however, there is one poem where a Urizenic pessimism and anxiety seem to predominate. This is *The Mental Traveller*, written around 1803.

The poem is presented as an unearthly journey:

> I travel'd thro' a Land of Men,
> A Land of Men & Women too,
> And heard & saw such dreadful things
> As cold Earth wanderers never knew.

This sounds like a psychic experience, one that the 'I' of the poem, like the Ancient Mariner, now relates to 'cold Earth wanderers'.[93] The ballad's narrative structure is a double-pendulum cycle, in which male and female, whom fate has eternally linked, begin life at opposite ends of the temporal cycle (she a 'Woman Old', he a 'Babe'), meet and pass in the middle as youth and girl, reach opposite ends of the pendulum swing (he an 'aged Shadow', she a 'Female Babe'), then meet and pass again on their way back, until they resume their original positions, at which point the cycle begins all over again. On one level, this disturbing poem is an allegory of human history seen as an eternal contest, perpetually unresolved, between two principles: the male, which is energetic and progressive, and the female, which thwarts, holds back and uses up the male's creative energy, turning generous production into selfish consumption. However, the deep structure of the poem is clearly psychological, a 'dreadful' vision of its speaker-narrator.

The babe's mother (an example of 'Female Will') is made into a cruel, persecutory and domineering figure (hence 'Old', perceived from the babe's 'vortex')[94] who forces him to experience the extra-uterine world ('She cuts his heart out at his side/To make it feel both cold & heat'),[95] yet who physically binds and stigmatises him (like Prometheus, Christ and Orc), holding back his ego-awareness by possessing and absorbing his emotions:

> Her fingers number every Nerve,
> Just as a Miser counts his gold;
> She lives upon his shrieks & cries,
> And she grows young as he grows old.

Seen from the vortex of the growing youth, the mother becomes 'a Virgin bright'. Rebelling, he 'rends up his Manacles' and appears to turn the tables, only to jump out of the frying-pan into the fire: it is a *mother-substitute* the 'bleeding youth', pre-oedipally fixated, his vulnerable ego still showing the wounds of infancy, has bound down 'for his delight'. His youthful energies are quickly expended (the author who writes this is now in his middle forties), but having stored up spiritual treasures ('the gems of the Human Soul'), he feeds others with his rich, tormented emotional history ('His grief is their eternal joy'). Yet does the 'countless gold of the akeing heart', of which he now has abundance —

enough to feed the spiritually poor and hungry — have a true, original worth, or is it locked in a pre-oedipal chest, and therefore *her* property — she who bound him in his infancy?[96] Alas, after this generous phase, his 'contrary' is re-born, a female 'Baby form' of fire, 'gems & gold' — *his* gems and gold — whom all fear like the plague, not daring to touch her. (Note that *she* has no parent, and is not bound down like the male babe.) She takes a lover and they drive out the 'aged Host'. Robbed of his creations, 'Which he by industry had got', he becomes a proletarian outcast reduced to spiritual beggary, symbolic of psychological guilt and collapse of creative confidence, from which the only escape is regression — which, of course, is no escape at all. A case of out of the fire and back into the frying-pan.

To renew his vigour, the poor old man takes in a new maiden, but his isolation and helplessness further weaken his already blurred ego boundaries, making it 'impossible for him to set limits to the process of identification'.[97] His Felpham-like cottage 'fades before his sight', and his shrunken feelings and timid perceptions are projected onto the outside world:

> For the Eye altering alters all;
> The Senses roll themselves in fear,
> And the flat Earth becomes a Ball.

Perception, in this schizoid world-view, has the magical power to determine the nature of everything perceived. Self and outer reality are barely differentiated: one is simply the magical sign of the other.[98] Meanwhile, love is an oral experience. Fulfilling oral needs and pleasures — not through verbal creation, but through kissing, eating and drinking — sets off an infantile regression:

> The honey of her Infant lips,
> The bread & wine of her sweet smile,
> The wild game of her roving Eye,
> Does him to Infancy beguile;
>
> For as he eats & drinks he grows
> Younger & younger every day . . .

(The clever pun on 'wild game' is revealed in the image of the girl as a fleeing stag, an image found in one of Wyatt's sonnets; 'game', then, is also food.) Regression is a common schizophrenic experience. In the words of one patient:

> I feel that I am constantly becoming younger and smaller. Now I am four years old. Shortly, I shall get into diapers and then back into mother.[99]

The elusive maiden teases and torments the possessive traveller by 'various arts of Love & Hate' (perhaps stirring his unconscious love-hate relationship with the maternal bosom) until 'he becomes a wayward Babe,/And she a weeping Woman Old'. The 'wide desert' of sterile, uncreative guilt and desolation now gives way to a cosy utopian fantasy: 'many a City there is Built,/And many a pleasant Shepherd's home'. The 'pleasant Shepherd's home' brings to mind Tharmas and Enion in Night IX of *The Four Zoas*, and casts a negative shadow on the whole Jerusalemite vision as a regressive fantasy. Everyone in the vicinity flees the re-born babe; as with the re-born female babe, theirs is a superego reaction, indicative that a powerful taboo has been broken. Yet his birth also terrifies because it is prophetic:

> For who dare touch the frowning form,
> His arm is wither'd to its root

— alluding to the man of God who withered the arm of King Jeroboam, the subject of one of Blake's most striking compositions.[100] The babe is nailed down again, like Orc and Prometheus, and will rebel again. Perhaps one day his rebellion will be enough to break the recurrent cycle of procreation merely for the selfish possession that binds others, and energetic production for selfish consumption, where, bound by the law of entropy, every energetic producer declines into a dissipated devourer. The poem has a weird fascination, yet if my reading of the 'dreadful things' it describes is correct, it questions the validity of the poet's entire artistic achievement up to this point.

Between the revolutionary years and the period prior to Waterloo, a number of changes occurred in Blake's outlook

which, when summarised, show that the author of *Jerusalem*
(most of it written *c.* 1809-15) is not the author of *The
Marriage*, nor even of *The Four Zoas*. The Jacobin of 1793
writes in 1810: 'I am really sorry to see my countrymen
trouble themselves about Politics.' The antinomian Devil
who hates religion is now the Christian who tells the deists:
'Man must & will have some Religion: if he has not the
Religion of Jesus, he will have the Religion of Satan.' (*The
Everlasting Gospel* is something of an exception here, in that
its antinomian Jesus is closer to the Devil of *The Marriage*
than he is to the Jesus of *Jerusalem*.)[101] In 1790-93 the tigers
of wrath and the flames of Orc are burning up the old society
and exposing pity as Urizenic ('Pity would be no more/If we
did not make somebody poor'). In *The Book of Urizen*, pity
separates off into a cold, moist web whose knotted fibres
twist into the Net of Religion, and in *The Four Zoas* Orc
rasps at Urizen: 'The Pity I contemn'. But in *Jerusalem*, Los
says of Albion's sons:

> They have divided themselves by Wrath, they must
> > be united by
> Pity; let us therefore take example & warning, O my
> > Spectre.
> O that I could abstain from wrath! O that the Lamb
> Of God would look upon me and pity me in my
> > fury . . .

E. P. Thompson plausibly cites the life-denying chapel in
The Garden of Love as evidence of Blake's abhorrence of
Methodism.[102] But Methodism attracts an emotional defence
in *Milton* and again in *Jerusalem* ('To the Deists'). *Visions
of the Daughters of Albion* (1793) repudiates the Christian
notion of sin, but in 1798 Blake can even write: 'The Earthquakes at Lisbon etc. were the Natural result of Sin.' In
Jerusalem he tells the deists that the Methodist Whitefield
'confessed his Sins before all the World', while 'The Book
written by Rousseau call'd his Confessions, is an apology &
cloke for his sin & not a confession.' Without the idea of sin
and guilt, forgiveness and confession of sin are redundant.
Yet both occupy a central place in Blake's last epic. In *The
French Revolution*, 'spectres of religious men' are 'driven out

of the abbeys' by 'the fiery cloud of Voltaire, and thund'rous rocks of Rousseau'; in *Jerusalem* Blake writes: 'Voltaire, Rousseau . . . charge the Spiritually religious with Hypocrisy; but how a Monk, or a Methodist either, can be a Hypocrite. I cannot conceive.' It is Voltaire and Rousseau who are the real hypocrites, while Rousseau's faith in the natural goodness of man is overturned by the Gnostic doctrine that natural man 'is altogether an Evil'.

Blake's increasingly virulent attacks on female will are another major shift. *Visions of the Daughters of Albion* gives poetic support to Mary Wollstonecraft and the sexual, as well as political and social emancipation of women: 'Enslav'd, the Daughters of Albion weep' is its first line. But in *Jerusalem*, these middle- and upper-class daughters of Albion have become perfectly monstrous tyrants who wield their charms against men and glory in the war, where, tormented by their hypocritical chastity, the men have been driven: 'I am drunk with unsatiated love,/I must rush again to War, for the Virgin has frown'd & refus'd', cries the warrior. Albion, seduced by Vala and hardened by a demonic 'Demonstrative Science', has cast out his Emanation and refuses to give Jerusalem the Bride to Jesus the Lamb, thus making the way clear for Rahab (as the Whore of Babylon) and Tirzah, emblems of the cruel, wilful seductress, who together make up Vala at her most degenerate. The rending of the veil is the rending of coy, hypocritical chastity and female 'secresy'; Vala (nature) is the mysterious, shadowy veil hiding Jerusalem (spiritual reality). Mystery is also rent when the Lamb of God appears. *Jerusalem* consciously echoes Hebrew prophecy after the Solomonite empire and the split into two kingdoms, when God's anger, embodied in the growing threat from Assyria and Babylon, was invoked against the Canaanite, Egyptian and other gods and rituals that had found their way even into the temple of Yahweh. Anath is the goddess of war in the Baal epic:

She waded up to the knees, up to the neck in blood. Human heads lay at her feet, human hands flew over her like locusts . . . her heart was full of joy, the liver of Anath was full of exultation . . .[103]

Vala and the daughters of Albion also delight in blood, and blood sacrifice. Vala, seeing and hearing 'blood & wounds & dismal cries & clarions of war' in Night VIII of *The Four Zoas*, 'joy'd in all the Conflict'; in Chapter 3 of *Jerusalem* 'the Daughters of Albion divide & unite at will,/ Naked & drunk with blood, Gwendolen dancing to the timbrel/Of War, reeling up the Streets of London'. Gwendolen repents in Chapter 4, but this time the Daughters have gone too far. Los informs Enitharmon, who not long before had proclaimed: 'This is Woman's World', that the sexes 'must vanish & cease/To be when Albion arises from his dread repose'. The mandatory Edenic solution to sexual conflict is simply to abolish sexual division altogether.

Much of *Jerusalem* consists of philosophy, and philosophy of an avowedly idealist, Neoplatonic kind. Blake held that by opening 'the immortal Eyes/Of Man inwards into the Worlds of Thought: into Eternity/Ever expanding in the Bosom of God', it was possible to catch a glimpse of the Eternal Idea in which the virtual knowledge of everything is contained, and nothing is forgotten. Los in Chapter 1 perceives

> . . . all that has existed in the space of six thousand
> years:
> Permanent, & not lost, not lost nor vanished, & every
> little act,
> Word, work, & wish, that has existed . . .
> For every thing exists & not one sign nor smile nor
> tear,
> One hair nor particle of dust, not one can pass away.

They cannot pass away because they have their platonic, real existence in the Divine Image or Eternal Idea. Perhaps this is why, in his poem *The Gray Monk*, Blake writes:

> For a Tear is an Intellectual Thing
> And a Sigh is the Sword of an Angel King
> And the bitter groan of the Martyrs woe
> Is an Arrow from the Almighties Bow.

Here, however, the emotional intensity and concentration of the language generate something new; we do not suspect it of being a mere dress for philosophical ideas. Blake is, in fact, incapable of sustained philosophical discourse. The following short passage is typical:

> Mental Things are alone Real; what is call'd Corporeal, Nobody Knows of its Dwelling Place: it is in Fallacy, & its Existence an Imposture. Where is the Existence Out of Mind or Thought? Where is it but in the Mind of a Fool?

The absence of any connecting links that might form a coherent chain of reasoning goes with the tone of irritable impatience and mockery, the bullying assumption that anyone who fails to see that the potatoes he is eating are mental ideas and nothing else must be either a fool, a blockhead or a dupe of Satan. Contrast this approach with that of Descartes, in the famous passage where he tells us how he came to realise that,

> in the very act of thinking everything false, I was aware of myself as something real; and observing that the truth: *I think, therefore I am*, was so firm and so assured that the most extravagant arguments of the sceptics were incapable of shaking it, I concluded that I might have no scruple in taking it as that first principle of philosophy for which I was looking.[104]

Whatever we make of the principle itself, Descartes takes us up to it step by step, showing us how he reached it, and then what its consequences were. But Blake's principle: 'Mental Things are alone Real' has no explicit psychological or rationalised cause. It is unconscious of itself. It can neither explain itself nor be explained. It just *is*.

One reason for this is Blake's reluctance, even inability, to rationalise or objectify his ego-cogito as 'something real'. Enlightenment philosophy, on the other hand, is lucidly self-conscious — witness d'Alembert's beautiful exposition of the Enlightenment's debt to Descartes in his *Discours preliminaire*. With Blake, we do not find that kind of self-objectification, the need to show where one's ideas have come from or how they have evolved and changed, which we find in writers such as Wordsworth and Joseph Priestley. Blake's ideological persona, as presented, is one whose ideas are innate or come from the world of eternal ideas, and who never doubts.

'Ideology,' said Marx, 'is a process accomplished by the so-called thinker consciously, indeed, but with a false consciousness. The real motives impelling him remain unknown to him.' Blake's class position enabled him initially to see many of the rationalists' blind spots, yet at the cost of remaining in a much more 'innocent' philosophical world.

Seen in context, Blake's idealism is only one side of a philosophical battle—the battle between idealism and materialism, whose lines can be drawn more clearly by setting the ideas of Priestley and those of Blake in two antithetical columns:

Priestley	Blake
The laws of nature are universal and inescapable.	Nature is the shadow of a higher spiritual reality.
The source of all our ideas is the external material world.	'Innate Ideas are in Every Man, Born with him; they are truly Himself' (annotations to Reynolds).
Hence the 'soul' or mind is also material and obeys the natural laws of necessity.	Hence the soul or mind is immaterial and obeys no natural laws. It transcends necessity.
The human mind, as the activity of the brain and the nervous system, is always bound by space and time. Like the body, it is finite.	The human mind, as the Poetic Genius or imagination, is not bound by space or time. It is infinite; only the body is finite.
When the body dies, the brain also dies. There is no life after death.	Death is the gateway to eternal life, when the soul finds perfect freedom.
True knowledge is acquired by practical means, through the study of physical, chemical, biological and social phenomena.	True knowledge is acquired through introspection: 'in your own Bosom you bear your Heaven/And Earth, & all you behold, tho it appears Without it is Within' (*Jerusalem*, Chapter 3).
Knowledge therefore has an objective, necessitarian foundation: 'To judge of the perceptive power without any regard to facts and appearances, is merely giving scope to our imaginations, without laying them under any restraint; and the consequences of building systems in this manner is but too obvious.'[105]	Knowledge is therefore the creation of free individuals: 'I must Create a System, or be enslav'd by another Man's/I will not Reason & Compare: my business is to Create' (*Jerusalem*, Chapter 1).
Freedom is won through the correct understanding of the laws of nature, i.e. necessity.	Freedom is won when imagination triumphs over the law and necessity imposed by 'Bacon, Newton & Locke'.
Perfectibility is thus possible in a material world given constant progress and improvement.	The material world is fallen. The perfect state is a spiritual one, achieved after the annihilation of this one.

Priestley's critique of idealism is the careful unthreading of a tangled web. Blake's critique of materialism too often degenerates into such splenetic outbursts as: 'Hartley a Man of Judgment! Then Judgment was a Fool What Nonsense!'

The various changes in attitude we summarised above also find their aesthetic reflection. Whereas *The Four Zoas* has a strong narrative and dramatic interest, in *Jerusalem* there is a marked loss of narrative dynamism and dramatic conflict. Although the poem consists mainly of speeches, they tend to be repetitive, non-dramatic and cyclic, rather like the choral odes in Aeschylean drama. Jerusalem's anguished nostalgia in Chapter 1: 'Then was a time of love: O why is it passed away!' is a sentiment repeated like a weeping refrain throughout the poem. Admission of guilt, an avowed sense of shame, despair of redemption and the impulse to confess afflict Albion right from Chapter 1, so that his repentance and conversion in Chapter 4 come as no surprise: the final symbolic release of the English people from monadic hardness, conservative stupor, cruelty, hypocrisy, bellicose imperialism and rationalistic science is a psychic event as bodiless as the Spectre of Reason itself. Which is not to say that the *critique* of these spiritually benighted people is not valid; indeed, it seems as valid now as it was when Blake was writing.

Two other major changes can be observed. There is no violent apocalypse as there is in *The Four Zoas*, while Urizen has disappeared, his place having been taken by Albion, or Albion's Spectre. Albion, however, lacks Urizen's archetypal power. He is almost characterless. Perhaps the Adam Kadmon of the Kabbala was too abstract and all-embracing a concept to be successfully mythologised. As Great Britain, or England, Albion seems to represent the ruling class rather than the common people. His patriarchal role, his hardening into 'Albion the punisher & judge' in Chapter 2, and the nature of his sons and daughters, confirm this.[106] But if we place the guilt-ridden Albion against the cool-headed Castlereagh, butcher of the Irish rebellion, or die-hard opponents of reform such as Wellington, Liverpool, Sidmouth and Eldon, one can only conclude that Blake, with his Christian faith, and possibly liberal-humanitarian illusions

(the product of a burgeoning middle-class strategy of divert-
ing working-class radicalism into non-revolutionary channels),
has lost sight of the enemy. A ruling class does not give up
power by repenting when Jesus appears.

One passage in Chapter 2, spoken by 'Bath, healing City'
(associated with the pacifist Richard Warner, who preached
a sermon there in 1804), is particularly revealing:

> When Africa in sleep
> Rose in the night of Beulah, and bound down the Sun
> and Moon
> His friends cut down his strong chains, & overwhelm'd
> his dark
> Machines in fury & destruction, and the Man reviving
> repented:
> He wept before his wrathful brethren, thankful &
> considerate
> For their well timed wrath. But Albion's sleep is not
> Like Africa's, and his machines are woven with his
> life.
> Nothing but mercy can save him! nothing but mercy
> interposing
> Lest he should slay Jerusalem in his fearful jealousy.

The 1807 Slave Trade Bill was not an act of emancipation or
the furious cutting of chains. It only halted the *trade*, which
rising production costs and a saturated sugar market had
made unprofitable. Planters on the old islands actually
welcomed the bill. Its prime movers, the conservative
Evangelicals and members of the Clapham Sect, sound here
almost like revolutionaries, yet the abolitionists 'for a long
time eschewed and repeatedly disowned any idea of emancipation . . . Wilberforce in 1807 publicly disowned such
intentions'.[107] Albion's 'emancipation', however, is even
more remote: nothing but 'mercy interposing' can prevent
him slaying liberty altogether.

Blake's theme of Jerusalem and Albion grew out of the
current mythology of 'British Israelism', which he strengthened by drawing new correspondences and analogies between
British and biblical events, figures and places (e.g. Tyburn
and Calvary, the mountains of Derbyshire and those of the

Holy Land). Richard Brothers, who believed that the ten lost tribes had settled in Ancient Britain, saw himself leading their descendants, including the Countess of Buckinghamshire ('descended from David, King of Israel'), back to a new Israel. For Blake this was not necessary, since Britain itself was 'the Primitive Seat of the Patriarchal Religion'. Jerusalem is thus 'the Emanation of the Giant Albion'. Before the Atlantean hills were flooded (the story of the lost Atlantic and the biblical flood are now one and the same), the 'giant Albion was Patriarch of the Atlantic'. 'Adam was a Druid, and Noah'; hence 'All things Begin & End in Albion's Ancient Druid Rocky Shore'. At one point in Chapter 4 Jerusalem laments:

> London cover'd the whole Earth: England
> encompass'd the Nations,
> And all the Nations of the Earth were seen in the
> Cities of Albion . . .

Denis Saurat, recognising Blake's special brand of 'Celtomania',[108] noticed 'a strange mystic imperialism, which reveals, at the back of the fantastic unfolding of the imagination of Blake, one of the most fundamental characteristics of the Anglo-Saxon race'.[109] The 'imperialism' is not a racial trait but a historical phenomenon. After the demise of mercantilism and the old empire (and with it the monopoly of the West Indian planters), British industrial capital began to think more and more in world terms. Although it had grown out of mercantile capital and slavery, it showed a preference for trade over dominion. Albion's 'machines' were now 'woven with his life', and that 'life' had a world dimension. In 1769 Matthew Boulton said of his steam engines: 'It would not be worth my while to make for three counties only, but I find it very well worth my while to make for the whole world.'[110] Eric Williams comments: 'Britain's mechanized might was making the whole world her footstool. She was clothing the world, exporting men and machines, and had become the world's banker.'[111]

All this lends a certain ambiguity to the Divine Voice's pronouncement: 'I elected Albion for my glory: I gave to him the Nations/Of the whole Earth.'[112] An unreformed, unrepentant, cruel, mechanised and exploitative Albion, who again acquires all the nations of the earth, was a grim prospect of which Blake was only too well aware, as he saw Albion's empire 'Shooting out fibres round the Earth, thro Gaul & Italy and Greece . . . to India, China & Japan'. What, then, apart from a Golden Age fantasy, gave him so much confidence that Albion, the crucifier of Luvah (at least on the sea, during the Peninsular War and in 1814-15) would send out his Emanation Jerusalem to free the nations of the earth?

There was, to begin with, the missionary enterprise. Missionary activity in this period was strongly represented by artisans, who gave the emergent *capitalist* (no longer mercantilist) empire an ardently plebeian, even radical, Christian-humanitarian image.[113] The Moravian Brethren, to whom Blake's father belonged, and from whom Blake probably derived concepts of brotherhood and community at an early age, had long undertaken missionary work on the Continent. After them came the Wesleyan Methodists. The first L.M.S. missionary ship, the *Duff*, set sail for the South Seas on 10 August 1796, and of its thirty missionaries, 'twenty-five were artisans, and one was a surgeon. Among the artisans were bricklayers, carpenters, tailors, weavers, [and] a blacksmith'.[114] One would like to know how far their hope of establishing Christ's kingdom in Tahiti, and some economic status for themselves, sprang from deferred hopes and political disillusionment at home. Blake's Albion turns his back on Christ 'into the Wastes of Moral Law' where 'Babylon is . . . founded in Human desolation'; but the faithful are secure in the knowledge that a 'Spiritual Fourfold/ London' will one day appear, and that Albion, in his primal innocence, gave Jerusalem 'to the whole Earth to walk up & down'. The missionary note, struck in the Methodist *Collection of Hymns* (1779) with:

> Then let it spread,
> Thy knowledge and dread,
> Till the earth is o'erflowed,
> And the universe filled with the glory of God

and:

Display thy salvation, and teach the new song
To every nation, and people and tongue

is taken up in Chapter 3 of *Jerusalem*, where a Jerusalemite
world empire is invoked:

Return, O Albion! let Jerusalem overspread all
                                        Nations
As in the times of old! O Albion awake! Reuben
                                        wanders,
The Nations wait for Jerusalem, they look up for
                                        the Bride . . .

Arabia, Palestine, Persia, Hindostan, China, Tartary,
                                        Siberia,
Egypt, Lybia, Ethiopia, Guinea, Caffraria, Negroland,
                                        Morocco,
Congo, Zaara . . .
All the Nations, Peoples & Tongues throughout all
                                        the Earth.

The L.M.S. missionary Van der Kemp went to 'Kaffraria'
or 'Kaffirland' in 1798; before that, Carey had gone to India
determined to proselytise, and in 1807 the L.M.S. sent
Morrison to China. West Africa, the Congo and Ethiopia
were also future missionary targets. Blake's visionary,
Jerusalemite empire annuls the one that came to an end in
1783, and gives a bright, utopian shine to the one that
finally came to an end this century.

The second cause for Blake's hope in Albion's redemption
is the memory of those who had faced long terms of transportation, imprisonment and even the scaffold in the cause
of reform:

Edinburgh, cloth'd
With fortitude as with a garment of immortal texture
Woven in looms of Eden, in spiritual deaths of
                                        mighty men
Who give themselves, in Golgotha, Victims to
                                        Justice . . .

Blake here pays homage to the National Convention held in
Edinburgh in 1793, and to five 'mighty men': Thomas Muir,

T. F. Palmer, W. Skirving, Maurice Margarot and Joseph Gerrald, who were transported for long terms by a vicious Scottish judiciary in 1793-4. Gerrald, whose transportation proved to be a death sentence, had said in his trial that Jesus had been a reformer, at which Braxfield, the Lord Justice-Clerk, turned to his fellow judges with: 'Muckle he made o' that; *he* was hanget'.[115] 'Erin' (Ireland) and Wales, symbols of nationalist revolt and Celtic resistance to Albion's 'machines', are also given prominence in Blake's scheme of things: Wales is the first to be allotted its biblical tribes in Chapter 1.

The third factor is less easy to define. Blake's profound religious faith in the change from a society of cruel exploiters and 'natural' enemies to a society of loving brothers cannot be explained; but it has a lot to do with a basic optimism rooted in the common people themselves. The optimism falls mid-way, historically, between an older belief in spiritual agency and the certainties of scientific socialism. As for the 'seeker' mentality that waits and hopes and prays rather than acting, that is clearly cast aside by Los's 'terrible labours' as he works at his anvil, takes the people's 'sighs & tears & bitter groans', and lifts them into his furnaces to form 'the spiritual sword' of intellectual war, waged until Jerusalem has been built in England's 'green & pleasant Land'.

Blake's dialectic has now given way to schematic contraries: cruelty and compassion; the blood sacrifices required by the accuser and the self-sacrifice offered by the forgiver; general demonstrations and minute particulars; Selfhood and Brotherhood; mystery and openness. The optimism lies in the conviction that one day Albion will pass from the first state into the second.[116] Imagistically, the shift is often effected through the somewhat mechanical device of joining the same concrete noun to a contrary abstract noun or nouns. For example, the Stonehenge of Druidical sacrifice is a 'building of eternal death'; Los's Golgonooza is 'a building of pity and compassion'. 'Mantles of despair' become 'mantles of life and death'. It almost becomes a kind of trick. Hills of sorrow can become hills of mercy, the couch of war the couch of peace, gates of hate gates of love, and so forth.

F. R. Leavis's comment, that the 'Eternal Man and Jerusalem can't even by Blake be *imagined*; there can be no presentation of them in terms of "minute particulars"',[117] has validity here.

D. H. Lawrence said that the Hebrews of the post-Davidic era 'looked at the world with the eyes of their neighbours. When the prophets had to see visions, they had to see Assyrian or Chaldean visions'.[118] Much of the imagery used to describe the four living creatures in Ezekiel 1:5-14, for example, and which Blake takes over in *The Four Zoas* and *Jerusalem*, is Babylonian. Likewise, the lingering, idealised image in Hebrew prophecy of the royal capital of David and Solomon is hardly suitable for that of a democratic republic. In Blake, certain confusions of imagery and style modulate into a political confusion when important symbolic values are not, we feel, sufficiently counterposed. The gates of the 'great City of Golgonooza' are adorned with bulls and lions of 'gold, silver, brass & iron', whereas Urizen's temple of deadly science has 'books of iron & brass/And silver & gold'. The reverse order is a trivial distinction, lacking the effect of those subtly distinguished 'minute particulars' we noted in Blake's visual art. Urizen's Mundane Shell, a 'wondrous building', has a 'Golden Hall', a 'White Couch', carvings, an altar of brass and 'high towers/In beauteous order'; Los's eternal days, months and years are similarly 'wondrous buildings'; his freed imagination builds 'a Couch of gold', 'a bright golden Gate carved with skill', 'Walls of brass & Gates of adamant', 'high Towers' and 'Bridges of silver & gold'. Does Los simply have more gold than Urizen? Urizen's iron pen, 'Pharoh in his iron Court', and the 'iron whips' of those captains who are feared more than the enemy, remind us that iron was at this time being used to make almost anything: pillars, bridges, water mains, iron pavings in London, and even a Methodist 'cast iron chapel' which the ironfounder Wilkinson built at Bradley.[119] J. H. Clapham said that 'Britain after Waterloo clanged with iron like a smithy'.[120] Is it that Los works metal to liberate whereas Urizen only uses it to oppress? With gold, the picture becomes clearer. In Revelation, Jerusalem's streets are made of solid gold, which means that gold no longer has any value as money. The gold is not mined; it descends from heaven. To the 'spiritual' alchemists, the metal that never rusts was the crown of their *magnum opus*, symbolising that state of the soul when it is free from base material thoughts. A world free of money becomes a world of everlasting purity.[121] In Blake's millen-arian utopia, the cash nexus is negated by the mutual, loving exchange of intellectual gifts and the fruits of cooperative labour:

> In my Exchanges every Land
> Shall walk, and mine in every Land,
> Mutual shall build Jerusalem,
> Both heart in heart & hand in hand.

The context of Blake's utopian vision is the transition from millenarianism and communitarianism to the utopian socialist experiments of the St-Simonians and Owenites. Lindsay also finds a parallel between Blake's earthly Eden and Thomas Spence's biblical Jubilee, with its 'pastoral and millenary coloration'.[122] The Shakers of the 1770s and the Buchanites of the 1780s were imbued with millenarian ideology. Intricate connections existed between British Israelism, followers of Brothers and Southcott and the Owenite movement.[123] Many followers of Brothers became Southcottians, such as William Sharp, who nevertheless failed to make Blake a follower of the prophetess.[124] George Turner of Leeds (d. 1821) was a Southcottian whose British Israelite doctrine was taken up by John Wroe, a Bradford woolcomber, who received visions and prophecies in 1819 and established a working-class community of 'Christian Israelites' in Ashton-under-Lyne, dividing them into the twelve tribes of Israel.[125] 'Shepherd' Smith was a Southcottian who became a Wroeite, then an Owenite, occupying for a short time an important place in the movement, though his position was closer to the St-Simonians. In Owenism, reform-ist rationalism and millenarian 'enthusiasm' again came together, just as they had done in the L.C.S., whose splits in the late 1790s to some extent reflected this division.[126] But by the 1820s and 1830s millenarianism had become merely a rhetorical dress for the new economic and social ideas:

While using the language of prophecy, revelation and scripture, the Owenites emptied the concept of millennium of all theological content, leaving it simply and essentially a description of a state of society in which the new system prevailed. No longer was the millennium the end of human history, but rather the latest and highest stage in historical evolution.[127]

It is perhaps symbolic that the word 'socialist' made its first appearance in November 1827, just three months after Blake's death, when the London *Cooperative Magazine* referred to 'Communionists or Socialists'. With that word, the millenarianism of countless generations of peasant farmers, craftsmen and artisans became the language and ideology of the past, at least in Europe. A new, working-class era had begun.

Notes

Introduction, pp. 1—13
1. Leon Trotsky, *Literature and Revolution*, Ann Arbor, Michigan 1960, 169.
2. J. M. Newton, 'The Landscape Paintings of Crome, Turner and Constable', *The Cambridge Quarterly*, viii, no. 1, 48.
3. The hostility of the artist to capitalist social relations, and the thesis that art flourishes only when it eludes the grip of capitalist production, is elaborated in A. S. Vazquez, *Art and Society* (1973). The thesis is derived from Marx himself: 'Capitalist production is hostile to certain branches of spiritual production, for example, art and poetry', *Theories of Surplus Value*, Part 1, Moscow 1963, 285. Vazquez writes: 'The romantic artist expressed both an attitude of disenchantment with the reality around him and a search for roots outside that reality. He rebelled against the present by taking refuge in the past and by projecting himself into the future. He rebelled against reason because reason was used to justify reality ... With capitalism, everything became abstract and impersonal, and the romantic, by unleashing an internal subjective volcano, attempted to reclaim everything vital or personal. In both its élitist and popular forms, romanticism expressed an antibourgeois attitude. For the first time, artists regarded social reality — capitalist social relations — as a world hostile to art' p. 166. Such claims for the Romantic artist may be contrasted with Christopher Caudwell's characterisation of the Romantics in *Illusion and Reality* (1936).
4. Jack Lindsay, *William Blake: His Life and Work*, London 1978, 48.

Chapter One, pp. 14—55
1. Hans Hess, *Picture as Arguments*, University of Sussex Press 1975, 11.
2. *Burke's Politics: Selected Writings and Speeches* ed. Ross and Levack, New York 1949, 297.
3. Trotsky, *Literature and Revolution*, loc. cit.
4. *Essai sur le principe générateur des constitutions politiques*, in Jack Lively, *The Enlightenment*, London 1966, 83.
5. *Don Juan*, 'Dedication'.
6. Keats, letter to Benjamin Bailey, 22 November 1817.
7. T. E. Hulme, 'Romanticism and Classicism', in David Lodge, ed., *20th Century Literary Criticism*, London 1972, 95.
8. Allan Rodway, *The Romantic Conflict*, London 1963, 22.

9. Ibid., 23.
10. 'The Prehistoric Aegean', 1954, in David Craig, ed., *Marxists on Literature: An Anthology*, Penguin 1975, 51.
11. H. G. Schenk, *The Mind of the European Romantics*, London 1966, 3.
12. T. J. Diffey, 'The roots of imagination: the philosophical context', in *The Romantics*, ed. Stephen Prickett, London 1981, 197.
13. Karl Marx, *The German Ideology*, 1846, in *Karl Marx: Selected Writings in Sociology and Social Philosophy*, ex. Bottomore and Rubel, Pelican 1963, 90.
14. Ibid., 72.
15. John Locke, *An Essay Concerning Human Understanding*, ed. A. D. Woozley, Fontana 1964, 90.
16. Locke's passive-perception model is refuted by modern science: 'The eye cannot detect light, the eye can only detect change of illumination; the eye is always wandering around, as it were monitoring the experience of the outside world. Seeing is not a passive perception — it is an act', J. D. Bernal, *The Extension of Man*, London 1972, 17.
17. Jacques Derrida, 'Force and Signification', in *Writing and Difference*, trans. Alan Bass, London 1978, 25.
18. John Locke, op. cit., 66.
19. Ibid., 67.
20. 'Disquisitions Relating to Matter and Spirit', 1777, in *Priestley's Writings on Philosophy, Science and Politics*, ed. John Passmore, London 1965, 113. Priestley concluded: 'the whole man is material unless it should appear that he has some powers or properties that are absolutely incompatible with matter', p. 115.
21. The discovery that perception is ideologically conditioned can lead in two different directions. Thus Arthur Koestler, in *The Invisible Writing* (1954), records how, during his travels in the Soviet Union in 1932-3, he saw entire villages deserted, begging families crowding railway stations and starving infants with 'puffed up bellies and cadaverous heads': 'I reacted to the brutal impact of reality on illusion in a manner typical of the true believer. I was surprised and bewildered — but the elastic shock-absorbers of my Party training began to operate at once. I had eyes to see, and a mind conditioned to explain away what they saw . . . I learnt to classify automatically everything that shocked me as "the heritage of the past" and everything I liked as "the seeds of the future"' p. 21. But the *reality*, as Koestler later realised, was a terrible famine resulting from Stalin's forced collectivisation of the land. The other view is Kantian: we never know *das Ding an sich* because we always impose mental categories on what we see. From here it is but a step — a step backwards — to Berkeleian idealism. If all perception is 'ideological', and if all ideology is illusion, any objective, scientific grasp of reality becomes impossible. An external reality distinct from our perception of that reality cannot be demonstrated. Hence an external reality does not exist beyond our perception of it.
22. J. J. Stoudt, *Sunrise to Eternity*, London 1957, 70.
23. Ibid., 71.
24. Ibid., 86.
25. Ibid., 112.

26. Stephen Prickett, 'Romantic literature', in *The Romantics*, 223.
27. Ibid., 225.
28. John Beer, *Blake's Humanism*, Manchester U.P. 1968, 6.
29. Bottomore and Rubel, 88
30. The horrors of surgery were legion in the eighteenth century: 'the patient conscious, or, if semi-conscious, then drunk, the surgeon performing with unsterile hands grasping unsterile instruments, wearing a frock coat stiff with the dried blood of previous patients, the whole atmosphere fraught with pain and thick with bacteria'. When, later, anaesthetics became available, surgical mortality still rose, because 'the surgeon could attempt a wider and more drastic range of operations', E. M. Sigsworth, 'Gateways to Death? Medicine, Hospitals and Mortality, 1700-1850', in *Science and Society 1600-1900*, ed. Peter Mathias, Cambridge U.P. 1972, 109.
31. John Locke, op. cit., 398.
32. Joseph Priestley, ed., *Hartley's Theory of the Human Mind, on the Principle of the Association of Ideas*, London 1775, 34.
33. *An Inquiry into the Nature and Causes of the Wealth of Nations*, London 1886, 4.
34. Karl Marx, *Capital*, vol i.
35. Ibid.
36. See J. F. C. Harrison, *The Second Coming: Popular Millenarianism 1780-1850*, London 1979, Chapter 3, 'Signs and Wonders'.
37. See Peter Mathias, 'Who unbound Prometheus? Science and Technical Change, 1600-1800', in *Science and Society 1600-1900*, 72-6.
38. Harrison stresses 'the gulf between polite and popular culture — and also between polite and popular religion, for there was a range of popular spiritual experience, embracing visions and supernatural manifestations, quite outside the orthodox churches', *The Second Coming*, 54.
39. Keith Thomas, *Religion and the Decline of Magic*, London 1971, 227.
40. *Political Works*, ed. Edwin Elliott, London 1876, 355.
41. Ibid., 356.

Chapter Two, pp. 56—84
1. Quoted in Dorothy George, *London Life in the Eighteenth Century*, Pelican 1964, 163.
2. M. D'Archenholz, *A Picture of England*, London 1791, 79.
3. Ibid., 179.
4. Ibid., 177.
5. Ibid., 196.
6. See the Tate Gallery exhibition catalogue (1978) for reproductions.
7. Richard Brothers, *A Revealed Knowledge, of the prophecies & Times*, London 1794, 26.
8. Thomas Taylor, *An Additional Testimony*, London 1795, 17.
9. Charles Dickens, *Bleak House*, Oxford U.P. 1948, 627-8.
10. *Letters, written from London*, 1807, 10.
11. E. P. Thompson, *The Making of the English Working Class*, Pelican, 1968, 491.
12. C. P. Moritz, *Journeys of a German in England in 1782*, trans. Reginald Nettel, London 1965, 34.

13. Engels, Friedrick, *The Condition of the Working Class in England in 1844*, London, 1845, 30.

Chapter Three, pp. 85—104
1. Hannah More, *Thoughts on the Importance of the Manners of the Great to General Society*, 5th ed., London 1788, 116-17.
2. Jean-Jacques Rousseau, *Emile*, Book 2.
3. Mrs Sherwood, *The History of the Fairchild Family: or, The Child's Manual*, 25th ed., London 1872, 60. Likewise, the children in *The History of Young Edwin and Little Jessy*, London 1802 are told to pray to their Almighty Father with the words: 'We confess that we are sinful children, constantly doing wrong, and unworthy of thy divine favour' pp. 8-9.
4. R. Coveney, *The Image of Childhood*, Pelican 1967, 56.
5. Isaac Watts, *A Discourse on the Way of Instruction by Catechisms*, 3rd ed., London 1736, 5-6.
6. D. G. Gillham, *Blake's Contrary States: The 'Songs of Innocence and of Experience' as Dramatic Poems*, Cambridge U.P. 1966, 48.
7. Geoffrey Keynes, ed., *William Blake, Songs of Innocence and of Experience*, Oxford U.P. 1977, 135.
8. John Holloway, *Blake: The Lyric Poetry*, London 1968, 27.
9. Ibid., 43-4.
10. Keynes, op. cit., 140.

Chapter Four, pp. 105—122
1. E. P. Thompson, *The Making of the English Working Class*, Pelican 1968, 487.
2. Quoted in Thompson, op. cit., 487.
3. Phillipe Ariès, *Centuries of Childhood*, Pelican 1962, 407.
4. William Godwin, *An Enquiry Concerning Political Justice*, London 1793, 850.
5. E. P. Thompson, op. cit., 21, quotes the example of a fourteen-year-old lad, Henry Eaton, who was summoned for interrogation by the Privy Council in May 1794, after Pitt had dismissed an uncooperative John Thelwall. *The Morning Post* for 16 May 1794 reported that the boy, who had been living with the Thelwalls, 'entered into a political harangue, in which he used very harsh language against Mr Pitt; upbraiding him with having taxed the people to an enormous extent'.
6. Laurence Clarkson, *A Single Eye all Light, no Darkness*, London 1650, quoted in A. L. Morton, *The World of the Ranters*, London 1970, 77.
7. Thomas Edwards, *Gangraena*, ii, 146, quoted in Christopher Hill, *The World Turned Upside Down*, Pelican 1975, 199.
8. John Eachard, *The Axe against Sin and Error*, London 1646, sig. (a)v, quoted in Hill, op. cit., 199.

Chapter Five, pp. 123—136
1. Kathleen Raine, 'Who Made the Tyger?', *Encounter*, June 1954.
2. Martin K. Nurmi, 'Blake's Revisions of "The Tyger"', *PMLA*, lxxi, 1956.
3. Nurmi, op. cit., 104-5.
4. *The Anti-Gallican; or, Strictures on the Present Form of Government Established in France*, London 1793, 22.

5. Samuel Romilly, *Memoirs*, 3rd ed., i, 349. Quoted in P. A. Brown, *The French Revolution in English History*, London 1918, 89. Romilly's horrified reaction was a temporary one. He 'recanted' later.

6. *The Prelude*, 1805, x, 11.91-3.

7. *The Anti-Gallican*, op. cit. 22-4.

8. *The Times*, 25 July 1793.

9. *The Anti-Gallican*, op. cit. 21. The complete melodramatic picture is of 'a Sans Culotte, with a dagger in his hand, and his eyes flaming with rage'.

10. Nurmi, op. cit. 105.

11. Acute anxiety and hysteria was one characteristic response to the 'deadly terrors' of Jacobinism, and is ably ridiculed in *Anti-Gallimania: Sketch of the Alarm; or, John Bull in Hysterics. An Heroi-Comic Poem*, London 1793.

12. *The Book of Urizen*, viii, 11.30-1.

13. The blacksmith-poet as a 'red son of the furnace . . . a voice from the deep Cyclopean forges', breathing the fire of working-class radicalism, was an image bestowed on the Sheffield poet and 'Corn-Law Rhymer' Ebenezer Elliott by Thomas Carlyle in *The Edinburgh Review* in 1832. Other versions of the archetype abound. The hammer-wielding proletarian is, of course, a common emblem in modern Soviet posters.

14. In an earlier draft of the stanza, Blake had written 'Did he laugh' instead of 'Did he smile', suggesting an almost hysterical response, a sense perhaps of tragic futility at the thought of irresponsible cosmic laughter amid so much 'sanguine woe'. This tendency was checked in the final draft, though a sense of lugubrious irony remains.

15. Jean H. Hagstrum, *William Blake: Poet and Painter*, University of Chicago Press 1964, 86.

Chapter Six, pp. 137–182

1. *The 'Heaven and Hell' of William Blake*, New York 1973, viii.

2. Ibid., 19. This interpretation, or discovery, brings us in fact back to the origins of hell. The sulphur mines near Athens, worked by slaves in 'infernal' conditions, provided much of the imagery for Hades and the Christian hell.

3. George Rudé, *Revolutionary Europe 1783-1815*, London 1964, Chapter 2.

4. E. P. Thompson, op. cit., 500.

5. A. L. Morton, *The World of the Ranters*, London 1970, 90.

6. W. J. T. Mitchell, 'Style as Epistemology: Blake and the Movement towards Abstraction in Romantic Art', in *Studies in Romanticism*, vol. 16, no. 2, Spring 1977, 160.

7. Quoted in Thompson, op. cit., 260.

8. W. H. Reid, *The Rise and Dissolution of the Infidel Societies in this Metropolis*, London 1800, 55.

9. John Wright, *A Revealed Knowledge*, London 1794, 4.

10. Ibid., 37.

11. William Bryan, *A Testimony of the Spirit of Truth, concerning Richard Brothers*, London 1795, 21.

12. Reid, op. cit., a2.

13. W. S. Baker, *William Sharp, Engraver*, Philadelphia 1875, 16.
14. Ibid., 17.
15. Paine, *Rights of Man*, Pelican 1969, 77.
16. By this I mean that the communist utopia of the Diggers, eloquently articulated by Winstanley, imagines the overthrow of *all* exploiting classes — in other words, a classless society. The revival of Blake's 'Eternal Hell' and even his prophetic cry: 'Empire is no more!' do not stretch that far.
17. A. S. Vasquez, *Art and Society*, London 1973, 176.
18. Pursuing the idea of literary images that are expanded to the cosmic level, Bachelard arrived at a 'reading hypothesis': 'when a fanatic dreamer sees the sun setting on the anvil of the horizon, will he take a legendary hammer to strike the last sparks from the incandescent block?' *La terre et les rêveries de la volonté*, Paris 1965, 156. He then began looking for confirmation of his hypothesis, and found it, among other places, in Thomas Hardy, in one line from a Russian poet, Maximilian Volostin: 'Where the blows of a hammer have forged dawns', and in a Provençal poet: 'You would think . . . that fantastic smiths were pounding on the red sun'. Bachelard concludes: 'The dreamer seems to be forcing the sun to crash, to bury itself. Absorbed in his cosmic dream, the dreamer ends his day by becoming conscious that his force dominates the universe' (p.164). Unfortunately, Bachelard misses examples from Blake. The basic image is there, in the posthumously printed *A Divine Image*, where we see Los, hammer in hand, about to strike the human-faced sun on the anvil of the horizon; and again, in *Jerusalem*, Plate 73, where Los is hammering away at the sun on its anvil-horizon, creating an expansive, prolific universe as an alternative to one that, finite and opaque, is composed of 'Rocky hardness . . . Accumulating without end' — suggesting the world of hard facts, hard bargains, and capital accumulation. Rather than hammering the setting sun, however, Los, like Volostin, would appear to be forging new dawns.
19. Gaston Bachelard, *On Poetic Imagination and Reverie*, trans. Colette Gaudin, New York 1971, 92-3.
20. Thompson, op. cit. 192.
21. David Davies, *The Case of Labourers in Husbandry*, London 1795, 70.
22. At one point in *Milton*, Blake defends Whitefield and Wesley, the founders of Methodism, as 'Men who devote/Their life's whole comfort to intire scorn & injury & death'. This defence of Methodism (continued in *Jerusalem*), the championing of labour and the repudiation of moral law, contain a sharp contradiction that needs pointing out. The 'Moral Report' of Coleham Cotton Manufactory, Shrewsbury, from June 1803 to June 1808 (when Blake was writing and etching *Milton*), refers to the chapel belonging to the 'manufactory' where a sermon was preached 'every Thursday evening, by a minister in the Wesleyan interest'. The moral law of the factory was enforced in Benthamite fashion by a system of punishments and rewards: a worker who was lucky enough not to be fined over a twelve-month period was rewarded with a new Bible or Common Prayer Book. 'The proprietors,' we are told, 'living on the spot, regularly superintend the works in person; and

particularly notice the moral conduct of their servants, and warn them to guard against evil of every description: on particular occasions, as for instance, when an unfortunate female was executed within sight of the works for the murder of her illegitimate child, all the hands were collected together; the cause of the awful scene, &c. was pointed out, and suitable observations were made', *The Tradesman, or, Commercial Magazine*, n. 12, 1 June 1809, 502-3. No doubt the 'minister in the Wesleyan interest', or someone similar (like George Eliot's aunt, the original of Dinah Morris in *Adam Bede*), aided the factory proprietors in making 'suitable observations' on this 'awful scene'.

23. Thompson, op. cit., 70-1.
24. Ibid., 72.
25. Trotsky, *Literature and Revolution*, 249-50.

Chapter Seven, pp. 183-191
1. W. J. T. Mitchell, op. cit., 148.
2. 'Blake's Visions of Eternity', *Sunday Times Magazine*, 5 March 1978, 46-9.
3. Nicos Hadjinicolaou, *Art History and Class Struggle*, London 1978, 81.
4. Ibid., 95-102.
5. 'Signs that are wholly arbitrary realise better than the others the ideal of the semiological process; that is why language, the most complex and universal of all systems of expression, is also the most characteristic; in this sense linguistics can become the master-pattern for all branches of semiology although language is only one particular semiological system', Ferdinand de Saussure, *Course in General Linguistics*, McGraw-Hill, New York. 68.
6 V. N. Vološinov, *Marxism and the Philosophy of Language*, New York 1973, 12.
7. Ibid., 21-2.
8. Ibid., 22.
9. Ibid., 22.
10. Hadjinicolaou, op. cit., 95.
11. Ibid., 101.
12. Ibid., 104.
13. A. S. Vazquez, *Art and Society*, 176.
14. Anne Kostelanetz Mellor, *Blake's Human Form Divine*, University of California Press 1974, 103.

Chapter Eight, pp. 192-238
1. See Robert Rosenblum, *Transformations in Late Eighteenth Century Art*, Princeton 1967, 146-91.
2. Peter Fuller, 'The Fine Arts after Modernism', *New Left Review*, 19, Jan-Feb. 1980, 45.
3. Ibid., 45.
4. David V. Erdman, *Blake: Prophet Against Empire*, 3rd ed., Princeton 1977, 39.
5. Sidney C. Hutchison, *The History of the Royal Academy 1768-1968*, London 1968, 36-7. The same attitude is seen in this, from a letter to the Free Society of Artists in 1762: 'do not affront your institution by displaying the fruits of it to the ignorant', W. T.

Whitley, *Artists and their Friends in England 1700-1799*, 1941, i, 178.

6. G. D. H. Cole and Raymond Postgate, *The Common People*, London 1961, 98.

7. See Erdman, op. cit. Chapter 3, and John Sutherland, 'Mortimer, Pine and some Political Aspects of English History Painting', *Burlington Magazine*, cxvi, June 1974, 317-26.

8. W. T. Whitley, op. cit., 170.

9. *Art and Revolution: Ernst Neizvestny and the Role of the Artist in the USSR*, Penguin 1969, 22-3.

10. Erdman, op. cit., 35.

11. W. T. Whitley, *Artists and Their Friends in England 1700-1799*, i, 290. Strange had produced an earlier pamphlet, *The Conduct of the Royal Academicians*, in 1771. One of those who helped in its preparation was George Stubbs, then Treasurer of the Society of Artists.

12. Opening lecture to the Royal Academy, January 1769. Quoted in John Pye, *Patronage of British Art*, 1845, facsimile ed., London 1970, 171.

13. *Public Address* (c. 1810), *The Complete Writings of William Blake*, ed. Geoffrey Keynes, Oxford U.P. 1966, 599.

14. Joshua Reynolds, *Discourses*, c. 1808, 258.

15. John Berger, *Ways of Seeing*, BBC Publications 1972, 53. In an important work that deserves to be better known, *An Inquiry into the Real and Imaginary Obstructions to the Acquisition of the Arts in England*, 1775, James Barry sets out an alternative to this dominant visual ideology. Regretting that English painting did not grow up 'whilst the genius of the nation was yet forming its character in strength, beauty and refinement' (pp. 124-5), he deprecates the 'frothy affectations and modish, corrupt, silly opinions' that have supplanted 'masculine vigour and purity of taste' (p. 125). The prime object of study to a history-painter being 'the entire man, body and mind, he can occasionally confine himself to any part of this subject, and carry a meaning, a dignity and a propriety into his work, which a mere portrait painter must be a stranger to, who has generally no ideas of looking further than the likeness and in its moments of still life' (p. 133). Naturalistic likeness cannot, therefore, give us 'the entire man, body and mind'. It is the *passionless* quality of upper-class art to which Barry objects, that stiff-upper-lip English reticence of those who speak 'almost without moving the lips', and among whom 'the circumstances of a murder [are] related with as little emotion as an ordinary mercantile transaction' (p. 215). A composition 'should always appear the true efflux of a mind so heated and full of the subject as to lose all regard and attention to every thing foreign'. 'On Composition', in *Lectures on Painting by the Royal Academicians*, ed. R. N. Wornum, London 1848, 153.

16. Pope, *Essay on Criticism*.

17. Frederick Antal, *Fuseli Studies*, London 1956.

18. Hugh Honour, *Neo-Classicism*, Pelican 1968, 19-20.

19. Ibid., 72.

20. Ibid., 71-2.

21. *Encyclopédie*, vol. xii, 1765, in *Art History and Class Struggle*, 160.

22. Ibid., 120.
23. Honour, op. cit., 36.
24. *Vérité agréables, ou le Salon vu en beau, par l'auteur de Coup-de-Patte*, Paris 1789, 3 (my translation). Quoted and discussed by Thomas Crow in 'The Oath of the Horatii in 1785: Painting and Pre-Revolutionary Politics in France', *Art History*, vol. i, no. 4, December 1978.
25. Hadjinicolaou, *Art History and Class Struggle*, 150.
26. Ibid., 160.
27. Ibid., 162.
28. Crow, op. cit., 428.
29. *Journal encyclopédique*, 15 December 1785, Hadjinicolaou, op. cit., 161.
30. Antal, op. cit., 1.
31. Ibid., 80.
32. Ibid., 80.
33. Ibid., 81.
34. Ibid., 69.
35. Ibid., 83.
36. See Rosenblum, op. cit.
37. David Erdman, *Blake: Prophet Against Empire*, 48-9.
38. *Lettre à Christophe, Oeuvres*, viii, 14.
39. Erdman, op. cit., 38.
40. Quoted in R. H. Wilenski, *English Painting*, London 1933, 124.
41. Reynolds, *Discourses*, Lecture 1. Opportunistic eclecticism, with one eye on the patrons and connoisseurs, another on the bank balance, is implied when Reynolds advises: 'With respect to the pictures that you are to choose for your models, I could wish that you would take the world's opinion rather than your own . . .'
42. And yet this was not, according to Michael Levey, a search for anything less artificial: 'Perhaps better based in observation of nature than Boucher, Gainsborough has no hesitation in refining it into something movingly artificial, scenes of country love which are not recorded but created by the artist. Both painters realized that such pictures give pleasure because they are recognizably not true — any more than is the theatre or a mechanical singing bird', *Rococo to Revolution*, London 1966, 111.
43. Blake, *Europe, a Prophecy* (1794). The identification of the 'Guardian of the secret codes' as Lord Thurlow was first made by Erdman.
44. This admittedly had become a eulogistic cliché, but Michelangelo seems to have been repeatedly drawn into the camp of the radicals and republicans. The Whig *Morning Chronicle*, opposed to the Tory *Morning Post*, which attacked Robert Strange in 1775, extravagently defended J. H. Mortimer as 'the most learned anatomist, the most powerful and perfect master of the human form that has ever appeared, either among the living or the dead', crowning this by saying that he 'excels Michelangelo' — presumably the highest praise one could bestow on any artist. W. T. Whitley, *Artists and Their Friends in England 1700-1799*, i, 339.
45. Lord Ronald Gower, *Romney and Lawrence*, London 1882, 21. See also J. Romney, *Memoirs of the Life and Works of George Romney*, London 1830.

46. J. Comyns Carr, *Papers on Art*, London 1885, 88.
47. Whitley, op. cit., i, 285.
48. Ibid., 286.
49. Ibid., 286.
50. Comyns Carr, *Papers on Art*, 81. One contemporary, writing in 1806, the year of Barry's death, said: 'In his person he was dirty and indifferent, in his deportment a savage, in his opinions fierce and obstinate; in his general conduct various, but always unpleasing, harsh and repulsive'; another, one Miss Corkings, said that his 'violence was dreadful, his oaths horrid, and his temper like insanity', but she conceded that sometimes 'his conversation was sublime', Whitley, op. cit., i, 287, 375. Barry, like Blake, was a true rebel, and an Irish patriot.
51. Letter of 17 August 1790, quoted in David Bindman, *William Blake as an Artist*, London 1978, 41.
52. Paul Ganz, *The Drawings of Henry Fuseli*, London 1949, 8.
53. Boydell, a print-seller who commissioned prints for engravers, was a man of big ideas and restless enterprise. His Shakespeare Gallery of 1786, to which artists such as Fuseli contributed, was a big money-spinner, linking painters to engravers through the commission system — in which only a middleman such as Boydell, never the engravers, could make a killing. In the war years, however, demand fell, and not even Boydell could make big profits any more.
54. Ozias Humphry's *Memoir* of George Stubbs, quoted in Ronald Paulson, *Emblem and Expression: Meaning in English Art of the Eighteenth Century*, London 1975, 156.

Chapter Nine, pp. 239-279
1. Bertolt Brecht, 'Building up a Part: Laughton's Galileo', in *Brecht on Theatre*, ed. John Willett, London 1978, 164.
2. Walter Benjamin, 'The Author as Producer', *New Left Review*, 62, 1970, 88. See also Stewart Crehan, 'The Artist as Producer', in *Art, Politics and Society Group: Conference Papers for 1978*, Liverpool University Press 1979.
3. Kathleen Raine, *William Blake*, Thames and Hudson 1971, 56.
4. Erdman's pun-seeking ingenuity (or is it Blake's?) is far too recondite for the ordinary viewer in this comment on Plate 32 of *Milton*: 'The divine imagination's entering Blake's tarsus and his falling upon the garden path (49:25) configure the conversation of Saul of Tarsus to Paul, a seizure totally annihilating the self/body, between pulsations of an artery', *The Illuminated Blake*, Oxford U.P. 1975, 248.
5. David Bindman, 'Blake's Visions of Eternity', *Sunday Times Magazine*, 5 March 1978, 46.
6. See Anne Kostelanetz Mellor, *Blake's Human Form Divine*, University of California Press 1974.
7. Erdman, op. cit., 144.
8. A Vision of the Last Judgment (1810), *William Blake, Complete Writings*, ed. Keynes, 611.
9. Janet Warner identifies the outstretched arms motif as a traditional Christian icon of the 'Cross, a symbol of divinity rich with associations of self-sacrifice or death and regeneration', 'Blake's Use of

Gesture', in *Blake's Visionary Forms Dramatic*, Princeton 1970, 177.

10. Lyson Tembo, *Poems*, Lusaka 1972, 4.
11. Cf. Blake, 'The wretched State of the Arts in this Country & in Europe, originating in the wretched State of Political Science, which is the Science of Sciences, Demands a *firm & determinate* conduct in the part of Artists to Resist the Contemptible Counter Arts . . .', *Public Address* (my italics).
12. Jonathan Swift, *Gulliver's Travels*, Part ii, Chapter 6.
13. Mellor, op. cit., 116.
14. Ibid., 116-17.
15. Ibid., 49. Mellor writes: 'Since Energy, the potentially divine force, is constantly expanding, it should present itself only in the most open and fluid of forms' (p. 49). Does this imply, then, a rejection of 'the bounding line' because it is 'the work of an 'oppressive reason'? Why, then is it always there? 'He portrays the fallen human form with the same precision, linear rhythm, incisive contour, and grandeur as the divine human form' says Mellor (p. 139). In other words, the bounding line is only 'oppressive' when it *expresses* something oppressive. The linearist technique, as such, has nothing to do with it.
16. Kant, *Prolegomena* (1783), trans. P. G. Lucas, Manchester U.P., 1953, 17.
17. Friedrich Engels, *Anti-Dühring*, Peking 1976, 47.
18. Robert Rosenblum, *Transformation, in Late Eighteenth Century Tradition*, London 1975, 41.
19. Ibid., 42.
20. Hans Hess, *Pictures as Arguments*, 27.
21. Robert Rosenblum, *Transformation in Late Eighteenth Century Art*, 187.
22. Erdman, op. cit., 156. Erdman's commentary is on the engraved design that serves as the frontispiece to *Europe* (1794).
23. Nathaniel Brassey Halhed, *Testimony of the Authenticity of the Prophecies of Richard Brothers*, 1795, 4-5. Halhed even testified that 'as Moses ascended from the ark of bull-rushes, so did Mr. Brothers rise from a ship, having been bred to the navy' (p. 36). Joseph Moser, in *Anecdotes of Richard Brothers in the Years 1791 and 1792*, 1795, notes how in times of 'disorder' people abandon their houses, fall into 'swoons and sweats', retiring to the fields, filling the streets, forming crowds, praying on week-days, and experimenting with 'families of love'. Thus some prophet will invariably appear in these times of distress, 'for some political vindictive or sinister purposes' (p. 12). H. F. Offley, in *Richard Brothers, neither a Madman nor an Imposter; with a few observations on the possibility of his being the Prophet of God*, 1795, says that since Brothers's prophecies of revolutionary war and the downfall of monarchies have come true, people now pay more attention to him: 'His books are now read with eagerness by all ranks of people, and all seem anxious to convince themselves of the reality of his mission' (p. xv). See also Thomas Taylor, *An Additional Testimony Given to Vindicate the Truth of the Prophecies of Richard Brothers*, 1795; C. F. Triebner, *Cursory and Introductory Thoughts on Richard Brothers' Prophecies*, 1795;

G. Coggan, *A Testimony of Richard Brothers*, 1795; anon., *Prophetical Passages, concerning the Present Times*, 1795; William Wetherall, *An Additional Testimony in favour of Richard Brothers*, 1795; J. Crease, *Prophecies Fulfilling; or, the Dawn of the Perfect Day*, 1795, and *The World's Doom; or the Cabinet of Fate unlocked*, 2 vols, 1795.

24. Gareth Wilkinson, in *William Blake: The Critical Heritage*, London 1978, 83. See also C. J. Wilkinson, *J. J. G. Wilkinson*, London, 1911.

25. Mellor, op. cit., 142.

Chapter Ten, pp. 280-331

1. Blake to Crabb Robinson, quoted in A. L. Morton, *The World of the Ranters*, 82.
2. Blake, *Jerusalem*, 'To the Christians'.
3. 'The Laocoon', *William Blake: Complete Writings*, ed. Keynes, 777.
4. Kathleen Raine, *Blake and Tradition*, London 1969, xxix.
5. D. G. Gillham, *Blake's Contrary States: The 'Songs of Innocence and of Experience' as Dramatic Poems*, Cambridge U.P., 1966, 174-5.
6. F. R. Leavis, 'Justifying One's Valuation of Blake', in *William Blake, Essays in honour of Sir Geoffrey Keynes*, ed. Morton D. Paley and Michael Philips, Oxford U.P., 1973, 80.
7. Keith Thomas, *Religion and the Decline of Magic*, 223.
8. Ibid., 224.
9. Ibid., 221.
10. Antinomianism, like Catharism, its Gnostic *alter ego*, arose in the thirteenth century. Adherents of the Free Spirit in Germany believed 'they had obtained such control over their senses that they could afford to them complete freedom, and that they were not subject to obedience, because "where the spirit of the Lord is, there is liberty"', Malcolm Lambert, *Medieval Heresy: Popular Movements from Bogomil to Hus*, London 1977, 178.
11. E. P. Thompson, *The Making of the English Working Class*, 113.
12. The Gnostic Blake describes the evolution of the human body as seven stages of 'dismal woe', the sexual act as a serpent forcing itself through 'white pillars' into a chapel of gold, 'Vomiting his poison out/On the bread & on the wine', and gestation and birth as a painful, ugly, disturbing trauma. The Creation trauma in *The Book of Urizen* becomes the birth trauma. (See, in this context, Macalpine and Hunter, *Schizophrenia 1677*, 110-15.) Gnostics also believed that Jesus had abolished the laws of Moses, an idea Blake repeats in *The Everlasing Gospel*: 'He mock'd the Sabbath, & he mock'd/The Sabbath's God'. This soon leads into antinomianism: 'Good & Evil are no more!/Sinai's trumpets, cease to roar!/Cease, finger of God, to write!/The Heavens are not clean in thy Sight', etc.
13. Malcolm Lambert, *Medieval Heresy*, 11.
14. 'Libertinism was an element in Gnostic heresy; from the tenet that all matter is evil and contact with it, including sexual relations, is to be condemned, it is possible to adopt another position, that for the elect, who have freed themselves from the

taint of matter, it has become wholly indifferent whether they engage in sexual relations or not. They are, so to speak, beyond sin, and the rules which must be observed by neophytes no longer apply to them', Lambert, op. cit., 131.

15. A. L. Morton, *The World of the Ranters*, 59.
16. *Jerusalem*, 'To the Christians'.
17. Morton, op. cit., 49.
18. Ibid., 49.
19. Saltmarsh, *Sparkles of Glory*, quoted in Morton, op. cit. 61. On the role of the various parties and sects in Judaea, see Rupert Furneaux, *The Other Side of the Story*, London 1953.
20. John Wesley, *The Journal of John Wesley*, ed. Curnock, London 1909-16, vol. iii, 238. See J. F. C. Harrison, *The Second Coming: Popular Millenarianism 1780-1850*, 14-16.
21. George Lavington, *The Enthusiasm of Methodists and Papists Compared*, London 1751, 145. See Harrison, op. cit., 16.
22. Quoted in Jack Lindsay, *William Blake: His Life and Work*, London 1978, 49.
23. Lindsay, op. cit., 49.
24. Morton, op. cit., 73.
25. Robert Hindmarsh, *The Rise and Progress of the New Jerusalem Church in England*, London 1861, 44.
26. Abiezer Coppe, *Fiery Flying Roll*, quoted in A. L. Morton, *The Matter of Britain*, London, 1966, 111.
27. Ibid., quoted in *The World of the Ranters*, 98.
28. Joseph Salmon, *Heights in Depths* (1651), quoted in *The World of the Ranters*, 95.
29. E. P. Thompson, *Making of the English Working Class*, 411-40.
30. The historical Jesus, who was merely one among several Jewish Messiahs (or popular nationalists) in the period from 4 B.C. to A.D. 70, belonged to a sect called the Nasoraeans. 'The term Nasoraean . . . particularly applied to the Rekhabites, the way-faring people of the desert comprising various itinerant craftsmen who were known as Noserin, the keepers or guardians of the secrets of their trade . . . The modern Mandaeans of Mesopotamia, the Nasoraia or keepers of secrets, are all craftsmen, carpenters, boat builders, smiths, and workers in metal, all professions found in the pedigree of the Rekhabites and Kemites. In Biblical times, the Kemites were a tribe of wandering craftsmen . . . They considered themselves the guardians of the pure religion of Yahveh . . . Their descendents, the modern Sleb, are the gipsies of the desert, craftsmen, healers, and story tellers who make their way through their life peacefully offering willing service to all. It was to this group that both John and Jesus belonged', Rupert Furneaux, *The Other Side of the Story*, 116.
31. Engels, on the origins of Christianity, in *Marx and Engels on Religion*, Moscow 1975, 291.
32. Winstanley, *Fire in the Bush. The Spirit Burning, not Consuming, but Purging Mankind*, in Christopher Hill, ed., *Winstanley: The Law of Freedom and Other Writings*, Pelican 1973, 221.
33. The phrase 'dark religions' is associated with the followers of the Everlasting Gospel, and particularly with Lawrence Clarkson, whose political and politico-religious development took him from

Presbyterian to Independent to Baptist to Seeker to Ranter and finally to Muggletonian. Dark religions or Churches (Blake counted twenty-seven) are the false dawn, foreshadowing yet holding back the coming new age of the Spirit.

34. E. P. Thompson, letter in *The Times Literary Supplement*, 7 March 1975.
35. Lambeth, or 'the house of the Lamb', had many associations for Blake, who lived there from 1790 to 1800. Los says in *Jerusalem*, Chapter 4: 'We builded Jerusalem as a City & a Temple; from Lambeth/We began our Foundations, lovely Lambeth'. Lambeth had been associated with radicals and reformers over a very long period. Hence 'Lambeth! the Bride, the Lamb's Wife, lovely thee'. The Asylum for Female Orphans, founded in 1758 by a group of noblemen, took in girls between the ages of nine and twelve, training them for domestic service, teaching them to read and write and how to master the first four rules of arithmetic. The girls did so much spinning and weaving, however, that for Blake the Asylum became a symbol of dreary labour and exploitation, hardly the benevolent charity its proposer, John Fielding, had originally intended. In *Milton*, Book 2, Los tells his labourers to begin reaping 'at Jerusalem's Inner Court, Lambeth, ruin'd and given/To detestable Gods of Priam, to Apollo, and at the Asylum/Given to Hercules, who labour in Tirzah's Looms for bread,/Who set Pleasures against Duty, who Create Olympic crowns/To make learning a burden & the Work of the Holy Spirit, Strife'. 'Hercules' may have been suggested by Hercules Buildings, where the Blakes lived, Hercules Road itself, and maybe Hercules Hall, the residence of Mr Philip Astley, owner of the nearby amphitheatre, from which Blake, in a rage, once rescued a circus boy whom Astley had punished by tying a log to his foot. The daughters of Los who toil hour after hour, 'labouring at the whirling Wheel' in *Jerusalem*, Chapter 3, may also include the poor female orphans who laboured 'in Tirzah's Looms for bread'.
36. A. L. Morton, *The Matter of Britain*, 111.
37. Richard Brothers, *A Revealed Knowledge of the Prophecies and Times*, London 1794, 46.
38. Ibid., 16.
39. On returning from sea around 1790, after an absence of three or four years, Brothers found that his wife was living with another man, who had given her several children. It was some time after this that he discovered his true identity as the Nephew of the Almighty, having been set up by Jehovah as 'the true Governor upon the Earth'. While living at the boarding house of Mrs Green, before the realisation of his prophetic mission, poor Brothers would remain indoors for days on end; on one occasion, according to his landlady, he lay on his side on the floor of his room for three days and nights (like Ezekiel?) in some kind of spiritual-catatonic stupor. His refusal to take the oath meant that his half-pay was stopped, which brought him to the workhouse, where he would often sit in silent contemplation, looking through the window, at which he received visits from a mysterious, beautiful lady (archetypal mother? ideal wife? Jerusalem the Bride?). Then, all of a sudden, he decided to leave, and at his new lodgings took on the

mantle of prophet extraordinary, leader of the British Hebrews, and newly-appointed 'Governor upon the Earth'. William McDougall, in *An Outline of Abnormal Psychology*, 2nd ed., London 1933, gives us the case of a schizoid archaeologist who fell in love with a girl but afterwards was told she had married. He plunged into work. Returning one day to the town where she lived, he suddenly found himself 'in the chaos of an overmastering dream, a sea of blood and fire; the world was out of joint; everywhere conflagrations, volcanic outbreaks, earthquakes and battles ... he was right in the midst of those fighting, wrestling, defending himself, enduring unutterable misery and pain'; then, exalted, he imagined himself seen by his loved one 'at the head of great armies which he could lead to victory' (379-80). The *real* battles and political earthquakes of the 1790s are, in Blake and Brothers, inevitably (con)fused with a psychic turmoil. McDougall quotes Kretschmer on the asocial type of schizophrenic: this type 'broods in a locked, ill-ventilated dungeon, over his own ideas', such as 'metaphysical trains of thought'. 'In active form, one finds these queer eccentrics and cranks leaving their corner with a sudden jerk, as 'enlightened' and 'converts'; and then, long-haired and sect-founding, they preach the ideals of humanity, raw dieting, gymnastics, and the religions of Mazdazdan or the Future, or all these at once' (p. 394).

40. Lindsay says that in Brothers Blake 'found a prophet on his side, a prophet who had evoked a vast agitated response, and who had gained wide support among the craftsmen and merchants of towns like Leeds and Hull' (op. cit., 93). How 'vast' the response was, and how wide the support, is impossible to say, though Thompson says that the 'influence of Brothers may have been much greater than has been supposed' (1968, 129). Going by the pamphlet evidence, support came from Nathaniel Brassey Halhed, member for Lymington; William Wetherell, Highgate surgeon; Henry Francis Offley, 'late of Oxford'; the Reverend Thomas Philip Foley, rector of Oldswinford, Worcestershire; the Reverend Stanhope Bruce, vicar of Inglesham; the Reverend Thomas Webster; George Turner, Leeds merchant; Peter Morrison, Liverpool cotton-printer; George Coggan, Hull merchant, and John Finlayson, well-to-do Scots lawyer. Wright and Bryan are the only craftsmen who wrote pamphlets, but Sharp we know was a supporter, and there must have been hundreds, or thousands of others of whom we know nothing. See Harrison, op. cit., 64-72. Blake's apparent refusal to give open support may have been the result of his own self-image as prophet rather than follower of other prophets, or there may have been a genuine difference: indeed, as we have seen, the differences were many.

41. Cf. the annotations to Watson: Paine 'has Extinguish'd Superstition'; 'Paine says that Christianity put a stop to improvement, & the Bishop has not shewn the contrary'; 'The manner of a miracle being performed is in modern times considered as an arbitrary command of the agent upon the patient, but this is an impossibility, not a miracle, neither did Jesus ever do such a miracle.'

42. Ibid., *Complete Writings*, 387.

43. All Religions are One, *Complete Writings*, 98.

44. Robert Lowth, *Lectures on the Sacred Poetry of the Hebrews*, trans. G. Gregory, London 1787, ii, 18.

45. Oliver Elton, *A Survey of English Literature 1780-1830*, i, London 1912, 156.

46. Blake defines the prophet's role in his annotations to Watson: 'Every honest man is a Prophet; he utters his opinion both of private & public matters. Thus: If you go on So, the result is So. He never says, such a thing shall happen let you do what you will. A Prophet is a Seer, not an Arbitrary Dictator'.

47. An apocalypse is an 'uncovering' or 'unveiling' of future events and of the unseen realms of heaven and hell; it is primarily a *written* form, intended to strengthen believers and encourage them to stand firm at a time of crisis and danger. A prophecy is primarily spoken, and appeals to men and especially to those in power to change their attitude. In a prophecy, the future is not fixed; in an apocalypse, the future is revealed as a divine, unalterable law. See *The Revelation of John*, commentary by T. F. Gleason, Cambridge U.P., 1965. On the crucial distinction between institutionalised and canonical Hebrew prophecy, see E. W. Heaton, *The Old Testament Prophets*, Pelican 1961.

48. E. V. Rieu, in his introduction to *The Odyssey* (Penguin 1946), says of Homer that 'the reader who tries to glean from his poems something of the man, as apart from his art, will find himself baffled by the most impersonal and objective of authors' (10).

49. One epic touch in *Jerusalem* is the 'breathing Bow of carved Gold' which Albion uses to annihilate the Spectre at the end of Chapter 4, recalling the great bow Odysseus used to kill the suitors in Book xxii of *The Odyssey*.

50. *The Four Zoas*, Night I.

51. *William Blake: The Complete Poems*, Penguin 1977, 921.

52. J. H. Robinson, quoted in Harry Elmer Barnes, *A History of Historical Writing*, New York 1962, 42.

53. Heinrich von Sybel, quoted in Barnes, op. cit., 56.

54. On British Israelism, see Denis Saurat, *Blake and Modern Thought*, 1929; Christopher Hill, *Milton and the English Revolution*, 1977; and J. F. C. Harrison, *The Second Coming*, 1979.

55. Christopher Hill, *Milton and the English Revolution*, London 1977, 355.

56. Cf. *Jerusalem*, Chapter 1: 'For not one sparrow can suffer & the whole Universe not suffer also/In all its regions, & its Father & Saviour not pity and weep'.

57. To Hayley, 4 December, 23 October, 1804.

58. Frances A. Macnab, *Estrangement and Relationship: Experience with Schizophrenics*, London 1965, 165.

59. Richard Brothers, *A Revealed Knowledge*, 49.

60. Lindsay, op. cit., 141.

61. When Homer's Zeus laments 'that men should blame the gods and regard *us* as the source of their troubles, when it is their own wickedness that brings them suffering', we do not feel the same discomfort.

62. R. D. Laing, *The Divided Self*, London 1960, 21.

63. Lindsay, op. cit., xvi.

64. Martin K. Nurmi, *William Blake*, London 1975, 123.

65. Schizophrenia is sometimes defined as the dissociation of thought, feeling and action, where thought and feeling find no practical outlet or resolution. The libido 'is consumed, in this conflict, in generating ineffective fantasies'; after months of 'fantastic self-absorbed brooding, which never finds free outward expression in effective action, but revolves always in the circle of incomplete inward activity, the mental powers in general atrophy', William McDougall, op. cit., 389. In the notebook, where Blake buried so many of his unacted desires, such as the things he *wanted* to say, but could never bring himself to say, to Hayley and others, the double-bind situation is poignantly summarised in his address 'To God': 'If you have form'd a Circle to go into, Go into it yourself & see how you would do.'

66. 'My Angels have told me that seeing such visions I could not subsist on the Earth,/But by my conjunction with Flaxman, who knows to forgive Nervous Fear', to Flaxman, 12 September 1800.

67. Habeas Corpus was suspended in 1794; the Two Acts of 1795 made it a treasonable offence to incite hatred or contempt of the king by speech or writing, and prohibited meetings over fifty persons unless permission was granted by a magistrate; the Combination Acts of 1799-1800 outlawed all workers' combinations on the pretext that they were being used for political subversion.

68. 'Melancholy' was also called a 'disease' by Richard Burton in his *Anatomy of Melancholy* (1621). It could denote a chronic state of depressive anxiety as well as the more 'normal' state of gloomy or pensive sadness.

69. Lindsay, op. cit., 188.

70. McDougall, op. cit., 395-6.

71. J. D. Bernal, *The Extension of Man*, London 1972, 24.

72. Brothers's work, written during his confinement, contains a detailed description of the Heavenly City, complete with streets, squares, palaces, cathedrals, and, in the centre, the Garden of Eden. Comparison between Brothers's often autobiographical *Description of Jerusalem* and Blake's *Jerusalem* is instructive. Brothers disowns his earlier fanaticism, which he says is 'the certain ruin of all that embrace it'. 'I should not have interfered with state affairs, nor meddled with politics', he now vows to his accusers, swearing his innocence in political matters. The desire for social peace and harmony goes with a refutation of the whole Copernican system, which, 'established by Newton, is the most erroneous, wild, and unnatural, that ever entered the imagination'. Brothers evidently wants the earth to stop moving, and asks: 'Who but myself, in this age of pride and conceit . . . dare, or daring know how, to contradict and confute the writings of the great Sir Isaac Newton?' The answer, of course, was a visionary artist born in the same year as Brothers (1757). Harrison says: 'We do not know how many people, like William Blake, rejected 'Single vision and Newton's sleep' . . . But at the popular level heaven and the angels remained just above in the sky, thunder was the voice of God, and Satan could be encountered in darkness and storm' (op. cit., 41). Even the tides, for Brothers, are due not to the moon's gravitational pull, but to the need 'to keep the sea sweet by circulation'. Brothers had been 'unjustly condemned' and

confined; Blake was unjustly charged, then tried for sedition at Chichester on 11 January 1804. Brothers saw himself as 'the slain Lamb', whose accusers would be punished by God; Blake said of himself: 'I act with benevolence & Virtue & get murder'd time after time', and put his accusers into his poem as the fallen sons of Albion.

73. Thomas Münzer, who saw the millennium as imminent, declared: 'Does not Christ say, 'I come not to bring peace, but a sword'? . . . Those who stand in the way of God's revelation must be destroyed mercilessly . . . else the Christian Church will never come back to its source' (quoted in Engels, 'The Peasant War in Germany', op. cit., 97). The spread of Pauline Christianity obscured and distorted this revolutionary side of Jesus' 'mission'. Says Furneaux: 'That Paul speaks of 'another Christ whom I have not preached'' indicates that there were in existence two totally opposed interpretations of the life and mission of Jesus' (op. cit., 38). Again: 'Between Jesus and Christianity stands Paul, the renegade Jew who turned the heroic death of a Jewish Messiah into the sacrifice of the mythical Christ as the scapegoat for the sin of primitive man' (p. 185). Blake seems to have vacillated between the Pauline idea of an other-worldly universal saviour and the historically more authentic image of Jesus as a radical leader. The revival of the radical reform movement after the battle of Waterloo confirmed this latter image in Blake's *The Everlasting Gospel* (1818). Although he swallowed the myth of Jesus as anti-Mosaic, antinomian lawbreaker — in other words, an *anti-Jewish* Christ, not the last Hebrew prophet (another Pauline travesty designed to attract Gentile sympathy and allay Roman hostility) — Blake is certainly not putting forward a Pauline Christ: 'The Vision of Christ that thou dost see/Is my Vision's Greatest Enemy'; 'Seeing this False Christ, In fury & Passion/I made my Voice heard all over the Nation'.

74. J. Steven Watson, *The Reign of George III 1760-1815*, Oxford U.P. 1960, 356.

75. N. Bukharin, *Historical Materialism*, Ann Arbor, Michigan 1970, 287-8. Quoted in Andrew Collier, *R. D. Laing: The Philosophy and Politics of Psychotherapy*, London 1977, 157.

76. 'It has been argued that the bark of the Two Acts was worse than their bite. The death penalty was never exacted under their provisions . . . It was, of course, the bark which Pitt wanted . . .' Thompson, op. cit., 161. This also implies, of course, that a bark was all that was *needed*.

77. See Erdman (1954), 272-8.

78. John Thelwall gave up the struggle in 1797, having come to the conclusion that his fellow countrymen were 'enslaved because degenerate', J. Steven Watson, op. cit., 361.

79. *The Divided Self*, 177. Laing is actually rather more positive: he says that Blake knew about this self-division while 'remaining sane'.

80. See J. F. C. Harrison, *Robert Owen and the Owenites in Britain and America*, London 1969.

81. 'The person who is now hated and feared as the persecutor was at one time loved and honoured', Freud, *Collected Papers*, vol. iii, London 1925, quoted by Paula Heimann, 'A Combination of

Defence Mechanisms in Paranoid Stakes', in *New Directions in Psycho-analysis*, ed. Melanie Klein, Paula Heimann and R. E. Money-Kyrle, London 1955, 256.

82. 'With those who are suffering from such schizophrenic disease, the affective attitude towards the outer world has very often this quality of 'insuring', of peeping distrustfully sideways out of half-sunken eyelids, and of tentatively projecting feelers and quickly withdrawing them'; however, 'behind the affectless numbed exterior, in the innermost sanctuary', there is 'a tender personality-nucleus, with the most vulnerable nervous sensitivity, which has withdrawn into itself, and lies there contorted', McDougall, op. cit., 384.

83. Geza Roheim, *Magic and Schizophrenia*, Bloomington, Indiana 1962, 112.

84. Laing, op. cit.

85. The terminology is Kleinian.

86. That Tharmas should become engulfed as — not merely *in* — a sea of oblivion and forgetfulness, is in a way wholly appropriate: his weakened ego has been overwhelmed, his guilty libido is showing, and he is terrified that *she* can see it. But even if Tharmas turns into a god of the sea, can we believe that it is possible to so dissolve, as Hamlet wished that his flesh would melt and 'resolve itself into a dew', or as Marlowe's Faustus, minutes before his date with hell, wished his soul could 'be changed to little water-drops/ And fall into the ocean'? No; the conflict is only continued through Los and Enitharmon, and Tharmas's further metamorphoses.

87. Herbert Rosenfeld, 'Psycho-Analysis of the Super-Ego Conflict in an Acute Schizophrenic Patient', *New Directions in Psycho-analysis*, 189.

88. Breeding and hatching (cf. the *couvade* ritual), as an aspect of schizoid procreation fantasies, are discussed in Ida Macalpine and Richard A. Hunter's study of the seventeenth-century painter Christoph Haizmann in *Schizophrenia 1677*, London 1956. As with Blake, so with Haizmann, the number nine takes on an important symbolic significance. If, as seems likely, the former artist's guilt was projected onto his wife, then it was *she* who had murdered the souls of the children she had not given birth to, whereas he was merely hatching monsters. If, on the other hand, prophetic books are children, then 'not producing', or closing the labial gates, means closure both of the lips ('the Gate of the Tongue') and of the female labia ('Luban's Gate'). Blake, however, never experienced the confusion of sex roles that Freud and Macalpine find in Haizmann and Schreber.

89. Depersonalisation is what Los seems to fight against in *The Book of Los* when he smashes the 'vast rock of eternity' that surrounds and stifles him. But a horrible vacuum opens up 'Beneath him, & on all sides round', and he falls into a 'horrid vacuity bottomless'. Laing, in *The Divided Self*, 52-4, quotes cases of such petrification dreams, in one of which the choked dreamer 'tries to break the crust . . . to let some air in', as examples of schizoid depersonalisation.

90. Antoine Nicolas Condorcet, *Sketch of a Historical Picture of the Progress of the Human Mind* (1795), quoted in Louis I. Bredvold,

The Brave New World of the Enlightenment, Ann Arbor, Michigan 1961, 111. Condorcet was also preoccupied with 'futurity'. If, he asked, 'man can predict with almost complete confidence the phenomena whose laws he knows ... why should it be thought a vain enterprise to trace with some verisimilitude a sketch of the future destiny of the human race from the results of its history?' Quoted in Jack Lively, *The Enlightenment*, London 1966, 74.

91. Erdman connects this with Napoleon's overthrow of the Directory and declaration of himself as Chief Consul on 9 November 1799, and his Concordat with the Pope a year later.

92. As D. H. Lawrence said, John of Patmos has a violent passion for 'the utter smiting of the Romans'; he 'insists on a Lamb "as it were slain": but we never see it slain, we only see it slaying mankind by the million'. *Apocalypse*, Penguin 1974, 35, 59.

93. Cf. Blake to Hayley, 11 December 1805: 'It will not be long before I shall be able to present the full history of my Spiritual Sufferings to the Dwellers upon Earth ...'

94. 'Vortex' was a term Blake borrowed from Descartes. See *Milton* Book 1:
   > The nature of infinity is this: That every thing has its
   > Own Vortex, and when once a traveller thro' Eternity
   > Has pass'd that Vortex, he percieves it roll backward behind
   > His path, into a globe itself infolding like a sun,
   > Or like a moon, or like a universe of starry majesty,
   > While he keeps onwards in his wondrous journey on the earth,
   > Or like a human form, a friend with whom he liv'd benevolent.

95. 'The moment of being separated from the mother involves ... an immense decrease of temperature ... against which the infant is defenceless. At the same time there is the phenomenon of thermo-lability, which means that the infant's own temperature depends on the temperature of its environment,' R. Bak, 'Regression of Ego-Orientation and Libido in Schizophrenia', in *International Journal of Psycho-Analysis*, xx, 1939, 69.

96. Cf. *To Tirzah* (1801): 'Thou, Mother of my Mortal part,/With Cruelty didst mould my Heart,/And with false self-deceiving tears/Didst bind my Nostrils, Eyes, & Ears.'

97. Geza Roheim, *Magic and Schizophrenia*, 101.

98. See ibid., 167-70.

99. V. Tausk, 'On the Origin of the "Influencing Machine" in Schizophrenia', in *The Psycho-analytic Reader*, ed. R. Fliess, New York 1949, 75.

100. *The Withering of the Arm of Jeroboam by the Man of God*, in the Manchester City Art Gallery.

101. If the poem was written in 1818, then the only way of explaining its apparent return to the spirit of *The Marriage* is the resurgence of popular radicalism, culminating in the St Peters Fields demonstration in Manchester in 1819 — scene of the Peterloo Massacre. But the true poet of *that* era was Shelley, not Blake.

102. 'So much has been said, in recent years, of Methodism's positive contribution to the working-class movement that it is necessary to remind ourselves that Blake and Cobbett, Leigh Hunt and Hazlitt, saw the matter differently,' E. P. Thompson, op. cit., 44-5.

103. Werner Keller, *The Bible as History*, London 1956, 264.
104. René Descartes, 'Discourse on Method', in Jack Lively, *The Enlightenment*, London 1966, 20.
105. Joseph Priestley, *Disquisitions Relating to Matter and Spirit* (1777), in John A. Passmore, ed., *Priestley's Writings on Philosophy, Science and Politics*, London 1965, 124.
106. Albion's sons are mostly Blake's personal enemies, reflecting his growing sense of persecution and resentment. These are: Hand, who is the Hunt brothers, one of whom (Robert) called Blake 'an unfortunate lunatic' in 1809 after seeing his exhibition; Hyle, who is Hayley; judges at Blake's trial for sedition at Chichester in 1804; Coban, who may be Cromek; and lastly, private Schofield and trooper Cox, his accusers. These sons of Albion are really projections of Blake's paranoid hatred, and his belief that 'a concerted, treacherous and murderous campaign' had been launched against him at Felpham, culminating in the 1809 attack in *The Examiner* (Lindsay, p. 217). Blake's persecution fantasies were a well-kept secret, but they expose a nauseating insincerity in his letters. In *Milton*, whose title page is dated 1804, Hayley is cast as a subtle liar, an artistic failure, and a satanic hypocrite; yet on 7 April 1804 Blake writes to his patron: 'You can have no Idea, unless you was in London as I am, how much your name is lov'd & respected.' In the notebook Blake says of Hayley that 'when he could not act upon my wife' he 'Hired a Villain to bereave my Life'. The man who was his patron, housed him and stood bail for him for £50, had, according to Blake, tried to seduce his wife and, when that failed, planted Schofield in Blake's garden to get him hanged for treason. His hatred of Cromek and Schiavonetti was such, says Lindsay, that their deaths in 1810 and 1812 respectively 'aroused in him an unholy joy and a sense of magical power' (p. 215). At one point Blake firmly believed that Stothard was casting a malignant spell on his work (p. 196). *Jerusalem* preaches forgiveness of sins, but 'when it is a matter of his own wrongs, or what he conceives to be his wrongs,' says Lindsay, 'Blake forgives nobody' (p. 196).
107. Eric Williams, *Capitalism and Slavery*, London 1964, 186.
108. The search into Britain's past unveiled a Celtic civilisation, whose rediscovery revived the struggles of the Celts against their Roman colonisers (and hence against Graeco-Roman culture), and encouraging parallels with the Jews and early Christians. William Stukeley felt a mysterious presence as he walked the turfy silences of Wiltshire. Blake's imagination evoked a moral presence: Celtic Britons whose religion 'was the religion of Jesus, the Everlasting Gospel', 'naked civilized men, learned, studious, abstruse in thought and contemplation'. These naked, learned Britons were 'overwhelmed by brutal arms, all but a small remnant', a remnant that remains 'for ever unsubdued, age after age' (*A Descriptive Catalogue*). William Owen Pughe, probably an acquaintance of Blake, was both a millenarian (as a follower of Joanna Southcott) and a 'Celtomaniac': 'a Welsh antiquary and lexicographer, [he] explored bardic culture, using the theories of the mythologists to weave a fantastic pattern of

Druidic history and Arthurian lore,' (Harrison, *The Second Coming*, 82).

109. *Blake and Modern Thought*, London 1929, 81.
110. Quoted in A. Redford, *The Economic History of England, 1760-1860*, London 1931, 45.
111. Op. cit., 131.
112. This marks yet another change in Blake's attitude, if we recall what he wrote against Bishop Watson in 1798: 'That the Jews assumed a right Exclusively to the benefits of God will be a lasting witness against them & the same will it be against Christians.'
113. This was especially true in the Cape, where Evangelical missionaries opposed the slavery instituted by the Boer settlers.
114. C. Silvester Horne, *The Story of the L.M.S. 1795-1895*, London 1895, 23.
115. Thompson, op. cit., 140.
116. Blake conceived of four main 'states': Eden, Beulah, Generation and Ulro. 'We are not Individuals but States, Combinations of Individuals', say the Seven Angels in *Milton*, Book 2; 'Distinguish therefore States from Individuals in those States./States Change, but Individual Identities never change nor cease.'
117. F. R. Leavis, *Nor Shall My Sword*, London 1972, 18.
118. D. H. Lawrence, *Apocalypse*, 35.
119. Redford, op. cit., 42.
120. *Cambridge History of the British Empire*, ii, 223; in Williams, op. cit., 129.
121. One alchemist, writing in 1645, hoped that with alchemy's success 'money will be like dross', thereby dashing into pieces 'that prop of the antichristian Beast'. Come 'our so long expected and so suddenly approaching redemption . . . the new Jerusalem shall abound with gold in the streets'. Hill, *The World Turned Upside Down*, Pelican 1975, 290.
122. Lindsay, op. cit., 47.
123. See Harrison, *Robert Owen and the Owenites in Britain and America*.
124. Blake's scornful dismissal of Joanna Southcott is evident in his notebook verse, 'On the Virginity of the Virgin Mary & Johanna Southcott', written *c*. 1804.
125. Harrison, *The Second Coming*, 141.
126. Methodist members of the London branch of the L.C.S. requested 'the expulsion of Atheists & Deists from the Society' in September 1795; when their resolution was rejected, they seceded to form 'The Friends of Religious & Civil Liberty', Thompson, p. 163. But Thompson adds: 'The dissension was not uncreative. It arose in part from religious — or anti-religious — issues. These men had pitted themselves against the State; now many of them were eager to pit their minds against the State religion' (p. 163).
127. Harrison, *Robert Owen and the Owenites in Britain and America*, 134.

Select Bibliography

Where no place of publication is given read London.

Antal, Frederick, *Fuseli Studies*, 1956

Ariès, Philippe, *Centuries of Childhood*, Peregrine, 1962

Baker, W., *William Sharp, Engraver*, Philadelphia, 1875

Barry, James, *An Inquiry into the Real and Imaginary Obstructions to the Association of the Arts in England*, 1775; *Lectures*, ed. R. N. Wornum, 1848

Beer, John, *Blake's Humanism*, Manchester U.P. 1968

Bentley, G. E., *Blake Records*, Oxford U.P. 1969

Berger, John, *Ways of Seeing*, BBC Publications, 1972; *Art and Revolution: Ernest Neizvestny and the Role of the Artist in the USSR*, Penguin, 1969

Bernal, J. D., *The Extension of Man*, 1972

Bindman, David, *Blake as Artist*, 1977

Blake, William, *Complete Writings*, ed. Geoffrey Keynes, Oxford U.P. 1966; *Songs of Innocence and Experience*, ed. Geoffrey Keynes, Oxford U.P. 1970; *The Marriage of Heaven and Hell*, ed. Geoffrey Keynes, Oxford U.P, 1975

Bloom, Harold, *Blake's Apocalypse*, New York, 1963

Blunt, Anthony, *The Art of William Blake*, Columbia U.P. 1959

Bredvold, Louis I., *The Brave New World of the Enlightenment*, Ann Arbor, Michigan 1961

Bronowski, B., *William Blake: Man Without a Mask*, Pelican, 1954

Brown, Anthony Philip, *The French Revolution in English History*, 1965

Burke, Edmund, *Reflections on the Revolution in France*, 1790

Carr, J. Comyns, *Papers on Art*, 1885

Caudwell, Christopher, *Illusion and Reality*, 1936

Coveney, R., *The Image of Childhood*, Penguin, 1967

Craig, David, ed., *Marxists on Literature: An Anthology*, Penguin, 1975

Crehan, Stewart, *William Blake: Selected Poetry and Letters*, Pergamon, 1976; 'The Artist as Producer', *APSG Conference Papers for 1978*, Liverpool U.P. 1979

Damon, S. Foster, *A Blake Dictionary*, 1973

D'Archenholz, M., *A Picture of England*, 1791

Davies, J. G., *The Theology of William Blake*, 1940

Engels, F., *The Condition of the Working Class in England in 1844*, 1845; *On the History of Early Christianity*, in *Marx and Engels* on *Religion*, Moscow 1975; *Socialism: Utopian and Scientific*, 1892; *Anti-Dühring*, Peking 1976

Erdman, David, *Blake: Prophet Against Empire*, Princeton 1954, 3rd ed. 1977; *The Illuminated Blake*, Oxford U.P. 1975

Frye, Northrop, *Fearful Symmetry*, Princeton 1963

Furneaux, Rupert, *The Other Side of the Story*, 1956

Ganz, Paul L., *The Drawings of Henry Fuseli*, 1949

George, Dorothy, *London Life in the Eighteenth Century*, Peregrine, 1964

Gillham, D. G., *Blake's Contrary States: The 'Songs of Innocence and of Experience' as Dramatic Poems*, Cambridge U.P. 1966

Gleason, T. F., ed., *The Revelation of John*, Cambridge U.P. 1965

Gleckner, Robert F., and Gerald E. Enscoe, eds., *Romanticism: Points of View*, 2nd. ed. Prentice-Hall, New Jersey, 1970

Hadjinicolaou, Nicos, *Art History and Class Stuggle*, 1978

Hagstrum, Jean H., *William Blake: Poet and Painter*, Chicago, 1964

Hall, W. P., *British Radicalism 1791-1797*, 1973

Harrison, J. F. C., *Robert Owen and the Owenites in Britain and America*, 1969; *The Second Coming: Popular Millenarianism 1780-1850*, 1979

Hauser, Arnold, *The Social History of Art*, vol iii, 1958

Hess, Hans, *Pictures as Arguments*, Univ. of Sussex Press, 1975

Hill, Christopher, ed., *Winstanley: The Law of Freedom and Other Writings*, Penguin Books, Harmondsworth, Middlesex, 1973; *The World Turned Upside Down*, Penguin Books, 1975; *Milton and the English Revolution*, 1977

Hirsch, E. D., *Innocence and Experience: An Introduction to Blake*, New Haven, 1964

Holloway, John, *Blake: The Lyric Poetry*, 1968

Honour, Hugh, *Neo-Classicism*, Penguin Books, Harmondsworth, Middlesex, 1968

Hutchison, Sidney C., *The History of the Royal Academy 1769-1968*, 1968

Keynes, Geoffrey, ed., *William Blake: Complete Writings*, see Blake, William

Kisker, Gary W., *The Disorganised Personality*, New York 1964

Klein, Melanie, Paul Heimann and R. G. Money-Kyrle, eds., *New Directions in Psycho-analysis*, 1955

Laing, R. D., *The Divided Self*, 1960

Lambert, Malcolm, *Medieval Heresy: Popular Movements from Bogomil to Hus*, 1977

Lawrence, D. H., *Apocalypse*, Penguin 1974

Leavis, F. R., *Nor Shall My Sword*, 1972

Levey, Michael, *Rococo to Revolution*, 1977

Lindsay, Jack, *William Blake: His Life and Work*, 1978

Lively, Jack, *The Enlightenment*, 1966

Locke, John, *An Essay Concerning Human Understanding*, ed. A. D. Woozley, Fontana 1964

Macalpine, Ida, and Richard Hunter, *Schizophrenia 1677*, 1956

McDougall, William, *An Outline of Abnormal Psychology*, 2nd ed. 1933

Marx, Karl, *Capital*, vol. i; *Selected Writings in Sociology and Social Philosophy*, ed. Bottomore and Rubel, Penguin Books,

Harmondsworth, Middlesex, 1963; *Theories of Surplus Value*, 3 vols, Moscow 1963; *Marx and Engels on Religion*, Moscow 1975

Mathias, Peter, ed., *Science and Society 1600-1900*, 1972

Mellor, A. K., *Blake's Human Form Divine*, Univ. of California Press 1974

Moritz, C. P., *Journeys of a German in England in 1782*, trans. Reginald Nettel, 1965.

Morton, A. L., *The Matter of Britain*, 1966; *The World of the Ranters*, 1970

Nurmi, Martin K., 'Blake's Revisions of "The Tyger"', *PMLA* lxxi, 1956; *William Blake*, 1975

Ostriker, Alicia, *William Blake: The Complete Poems*, Penguin Books, Harmondsworth, Middlesex 1977

Paine, Thomas, *Rights of Man* (1791-2), Penguin Books, Harmondsworth, Middlesex 1969

Paley, Morton D., *Energy and the Imagination*, Oxford U.P. 1970; and Michael Phillips (eds.), *William Blake: Essays in honour of Sir Geoffrey Keynes*, Oxford U.P. 1973

Passmore, John A., ed., *Priestley's Writings on Philosophy, Science and Politics*, 1965

Paulson, Ronald, *Emblem and Expression: Meaning in English Art of the Eighteenth Century*, 1975

Pevsner, N., *The Englishness of English Art*, New York 1962

Pinto, Vivian De Sola, ed., *The Romantics*, 1981

Prickett, Stephen, ed., *The Romantics*, 1981

Pye, John, *Patronage of British Art*, 1845, facs. ed. 1970

Raine, Kathleen, *Blake and Tradition*, Princeton, 1968; *William Blake*, 1971

Rattenbury, J. E., ed., *The Eucharistic Hymns of John and Charles Wesley*, 1948.

Reid, William Hamilton, *The Rise and Dissolution of the Infidel Societies of the Metropolis*, 1800

Roheim, Geza, *Magic and Schizophrenia*, Bloomington, Indiana 1962

Rosenblum, Robert, *Transformations in Late Eighteenth Century Art*, Princeton 1967

Rudé, George, *Revolutionary Europe 1783-1815*, 1964

Saurat, Denis, *Blake and Modern Thought*, 1929

Slaughter, Cliff, *Marxism, Literature and Ideology*, 1980

Smith, Alan, *The Established Church and Popular Religion 1705-1850*, 1971

Stoudt, J. J., *Sunrise to Eternity*, 1957

Strange, Robert, *The Conduct of the Royal Academicians*, 1771; *Inquiry into the Rise and Establishment of the Royal Academy of Arts*, 1775

Sutherland, John, 'Mortimer, Pine and some Political Aspects of English History Painting', *Burlington Magazine*, June 1974

Tabrizi, G. R. Sabri-, *The 'Heaven' and 'Hell' of William Blake*, New York 1973

Thomas, Keith, *Religion and the Decline of Magic*, 1971

Thompson, E. P., *The Making of the English Working Class*, Penguin Books, Harmondsworth, Middlesex 1968

Trotsky, Leon, *Literature and Revolution*, Ann Arbor, Michigan, 1960

Vazquez, A. S., *Art and Society: Essays in Marxist Aethetics*, 1973

Vološinov, V. N., *Marxism and the Philosophy of Language*, New York 1973

Waters, Charlotte M., *An Economic History of England 1066-1874*, 1925

Watson, J. Steven, *The Reign of George III 1760-1824*, Oxford U.P. 1960

Watts, Isaac, *Divine and Moral Songs for the Use of Children*, 1715

Wesley, John, *A Collection of Hymns, for the Use of the People Called Methodists*, 8th ed. 1793

Whitley, W. T., *Artists and their Friends in England 1700-1799*, 1941

Wicksteed, J., *Blake's Innocence and Experience*, 1928

Wilenski, R. H., *English Painting*, 1933

Williams, Eric, *Capitalism and Slavery*, 1964

Williams, Gwyn A., *Artisans and Sans-Culottes*, 1968

Wilson, Mona, *The Life of William Blake*, 1948

Wornum, R. N., ed., *Lectures on Painting by the Royal Academicians*, 1848

Index